SHOUT-OUTS FOR *FDR: A NEW POLITICAL LIFE*

"FDR: A New Political Life *is the most illuminating one-volume history of FDR ever written. American historians have come to recognize that Roosevelt's New Deal did not end the Great Depression, but prolonged it. David Beito carefully explains why so many FDR programs and power grabs were so counterproductive. To go from the older FDR histories by Schlesinger and Leuchtenberg to David Beito's wonderful new work is to make a historiographic leap from the Dark Ages to the Atomic Age."*

—BURTON W. FOLSOM, Jr., Hillsdale College, author of *New Deal or Raw Deal?* (2008)

"Beito's well-researched yet succinct FDR *both informs and enchants while showing that, contrary to legend, Roosevelt did not save the nation from depression or foreign subjugation. America survived despite being ruled for a dozen years by a patrician politician more interested in winning elections and augmenting his power than in helping his country, the downtrodden, or even his own advisers or wife. Truth, civil liberties, the economy, and the future all suffered at FDR's hands."*

—ROBERT E. WRIGHT, author of *FDR's Long New Deal: A Public Choice Perspective* (2024)

"When it came to race and Western influence, FDR's vision of the world order was muddied by delusional phenomena. He was not a man of empire or of genocide, like his wartime allies Churchill and Stalin, but rather a dreadfully old-fashioned Victorian quack, an amateur phrenologist, who believed that repopulating the Pacific Rim with certain choice 'cross-breedings' would create a better world for all. In this instructive and revelatory history, David Beito takes us further than his predecessors along the breadcrumb path into Franklin Roosevelt's 'thickly forested interior'."

—DAVID MICHAELIS, author of several best-selling biographies, including *Eleanor* (2021)

"David Beito, one of the premier chroniclers of American life in the first half of the twentieth century, has worked his magic again. In FDR: A New Political Life, *he shows how President Franklin Roosevelt used the power of the federal government to harass enemies and reward friends, often in the pursuit of economically disastrous and constitutionally dubious New Deal or wartime initiatives."*

—RICHARD K. VEDDER, Distinguished Emeritus Professor, Ohio University, co-author of *Out of Work: Unemployment and Government in Twentieth-Century America* (1997)

"Judicious, skeptical, and empirically rich—Beito's new book gives us a genuinely new 'political life' of FDR. The chapters on The Black Inquisition and the unlikely free-speech coalition in particular, are humane but unsparing. By weaving race policy, administrative ambition, party strategy, and national security into one narrative, Beito reframes Roosevelt not as a myth but as a statesman with traceable incentives and constraints, showing how careful attention to neglected sources can change a story we all thought we knew."

—MICHAEL C. MUNGER, Professor, Political Science and Economics, Duke University

"A powerful and provocative takedown of the FDR myth. Beito masterfully shows how a revered political saint built a dictatorial presidency and ruthlessly weaponized the government against his enemies. Brilliantly researched and utterly compelling, this is also the story of how a bipartisan coalition rose up to restrict Roosevelt's seemingly unlimited power.

"This is not your father's biography of Franklin D. Roosevelt. In his sweeping and meticulously researched account, Beito dismantles the myth of the benevolent president. From the Newport Sex Scandal to the disastrous wartime policy of Unconditional Surrender, he reveals a leader driven by a ruthless pursuit of personal and political advancement. A landmark work of revisionist history that will force you to rethink everything you thought you knew about the 32nd president."

—JONATHAN BEAN, editor of *Race and Liberty in America: The Essential Reader* (2025)

"In this highly critical study of Franklin D. Roosvelt's presidency, historian and libertarian influencer David Beito challenges New Deal economic policies and Franklin Roosevelt's leadership. Well written and well researched, this book revisits a major turning point in American political and economic history, the New Deal."

—DONALD T. CRITCHLOW, Faculty of History, Arizona State University, author of *When Hollywood Was Right* (2013)

"In David T. Beito we have both a highly-accomplished, trustworthy, old-school scholar and a spirit with a youthful vibrance for finding and exposing important truths—perfect for a fresh look at FDR."

—DANIEL KLEIN, George Mason University, author of *The Spirit of Smithian Laws* (2025)

"FDR: A New Political Life *presents a critical reassessment of Franklin D. Roosevelt's political career. David Beito examines some of Roosevelt's most controversial actions, including the suppression of free speech, the strategic deployment of federal power for political retribution, a disregard for civil rights, and the manipulation of public opinion for political gain. By presenting a fresh perspective on Roosevelt, this important book serves as a broader cautionary tale about the dangers of centralized political power.*"

—CHRISTOPHER COYNE, author of *In Search of Monsters to Destroy: The Folly of American Empire and the Paths to Peace* (2022)

"Apart from their New York origins, no two presidents could seem less alike than Franklin Delano Roosevelt and Donald J. Trump: an editorialist has even gone so far as to dub Trump the 'anti-FDR'. Yet, as David Beito shows in his disturbing new biography of the United States' 32nd President, FDR set the stage for many of Trump's most flagrant abuses of executive authority, including his unprecedented resort to 'rule by executive order'; his open contempt for the Supreme Court; his politically-motivated attempts to fire heads of independent

agencies; and his support of a plan to criminalize fake ('false') news, defined to include news critical of his policies. The practical lesson seems clear: even had Roosevelt's stretching of the limits of executive authority served only desirable ends—an assumption Beito also debunks—a proper inventory of his administration's achievements must take account of chickens hatched during it that are still coming home to roost."

—George Selgin, author of *False Dawn: The New Deal and the Promise of Recovery* (2025)

"Historian David Beito, who previously exposed how President Franklin Roosevelt ravaged Americans' constitutional rights, is back with a new book vividly exposing FDR's personal perfidy from the dawn of the Woodrow Wilson administration to the 1945 betrayal at Yalta and beyond. With volleys of research, Beito demolishes Roosevelt's reputation as one of the great presidents."

—James Bovard, author of *Last Rights: The Death of American Liberty* (2023)

"In FDR: A New Political Life*, David Beito brings an enlightening classical liberal perspective to the life and misunderstood legacy of one of the twentieth century's most successful politicians. Beito's reassessment of Roosevelt examines a popular president in a new—and needed—light."*

—Art Carden, co-author of *Mere Economics* (2025)

FDR

FDR

A New Political Life

DAVID T. BEITO

OPEN UNIVERSE
Chicago

To find out more about Open Universe and Carus Books, visit our website at www.carusboooks.com.

Printed and bound in the United States of America. Printed on acid-free paper.

FDR: A New Political Life

ISBN: 978-1-63770-069-3

This book is also available as an e-book (978-1-63770-070-9).

Library of Congress Control Number: 2025931904

Contents

Preface, with Thanks vii

Illustrations ix

1. From Country Squire to President 1

2. Fear and Emergency: The First New Deal 33

3. The Second New Deal: Free Markets Plowed Under 59

4. The Politics of Retaliation: The Black Inquisition 83

5. Roosevelt Confronts a Right-Left Free Speech Coalition 103

6. "Again, and Again, and Again": The Politics of War 125

7. FDR's Wartime State and the Poisoned Fruit of Unconditional Surrender 157

8. The Culmination of a Failed Presidency 183

Endnotes 217

Partial Bibliography 253

Index 267

Preface, with Thanks

This book was the fulfillment of this biographer's dream. Shortly after the publication of *The New Deal's War on the Bill of Rights: The Untold Story of FDR's Concentration Camps, Censorship, and Mass Surveillance* (2023), David Ramsay Steele of Carus Books gave me the opportunity (and freedom) to delve deeper into the record of a president often ranked by my colleagues in the "great" category.

This new, much more ambitious, project allowed me to examine FDR's presidency in a fuller context as well as to gain new understanding of his background, personal character, and climb up the political ladder. Throughout the research and writing process, David has been a fount of encouragement and wise counsel.

I have had much invaluable help along the way. Jonathan Bean, who is thoroughly familiar with FDR's economic and civil rights record, read drafts and was a source of much valuable feedback. Mary Grabar, who knows more than just about anyone about Roosevelt, especially during his formative years, was extremely generous with her time. Others who read drafts and/or provided helpful comments and encouragement include Marcus Witcher, Christopher Briggs, Mary Theroux, Graham Walker, Robert E. Wright, and Judge Glock. My apologies to anyone whom I missed.

Most of all I want to thank my wife, Linda Royster Beito, and my daughter, Quale Linda Beito, for their patience and forbearance, given the time I devoted to this project.

Illustrations

Front Cover: **FDR as State Senator, 1910–1913.** Underwood and Underwood, National Portrait Gallery/Smithsonian.

Page 9. **FDR's sometime mistress, Lucy Mercer Rutherford.** When Eleanor discovered FDR's affair with Lucy during World War I, it almost ended their marriage. Lucy was with him when he died. Wikimedia Commons.

Page 25. **Anticipating victory with daughter and wife just before the 1932 election**. FDR with Anna Roosevelt Boettiger and Eleanor in Warm Springs. Wikimedia Commons.

Page 40. **New Deal blamed for loss of African American jobs.** In 1934, the *Chicago Defender*, a leading African American newspaper, identified the minimum wage and maximum hours mandates of FDR's National Recovery Administration as the cause of many job losses. *Chicago Defender*, January 27th, 1934.

Page 79. **Ernest Hemingway indicts Hopkins and FDR for the deaths of 256 veterans.** After veterans at a New Deal work camp in the Florida Keys perished in a hurricane, Hemingway charged that "Harry Hopkins and Roosevelt who sent those poor bonus march guys down there to get rid of them, got rid of them all right." Wikimedia Commons.

Page 92. **Senator Hugo Black's Klan connections.** When the Black Committee examined millions of private telegrams in 1936, the *Chicago Daily Tribune* highlighted allegations (subseuqntly proven to be true) that the senator had a history with the Ku Klux Klan. Black was later rewarded for his New Deal zeal with a seat on the Supreme Court. *Chicago Daily Tribune,* March 7th, 1936.

Page 142. **J.B. Martin (far left), in front of his South Memphis Drug Store.** Democratic Boss Ed Crump ordered the "policing" of Martin's store after Martin, African American head of the Memphis GOP, refused to call off a rally for Republican presidential candidate Wendell Willkie. FDR took no action against Crump, a longtime ally of both FDR and Eleanor. Memphis and Shelby County Room, Memphis Public Libtary and Information Center.

Page 165. **Dr. Seuss (Theodor Geisel) depicts Japanese Americans as dangerous Fifth Columnists.** This cartoon for a pro-New Deal newspaper appeared one week before Roosevelt's decision to order internment. Special Collections and Archives, UC San Diego.

Page 207. **FDR, Stalin, and Churchill meet at Yalta, February 1945, to plan the postwar world.** After he saw the enfeebled American president, Churchill's physician commented: "I give him only a few months to live." Wikimedia Commons.

1

From Country Squire to President

On July 13th 1921, Franklin D. Roosevelt, who several months before had left office as Assistant Secretary of Navy, received a most disturbing telegram while on vacation at Campobello Island in Canada. It came from his old boss, former Secretary of the Navy Josephus Daniels. Daniels warned that the Senate Committee on Naval Affairs was about to issue a damning report about FDR's past alleged misconduct in a series of events that had become known as the Newport Sex Scandal.

The Committee had singled him out for reliance on entrapment and other devious methods to root out same-sex relationships while he had been Assistant Secretary of the Navy. The future president had justified cause to fear that his hopes for higher political office were at risk. He needed to act, and act quickly.[1]

Formative Years

In the four decades prior to the culmination of the Newport Sex Scandal, Roosevelt had made a continuous upward climb in life that had started under conditions unusually happy and prosperous. He was born in 1882 to the Hyde Park, New York, branch of the Roosevelt family. The political career of his fifth cousin, Theodore Roosevelt of Oyster Bay, who was then in his first term in the New York State Assembly and was to become president nineteen years later, had just started.[2]

Franklin was the second of two children of James Roosevelt (an older brother from his father's previous marriage was already an adult) and Sara Delano. Although James held top executive positions in both railroad and canal companies, his income came primarily from inherited wealth in coal mining, the West Indian sugar trade, and Manhattan real estate. James had the luxury of periodic business plunges (usually guessing wrong) but, like his son (who also usually guessed wrong), never had a sufficient income to dispense much in the way of philanthropy.[3]

FDR's mother Sara came from the highly prosperous and equally aristocratic Delano family of New England. Her father had made his fortune in China, including in the opium trade, and she shared many stories with Franklin about her experiences. Sara was a powerful influence and had great ambitions for her progeny. Her role became even more dominant after her husband James died when Franklin was only eighteen.[4]

Franklin's educational trajectory followed logically from his elite background. At age fourteen, he headed off to Groton in Massachusetts, probably the most exclusive prep school in the United States. He followed by attending Harvard and finally Columbia Law School. Well liked by fellow students, his grades were generally average. Classes for him, James MacGregor Burns writes, were mainly "obstacles to be run." Franklin devoted much of his free time to such personal hobbies as stamp collecting and sailing, but he was not immune to the spread of progressive ideas all around him.[5]

Greatly facilitating that spread of these ideas was the popularity of Germany as a destination for study abroad. At the time, a dominant figure in that country was the "Iron Chancellor" Otto von Bismarck who promoted a regime based on paternalism and military-style efficiency. Attracted by the prospect of an affordable and first-rate education, some fifteen thousand Americans flocked to Germany during these years. Their professors taught doctrines of political economy dramatically at odds with the more predominant classical liberal traditions of limited government in the United States. More than a few Americans returned home eager to apply such German-inspired policies as compulsory insurance, public housing, and zoning.[6]

Concurrent in time, advocates of the Social Gospel in the United States, such as Washington Gladden and Walter Rauschenbush, were gaining influence among Protestant elites, including many academics. A uniquely American phenomenon, the Social Gospelites tried to weave together ideas of democracy, Christianity, social reform, and interventionist government. They hoped through political uplift to usher in a postmillennial kingdom of Heaven on Earth. Many of them had also studied in Germany, most notably Richard Ely, who, in 1885, had drafted the founding document of the American Economic Association. It declared:

> We regard the state as an educational and ethical agency whose positive aid is an indispensable condition of human progress. While we recognize the necessity of individual initiative in industrial life, we hold that the doctrine of laissez-faire is unsafe in politics and unsound in morals; and that it suggests an inadequate explanation of the relations between the state and the citizens.

Ely was one of Woodrow Wilson's seminar professors at Johns Hopkins University and was instrumental in shaping the "Wisconsin Idea" of administrative efficiency and expertise (as embodied by appointed regulatory commissions) under Governor Robert M. La Follette. For his part, Theodore Roosevelt declared, "I know Dr. Ely. He first introduced me to radicalism in economics and then made me sane in my radicalism."[7]

Uncle Ted as Role Model and Patron

Franklin was so smitten by cousin Theodore's accomplishments (often referring to him as "Uncle Ted") that he broke from the Democratic family tradition and campaigned for the McKinley-Roosevelt Republican ticket in 1900. He also joined Harvard's Republican Club and, in 1904, cast his first presidential vote for Uncle Ted and his "New Nationalist" agenda.

The New Nationalists emphasized (in the words of journalist Herbert Croly) "Hamiltonian means" (big government) to advance "Jeffersonian ends" which they interpreted as equality, democracy, and extensive regulation. TR unwillingly contributed, albeit in a more circuitous way, to one of Franklin's most notable accomplishments at Harvard. During a visit to the White House, the younger Roosevelt found out that the president was planning to give a series of lectures on campus. Franklin, then a reporter for the Harvard *Crimson*, leveraged this scoop to become editor-in-chief. Because of these journalistic experiences, he came to fancy himself a comrade-in-arms to the press, much later ostentatiously boasting of his background as "a reporter in Boston ten or twelve years."[8]

A Political Marriage

The relationship between the younger and older Roosevelt took on more of a personal dimension when Franklin began courting the president's niece, Eleanor Roosevelt. Her childhood, though prosperous, was, in contrast to his, traumatic, unstable, and unhappy. Before she was ten, her mother had succumbed to diphtheria and her chronically alcoholic father, Elliott, TR's younger brother, committed suicide. Thereafter, her aunts traded off responsibility for raising her. At their White House wedding in 1905, TR, filling in for his late brother, gave away the bride. Through this marriage, as Jean Edward Smith notes, "FDR would acquire even greater access to the man he most admired . . . Eleanor was not rich like the Astors, but her trust fund provided an annual income of about $8,000 [$253,000 in 2025 dollars] which was considerably more than Franklin's." From beginning to end, it had the markings of a "political marriage."[9]

The imperious Sara Delano Roosevelt held most of the purse strings and she imposed a steep price for any largess. She gave the newlyweds a commodious mansion in New York City, but had it designed as a "double house" with two separate addresses, one for Franklin and Eleanor, and the other for her. The two domiciles shared adjoining dining and drawing rooms. "Unsettlingly," writes historian David Michaelis, "when they passed back through to their side after dinner, Eleanor could not know when, day or night, or through which door, she would next see her mother-in-law."[10]

From Lawyer to State Senator

When Roosevelt passed the bar exam in 1906, he decided to rely on his family connections in the job market and dropped out of Columbia Law School where he had consistently earned poor to mediocre grades. In 1929, Columbia's president Nicholas Murray Butler jokingly told FDR at an alumni dinner that he could never call himself an intellectual unless he came back and completed his course work. "That just shows," Roosevelt quipped, "how unimportant the law really is."

He went to work for the prestigious firm of Carter, Ledyard, and Milburn. The life of a lawyer, however, never excited him and he always saw it as a means to something else. A colleague in the firm, and former Harvard classmate, Grenville Clark remembered him saying "with engaging frankness that he wasn't going to practice law forever, that he intended to run for office at the first opportunity, and that he wanted to be and thought that he had a real chance to be President." Franklin described "very accurately the steps that would lead to this goal. They were: first, a seat in the State Assembly, then an appointment as Assistant Secretary of the Navy . . . and finally the governorship of New York."[11]

Hence, it came as no surprise that FDR was ready to pounce when the local Democrats recruited him to run for the New York State Senate representing Dutchess County (which included Hyde Park). The choice of party was more by happenstance than plan. He might just as well have run as a Republican if someone had tried to recruit him, but 1910 was a Democratic year and the local party asked first. When Uncle Ted spoke in Dutchess County during the election, he helped ensure a narrow victory by failing to mention either Franklin or his opponent.[12]

Less Threatening Progressivism

Once in office, FDR (then only twenty-eight) carefully steered a middle course. He spoke out against the party bosses, but not stridently so, and was usually a reliable vote for measures to increase the size and scope of government, though he proposed very few initiatives of his own. But Roosevelt was already showing a knack for repackaging in less threatening form more controversial ideas. In a speech to the Peoples Forum, for example, he reassured the audience that because "the liberty of the individual had been accomplished" the next stage was a society centered on cooperation rather than excessive competition. Any further political gains for progressives were impossible, however, unless they abandoned phrases which smacked of socialism and sentimentality such as "the brotherhood of man," "community interest," or even "regulation."

The best approach was to adopt less threatening verbiage. "If we call the method *regulation,*" he elaborated for illustration, "people will hold up their hands in horror and say 'unAmerican' or 'dangerous'. But if we call the same process co-operation these same old fogeys will cry out 'Well done!'." Roosevelt lauded Germany because it had "passed beyond the liberty of the individual to do as he pleased with his own property and found it was necessary to check this liberty for the benefit of the freedom of the whole people."[13]

Roosevelt leaned on his abundant aristocratic charm to speed his rise. Unlike Uncle Ted, he never sought the persona of a rough-hewn cowboy or adventurer. He readily embraced, and perfected, his patrician strengths as a "Hudson River country gentleman." In his aptly titled *Country Squire in the White House*, John T. Flynn, said that FDR saw himself as "the kind gentleman in the big mansion in the midst of the village—the rich man who is resolved to treat the village folk generously."[14]

Relationship with Louis Howe

During this period, FDR first demonstrated his seemingly innate political acumen by selecting reporter Louis Howe to manage his reelection campaign. It was the start of a relationship which lasted for more than a quarter of a century. Chosen primarily for his electoral skills and personal compatibility with the candidate, Howe was largely indifferent to ideology. He recalled that "I made up my mind that nothing but an accident could keep him from becoming President.[15]

Meanwhile, Governor Woodrow Wilson of New Jersey, recently president of Princeton University, was making a national impression. Even as FDR carefully maintained friendly ties with Uncle Ted, Wilson became another political role model. "Those tracing the origins of New Deal ideas," writes Frank Freidel, "go back to two main fountainheads—Wilson's New Freedom and Theodore Roosevelt's New Nationalism. The ideology and techniques of both men left a deep impress upon Franklin D. Roosevelt."[16]

In 1911, FDR attained the rare status of becoming an "original Wilson man" when he went on record for the New Jersey governor's presidential aspirations. He attended the Democratic convention the following year (but not as a delegate) and brought 150 Wilson supporters along from New York. Although he was not an important contributor to Wilson's winning the nomination, he successfully jockeyed for an appointment as assistant secretary of the navy in the new administration. Thus, he continued to self-consciously emulate the educational and career trajectory of Uncle Ted, who had held that office after also both attending Harvard and serving in the New York legislature. FDR brought Louis Howe along to Washington, D.C. as a special assistant.[17]

"A Case of Love at First Sight"

The man chiefly responsible for arranging FDR's appointment was Secretary of the Navy Josephus Daniels. Like many powerful men, he was drawn by FDR's charm and personal magnetism. He also saw himself as something of a father figure. When the two first met at the Democratic convention in 1912, Daniels called it "a case of love at first sight." He said that Franklin "always had about him what women would call glamour and charm—to the nth degree—

one of the greatest things a politician can have . . . Roosevelt had it just like an actress."[18]

Prior to this period, Daniels main claim to fame was as the Democratic publisher and editor of the Raleigh, North Carolina *News and Observer*. In 1898, he had waged an unusually vicious (even by the low standards prevailing in that region) white supremacist propaganda campaign to banish African Americans from the legislature and overthrow the state's multiracial government. The resulting hysteria emboldened a white mob of two thousand to both murder sixty African Americans and intimidate black city officials into resigning from their posts.

In subsequent years, Daniels won national recognition for advocating progressive reform and Wilsonianism. His racism was on full display, however, when the Roosevelts came to dinner in 1913. Daniels upbraided Eleanor for bringing along her New York white servant, considering it unnatural to require whites to serve members of their own race in a home when black domestics were available to carry the load. "Whom else," he emphasized, "could one kick?"[19]

Imposing Segregation in the Department of Navy

The Wilson administration came to power at the low point in the political rights of African Americans during the twentieth century. A vast system of segregation and disfranchisement in the South, which had started to take root in the late 1870s, reached its culmination after the turn of the century. Wilson, a native of Virginia who grew up in Georgia and South Carolina, applauded this trend in his book, which became a standard text, *A History of the American People*. It praised Southern whites for ridding "themselves, by means fair or foul, of the intolerable burden of governments sustained by the votes of ignorant negroes. Every country-side wished to have its own Ku Klux . . . until at last there had sprung into existence a great *Ku Klux Klan*, an Invisible Empire of the South."[20]

Daniels quite clearly did not need any prompting from Wilson to enforce rigid white supremacy in his department. He began to systematically purge the few remaining black employees. The most prominent to get the ax was Ralph W. Tyler, the Auditor of the Navy, a position traditionally reserved for African Americans. Tyler, first appointed by TR in 1907, did not go quietly. In response to accusations that black employees were overpaid, he described it as "strange that in all these years these negro clerks have been efficiently and unobtrusively serving, only now their presence becomes distasteful." The Wilson administration coincided with what historians have described as the "nadir" or low point in the rights of African Americans during the twentieth century.[21]

FDR not only failed to object to these racist policies, but he obligingly lent assistance. In 1916, for example, he carried out an order to designate at considerable expense separate toilets for "the use of [white] women, white men and colored." A "watch force" took charge of enforcement. The NAACP and civil rights organizations objected so strenuously that the order was rescinded without explanation only a month later.[22]

"We've Got to Get into This War"

FDR's passivity and complicity on matters related to racial equal treatment stood in contrast to his belligerent, sometimes downright insubordinate, pushback against Daniels's more pacifistic approach to military and foreign policy. In February 1914, FDR penned an article for *Scientific American* declaring that U.S. national defense "must extend all over the Western Hemisphere, must go out a thousand miles to sea, must embrace the Philippines wherever our commerce may be . . . We must create a navy not only to protect our shores and our possessions but our merchant ships in time of war, no matter where they may go."[23]

In the two years after the breakout of war in Europe, Roosevelt tirelessly pushed for U.S. intervention in that conflict. "We've got to get into this war," he told Daniels in 1916. He also confided to Eleanor at a time when President Wilson was publicly urging neutrality in thought as well as deed, that it was likely that "I shall do some awful unneutral thing before I get through." FDR did little to conceal his low opinion of Daniels. A letter to Eleanor paired Daniels with the similarly antiwar Secretary of State William Jennings Bryan as having "as much conception of what a general European war means as Elliott [his four-year old son] has of higher mathematics. They really believe that because we are neutral we can go about our business as usual." Roosevelt also revealed his attitude toward Daniels by regaling friends at the elite Metropolitan Club with a "killing" imitation of his boss's hillbilly mannerisms. He eventually ceased after his friend, Secretary of Interior Franklin K. Lane, chastised him for showing disrespect.[24]

Once the U.S. entered World War I, Roosevelt, then only thirty-five, contemplated volunteering for the infantry. Uncle Ted, citing his service in 1898, declared: "You must resign. You must get into uniform at once." TR was so adamant that he entreated Eleanor to put pressure on her husband. But Daniels, backed up by Wilson, rejected the idea, characterizing his young assistant as essential to the war effort. FDR, who did not need much persuading, stayed at his post. As H.W. Brands puts it, "he was a different kind of man than Uncle Ted. Theodore, too, had been told that abandoning the Navy Department for the cavalry would be irresponsible, but he refused to listen."[25]

An Affair with Lucy Mercer

Franklin's career suffered almost a mortal blow after Eleanor found out about his affair with Lucy Mercer. Lucy's father Carroll Mercer had fought alongside Uncle Ted in Cuba, and she had close ties to Washington, D.C., society. After Franklin began his duties as assistant Secretary of the Navy, Eleanor, needing an introduction to the local elite, hired Lucy as her private secretary. It did not take long for Franklin to notice Eleanor's charming and beautiful twenty-two-year-old employee and they began a secret affair. Eleanor revealed her suspicions to her husband, but he denied everything. Not convinced, she fired Lucy in 1917, but Franklin promptly got his mistress a job in the office of the Assistant Secretary of the Navy! The puritanical Daniels seemed to sense something untoward and fired Lucy soon thereafter, despite her recent promotion and a perfect performance grade.[26]

FDR's sometime mistress, Lucy Mercer Rutherford

The affair took a new turn, however, when Eleanor found a cache of letters from Lucy. Divorce seemed likely, but Sara put her foot down, threatening to cut off her son from any inheritance if he left his wife. Louis Howe joined forces with Sara and pushed to keep the marriage together. Eleanor agreed to reconcile, and Franklin promised never to see Lucy again. "He did not want to be bothered," wrote son James Roosevelt. "He cared more about his life than he did his wife." Eleanor began to create her own circle of friends and like-minded associates, which included an intimate, possibly romantic, relationship with reporter Lorena Hickok.[27]

Repression, Race, Violence

FDR gave unquestioning support to President Wilson's crackdown on free speech during World War I, including his enforcement of the Sedition and Espionage Acts. According to Kenneth S. Davis, Roosevelt "went along with prevailing trends in the realm of the national spirit, uninhibited by any strong ideological commitment to the Bill of Rights." After reading about the conviction of the publisher of an antiwar socialist pamphlet, for example, he sent a congratulatory letter to the federal prosecutor. When a perceived offense involved a personal slight, FDR outdid his governmental peers in endorsing repressive measures. After an anarchist journal published a satirical article implying that Roosevelt's call for compulsory military service illustrated hypocrisy because he was not himself in uniform, he entreated the Department of Justice to "send the writer and his whole plant to [the federal penitentiary in] Atlanta for the rest of their natural lives." Assistant Attorney General Charles Warren replied that the department had no legal basis for prosecution.[28]

FDR's actions, and inactions, during a wave of notorious white violence against African Americans in 1919, known as the "Red Summer," showed complicity with the worsening plight of African Americans. The trouble began on July 19th when white sailors attacked black streetcar passengers and pedestrians after hearing rumors that a black man had assaulted a white woman. As the violence eventually spread to twenty-six cities, the NAACP demanded that Secretary Daniels arrest the sailors and marines who were responsible. Daniels refused, and Wilson, then in Paris for the Versailles conference, deferred to his judgement. Roosevelt revealed his state-of-mind in a letter to a Harvard classmate: "With your experience in handling Africans in Arkansas, I think you had better come here and take charge of the Police force." Secretary of

War Newton D. Baker finally stepped in to quell the disorder by deploying two thousand troops. According to Michaelis, Roosevelt's inaction revealed "at worst a dangerous dereliction of duty and, scarcely better, the distancing jockey banter of upper-class bigotry."[29]

The Newport Sex Scandal

On issues he truly cared about, however, Roosevelt was more than willing to seize the initiative. He was particularly eager to indulge his fascination with cloak-and-dagger intrigue. Novelist John Steinbeck later observed that FDR "simply liked mystery, subterfuge, and indirect tactics . . . for their own sake." Roosevelt's participation in the "spy business," was often more fanciful, at least in retrospect, than real. A favorite story he later related was how the Secret Service had brought to his attention a document "in the safe of the German consul in New York entitled: To Be Eliminated." The first name on this hit list was Frank Polk, intelligence coordinator at the State Department while "Mine was the second." Again, as told by FDR, he was in so much personal danger that the Secret Service gave him a holstered revolver. "We have only Franklin's word for this story," writes Roosevelt biographer Geoffrey C. Ward, "and it is a little hard to understand why the Germans should have chosen to eliminate two sub-Cabinet officials in advance of their superiors."[30]

FDR's foray into the "spy business" culminated in the Newport Sex Scandal. The catalyst was an informal investigation by Ervin Arnold, a chief petty officer and ex detective to find "perverts" at the Newport Naval base. Arnold boasted that he could "recognize degenerates by the way they walk along the streets." His operatives began to use methods of entrapment to obtain evidence including same-sex acts. They received instructions to "go forth into Newport and to allow immoral actions to be performed upon them, if in their judgement it was necessary for the purpose of running down and trapping certain specified alleged sex perverts." Although Arnold's immediate superiors approved of his efforts, Attorney General A. Mitchell Palmer failed to provide sufficient financial resources to conduct a formal query.[31]

At this point, Roosevelt, almost single-handed, saved the investigation by interceding with Daniels to create Section A (eventually nicknamed the Newport Sex Squad) under his leadership. As historian Irwin F. Gellman concludes, Roosevelt, like most other Americans, took for granted that "homosexuality was immoral and he would expend every effort to ferret out offenders." Section A allowed him to satiate his fascination with espionage and, potentially, to enhance his political resume. Working with Arnold, who often emphasized his close ties with the Assistant Secretary, he deployed a large team of amateur detectives, including several Harvard classmates. The heavy-handed tactics of Section A soon backfired as illustrated by a public backlash from the prosecution of Rev. Samuel N. Kent (though he was a civilian), a well-respected Episcopalian priest. He was eventually tried on vague and convoluted federal charges of abetting "lewdness" near military installations. The *Providence Journal* as well as the national Episcopalian hierarchy and local clergy rallied to the priest and demanded the Department of the Navy issue an official apology. In a series of articles, John Rathom, the editor of the *Journal*, used the prosecution of Kent, who was eventually acquitted, as an opportunity to excoriate Roosevelt's entrapment methods.[32]

The resulting controversy led to a naval board of inquiry under Admiral Herbert O. Dunn. In his testimony, Roosevelt denied any knowledge that his investigators had engaged in same-sex acts to obtain evidence. But the skeptical judge advocate pressed him further: "How did you think evidence of unnatural crimes could be obtained?" Roosevelt replied revealingly that "I didn't think." At another point, he explained: "I was only interested in getting results. I was not concerned any more than in finding out about how the commanding officer of a fleet takes the fleet from New York to Newport." Roosevelt did not seem unduly worried, however.[33]

The 1920 Presidential Election

As the Senate Committee on Naval Affairs was quietly undertaking its own probe, FDR felt confident enough to seek the role of kingmaker in the 1920 presidential campaign. In early 1920, he set out to recruit Herbert Hoover, whom he considered a "wonder," to run for the nomination. Roosevelt's interest in Hoover made good political sense. The "Great Engineer" had soared to popularity during World War I as director of Belgian relief. FDR and Hoover had much in common, including a history of fluid partisan loyalties, similar moderate progressive views, and friendly political ties to both TR and Wilson. In March, the Roosevelts invited the Hoovers to dinner to make a pitch. Their guest seemed receptive but was careful not to reveal himself. Unfortunately for Roosevelt, Hoover announced later that month that he was a Republican.[34]

But four months later, opportunity knocked when the Democratic nominee, Governor James M. Cox of Ohio, chose FDR as his running mate. The day after the nomination, John Rathom of the *Providence Journal* tried, mostly in vain, to remind voters of FDR's role in the Newport scandal. "His deliberate attempts to cover up the true conditions existing in the Navy department," the *Journal* declared, "and the lengths to which he has gone in this direction, have shocked hundreds of naval officers who know the truth." The Republican ticket of Senator Warren G. Harding of Ohio and Governor Calvin Coolidge of Massachusetts pledged normalcy after four years of Democratic world saving and anti-civil liberties excesses. The Democrats, weighed down by the albatross of the unpopular Wilson, were in an almost impossible fight and Roosevelt, who had his eyes on the future, knew it.[35]

Instead of running away from the record of the sitting president, however, Roosevelt both defended it and embraced the more repressive aspects. In a speech in Centralia, Washington, for example, he lauded the actions of a mob of American Legionnaires who had attacked the headquarters of the Industrial Workers of the World (the Wobblies) in Centralia. After a pitched battle, a Wobbly, who had tried to escape, was castrated and hanged from a telephone pole. In his speech, Roosevelt described his visit to Centralia "as a pilgrimage to the very graves of the martyred members of the American Legion who gave their lives in the sacred cause of Americanism."[36]

Roosevelt's biggest misstep during the 1920 campaign was his boastful statement that he had "something to do with the running of a couple of little republics. . . . I wrote Haiti's Constitution myself and, if I do say it, I think it is a pretty good constitution." He repeated this claim of constitution authorship (which FDR biographer Kenneth S. Davis labels an "utter falsehood") on several occasions. When challenged, he denied ever saying any such thing, but more than twelve Democratic and Republican reporters issued a statement that they had heard him. Speaking from his front porch in Marion, Ohio, Warren G. Harding commented that FDR had made "the first official admission of the rape of Hayti [sic] and San Domingo by the present Administration." An African American newspaper piled on: "Now comes Franklin D. Roosevelt, Democratic nominee for vice president, who boasts that he wrote the new constitution of Haiti which was forced on an unwilling people at the points of bayonets."[37]

"Lay Naval Scandal to F.D. Roosevelt—Details Are Unprintable"

In November 1920, Harding and Coolidge buried the Cox and Roosevelt ticket in a landslide. Few blamed FDR, who had generally campaigned ably, for the loss. He accepted a lucrative position with Fidelity and Deposit, the third largest investment company of its kind in the United States. To keep his name in the news, he allotted many of his evenings to political speeches.[38]

The stirring up of the Newport Scandal, however, soon disrupted his new routine. In February 1921, the final report of the Dunn Naval Board of Inquiry, although leaving Roosevelt mostly unscathed, found it "unfortunate and ill-advised" that he had "either directed or permitted the use of enlisted personnel to investigate perversion." At the same time, the Court did not recommend punishment of those personnel because they had acted with a good purpose.[39]

Roosevelt feared that Attorney General Mitchell A. Palmer might prosecute the amateur investigators in Section A for entrapment. A letter to Daniels emphasized that the Court had faulted the "use of enlisted personnel" and "NOT the METHODS, which were employed." His focus on the ends, rather than the means, was becoming a defining trait. Roosevelt concluded that since the motivations and final goals of the investigation were proper, so too were its methods. The "only clear distinction in law relates to the question of intent," he wrote to his boss. "In other words, if the intent of those authorized to investigate crime is honestly to obtain evidence without active solicitation, then the basic law declares that no crime has been committed." Roosevelt compared Section A to a police department which orders officers to justifiably break into a home because of foreknowledge of a robbery.[40]

If Roosevelt assumed that interest in the Newport Sex Scandal was waning, the report of the Senate Committee of Affairs in July 1921, which had been quietly gathering up evidence since January 1920, showed otherwise. In a stunning rebuke, it declared that his office had violated "the moral code of the American citizen, and the rights of every American boy who enlisted in the Navy to fight for his country." The report found Roosevelt to be "morally responsible" for the use of entrapment and other "immoral acts" and concluded that he "must have known" the methods used. More devastating, the committee suggested that Roosevelt was unfit for any public office.

After Roosevelt got the advance warning from Daniels while vacationing at Campobello, he asked the committee to delay the report's release so he could testify. Thinking that he had an agreement, he worked into the night with a prepared statement and rushed by train in the exhausting summer heat to the Capitol building to testify but it proved futile. The Committee had already released the report to the press. Roosevelt, "white with exhaustion," read it anyway and then left.[41]

A blaring front-page headline of the *New York Times* on the next day left no doubt about blame: "Lay Navy Scandal to F.D. Roosevelt—Details Are Unprintable." The findings stressed Roosevelt's close involvement. Michaelis concludes that FDR, "a subcabinet official . . . knew perfectly well—indeed had, tried to cover up—that his own secret orders for the sting operation had put young enlisted men in 'a most deplorable, disgraceful, and unnatural' position.'" But the legendary Roosevelt luck carried him through. The Democrats closed ranks and charged that the Republicans had targeted their former vice-presidential candidate in a partisan smear. Moreover, the new Harding administration was dominating the headlines, pushing the story aside. While the controversy did no lasting damage to Roosevelt's upward political trajectory, the victims of Section A were not so lucky. The entrapped suffered dishonorable discharges and their veterans' benefits were revoked, including military funerals.[42]

Overcoming Polio

Less than a month after the damning report of the Senate Committee on Naval Affairs, Roosevelt had far greater problems on his mind. He showed the first symptoms of polio on August 9th and soon developed complete paralysis in his legs. He never walked on his own power again. But he always (or almost always) re-mained upbeat and determined to resume a normal life. "Of greater life-affirming courage of a political leader of the first rank," writes historian Kenneth S. Davis, "all history affords few examples." Although most experts now attribute the polio to contaminated water, combined with a weakened immune system, Roosevelt assigned primary blame to the Senate Committee on Naval Affairs investigators. He aimed his ire at Republican committee member Senator Henry W. Keyes (R-New Hampshire) for scapegoating him and not letting him testify before the committee. According to historian David Michaelis, "Franklin couldn't live with it. He wanted vengeance . . . for the next fifteen years, he held Keyes responsible for intensifying his susceptibility to viral disease."[43]

As he struggled to rebound, Roosevelt kept abreast of political developments and continued his business career. Like his father, his investment dabblings usually came to naught. He sank money into a lobster-packing plant betting on rising prices, but they fell instead, and it went bankrupt. More unusual was his investment in a company offering passenger travel in helium-filled dirigibles between Chicago and New York. In 1921, FDR had been "horrified" when his mother had flown a plane from London to Paris. "Wait until my dirigibles are running," he exuded to one of his law partners, "and then you will be able to take a form of transportation which is absolutely safe." The project fell apart because, among other factors, airships were vulnerable to shifting winds and incapable, despite their great physical size, of carrying more than a small number of passengers. These business failures did not surprise many of those closest to FDR. Wilson's Secretary of Interior Lane said that "Roosevelt knows nothing about finance, but he doesn't *know* he doesn't know."[44]

Despite his health problems, FDR continued to be active on the Harvard University Board of Overseers. Alarmed by information in 1923 that the proportion of Jews had risen to one third of the entering class, Roosevelt supported a plan to impose quotas. While he had grown up in an atmosphere of elite "social antisemitism," his belief in the proposed quota system ran deeper than that. In 1941, he was still defending it to Secretary of Treasury Henry J. Morgenthau (a Jew), arguing that "You can't get a disproportionate number of any religion" hence he had found it necessary to limit new Jewish students to "one or two percent a year until it [the percentage] was down to 15%."[45]

Construction Czar

FDR, his admiration undaunted, reconnected again with Hoover in 1922. He teamed up with the new Republican Secretary of Commerce, to form the American Construction Council. Roosevelt went on to become president of that organization. Like many trade associations during the period, the Council's mission was "to stabilize the entire construction industry by eliminating the 'peak and valley' conditions, to the advantage of capital, labor, and the public." It presided over about 250 trade associations in the building industry including architects, contractors, equipment dealers, and various building divisions in government. FDR made the cover of *Time* (smoking a pipe!) for the first time largely because of his activities as "construction czar."[46]

Although some critics said that the Council was an entering wedge for "socialism," Roosevelt portrayed it as a means to get industry to regulate itself through voluntary cooperation. But sometimes the line between voluntary and coercive was murky. To New York journalist John T. Flynn, Roosevelt's tenure anticipated the format and goals of the National Recovery Administration of the New Deal. Roosevelt himself hinted that his efforts might be a precursor to something else. While specifying that the Council wanted to help businesses "keep their own house in order," he also warned that in the case of failure "an exasperated public will some day regulate their house for them." But Roosevelt had no such power. He received no salary from the Council and could only exhort. He soon grew bored and started to skip meetings, though he remained titular president until 1928.[47]

Mounting a Political Comeback; The Warm Springs Resort

Electioneering was a different matter. It never bored him. His political comeback began in 1924 when New York Democratic governor and presidential candidate Alfred E. Smith, at the suggestion of his advisor Judge Joseph M. Proskauer, asked him for a nomination speech at the Democratic convention. Proskauer, who had recommended the selection of Roosevelt as helpful to win over Protestant delegates, was the main author of the speech, including its most iconic line. The crowd erupted in applause as FDR, held up only by braces, hobbled slowly on his crutches across the stage to make an appeal for "the 'Happy Warrior' of the political battlefield." But this was not Smith's year. On the 103rd ballot, the delegates nominated the moderately conservative distinguished lawyer, John W. Davis who went on to a landslide loss to Republican president Calvin Coolidge.[48]

During this time, Roosevelt was making regular trips to a resort in Warm Springs, Georgia, to treat his polio. He exercised in a pool fed by a constant flow of springs thought to have curative qualities. He soon developed a friendship and business relationship with Thomas Wesley Loyless, a manager and part owner of the resort, who also wrote a column for the *Macon Telegraph*. In 1925, the ailing Loyless, finding the writing schedule to be too grueling, persuaded FDR to "have fun" and temporarily take over, under the heading "Roosevelt Says." Roosevelt so enjoyed the experience that he tried without success to arrange a syndication deal.[49]

His columns had some revealing comments, especially given subsequent history, about Japanese Americans. The future president wrote that "Anyone who has travelled in the Far East knows that the mingling of Asiatic blood with European or American blood produces, in nine cases out of ten, the most unfortunate results." Regarding laws on the West Coast banning land ownership by Japanese noncitizens, Roosevelt asserted that "Californians have properly objected on the sound basic grounds that Japanese immigrants are not capable of assimilation into the American population."[50]

At Smith's urging, Roosevelt ran as the Democratic candidate for Governor of New York in 1928. He narrowly edged out his opponent while his old friend Hoover won handily for president. As governor, Roosevelt steered a straight middle course, including on such hot button issues as prohibition. His record, according to historian James MacGregor Burns, was that of a moderate "in a moderately liberal party. He believed that the party should be for 'progressivism with a brake on', 'not conservatism with a move on'."[51]

"The Little Flurry Down Town"

On the single day of October 24th, only about eleven months after Roosevelt took office as governor, the Dow Jones Industrial Average suffered a decline of nearly 13 percent. Severe reverses followed in the next few days. The governor showed little alarm, dismissing the crash as a "little Flurry down town," Of course, he, like many other Americans, was wrong. When the market finally bottomed out in July 1932, the Dow, despite occasional gyrations, was down nearly 85 percent from its monthly peak in 1929.[52]

FDR's tenure of government coincided not only with a sharp drop in the New York stock market but the worst overall economic decline in American history. The most visible indicator of the nationwide impact was the spectacular rise in unemployment from 3.2 percent in 1929 to a still standing annual record of 24.9 percent in 1933. Real GDP declined by 29 percent during these years. A fiscal crisis of epic proportions was wreaking havoc with local and state governments. By 1933, the rate of property tax delinquency (the percentage of taxes levied but not collected) had advanced to 26.3 percent. In 1929, 659 banks had failed and in 1930 that number had doubled. The numbers of banks which shut their doors doubled again the next year, reaching nearly three thousand. For a time, the crisis appeared to abate but, in 1933, a third wave of failures led to the closing of an additional four thousand banks.[53]

Severe Pressure on Mutual Aid Systems and Banking

The economic decline put incredible strain on the mutual-aid systems embodied by fraternal societies which had proved so valuable in helping Americans to weather previous depressions. Groups such as the Odd Fellows, the Loyal Order of Moose, and the Polish National Alliance, provided health and other social welfare benefits on a mass scale. While these societies generally survived the depression intact, they suffered tremendous losses in membership, falling from about 17.3 million in 1930 to only 12.5 million in 1940. In past depressions, workers kept their dues current by drawing from savings, borrowing money or kin networks or, if that failed, persuading local lodges to temporarily carry them on the rolls. While workers in the 1930s also used these traditional methods, they started to buckle because of the unprecedented duration of unusually high unemployment. Credit and savings dried up, and family networks frayed.[54]

The banking collapse during the depression was a classic example of a politically engineered crisis. Leading culprits were "unit banking" laws in multiple states (including New York) which impeded the diversity of assets by prohibiting, or severely limiting, the establishment of branches beyond a single "unit" or office. These laws, which arose from a deeply held "anti-monopoly" Jacksonian tradition of aversion to big banks and eastern finance, had wide support, particularly in rural areas. Unfortunately, however, as Jim Powell points out, the result was to make banks "highly vulnerable to failure when local business conditions were bad, because all their loans were to local people, many of whom were in default, and all their deposits came from local people who were withdrawing their money." A striking 90 percent of bank failures during the depression were by small-town banks. The federal government gave an official imprimatur to unit banking when it enacted the McFadden Act (1927) which prohibited branching across state lines.[55]

A Hoover New Deal?

In finding solutions to the depression, President Hoover had the recent precedent of Harding's response to the Depression of 1921 and 1922 who had faced a downturn just as severe as that experienced in the first two years of the Great Depression. Between 1920 and 1921, unemployment increased from 4.0 to 11.9 percent while the Federal Reserve's index of industrial production plummeted by 31.6 percent. By comparison, between 1929 and 1930, unemployment rose from 3.2 to 8.9 while the index of industrial production fell by 21 percent. After that, however, the trend line of the two downturns sharply diverged. In 1922, for example, unemployment was rapidly falling but in 1931, it was scaling new heights.[56]

In 1921, President Harding, following the pattern of previous presidents, had responded to the downturn by a policy of letting wages, prices, and profits fall to what he saw as more sustainable levels. Hoover, by contrast, pursued a different course. In doing so, he established policy precedents later expanded upon by FDR. Hoover's premise was that the federal government was obligated to stop the slide in wages, prices, and profits. He vehemently rejected the "leave it-alone liquidationist" approaches of Harding as well as his own Secretary of Treasury Andrew Mellon. Instead, he wanted to stabilize or raise wage rates to restore prosperity.[57]

Hoover's "High Wage" Policy Hobbles Recovery

Only three weeks after the Stock Market Crash, for example, Hoover convened the first of many conferences to secure business pledges not to cut wages. Henry Ford even boldly announced a wage increase. In addition to exhortation, Hoover also implemented unprecedented subsidy and regulatory programs to achieve the same ends. These included the Federal Farm Board (an agency which predated the 1929 Crash), the Home Loan Board, the Reconstruction Finance Corporation, the Emergency Relief and Construction Act of 1932, for public works and direct relief, and the Davis-Bacon and Norris-LaGuardia acts to subsidize labor unions and push up wages.

Hoover spent more on public works than all the previous nine presidents combined. "We might have done nothing," he declared in his 1932 renomination speech. "That would have been utter ruin. Instead, we met the situation with proposals to private business and to the Congress of the most gigantic program of economic defense and counterattack ever evolved in the history of the Republic."[58]

Perhaps Hoover's most aggressive attempt to boost wages and production was the Smoot-Hawley Tariff. His signing statement of

1930 quoted the GOP platform which emphasized the need to protect "industries which cannot now successfully compete with foreign producers because of lower foreign wages and a lower cost of living abroad." Smoot-Hawley led to a wave of retaliation which eventually engulfed the world. Between 1929 and 1932, American exports dropped catastrophically from $7 billion to 2.5 billion. The inability of Europeans to make further purchases of many key manufacturing products had a contagion effect. American car sales, for example, dived from over 5 million in 1929 to just under 2 million in 1932. By late 1930, a recession had turned into a steep depression with no end in sight.[59]

Governor Roosevelt's views on trade policy at this time were virtually indistinguishable from those of Hoover. In March 1930, as Smoot-Hawley was under debate, he was carefully distancing himself from the low tariff wing of the Democratic Party. In a letter in June 1930 to a protectionist Republican banker and farmer from Nebraska, he volunteered, with more than a touch of prevarication, his desire to "make it perfectly clear that we [Democrats] are not for free trade; that we are for protection but that protection does not mean the right for manufacturers to sell their goods here at a higher price than they sell the same goods in other countries."[60]

Measured by the goal of maintaining high wages, Hoover was successful, only too successful. The average real wage rose to record levels in 1932 and was still higher in 1933 than at the height of prosperity in 1929. As historians Richard K. Vedder and Lowell E. Gallaway point out, employers, in contrast to previous depressions, had saved on payroll cuts by discharging workers rather than cutting wages. Hoover's dependence on higher wages as a spur to recovery proved a chimera, and worse.[61]

To finance his programs, as well as a mounting deficit, Hoover's Revenue Act of 1932 imposed the highest tax increase in peacetime. It more than doubled the top rate, which increased from 25 percent to 63 percent in a single stroke, included a bewildering array of excise taxes on gasoline, theater admissions, tires, toiletries, and stock transfers. The effect of these added tax burdens was to further impede recovery. It also represented a complete repudiation of the Harding-Coolidge strategy to dramatically lower marginal rates.[62]

If Hoover rejected Harding's approach of letting wages and prices fall, he also did not consider emulation of Canada's comparatively successful banking system. In contrast to the U.S., Canada didn't have a single bank failure primarily because it allowed branching both within provinces and nationally. Canada's ten largest banks had some three thousand branches throughout the country and thus less vulnerable to local shocks and runs. As Milton Friedman points out, Canada "experienced roughly the same decline in the quantity of money as the United States and had a depression of essentially the same severity." If a similar structure had existed in the U.S., he added, there would have been "few if any bank failures, no banking holidays."[63]

Moreover, had Hoover embraced the Canadian model he might have found prominent allies in the press and among politicians. Democrat Senator Carter Glass (D-Virginia) of the Banking and Currency Committee had conducted since 1930 well-publicized hearings to consider legislation along Canadian lines. In January 1932, Glass proposed an early version of a bill to permit branch banking across states. It stalled in committee, however, because of opposition from Hoover, who was then preoccupied with a status quo strategy of shoring up the existing unit banking structure.[64]

The Bank of United States Scandal

Although New York was the nerve center of the American economy, Roosevelt's record as governor did not particularly stand out. John T. Flynn observes: "There was nothing at all spectacular about Roosevelt's regime. Generally he followed Al Smith's policies." The policies of Governor Roosevelt were not that different from those of his old ally, Hoover. FDR was initially resistant to federal and state measures to spend more on relief and unemployment insurance.[65]

President Roosevelt had a reputation for boldness in the banking crisis of 1933, but Governor Roosevelt's response in 1929 was timid, indecisive, and politically petty. Personal feelings and grudges often drove him forward after the failure of City Trust in April 1929, a bank with primarily Italian immigrant depositors. He was upset by the decision of Lieutenant Governor Herbert Lehman, acting in his absence in Warm Springs, to appoint Robert Moses, the chairman of the New York State Council of Parks, to lead an investigation into the circumstances of this collapse. A grudge still festered from the Smith years when Moses had spurned a request from Roosevelt, then commissioner of Taconic Park, to appoint Louis Howe as secretary to assist him.[66]

When Moses presented his report in July, the press widely praised its professionalism and thoroughness. After highlighting the role played by mismanagement and corruption in the failure of City Trust, it pointedly warned about the financial shakiness of the much larger New York-based Bank of United States. Roosevelt's response to the report was astonishing. He set up a commission to investigate banking issues in New York but, flouting the recommendation of Moses, named as a member the director and counsel of the Bank of United States! Flynn, a well-known economic reporter at the time for publications such as *Harper's* and *New Republic*, found it inexplicable that FDR had appointed "a director of the Bank of United States on a commission to investigate a condition of which the bank was supposed to be the worst exemplar." Roosevelt did not, Flynn writes "perceive the impropriety of this practice—there is some blind spot or mental obfuscation on the point that is not easily explained." In the end, FDR's banking commission rejected all of Moses's recommendations, even minor ones.[67]

Only a month after FDR's reelection as governor, the Bank of United States collapsed following a run by depositors. It was the biggest such failure up to that time in U.S. history and contributed to a chain reaction that brought the first major banking crisis of the Great Depression. According to Owen D. Young, the deputy director of the New York Bank of the Federal Reserve, the collapse shook "confidence in the Federal Reserve System more than any other occurrence." As the eminent American historian Richard Hofstadter points out, however, FDR refused to take any responsibility. He sent the legislature a "self-assured, unabashed, impenitent" and "righteously impatient" appeal, writes Hofstadter, implying that it was to blame for the bank's failure. This disastrous outcome might have derailed Roosevelt's career, but these were not normal times. Americans understandably looked first to blame President Hoover and the rest of the Republican party for any economic problems. As with the Newport Sex Scandal, Roosevelt suffered no setback to his political ambitions.[68]

Presidential Candidate: Something for Everyone

One of FDR's distinctive advantages was that he had not alienated any important faction in the Democratic party. The day after his reelection to governor in 1930, his campaign chairman James A. Farley, an experienced Democratic politico, proclaimed to an impromptu press conference that there was no way that "Mr. Roosevelt can escape becoming the next presidential nominee of his party." Although FDR did not formally announce until February 1932, he responded by phone: "Whatever you said, Jim, is all right with me."[69]

Roosevelt was the man to beat. Nevertheless, to ensure success, he had to carefully mollify the leading factions and power brokers of a highly divided political party. For decades the solid Democratic South had exercised disproportionate power both at nominating conventions and in Congress. The predominantly Protestant region spoke with a single voice in favor of segregation and African American disenfranchisement and nearly a single voice for upholding the Eighteenth Amendment of 1919 imposing prohibition of alcoholic beverages. The Northern Democrats, by contrast, drew from a heavily immigrant, Catholic, and big-city base. Their animus toward the Eighteenth Amendment grew in intensity with each passing year.

The Democratic Party also had ideological divisions which cut across geography. Self-described, but sometimes vaguely defined, progressive factions squared off against more conservative elements on issues ranging from the currency to economic regulation and taxes.

Roosevelt relied heavily on an inner group of advisors, dubbed by the press the "Brain Trust," for speeches and advice. Three professors at Columbia University were at its core but others eventually came on board. The unofficial head, and chief recruiter, was law professor Raymond Moley. Perhaps the least radical person in the group, though still on the political left, Moley recalled that as a young man he "had absorbed the idea and spirit of the Progressive Movement, although I was never an admirer of Theodore Roosevelt. I doubted his sincerity and was repelled by his ham acting. I preferred Wilson's more intelligent approach to reform."[70]

Much friendlier to unbridled big governmental planning was Rexford Tugwell, a specialist in agricultural economics. His book, co-authored with Gardiner C. Means, *American Economic Life and the Means of Improvement* (1928), lauded the Soviet Union for producing "goods in greater quantities" while, at the same time, acknowledging a regrettable "disregard for liberties and rights." Tugwell liked to shock those around him by musing about his plans for "doing America over."[71]

Rounding out the Columbia University group was law professor Adolf A. Berle Jr., a strident critic of free markets. *Time* magazine described his landmark book, *The Modern Corporation and Private Property* (1932) as "the economic Bible of the Roosevelt administration." Berle stated matter-of-factly that the two hundred largest corporations exercised monopoly power, and were controlled by salaried managers motivated by parochial self-interest, rather than the interests of shareholders. Berle's recommended solution was for the federal government to regulate big business and harness it for the public good. Along with Tugwell, Berle favored deficit-financed public works spending.[72]

Promising a "New Deal for America"

When Roosevelt arrived in Chicago in June 1932 for the Democratic convention, his lead was formidable but still not insurmountable. His main opponents were Rep. John Nance Garner (D-Texas), the speaker of the U.S. House, who had strong support in the South, and Alfred E. Smith, Roosevelt's former mentor. Roosevelt's main obstacle was the two-thirds rule which served to enhance the power of Southern Democrats. But Garner's decision to release his delegates, combined with an earlier endorsement of FDR by Senator Huey Long (D-Louisiana) and William Randolph Hearst, dashed any chance of blocking him. The victor obligingly chose the conservative Texan as his vice-presidential candidate.[73]

Breaking precedent, FDR became the first major party nominee in history to deliver his acceptance speech at the convention. The most memorable passage was the endorsement of "a new deal for America." The phrase came from a recent article by Stuart Chase in *The New Republic* which had praised Soviet central planning. FDR's "new deal," however, was politically conventional, avoiding specifics or giving offense. His rhetoric wove together criticism of the GOP for tilting toward "a favored few" and calls to abolish "useless offices" and "eliminate unnecessary functions of Government."[74]

Anticipating victory with daughter and wife just before the 1932 election.

Nor did FDR's subsequent campaign speeches anticipate the future New Deal in any discernible way. They endorsed without qualification the party platform which called for deep cuts in federal spending. In one of the few early speeches memorialized on audio, he demanded "a saving of not less than 25 per cent in the cost of the Federal government" and accused Hoover of presiding over "the greatest spending administration in peace times in all our history." He appealed to voters "very simply to assign to me the task of reducing the annual operating expenses of your national government."[75]

"Herbie the Hoov"

Smattered in his pre-election prose, but only smattered, were verbal gestures that tilted more to the left. His speech to the Commonwealth Club is the leading example, though it too was mostly vague. It proclaimed that "we are coming to a view through the drift of our legislation and our public thinking in the past quarter century that private economic power is, to enlarge an old phrase, a public trust as well." A bit more specific was another speech which promised to "study" the possible implementation of unemployment insurance. "You could not quarrel with a single one of his generalities," wrote reporter Elmer Davis, "you seldom can. But what they mean (if anything) is known only to Franklin D. Roosevelt and his God."[76]

Like a much later president from New York, FDR enjoyed tagging his chief opponent with an unflattering nickname. When someone asked his reaction to a recent article about President Hoover, he burst out in "mighty laughter" because of "a statement in there that the life of Herbie the Hoov was one of hard knocks. Did you know that Herbert Hoover is the eleventh richest man in the United States?" Basing his evidence on Hoover, he concluded that "these rich men" now had "to face realities and they won't like what they're going to have to see." FDR's reliance on Hoover as a whipping boy in these comments, however, rested on two patent falsehoods. Born in modest circumstances, Hoover was orphaned at age ten and raised successively by two uncles. Moreover, the extent of his fortune, a maximum of about 4 million in 1913 (falling to about 700 thousand dollars in 1932), was a far cry from that of the eleven wealthiest individuals at the time who each had a net worth exceeding 60 million dollars.[77]

Hoover's policy reaction to the bonus marchers at the outset of the general election campaign had dealt a body blow to his already slim chances. By the middle of 1932, a "Bonus Army" of some twenty thousand World War I veterans had gathered in Washington, D.C. to demand an early payment of their federal bonus due in 1945. Hoover ordered the Army to clear their camps. On July 28th, troops commanded by General Douglas MacArthur, backed by tanks, moved in. Using tear gas, and equipped with fixed bayonets, they torched the Anacostia shantytown of the marchers to prevent them from returning. Appalled Americans throughout the country watched the spectacle in theater newsreels.[78]

Most everyone expected Roosevelt to win in November, but he was not taking any chances. Despite the affinity of the Brain Trusters for bigger government, these views were not discernable in the speeches they wrote for FDR. In September, Frank R. Kent observed that "Republicans are in high state of exacerbation over his refusal to say anything of which an issue can be made . . . in this matter of not offending any element, Mr. Roosevelt and the [Columbia] professors seem to be doing a swell job."[79]

Only three weeks before the election, FDR's speech in Pittsburgh condemned Hoover's "reckless" federal spending and deficits and pledged to carry out "the plain precept of our Party, which is to reduce the cost of current Federal Government operations by 25 percent." The federal government needed to tighten its belt, he elaborated, much like families had. He warned that "all business—big business and little business and family business and the individual's business—is at the mercy of our big Government down at Washington, D.C." Following this event was his highly calculated "Covenant speech" so named because of the covenant (or promise) implicit in the gold clause. It promoted "sound money" over Hoover's "rubber dollars" and promised not to tinker with gold prices.[80]

A Landslide Victory (Except Among African Americans)

The election results in November proved that FDR had no reason to be cautious. He won an impressive 57 percent of the popular vote, carrying forty-two out of forty-eight states and Democrats gained lopsided majorities in both houses. A rare shortcoming for the Democrats was among African Americans. FDR won only 23 percent of the black vote and, in some northern cities, fell behind Smith's showing in 1928. Despite wide discontent with Hoover's commitment to civil rights, African Americans still had fresh memories about FDR's complicity with segregation as Assistant

Secretary of the Navy and his close ties with the segregationist South. As Nancy Weiss put it in her landmark study, *Farewell to the Party of Lincoln,* FDR's prior "political career had shown no sensitivity to the problems of blacks."[81]

A Period of Flux, The Tragic Interregnum

Historical accounts of FDR's 1932 election victory often leave the impression that Roosevelt's voters had endorsed the welfare-regulatory philosophy of the New Deal or something like it. But before his election, Roosevelt gave few clues about his eventual destination as president in 1933. Campaign statements that seemed to foreshadow elements of the New Deal coexisted with, and were often overshadowed by, contradictory pledges to carry out the Democratic platform's pledge to slash government spending and maintain sound money. Perhaps because of a tendency to look backward from the New Deal, historians have not adequately considered whether another choice was available to Americans prior to 1933, beyond the "big three" of fascism, socialism, or the modern welfare-regulatory state. An ideological shift favorable to statism was underway by 1933 but the years immediately before that are harder to classify. The period from 1929 to 1932 can best be characterized as an interlude of ideological flux, when few options could be entirely ruled out.

Americans may have wanted change in 1932 but that did not necessarily entail support for more governmental intervention. To voters, change entailed a wide range of possibilities. In the state houses, it included the policies of progressives, such as Governor Philip La Follette of Wisconsin, as well as those of economizers such as Harry G. Leslie of Indiana. The most radical species of this economizing tendency was tax resistance, which centered primarily on a rising de facto burden of property taxes. The source of this burden was that although real estate values had fallen dramatically, tax assessments and tax rates had remained at the old level. In 1932, *New York Times* journalist Anne O'Hare McCormick stated that the "nearest thing to a political revolution in the country is the tax revolt . . . taxpayers are wrought up to the point of willingness to give up public services. 'We'll do without county agents', they say. 'We'll give up the public health service'." Throughout the country, Americans formed "taxpayers' leagues" to demand spending cuts.[82]

During the long transition from November 1932 to March 1933, Roosevelt's statements and behavior both failed to counter existing levels of flux and also heightened them. His iciness toward

Hoover during the transition was in stark contrast to the cordiality between them a decade earlier. At times, he showed more interest in President Hoover's discomfort than in reassuring the nation. When reporters asked him about the issue of international debt, he quipped, "That's not my baby."[83]

Roosevelt's behavior helped undermine clear signs of recovery from July to November 1932, including a big rise in industrial production and fall in unemployment. A good example of FDR's attitude toward the crisis was his response to a new communication from Hoover. On February 19th, the Secret Service delivered to the president-elect, while he was enjoying a stage show at the Hotel Astor, a ten-page hand-written message from the president. It began: "A most critical situation has arisen in the country of which I feel to advise you confidentially." As evidence of a "steadily degenerating confidence in the future," the president elaborated that "the bank structure is weakened as witness Detroit and increased failures in other localities." Hoover urged the president elect to reassure financial markets and reduce this "state of alarm" by stating that he still planned to balance the budget and avoid any resort to inflation (both promises that FDR had made during the campaign).[84]

Raymond Moley, who saw Roosevelt read the message, had expected to see some recognition about the "grim news in his face or manner. And there was nothing—nothing but laughter and applause for the play actors, pleasant bantering with those who sat at the table with him, and the gay, unhurried, autographing of programs for half a hundred fellow guests." FDR delayed for another twelve days before responding. He innocently, and quite disingenuously if Moley's account is true, claimed that his secretary had "mislaid" his reply. As before, the wording of the president elect's reply stood firm against cooperating in any joint effort.[85]

In failing to advance any constructive solutions, FDR not only rebuffed Hoover but also members of his own party. Alarmed by the banking crisis, Senator Carter Glass (then widely mentioned as a possible secretary of treasury) made a renewed push for his banking bill in January 1933. This time Hoover publicly backed the measure. After the bill passed the House, however, the populist-minded Senator Huey Long (a crucial ally of FDR at the Democratic convention) launched a determined filibuster. Glass and Long each pressed FDR for support, but he answered them with obfuscation and mixed signals. Despite his background as a border state governor, and frequent sojourns there, Roosevelt had never shown any discernible interest in the generally well publicized Canadian approach to banking. After Long's filibuster dragged on for two weeks during a period of mounting crisis, FDR finally acted but in a destructive way. He scuttled the Glass bill by coming out against branching across county lines. Had either FDR or Hoover vigorously pushed the Canadian branch banking model, and done it much earlier, the course of the financial crisis during the transition might have been much less bleak.[86]

Not surprisingly, the banking collapse rapidly accelerated in the days before the inauguration on March 3rd 1933. In early February, Louisiana declared a state "holiday" closing the banks and by the beginning of March, twenty-five other states had done the same. Millions of Americans lost their deposits. "At the moment of Roosevelt's inauguration," writes H.W. Brands, "the American banking system verged on dissolution." But Roosevelt seemed unmoved. Hoover struggled for a middle ground sending clear signals that he wanted to cooperate with Roosevelt in measures such as invoking the Trading with the Enemy Act, enacted during World War I to give the president the power to restrict trade between the United States and its enemies, to control bank exchanges and withdrawals. Roosevelt again refused.[87]

Top Roosevelt aides had similar accounts of their candidate's apparent indifference during the transition. Tugwell confided to industrialist James Rand Jr. that Roosevelt was "fully aware" that the banking system "would undoubtedly collapse in a few days." This did not bother him because it "would place the responsibility in the lap of President Hoover" and thus give him "a free hand" and full credit for "rehabilitating the country on March 4th." Roosevelt himself told another advisor that it was time to "let them (the banks) bust—then we'll get things on a sound basis." Similarly, Charles Michelson, a leading Democratic publicist said that the "President-elect told me on more than one occasion that the bank crisis was due to culminate just about inauguration day . . . Naturally he did not care to have the dramatic effect of his intended proposals spoiled by a premature discussion of them in advance of their delivery." Moley speculated that after reading Hoover's message in February Roosevelt "either did not realize how serious the situation was or that he preferred to have conditions deteriorate and gain for himself the entire credit for the rescue operation."[88]

"A Thin, Steel-edged Cruelty"

Several historians attribute Roosevelt's behavior during the transition to a fear of being "locked into" the policies of the previous administration including commitment to the gold standard and a balanced budget. According to Brands, "Hoover wanted Roosevelt to share responsibility for policies over which he had no authority; and Roosevelt refused." Brands elaborates: "Roosevelt naturally resisted. The voters had selected him and rejected Hoover." Jean Edward Smith takes it further: "Hoover's doctrinaire attachment to the free market precluded government intervention. Even more serious in terms of long-term recovery. The president did his utmost to inveigle FDR into endorsing the administration's policy." Elevating it to yet another level entirely, Jonathan Alter, although agreeing that Roosevelt "intentionally allowed the economy to shift lower," puts ultimate blame on Hoover for not acting. Hoover, Alter asserts "was so shaken and confused that he believed that FDR, though he wasn't president, should also sign off on it. If Hoover had taken the action on his own, he would have left the presidency on a higher note."[89]

These interpretations often overstate policy differences between Hoover and Roosevelt and understate the considerable evidence of potential common ground. Examples of this common ground were Roosevelt's recent campaign statements, including a renewed commitment to "sound money," his vow not to tinker with the value of the currency, and his verbal commitment to balanced budgets. While these pronouncements stopped just short of a firm commitment to the gold standard, the same could be said for the GOP platform in 1932 which had endorsed a "sound currency" without specifying gold. Moreover, both Hoover and Roosevelt had promoted unprecedented governmental intervention to raise prices and wages and condemned the strategy of previous presidents to let them fall. Hoover's actions were not those of a "doctrinaire" free market advocate.

FDR had repeated openings, such as one encouraged by Secretary of State Henry Stimson, to meet Hoover halfway without making any firm long-term policy commitments. An agreement to issue a joint statement or endorse a presidential executive order did not have to entail a long-term commitment to the gold standard or even a balanced budget. There is no documented case of FDR ever seriously pondering the possibility of such a cooperative agreement. As Hoover pointed out on March 1st, FDR had simply ruled out any *modus vivendi* regardless of the details: "It would be futile to present anything unless the President-elect will publicly declare that it is his desire that it should be undertaken."[90]

When given chances to compromise to relieve immediate suffering, Roosevelt repeatedly chose instead to seek political advantage and expediency, and sometimes worse. This attitude fits a consistent pattern. A passage from a leading FDR biography, Kenneth S. Davis, comes uncomfortably close to providing an explanation: "there also ran through the complicated Roosevelt personality a thin, steel-edged cruelty, a narrow and deeply buried streak of sadism which seemed to contradict his empathic sensitivity, which did flatly contradict his general kindliness, but which was consistent with his instinct for power and with the masked vindictiveness of his dealings with those (they were very few) who had shamed him or otherwise made him feel small."[91]

FDR's callousness toward the suffering of Americans, such as that he demonstrated during the transition, obsession with personal political gain, and settling old grudges, were common threads in his political career. These qualities characterized his response to discrimination against African Americans during the Wilson administration, Newport Sex Scandal, protection of free speech during World War I, and the New York banking crisis. In these cases, he had revealed much pettiness, coldness, and predilection toward settling personal and political scores. While Roosevelt had admirable traits (most especially his inspiring fight against polio) it does no favors to an understanding of history to discount those less flattering aspects of his political personality which so often governed his behavior.

2

Fear and Emergency: The First New Deal

FDR's inauguration address on March 4th 1933 has captured the imagination of scholars and the informed public for decades. The website, American Rhetoric, ranks it as the "third greatest" speech in the twentieth century, over such competitors as Kennedy's "Ich bin ein Berliner" or Eisenhower's "Farewell Address." A survey of 137 scholars, including specialists in rhetoric, pegged it at number three. The National Constitution Center ranked it as the sixth greatest American speech, edging out both Martin Luther King Jr.'s "I Have a Dream" and Reagan's "Tear Down This Wall."[1]

The best-known passage, sometimes remembered to the exclusion of all else, is, "The only thing we have to fear is fear itself." As a result, some call it the "Fear itself speech." How these words came to be included is a matter of some debate. Eleanor Roosevelt said that her husband had drawn inspiration from Henry David Thoreau's diary: "Nothing is so much to be feared as fear." Raymond Moley, who was central to the drafting process, remembered that Louis Howe had lifted it from a department store advertisement. "I am sure," he adds, "that neither Howe at that time nor Roosevelt was familiar with Thoreau's passage." While a database search does not show "fear itself" in any advertisement, those words do appear in the "Wise Words" filler column from 1932 which quoted Francis Bacon: "Nothing is terrible except fear itself."[2]

By the twenty-first century, the phrase had taken on a life of its own including titles for movies, comic books, novels and the Bancroft-prize winning *Fear Itself: The New Deal and the Origins of Our Time* (2013) by Ira Katznelson. "'Fear itself': evocative and shocking," he writes, "it is a visceral phrase . . . As the president spoke, there already was more than enough cause to evoke 'fear itself'."

But Americans in 1933 did not necessarily see it in those terms. The newspapers had fewer references to "fear itself," according to a database search of March 3rd and March 4th, than to Roosevelt's call for "broad Executive power to wage a war against the emergency, as great as the power that would be given to me if we were in fact invaded by a foreign foe." The only newsreels known to currently exist (Universal and Hearst Metrotone) completely omitted the "fear itself" portion. Adding to this evidence was Eleanor Roosevelt's observation that the loudest applause came when "Franklin got to the part of his speech when he said it might become necessary for him to assume powers ordinarily granted to a President in war time." Another "analogue of war" in the speech was an appeal to martial virtues: "if we are to go forward, we must move as trained and loyal army willing to sacrifice for the good of a common discipline . . . We are, I know, ready and willing to submit our lives and our property to such discipline."[3]

Perhaps FDR's only undisputed original contribution to the address was the very first line inserted in his own handwriting at almost the last minute: "This is a day of national consecration." According to Davis Houck, the point of this was "to mark this moment as sacred, ordained by [God] . . . God should be invoked from the outset of his administration." Mary Grabar interprets this wording more negatively as breaking from the emphasis on humility in previous religious references in presidential addresses.[4]

"Congratulate Me: We're Off the Gold Standard!"

Roosevelt set off an avalanche of legislation in his first one hundred days in office, typically known as the First New Deal. Though FDR was never the kind of man to share credit, Hoover was both a pioneer and enabler. Hoover's outgoing staff aided closely in the implementation of the executive order on March 6th, closing all banks (the Bank Holiday). The main authors of the Emergency Banking Act of 1933 were Hoover's Secretary of the Treasury Ogden Mills and Undersecretary Arthur Ballantine.

The Act created a new precedent in legislative overreach by invoking the World War I Trading with the Enemy Act, which gave the president the power to restrict or regulate trade with enemy nations. In addition to his key drafting role in the Emergency Banking Act, Ballantine also wrote the first draft of FDR's Fireside Chat explaining the legislation. On April 5th, Executive Order 6102, following the same Trading with the Enemy Act "national emergency" template, banned private gold ownership (with some exceptions such as jewelry). It required Americans to surrender their gold by May 1st or face a possible ten-thousand-dollar fine or a ten-year prison term. FDR carefully reassured doubters that his bold actions were "temporary" rather than a radical break while William Woodin, his secretary of the treasury, called it "ridiculous and misleading to say that we have gone off the gold standard."[5]

The president had no intention of keeping Woodin's promise, however. On April 18th, he shocked his advisors by announcing "Congratulate me. We are off the gold standard." He mischievously needled the more conservative Secretary of State Cordell Hull. Pulling out a ten-dollar bill, he exclaimed "'Ha!"—the bill was from a Tennessee bank—"in your state, Cordell. How do *I* know it's any good? Only the fact that I think it is makes it so." One day later, the president officially announced that the U.S. was off the gold standard. Congress soon followed up by declaring invalid all current and future contracts requiring payment in gold, thus negating the same "gold clause" FDR had defended in his pre-election critique of Hoover's "rubber dollars."[6]

Roosevelt regarded the economic crisis as an opportunity for long-term transformation as much as an obstacle to be overcome. An early manifestation was the Civilian Conservation Corps (CCC) in March which he intended as "a permanent part" of the federal government. "The bill interested Roosevelt himself," writes James MacGregor Burns, "as much as any single measure of the Hundred Days." Under it, the unemployed, who wore army uniforms and slept in barracks, worked on various projects including reforestation. By July, there were over 1,400 camps, each commanded by a reserve army officer.[7]

A formidable financial engine of, and slush fund for, the First New Deal was the Federal Emergency Relief Administration (FERA). At its head was Harry Hopkins, a social-work veteran carried over from the administration of Governor Roosevelt. Created in May 1933, the FERA dispensed over $500 million in grants-in-aid for a variety of projects in both agriculture and industry but, under standards imposed by Hopkins, it selectively raised and lowered the bar for states to secure matching funds. For example, relatively poor Tennessee had to contribute an unusually high 33 percent in matching funds for relief while richer Pennsylvania only had to pay 10 percent. A pertinent difference was that Tennessee was safely Democratic (and thus could be taken for granted by FDR) while Pennsylvania, which had narrowly voted for Hoover in 1932, might be lured to the Democratic column in 1936.[8]

Roosevelt relied on the CCC and FERA to handle a political hot potato, the persistent push of World War I veterans for early payment of their bonus. Like Hoover, Roosevelt opposed early payment citing the massive potential expense. An added motivation was that it would divert resources from his other New Deal legislative priorities. A major difference with Hoover was that Roosevelt was much more skilled in defusing any potential trouble. He responded to a second contingent of marchers by giving them food and temporary shelter in safely distant Fort Hunt, Virginia (thus keeping them out of the nation's capital). After the First Lady led the veterans in a singalong, one veteran quipped, "Hoover sent the Army. Roosevelt sent his wife." Both the CCC and the FERA erected "transient camps" which gave veterans special preference. Over the next two years, these methods quieted potential discontent by dispersing the veterans throughout the country.[9]

The Welfare State as a Way of Life

Dependence on largesse from "alphabet soup" programs, including the FERA, the CCC, the Public Works Administration (PWA), and the Civil Works Administration (CWA), became a way of life for millions of Americans. Because earlier depressions had generally lasted two or three years, the unemployed had found it comparatively easy to fall back on charity, savings, family networks, insurance, and mutual aid. A decade-long Great Depression of double-digit unemployment, by contrast, put these old survival strategies under much greater stress. By the middle of 1934 (five years into the downturn) about one out of every seven Americans was on relief.[10]

The First New Deal brought the most consequential banking regulation in U.S. history: the Glass-Steagall Act (not to be confused with the earlier Glass Bill). While intended to correct weaknesses in the banking structure, it repeatedly compounded them. Glass-Steagall enshrined the primacy of unit banks and, arguably, heightened their vulnerability by spinning off the generally stronger, and more diverse, investment banking sector. The Act also created the Federal Deposit Insurance Corporation to partially or completely insure all deposits.

Although Roosevelt later took credit for deposit insurance, he had originally condemned the whole concept as an alarming entrée for shifting costs onto the taxpayers. Decades later, FDR's earlier warning came true when taxpayers forked out hundreds of billions of dollars for the savings and loan associations during the 1980s and failing banks in the Great Recession of 2008. The U.S. had chosen not to follow the examples set by Australia, the United Kingdom, Canada, and South Africa which, though shunning deposit insurance, had many fewer failures during the depression because they allowed banks to spread the risk, and thus protect depositors, through branching.[11]

Few programs of the First New Deal more directly touched the lives of the middle class than the Home Owners Loan Corporation (HOLC) of June 1933. It invited millions of distressed owners and lenders to apply for a government takeover of their mortgages. The HOLC also dispensed hefty bailouts to real-estate interests and local governments besieged by tax delinquency and tax resistance. An amendment pushed by urban officials required loan applicants to put priority on paying down outstanding tax arrears. The effect was not only to reduce tax delinquency but also, not coincidentally, to stem possible future tax revolts and tax strikes. Between 1933 and 1935, the HOLC lent over $200 million to taxpayers to pay their outstanding delinquent property taxes, all of which flowed in local treasuries.[12]

Transforming the U.S. through Public Power

FDR's preoccupation with extending "public power" over electricity was one of the main transformative features of the First New Deal. He forged a close alliance with Senator George Norris (R-Nebraska), the premier advocate of more governmental control over production and distribution. On being asked after their meeting in January if the president elect agreed with him, Norris replied, "He is more than with me, because he plans to go even farther [in extending federal control] than I did."

FDR's joint effort with Norris culminated in May 1933 with the Tennessee Valley Authority (TVA). Politics and presidential spite had much to do with determining where it was located. Hoover Dam on the Colorado River arguably made the most sense but was too closely associated with the former president. This animus was so visceral that Secretary of Interior Harold Ickes started to call it Boulder Dam and FDR followed suit. Two years after FDR's death, Truman, who had cultivated a friendly relationship with Hoover, returned the official name to Hoover Dam. Roosevelt envisioned the TVA as the first in a "step by step" plan . . . to ultimately transform the whole of the national structure."[13]

Historian Ira Katznelson observes that Southern Democrats, so essential in birthing the TVA, "assumed that the law would do nothing to disturb the racial order. They were correct." The TVA relegated African American employees to menial occupations under iron-clad segregation and the much touted "planned model community" of Norris, Tennessee (named in honor of Senator Norris), was an all-white "sundown town." As Anthony Gregory points out:

> the TVA expropriated black homeowners to make room for white workers. Among those harmed were a significant community of independent farmers: two thirds of East Tennessee's Black Americans worked their own farms. The relocation turned middling property-owning Black farmers into landless wage earners.[14]

Dragging Down Recovery

The economic rebound, which had started under Hoover in July 1932 but stalled because of uncertainty during the transition, resumed in March 1933. Impressively, unemployment dipped from 28.3 percent in March 1933 to 23.3 percent in July. A chief factor in this recovery was the stability brought by the Banking Holiday. Had that rate of recovery continued, unemployment would have fallen to under 5 percent by October 1934.

But, of course, nothing like that happened. The economy stayed in the doldrums, and joblessness in double digits, until the beginning of the next decade. After 1932, the U.S. lagged behind Japan, Sweden, New Zealand, Chile, and many other countries in the growth of industrial production. The Dow did not return to its 1929 level until several years after FDR's death. "The big question about the American depression is not whether war with Germany and Japan ended it," writes Amity Shlaes. "It is why the depression lasted until the war." In his Pulitzer Prize–winning overview of the period *Freedom from Fear*, historian David M. Kennedy concludes that "Whatever it was, [the New Deal] was not a recovery program, or at any rate not an effective one."[15]

A "Vote Adding Machine"

Four policies, all occurring in a six-month period in 1933, conspired together against a sustainable recovery: the Agricultural Adjustment Act (AAA) (May), the National Industrial Recovery Administration (NIRA) (June), the scuttling of the London

Economic Conference (July), and the gold buying spree (October). The AAA exercised unprecedented federal powers in peacetime, and pegged prices at the unusually high level of the prosperous pre-World War I period. It set out to reduce supply, and thus boost sagging agricultural prices, by paying farmers not to produce on part of their land. The AAA's gargantuan bureaucracy, funded by a tax on distributors (often demonized as "middlemen"), deployed thousands of inspectors to America's farms. Journalist H.V. Kaltenborn observed that "accountants had to keep track of what each inspector reported about, what each farmer was growing, and what benefits every grower or nongrower was entitled to receive."[16]

Gaming the system through the AAA often became a full-time occupation. Some farmers were able to skirt the limits by paying off inspectors and others secured subsidies on poor quality land they never farmed anyway. Still others reacted by purchasing more fertilizer to intensify yields thus running counter to the AAA goal of reducing production. In the South, planters, operating on a toothless honor system, ignored the requirement to pay fifty percent of any government benefits to their sharecroppers or tenants who, according to sociologist Rupert B. Vance, received "but a fraction of the benefit paid to landowners for retiring part of their acreage they cultivate."

The AAA gave planters wide discretion to racially discriminate in firing and retention. The effect was to throw more than a million people in agriculture out of work but, because they were politically powerless, FDR could safely ignore them. The president, as FDR admirer Robert McElvaine puts it, responded to this situation like a "vote adding machine" and "very few blacks in the South, and poor whites in the region could be counted on to vote Democratic even if the President did not do more for them."[17]

The AAA's all-out war on production led to appalling waste, including paying farmers to plow up ten million acres of crops and slaughter six million piglets. Most of the carcasses were thrown away while others were converted into fertilizer. Only about one tenth of this meat found its way to families on relief and that tenth was due to the last-minute intervention of AAA general counsel Jerome Frank. Ironically, while the AAA reduced production in some crops, it created incentives to turn to foreign sources. Imports rose for the first time in memory for such products as ham, cotton, butter, and corn. Only in 1941 did farm income reach the level of 1929 (not an especially good year).[18]

How the South Interprets the New Deal

New Deal blamed for loss of African American jobs.

"A Certain Little Sweater Factory"

No other legislation better summarized FDR's suspicion of free markets and voluntary cooperation than the National Industrial Recovery Act of June 1933 which created the National Recovery Administration (NRA). In April, he had tipped off reporters that he was considering a scheme for the "regulation of production or, to put it better, the prevention or foolish over-production." He related "a story which was told me the other day" about "a certain little sweater factory in a little town." The owners and the employees "had always been on exceedingly good terms" but the factory was teetering toward bankruptcy and "the population in this little town was practically starving to death." To prevent a shutdown, the workers had agreed to a wage cut and the factory became so successful that it stayed open all day and undersold "every other sweater factory."

Some might regard this as an inspiring success story of community and entrepreneurial resourcefulness, but FDR most certainly did not. He concluded that it was "bad business, in all ways" because of a reduced "scale of living" that had "put two other sweater factories completely out of business." To Roosevelt, the story was an urgent warning to "work out some kind of a plan" to redistribute the "volume of consumption in a given industry over the whole industry."[19]

The NRA, in Roosevelt's view, was just such a plan. It was meant to reproduce that spirit of collective sacrifice which he so fondly remembered from World War I: "Must we go on in many groping, disorganized, separate units to defeat or shall we move as one great team to victory?" The program had close parallels in design to Woodrow Wilson's old War Industries Board (WIB) led by Bernard Baruch. Roosevelt cemented the wartime connection by entrusting the agency to Baruch's main assistant at the WIB, General Hugh S. Johnson. Working alongside Johnson was Chief Counsel Donald Richberg, who was also a close FDR confidante. Johnson's explosive bluster on behalf of the NRA worked in tandem with Richberg's (and Roosevelt's) more subtle approach.[20]

Under the NRA, the executive branch had sweeping discretion to authorize industry-specific codes of fair competition and make those binding on both those who signed them and those who did not. But the goals of the various codes often ran at cross purposes: stimulate consumer "purchasing power," eliminate "cutthroat competition," (sometimes called "economic murder"), raise wages, boost production, hold up prices and spur employment. Signers of the "President's Re-employment Agreement" received in exchange a Blue Eagle poster. The NRA required each post office to prominently display a list of the signers, along with the names of their businesses. The campaign may have purported to be voluntary but, as one historian noted, "those who did not volunteer to cooperate were to be forced into participation."[21]

The labor regulations of the NRA, Section 7(a), institutionalized a system of collective bargaining under which a single union represented all workers in a particular organizing unit. Such an arrangement differed from the "plural bargaining" approach of many European countries which allowed workers to choose between competing, legally recognized, unions. Section 7(a) also authorized minimum wages and maximum hours. The NRA gave a tremendous spur to the American Federation of Labor which rapidly added two million members in the period after its implementation.

A small band of academic critics proved, in retrospect, to be prescient. “The policies of the New Deal,” wrote Harvard economics professor Joseph Schumpeter, “by attempting to fix wages and prices, have interfered with the automatic mechanisms of adjustment in a capitalist economy. Such interventions, while well-intentioned, often prolong the very maladjustments they seek to cure.” Similarly, British economist Lionel Robbins wrote in 1934 that Roosevelt’s effort “to maintain wages at levels above those which the market can sustain has been a potent cause of unemployment. By preventing the necessary adjustments in costs, such policies retard the recovery of industry and commerce.”[22]

“They’ll Get a Sock in the Nose”

Perhaps recalling his frustrations with the comparatively powerless American Construction Council during the 1920s, Roosevelt hailed the NRA’s code-making boards as “modern guilds” for the “general good.” Cooperating businesses received exemption from antitrust laws. Only 10 percent of the code writing and enforcement boards had representatives from labor and just 2 percent from consumers. Many in business abandoned their previous paeons to free enterprise and rallied to the program. Indicative of the early enthusiasm were endorsements by both the National Association of Manufacturers and the U.S. Chamber of Commerce, the latter hailing it as the “Magna Carta of Industry and Labor.”[23]

In contrast to Johnson’s swaggering, FDR was the NRA’s “good cop,” taking the high road of stressing generalized appeals to community spirit and neighborliness rather than the coercive aspects. Roosevelt considered it “wholly wrong to call the measures that we have taken Government control of farming, industry, and transportation. It is rather a partnership . . . not a partnership in profits, for the profits still go to the citizens, but rather a partnership in planning.” Yet, both FDR and Johnson shared a common mission of getting more businesses to display the NRA’s Blue Eagle emblem, “We Do Our Part.” In his Fireside Chat of July 24th 1933, FDR waxed that “In war, in the gloom of night attack, soldiers wear a bright badge on their shoulder to be sure that comrades do not fire on comrades. On that principle, those who cooperate in this program must know each other at a glance. That is why we have provided a badge of honor for this purpose, a simple design with a legend. 'We do our part', and I ask that all those who join with me shall display that badge prominently."[24]

Gyrating between ballyhoo and high-pressure tactics, Johnson excelled at the NRA's bad cop. "The general, drunk or sober," the president's son Elliott reminisced, "ran his operation like a circus. When he was not standing stage center in Washington, joking, cajoling, and badgering businessmen and labor leaders, he was crisscrossing the land in an army plane making headlines at every stop." Johnson also exhorted Americans to shelve as archaic deeply ingrained habits of thrift, delayed gratification, and restraint. "We must shake ourselves of this four-year-old idea of doing without against a rainy day," he declared, "and must do that overnight . . . Buy! Buy now! Buy within prudence everything you need and have so long denied yourselves." For a time, Johnson held tremendous sway. Even former president Hoover, who later depicted the NRA as a species of fascism, signed the NRA's pledge for consumer cooperation during this period. Hollywood movie owners joined in by mandating that the opening frames of each new film feature the Blue Eagle.[25]

Johnson's motto was "Those who are not with us are against us," and he meant it. As to recalcitrants, "They'll get a sock in the nose." Even more than FDR, he brushed aside analogies between the NRA and the previous trade association approach. Those groups, unlike the NRA, were about as effective "as the Old Ladies' Knitting Society." To underline this point, Johnson threw down the gauntlet to the "Captains of Industry" [now demoted to "Corporals of Disaster"] . . . You might be trampled underfoot—not knowingly but inadvertently—because of your small stature and of the uplifted glance of a people whose 'eyes have seen the glory' and whose purpose is intent on the inspired leadership of your friend and neighbor Franklin Roosevelt." But Johnson also admitted that the NRA was "absolutely unenforceable without a strong surge of public opinion behind it."[26]

The NRA's codes encompassed such variables as the hours of machine operation. production quotas, and permission to open or close plants. John T. Flynn recalled that "Flying squadrons of these private [code enforcement] coat-and-suit police went through the [New York Garment] district at night, battering down doors with axes looking for men who were committing the crime of sewing together a pair of pants at night." Sometimes the minutia encompassed the smallest of details including the precise components necessary to define macaroni. "Izzy" Herk, executive secretary of the local code authority for the burlesque industry in New York City, limited performers on a given night to only "four strips."[27]

Propaganda for the NRA was, of course, also propaganda for Franklin D. Roosevelt. The Warner Brothers hit movie, *Footlight Parade,* starring Jimmy Cagney, Ruby Keeler, and Joan Blondell, featured a lavish production number of dancers joining together to create an image of the Blue Eagle and then reversing it to reveal FDR's visage. This was subtle compared to a movie short, "Give a Man a Job!" an MGM production "Patriotically Contributed by the Motion Picture Industry." The pugnacious master of ceremonies, comedian Jimmy Durante, alternates between singing "Give a Man a Job," written by Richard Rodgers and Lorenz Hart, and mercilessly hectoring a banker, an exterminator (played by Moe Howard of Three Stooges fame), and a "hypochondriac." Durante admonishes the banker to hire a chauffeur "to keep a man from becoming a loafer." He pesters the exterminator to hire an assistant pointing out that NRA meant "No Rats Allowed." The hypochondriac's assigned mission is to hire separate doctors to treat her imagined "neuritis, bronchitis, phlebitis, St. Vitus or any other kind of an-itis, that will delight us." The finale reminds the audience that "we have a president now" who "gave the land a New Deal . . . If the old name of Roosevelt makes the old heart throb, you take this message straight from the President and give a man a job." At the conclusion, Durante pulls a cord raising a large "We Do Our Part" NRA banner to reveal FDR's portrait underneath draped in two American flags.[28]

The London Bombshell

FDR's single-mindedness in protecting the NRA and AAA animated his response to the London Economic Conference in June 1933. The delegates had arrived expecting that the U.S. would promote goals long favored by Cordell Hull, such as currency stabilization, paying down debt, and reducing tariffs. Even before it began, Hull had persuaded other countries to temporarily halt additional restrictions and currency manipulations. He viewed the conference as possibly the last chance to hold back the tide of protectionism. Agreeing, Roosevelt's director of the budget Lewis Douglas predicted that "if the London Economic Conference was not successful . . . Hitler would doubtless move his frontiers out by force."[29]

Hull, sincere in his belief that he had presidential backing, carried a copy in his pocket of a proposed bill soon to be pushed in Congress for reciprocal tariffs, as an intended centerpiece for discussion. Roosevelt, however, sent a telegram while Hull was in transit torpedoing that agenda and stating that he did not intend to support the bill. "I left for London with the highest of hopes," the Secretary of State later lamented, "but arrived with empty hands." Finally, the delegates, then desperate for almost any fig leaf, agreed to an innocuous statement that, in the words of Moley, would pass muster with "the most fanatical inflationist."[30]

But it was becoming apparent that FDR did not want any deal at all. In a "bombshell message," the president summarily rejected the weak compromise approved by the delegates as tainted by the "old fetishes of so-called international bankers" and contrary to each nation's sovereign right to regulate its own economic affairs. Even Arthur Schlesinger Jr., perhaps FDR's most famous historian defender, condemned this sabotage as "deplorable." The president had made the Europeans, then ready to agree to almost anything, look like fools.

The London Economic Conference was an opportunity never to be repeated. If the U.S. had used it to push for lower tariffs, wrote Hull many years later, "it would have greatly encouraged the whole spirit and doctrine of international cooperation. This might have been a splendid beginning, with greater possibilities ahead." Similarly, Kenneth S. Davis asks whether FDR had missed a chance "to stem or slow the tide of vicious aggressive nationalism, which was then rising so ominously in Hitler's Germany, in Mussolini's Italy, in militaristic Japan? The question must remain forever open. All this is certain that effort was never made."[31]

A Gold-Buying Spree

There was a method to FDR's madness, however. He regarded any move toward lower tariffs and a stabilized dollar as directly at odds with the NRA's and AAA's goals of higher prices and wages. FDR viewed the First New Deal as akin to a controlled laboratory experiment to be shielded from outside contagion of open international trade. Roosevelt had foreshadowed the often-profound nationalism of his agenda in a passage in his inaugural address stressing "that putting our own national house in order" and "first things first" had primacy over international relations or trade. A much blunter expression of this nationalism was Johnson's admonition to Moley that an "agreement to stabilize now on the lines your boy friends in London are suggesting would bust to hell and gone the prices we're sweating to raise."[32]

Critical to understanding FDR's motivations were the theories of George Frederick Warren, a professor of agricultural economics at Cornell University who asserted that stabilization would undermine the president's discretion in domestic affairs. For a time, the now largely forgotten Cornell professor became the most influential economist in the world. FDR leaned heavily on Warren's counsel to launch the most surreal phase of the First New Deal: the gold buying spree. Warren's idea was deceptively simple: if the price of gold rose so would the prices of other commodities including farm goods. This was music to Roosevelt's ears. When James Warburg, a key financial advisor to the president, urged gold stabilization in relation to the dollar at a definite price to enable people to plan future contracts, FDR retorted, "Poppycock. The bankers want to know everything beforehand and I've told them to go to hell." FDR was almost alone in the top reaches of the administration in his enthusiasm for Warren. Rexford Tugwell regarded the Cornell professor's theories as "nonsense," John Maynard Keynes found them to be "crack brained" while Hull was completely dismissive.[33]

But FDR, with the zeal of a convert, pushed ahead with abandon. On August 29th 1933, he issued Executive Order 6261 mandating that gold producers sell their output at a price he determined. So began a regular ritual. Every morning Secretary of Treasury Henry Morgenthau, Jesse H. Jones of the Reconstruction Finance Corporation, which carried out the purchases, convened in the president's bedroom to set the day's price of gold. When Morgenthau suggested an increase of between 19 and 22 cents, for example, Roosevelt settled on 21 cents, "a lucky number because it's three times seven." Morgenthau suspected the president was joking but it was hard to be sure. This statement was consistent, after all, with FDR's superstitious bent for lucky days, lucky clothes, and lucky hats. In December 1933, the gold buying spree, which Keynes belittled as "blind man's bluff," ended. FDR had lost faith in Warren's theories because the purchases had barely dented the world gold price or the domestic price of commodities. The Cornell professor soon faded back into relative obscurity.[34]

"That Admirable Italian Gentleman"

The era of the New Deal was also one of totalitarianism and authoritarianism in much of the rest of the world. On the left,

Lenin (1917), followed by Stalin (1927), consolidated total power in Russia, while on the right, Mussolini (1923) and later Hitler (1933), had established their own brands of dictatorship.

The United States never abandoned democracy, as did Russia, Italy, and Germany, but it did not exist in an ideological vacuum. Both Senator Robert F. Wagner (D-New York) and AFL head William Green, for example, had consulted the "corporative laws of Fascist Italy" when drafting Section 7(a). As Howard Dickman notes, Italy, by embracing this approach had become the "only significantly industrialized country before America to establish the principal exclusive representation in its labor law."[35]

These similarities in approaches to the New Deal were not lost on either Americans or Italians. In his diary, Tugwell called fascism "the cleanest, neatest, most effectively operating piece of social machinery I've ever seen. It makes me envious." FDR told a White House correspondent that he was keeping close track of Mussolini, "that admirable Italian gentleman." After Breckinridge Long, the new U.S. ambassador to Italy, met with the dictator, the president confided that he was "much interested and deeply impressed by what he has accomplished and by his evidenced honest purpose of restoring Italy." According to FDR's son, Elliott, this admiration for Mussolini only flagged after Italy's invasion of Ethiopia.[36]

Italian political and media elites reciprocated Roosevelt's praise. In his review of FDR's book, *Looking Forward,* Mussolini hailed the president's "appeal to the decisiveness and sobriety of the nation's youth" as "reminiscent of the ways and means by which Fascism awakened the Italian people." When he heard that the president had complete power to reject and rewrite a Fair Code of Competition, the Duce proclaimed: "Behold a dictator!" *Il Giornale d'Italia*, a leading newspaper in Italy, praised FDR's call for broad powers in his inaugural address: "the whole world feels the need for executive authority capable of acting with full powers of cutting short the purposeless chatter of legislative assemblies . . . this method of government may well be defined as Fascist."[37]

Hitler had also offered kind words, telling American ambassador William Dodd that he agreed with "the President in the view that the virtue of duty, readiness for sacrifice, and discipline should dominate the entire people." Hitler saw that approach as in accord with the Nazi philosophy that "The Public Weal Transcends the Interest of the Individual." One of Roosevelt's best qualities, the Fuehrer added, was that "he marches straight to his objective over Congress, over lobbies, over stubborn bureaucracies." In 1934, the main Nazi newspaper, the *Völkischer Beobachter*, hailed "Roosevelt's adoption of National Socialist strains of thought in his economic and social policies . . . The president's fundamental political course still contains democratic tendencies but is thoroughly infected by a strong national socialism.'"[38]

Enforcing Ideological Uniformity on Radio

FDR was unexcelled in his mastery of promoting his ideas through radio. His warm and finely honed voice, "sincere . . . and good natured even in attack," gained easy access to millions of living rooms. It was often said that he had the requisite natural talent to thrive as a radio announcer. Roosevelt both finished the regulatory edifice built by Hoover and Coolidge, who had worked together to create the Federal Radio Commission (FRC), the predecessor of the Federal Communications Commission, in 1927 and put his own peculiar stamp on it.[39]

Roosevelt had few, if any, scruples about hatching covert schemes to sideline dissenting radio voices. He was the master of behind-the-scenes intrigue, usually via private sector or governmental intermediaries, and adeptly manipulated the revolving door of regulators and industry executives. Illustrative of the president's extensive power was his relationship with Herbert L. Pettey, his appointee as the FRC's secretary. Pettey had overseen radio for Roosevelt in the 1932 campaign and continued to work in tandem with the administration after his appointment to the Democratic National Committee (DNC) to handle "radio matters."[40]

Almost in lockstep, broadcasters aligned themselves with the new regime. Former FRC commissioner, and CBS vice president, Henry A. Bellows, a Democrat and Harvard classmate of FDR, promised to reject any broadcast over the network "that in any way was critical of any policy of the Administration." He elaborated that all stations were "at the disposal of President Roosevelt and his administration." Bellows specified that CBS had a duty to support Roosevelt, right or wrong, and privately assured presidential press secretary Stephen Early that "the close contact between you and the broadcasters has tremendous possibilities of value to the administration, and as a life-long Democrat, I want to pledge my best efforts in making this cooperation successful."[41]

The day after Roosevelt took office, the networks and the National Association of Broadcasters (NAB) jointly announced that all broadcasting facilities were on "an instant's notice" at the service of the administration. They adopted a "right of way" policy of requiring affiliates to break into their regular broadcasts for the president's speeches. In the first year alone, the networks carried fifty-one of Roosevelt's speeches, far more than they had for Hoover in a similar period. This permissive access to the airwaves extended to the president's political allies and family members. At NBC's invitation, Louis Howe hosted a weekly series that often floated "useful trial balloons" for the president. At Howe's suggestion, the FRC asked each station to supply copies of "all addresses on public affairs," a practice that allowed administration friends to head off critical commentary by making friendly warnings to the stations.[42]

It was the president's fireside chats, however, that especially had priority both for the networks and for FDR. This format was ideal for making a personal pitch to the voters and bypassing the newspapers. According to media historian Betty Houchin Winfield, it cast the president simultaneously as "the newsgatherer, the reporter, as well as the editor." When Roosevelt later proposed a weekly newspaper to publisher J. David Stern to refute the "poisonous propaganda of the conservative press," Stern quipped that he did not need "such a vehicle. You did it alone on the radio."[43]

Radio proved indispensable for the promotion of the NRA. In August 1933, FRC Commissioner Harold A. Lafount warned that stations had a "patriotic, if not the bounden and legal duty," to reject advertisements from those "disposed to defy, ignore or modify the codes established by the N.R.A." Lest the consequences were insufficiently plain, he elaborated that "radio stations, using valuable facilities loaned to them temporarily by the government," must "not unwittingly be placed in an embarrassing position because of greed or lack of patriotism on the part of a few unscrupulous advertisers." In her study of radio censorship in 1937, *Not to Be Broadcast*, Ruth Brindze pointed out that "any similar effort to control the [print] press would have created a sensation. Not so with radio." The main issues under debate showed close parallels to those in the early twenty-first century discourse on the censorship of social media platforms.[44]

A radio voice that FDR encouraged was that of Father Charles E. Coughlin. Coughlin had started to broadcast his sermons in 1928 and rapidly gained an audience. He purchased time on dozens of hookups of independent stations and reached millions of listeners (including presidential candidate Roosevelt) who tuned in for his populist jeremiads against the "international bankers." "Once Roosevelt had decided that Coughlin would be useful to his political strategy," Alan Brinkley observes, "he showered the priest with attention and compliments and soon won him over completely." Coughlin was fulsome in his praise, proclaiming "Roosevelt or Ruin!" and "The New Deal is Christ's Deal." He seemed overjoyed when Roosevelt broke with the gold standard and characterized the gold-buying spree as "inspired leadership."[45]

"That's Legalized Murder"

The early part of 1934 had some rough patches for the president. For the first time, he paid a steep price for his own hubris during the airmail scandal. The background for this controversy was a highly publicized investigation led by Senator Hugo L. Black (D-Alabama), publicizing a lack of competitive bids for mail contracts, wasteful subsidies to private companies, as well as bribery and favoritism. Black recommended steps to open up the bidding process. Rejecting privatization and competition as an option, the president abruptly canceled all federal contracts and ordered Army fliers to henceforth deliver the mail.

The Magazine of Wall Street asked: "if private industry is thus to be summarily punished without even a fair hearing, what industry can confidently enter into contracts with its Government?" Aviator Charles Lindbergh, who worked for Trans World Airlines, sent a telegram to the president and press predicting that the new system would "unnecessarily and greatly damage American aviation." Roosevelt brushed this aside as well as a warning from veteran pilot, Eddie Rickenbacker, that young Army fliers lacked the necessary equipment and training to cope with foggy weather and other dangers.[46]

Rickenbacker characterized the resulting orgy of death as "legalized murder." Three pilots died on the first day in two separate crashes. The next week brought the death of six more pilots and the severe injuries of five others. The mounting pressure on the president included a lecture from his son Elliott who called it "probably as great a mistake as you've ever made." But FDR dug in his heels. Writing to Harvard law professor Felix Frankfurter, he complained that "the aviation companies have been shrieking to high heaven, using Chambers of Commerce in every small community with a flying field to demand the return of the contracts." When Rickenbacker tried to deliver a radio speech condemning the policy, a network executive at NBC informed him that "orders had come from Washington" not to allow any controversial commentary on that issue.[47]

As the death toll rose to twelve, FDR finally realized that he had to back off. He crafted a revised deal which simultaneously restored private contracts (with more competitive bidding) and exposed his pettiness. The wording excluded participation by any airline covered by the old arrangement, an impossibility since only the major airlines were immediately capable of doing the job. But to please FDR, each of them played along with the charade. Hence, Eastern Air Transport changed its name to Eastern Airlines and United Aircraft and Transport became United Airlines. Lindbergh described that ploy as "reminiscent of something to be found in Alice in Wonderland." The scandal had, according to Schlesinger, "dented the myth of Roosevelt's invulnerability and strengthened the business community's dislike of what it considered personal and arbitrary actions by the New Deal."[48]

Mounting Resistance to the New Deal

By this time, FDR was also facing considerable public resistance to the dictates of the NRA. Enthusiasm for the codes, always dependent on public compliance, was slackening. By late 1933, Senator William Borah (R-Idaho), who had fought the NRA from the beginning, had accumulated about nine thousand complaints about the law's enforcement.

Two detractors of the NRA were leading voices in the Democratic Party but had kept quiet publicly for sake of party loyalty. Senator Carter Glass, perhaps also still smarting from Roosevelt's duplicity when he capitulated to Huey Long's anti-branch banking filibuster earlier in the year, wrote to Hugh S. Johnson "that your blue buzzard will not fly from the mastheads of my two newspapers." He castigated the NRA as "unconstitutional, and tyrannical and literally brutal." Another critic was Hull who regarded attempts by the AAA and NRA to push up prices and wages as obstructive to low tariffs.[49]

By the beginning of 1934, the press was giving much more coverage to the plight of individual NRA victims. Jacob Maged, a tailor in Jersey City, New Jersey, went to jail for charging 35 cents for pressing a suit. The NRA code had mandated a price of not less than 40 cents. The *Washington Post* commented that "if Maged had to charge less than the bright and shiny tailor shop up the street if he wanted to continue to exist. The law said he couldn't." Also jailed was Fred Perkins, who owned a factory which manufactured batteries. His offense was that he had negotiated a cost-saving deal in cooperation with his workers who accepted wages under the NRA minimum to keep the factory running. It was not unlike the worker-management agreement described, and deplored, by FDR in his pre-NRA parable. Unlike Fred Perkins, the executives of Montgomery Ward, one of the largest retailers in the U.S., were not willing to go to jail. However, the company posted an advertisement stating that though it preferred "to continue the low prices" on tires, it had to raise them because of "the NRA order fixing these prices becomes effective next Monday."[50]

To mollify critics, FDR established the National Recovery Review Board to investigate the complaints. If this were a ploy to protect the program, however, it backfired spectacularly. Johnson, acting under "a moment of total aberration," endorsed the appointment of legendary defense attorney Clarence Darrow. FDR signed off, perhaps lulled by the seventy-seven-year-old legal lion's progressive credentials. Darrow's final report excoriated the NRA from top to bottom, depicting it as a business scheme to quash competition, raise prices, and to "seize control of an industry or to augment and extend a control already obtained." Richberg, who had also recommended Darrow's appointment, lamented that "a noted socialist who advocates complete government control of business" had authored a report "for philosophical anarchists, who apparently oppose any government control of anybody, including criminals."[51]

A Raw Deal for African Americans?

NRA enforcement brought many complaints from African Americans, a growing potential voting constituency for FDR, that it was pricing them out of the job market. In January 1934, the *Chicago Defender*, a paper which had endorsed FDR in 1932, ran one in a series of scathing anti-New Deal editorial cartoons entitled "How the South Interprets the New Deal." The top panel shows a black man speaking to his wife before going to work: "Dear, the old factory is now a member of the 'NRA', which means I'll get better wages and better hours." The second panel puts the man at the front of a line of discharged workers staring at a sign which read: "Under the 'NRA', this factory shall advance wages and minimize hours of all employees. Henceforth we shall employ white help only." The cartoon encapsulated a genuine problem faced by African Americans. In the low-wage South especially, employers adapted to the NRA's high minimum wages through mechanization and firing unskilled workers.[52]

Writing for the *Crisis*, the NAACP's official publication, W.E.B. Du Bois charged that the American Federation of Labor (AFL) and other predominantly white unions, were manipulating the NRA's collective bargaining rules to force African Americans out of the marketplace: "Seeking to avail itself of the powers granted under Section 7(a) of the NRA, union labor strategy seems to be to form a union in a given plant, strike to obtain the right to bargain with the employer as the sole representative of labor, and then to close the union to black workers, effectively cutting them off from employment." A member of the Chicago Urban League recommended that blacks take jobs as strikebreakers "provided that they were retained when the strike was over." Labor historian Herbert Hill concludes that the NRA's codes "intended to be the keystone of President Roosevelt's program to protect and uplift the working class had become a millstone around the Black worker's neck."[53]

The immediate harm inflicted on African Americans by the NRA and AAA was insignificant compared to that wrought by the Federal Housing Administration (FHA) launched in August 1934. In contrast to the HOLC, which focused on mortgage refinancing, that agency set out to enable Americans to buy their first home by insuring bank mortgages up to 80 percent of the purchase price. The rules threw multiple obstacles in the way of African American applicants, however. The FHA's appraisal standards included a whites-only provision and its *Underwriting Manual* (often used by banks in lending decisions) warned against mortgages in neighborhoods with too many "inharmonious racial or nationality groups." Because of the FHA, as Richard Rothstein puts it in *The Color of Law: The Forgotten History of How Our Government Segregated America* "racial segregation now became an official requirement of the federal mortgage insurance program."[54]

Inertia was FDR's default position, on the other hand, when it came to supporting any law intended to unambiguously help African Americans. For more than a decade, Republicans and some northern Democrats had pushed for a federal law to ban lynching. In 1922, a bill had passed the House, and secured the active backing of President Warren G. Harding, but a Senate filibuster led by Southern Democrats stopped it dead.

The situation had not greatly changed ten years later. While educated Southern opinion increasingly condemned lynchings, and the numbers of lynchings had declined somewhat, de facto checks on determined mobs remained extremely weak. "At no point during the entire period," writes historian Neal R. McMillen, "did vigilantes have cause to expect punishment . . . Even the most prudent investigations by antilynching reformers generally met a wall of silence." A new push for a federal anti-lynching bill came up in December 1933 but FDR, unlike Harding, was silent. While it passed the House judiciary committee, it never came to a floor vote in the House (where it would have had certain passage) because Democrats in the Senate vowed to block it. At a meeting in mid-1934 arranged by the First Lady with NAACP head Walter White, FDR fell back on an already threadbare excuse: "If I come out for an anti-lynching bill now, they [Southern Democrats) will block every bill I ask Congress to pass to keep America from collapsing."[55]

Several widely publicized racial outrages later in the year did nothing to shake this presidential silence. FDR was apparently unmoved, for example, after a mob seized Claude Neal, a black man accused of murdering a white woman in Florida and then forced him to eat parts of his penis and testicles. A few days later, the president brushed aside questions about the torture-killing by telling a reporter that he had to "check up and see what I did last year. I have forgotten." Affirming this callousness, White House press secretary, Stephen Early, a Virginian "was always on the alert for any piece of legislation, White House appointment, or firm pronouncement that risked an impression of special concern for racial discrimination" while key FDR speechwriter Senator Jimmy Byrnes (D-South Carolina) "believed unquestionably in the supremacy of the Caucasian race." Eleanor Roosevelt, despite much more tolerant attitudes, repeatedly let politics and caution triumph in moments of decision. Walter White invited her to a meeting to protest the Neal killing but after the president intervened to tell her it was "dynamite," she answered: "I do not feel it is wise to speak on pending legislation."[56]

The "Black Cabinet" Charade

Nevertheless, both Eleanor and Franklin recognized the need to make symbolic gestures. African Americans, though they had stayed with Hoover in 1932, were increasingly receptive to Democrats. The most important of these gestures was the informal launching of the so-called "Black Cabinet." Popularized by African American educator Mary McLeod Bethune, it was, more or less, shorthand for the Federal Council of Negro Affairs, a group of black federal employees who met informally. The term "Black Cabinet" was, of course, a misnomer. It was not an actual cabinet, nor did FDR ever acknowledge it as such. It was also not an original idea. For more than a quarter century, the Black press had periodically referred to African American advisors to Republican presidents as members of a "Black Cabinet."[57]

While the Black Cabinet was politically useful for FDR, it was almost wholly a charade, and an often cruel one at that. In an article in April 1934, African American journalist Eugene Davidson perceptively referred to it as "the mythical Black Cabinet." Over the time of its existence, any real accomplishments were by members in their individual capacities. Put in perspective, during his entire time in office, FDR did not nominate a single African American to either his own official cabinet or to a sub-cabinet position. As Nancy Weiss cautions, interpreting the Black Cabinet "as evidence of a genuine commitment by the New Deal to racial progress would be to overstate the case. Rather, it shows, again, the skill of Franklin D. Roosevelt in turning limited departures from past racial practices to his own political advantage."[58]

An "Embargo Fence" to Protect the New Deal?

Throughout 1934, Hull was desperately trying to curry favor with FDR in his fight for freer trade. The economic nationalists had prevailed in the early rounds but Hull, after almost resigning because of his humiliation at the London Economic Conference, initiated a spirited counterattack. He benefited from considerable clout in Congress and generally good press. In his fight for freer trade, Hull also had some powerful allies on the political left, including Secretary of Agriculture Henry Wallace who regarded low tariffs as the best hope for farmers to sell their surpluses.

In April, however, FDR undermined Hull again by naming George N. Peek, an ardent advocate of protectionist economic warfare as Foreign Trade Advisor. As the former administrator of the AAA, Peek, like his friend Hugh S. Johnson, promoted an "embargo fence" (with partial exceptions for bi-lateral carve-outs) as a necessary aid for the New Deal's high price and high wage policy. Hull recalled that he could not have been more stunned "if Mr. Roosevelt had hit me between the eyes with a sledge hammer." Peek's "efforts, and those of associates, aided at times by the President, came perilously near supplanting my whole set of international economic policies."[59]

FDR simultaneously dangled hope in front of both Hull and Peek when he signed the Reciprocal Trade Agreement Act (RTAA) in June 1934, authorizing the president to raise or lower tariffs by fifty percent at his discretion. Technically an amendment to the

Smoot-Hawley law, it was, as Amity Shlaes writes, "classic Roosevelt" because it "strengthened the power of the executive."

The RTAA (as well as subsequent trade laws) anticipated the wide and, for a time, unhindered executive leeway exercised by President Donald Trump to raise or lower tariffs to wage economic warfare. Hull, in contrast to Peek, envisioned the RTAA as enabling the negotiation of agreements to free up free trade, nation-by-nation, based on the Most Favored Nation (MFN) principle. If the U.S. had a MFN deal with another country to lower tariffs, for example, every other country which also signed an MFN agreement with the U.S. got the exact same "unconditional" terms. Hull's long-term goal was multilateral reduction in trade barriers. Peek, however, looked on the RTAA as an opening to negotiate bilateral "horse trading" exclusive bargains for the U.S. to purchase scarce goods and dispose of surpluses. As Arthur Schlesinger Jr. observes, Peek, and at times FDR, sought a "form of economic autarchy; they desired a nation where external controls could render internal planning safe from the economic tempests of the world outside."[60]

For the next year, Hull and Peek jockeyed in a kind of cold war over the future direction of trade policy. Both men gained maneuvering space because of the president's penchant for running away from tough choices. Building on relationships developed through the Good Neighbor policy in Latin America, Hull vigorously negotiated MFN agreements while Peek concentrated on negotiating bilateral "horse-trading" or *quid pro quo* deals with major manufacturing countries. These two contradictory approaches could not co-exist over time. For the time being, Hull had the upper hand, and he controlled the comparatively vast machinery of the State Department.[61]

During most of 1934, the economy showed signs of recovery caused in part by Roosevelt's abandonment of his gold-buying spree. Securing congressional authorization, he fixed the price at $35 per ounce relative to the dollar, thus giving investors greater certainty. Hull's success with MFN also contributed to recovery in a modest way. After dipping precipitously from 1929 to 1933, the U.S. share of world trade finally began to inch up in 1934. Another driver for recovery was one over which Roosevelt had no control. The panic induced by Hitler's consolidation of power led Europeans to seek relative safety by shipping their gold to the United States. The inflow increased after Stalin, desperate for foreign exchange, ramped up gold mining in the Soviet Union. America's gold stock jumped between 1934 and 1937 and this boosted lending and economic activity. "Between them, it seems," writes economic historian George Selgin, "Stalin and Hitler were then doing more to hasten the U.S. recovery than the American president himself!" There was no denying the overall anemic nature of the recovery, however. Unemployment in 1934 was 21 percent, a far cry from the 5 percent it would have been in October 1934 if the rate of recovery from March to July 1933 had continued unabated.[62]

Winning Elections through Strategic Patronage

The depression's persistence, combined with the historical tendency of the dominant party to lose ground in midterms, led many pundits to predict big GOP gains in 1934. But FDR moved aggressively to overcome these apparent disadvantages by turning for help to a pioneer of modern scientific polling, Emil Hurja, the deputy director of the Democratic National Committee. Hurja identified over sixty districts where Democratic candidates had a fighting chance and FDR then ensured that federal funds and projects flowed to them. Hurja sent charts for candidates as guides for their campaigns: "Federal appropriations segregated by departments for your state. You can use this any way you like—in speeches, radio talks or newspaper interviews."[63]

The first electoral test was in the normally Republican state of Maine which at the time voted in September rather than November. In the months before that election, FDR dispensed a bonanza of well-advertised federal projects. The Democratic candidate for governor reminded voters that the "Roosevelt policies are such that the state must have friendly contacts with Washington." The Democrat running for U.S. Congress boasted that "Maine has received $108 million from New Deal agencies." After both Democrats won unexpected victories in Republican Maine, FDR and Hurja repeated this technique to help other Democratic candidates throughout the country.[64]

The national application of this strategy after the Maine experience brought dramatic success in the 1934 elections. The results were consistently bad news for the Republicans. The Democrats gained nine seats each in the Senate and House and an equal number in the House, giving them a super majority in both chambers. The number of Republican governors fell to a dismal low of only seven. These electoral gains left FDR more emboldened than ever.

Despite a lagging economy, he had bucked the historical trend in a midterm election. That election taught him valuable lessons about the electoral potential to apply scientific polling, when combined with targeted federal spending and patronage. Throughout the balance of his time in office, he repeatedly fine-tuned and expanded these methods, which relied on the strategic dispersal of funds, for future electoral successes. FDR now seemed to enjoy a free hand to expand the New Deal.

3

The Second New Deal: Free Markets Plowed Under

Less than a week after the thumping Democratic victory in November 1934, FDR was on a leisurely Sunday drive with members of his staff. They had rarely seen him more elated and determined. He told them:

> Boys—this is our hour! We've got to get everything we want—a works program, social security, wages and hours, everything—now or never. Get your minds at work on developing a complete ticket to provide security for all the folks of this country up and down and across the board.[1]

Eleanor as FDR's Not So Secret Weapon

Notably absent from FDR's list of priorities was enacting an antilynching bill. Even so, the NAACP's executive secretary, Walter White, a friend of the First Lady, was confident that it too would find a place on the agenda. In December, he sent to the president a petition of 250 prominent leaders in politics and higher education urging legislation to address this issue as a "must."

As one year earlier, Roosevelt reacted with delay and silence. After additional rebuffs, White had lost nearly all hope. He wrote to the president that "in justice to the cause I serve I cannot continue to remain even a small part of your official family." He added "that the utterly shameless filibuster could not have withstood the pressure of public opinion had you spoken out against it." Driving White's urgency was the continued severity of the problem. In 1934, for example, there were fifteen documented lynchings across twelve states in the South, and in 1935 the number had increased to twenty-one.[2]

But Eleanor was FDR's not-so-secret weapon for such occasions, and she demonstrated why in handling White. Her sincere beliefs in racial justice coexisted uneasily with her role as a presidential troubleshooter during crucial moments. This was such a moment. Eleanor both cooled White's anger by expressing sincere regret and then softened the blow by wishing "better luck next time."[3]

The First Lady's approach to the Walter White case typified the ways in which she dealt with such cases. Depending on the situation, her methods included incremental amelioration, conciliation, symbolic gestures, promises, and, if necessary, well-managed strategies of delay. Nobody could more skillfully defuse anger by holding out the prospect of a light at the end of the tunnel. "The First Lady once warned," Anthony Gregory observes, "that the NAACP would dislike Roosevelt's current thinking, while suggesting he might change his mind." It's no exaggeration to state that Eleanor shifted the entire trajectory of American civil rights history. This was not always in a good way. Without her influence, for example, African Americans might have stayed with the GOP and brought reform to that party or, more provocatively, pursued a more militant course earlier, including direct action. In the here-and-now of the 1930s, however, her sincere expressions of compassion were not insignificant in a society which often ignored or belittled black concerns.[4]

Freer Trade or Economic War?

FDR had drawn from his bag of tricks to immobilize any meaningful anti-lynching bill, but that kind of approach was no longer sufficient to reconcile the opposing trade policies pushed by Cordell Hull and George Peek. The strategy of papering over the contradictions between freer trade through Most Favored Nation Agreements and closed door, bilateral protectionism had reached its final limits. The almost inevitable showdown came in December 1934 after Peek cut a deal with Germany to exchange 800,000 bales of American cotton for an equivalent of industrial goods. The Brazilian ambassador, citing U.S. discrimination against his country's cotton exports, reacted by threatening to pull out of a pending MFN agreement.[5]

While FDR had no great affinity for Hull's views on trade, conditions now compelled him to pick one side or the other. After initially approving the German deal, he reversed course and canceled it. Peek stayed at his federal post, perhaps encouraged by the muddled thinking evidenced by FDR's reassurance to Jesse Jones in

July 1935 that Peek's "position is so close to that of the State Department that the difference is one of detail and not of principle." Nevertheless, by November, Peek recognized that Hull had the upper hand and resigned. While Hull was to sign an impressive nineteen additional MFN agreements through 1939, that accomplishment barely dented the protectionist structure built by Smoot-Hawley and fortified by the collapse of the London Economic Conference. These treaties reduced U.S. tariffs from 46.7 percent in 1935 to 40.7 percent in 1940, but this was only about half the increase in the previous five years.[6]

"People Will Say It's Propaganda"

FDR officially launched the Second New Deal (or Second Hundred Days) on May 6th 1935, through an executive order establishing the Works Progress Administration (WPA) and entrusted Harry Hopkins to head it. The WPA embodied FDR's ideal of executive supremacy by eliminating the local and matching funds requirement in favor of giving the president complete discretion in the dispersal of funds.

With a budget of over four billion dollars and employing more than three million workers, the WPA soon overshadowed all previous work relief efforts. Local and state politicians vied to "woo Roosevelt" for the largesse. Frank Kent shed some light on the process: "Every city and state needs its portion of the incredibly great sum. They all want as much as they can get. Failure to secure its proportion places a state at great disadvantage. It means heavier local taxation." Of course, FDR expected something in return. The WPA was both a device to secure Democratic votes and to sell New Deal ideas to the public.[7]

The propaganda aspect of the WPA reached its apex in the Federal Theater Project (FTP). It soon mushroomed to over ten thousand employees (about half based in New York) including actors, directors, and ushers. While most of the FTP's productions represented relatively non-controversial fare, such as modern adaptations of Shakespeare, others had a decidedly left-wing slant. One of the most publicized was the long-running play "Triple A—Plowed Under," which, according to one of its musical composers, was "up to its ears in commies." When journalist Garet Garrett attended a performance, he noticed that the finale brought enthusiastic applause "by Communists who packed the audience because it happened to embody the idea of a militant workers'-and-farmers' alliance."[8]

The FTP mobilized to promote the next major initiative of the Second New Deal: The Rural Electrification Administration (REA) created by executive order in May 1935. Consistent with the "public power" template of the TVA, it authorized action "to initiate, formulate, administer, and supervise a program of approved projects with respect to the generation, transmission, and distribution of electric energy in rural areas." The order empowered the REA to seize "any real property" through eminent domain to carry out these goals.[9]

Roosevelt justified the REA on the theory that private enterprise was incapable of providing the "modern necessity" of electricity to rural areas. This same view was the raison d'etre of the FTP production of Arthur Arent's play, *Power*, described by a *New York Times* reviewer as "one of the most exuberant shows in town." The main theme depicted is a struggle between price-gouging utility executives, such as Wendell Willkie and Samuel Insull, who stubbornly refuse to extend service, and public-spirited crusaders for public power, such as Senator George Norris. The setting is Dayton, Tennessee, the recipient of one of the first REA loans. After the farmers win their fight for public power, they parade triumphantly around a filmed projection of a waterfall at Norris Dam, singing a "Kentucky folk tune" which includes the stanza:

> The Government employs us,
> Short Hours and certain pay;
> Oh things are up and comin',
> God bless the T.V.A.[10]

An ecstatic Harry Hopkins came backstage to congratulate the cast for a "great show." He added "you will take a lot of criticism on this play. People will say it's propaganda. Well, I say what of it? It's propaganda to educate the consumer who's paying for power. It's about time someone had some propaganda for him."[11]

Few New Deal programs have received more praise from historians than the Rural Electrification Administration. Schlesinger set an early standard by concluding that "rural electrification, if it was to come in anyone's lifetime, would have to be brought about by government . . . No single event, save perhaps for the invention of the automobile, so effectively diminished the aching resentment of the farmers and so swiftly closed the gap between country and city. No single public agency ever so enriched and brightened the quality of rural living." That assessment, and many like it, however, considerably overstates REA's accomplishments and understates the tremendous strides in rural electrification during the preceding period.

Private companies had led a four-fold increase in electrification, some of which occurred during a so-called "agricultural depression" between 1924 (2.8 percent of rural homes) and 1932 (11.8 of rural homes). Had this original rate of increase continued (it slowed but did not decline during the early 1930s) nearly all farms would have been electrified by the 1940s.[12]

The Rise and Demise of Decentralized Electricity

While extending lines to low density rural areas presented many challenges, private companies in the pre-REA era found creative ways to overcome them. One of these was to piggyback service for family farms by tying it to the demands of more profitable consumers. By 1931, for example, companies had connected a large majority of rural homes in California and Utah to lines originally brought in for high-usage operations to pump water for irrigation. Private enterprise pioneered in such cost-reducing innovations (some later inaccurately attributed to the REA) as installing lines spanning up to six hundred feet between poles, improvements to insulation and wiring and lowering right-of-way costs by building along existing roadways.[13]

For good or ill, the REA, and the TVA before it, reduced incentives for consumers to "stay off the grid." At the time those agencies came on the scene, more than half of all electrified farm homes had individual generators. Manufactured by commercial companies and sold directly to consumers, these so-called "individual lighting plants" used such diverse power sources as wind, water, gasoline, or kerosene. One of the most popular was Delco-Light which in 1926 sold individual lighting plants to more than a third of the 1,786 electrified farms in New York state, including for such amenities as washing machines, irons, radios, and cream separators. "Prior to the construction of expensive transmission grids," writes economic historian Robert E. Wright, "farms . . . produced their own electricity with windmills, mechanical energy, and diesel or gasoline generators, or they bought it in town on weekends and stored it in large batteries, rendering untrue the babblings of a New Dealer who claimed that 'one doesn't go into a retail store and buy a package of electricity over the counter'."[14]

From the outset, REA administrators followed a rigid policy of rebuffing private sector participation, including a proposal in July

1935 by utility companies to extend power to about a quarter of a million farms in eighteen months. Instead, the REA spent the next two decades lavishing funds and legal privileges on quasi-non-governmental cooperatives through loans and subsidies. As a result, private suppliers fell from 100 percent of the market in 1935 to just over 40 percent in 1950 and sales to consumers of individual lighting plants withered away as existing equipment, such as windmills, gradually went to rust.[15]

Historian Richard F. Hirsh in his extensive survey, *Powering American Farms,* asks what might have happened had the REA never existed. "Conceivably, "he writes, "if private utility companies had not continued their pre-Depression pace of supplying electricity to farmers or if the federal government had not intervened, a larger number of farmers would have purchased independent means to generate power. As ruralites came out of the Depression and World War II with greater prosperity . . . more of them would have had the wherewithal to purchase products such as Delco-Light sets . . . Consequently, rural America would have become electrified through a hodgepodge of interconnected and isolated power systems."[16]

"Joseph and His Brethren"

The first half of the roller coaster month of May 1935 included the executive orders creating two of FDR's greatest triumphs, the WPA and the REA, but ended with his first significant defeat. On May 27th, the Supreme Court struck down the NRA as unconstitutional in *A.L.A. Schechter Poultry Corp. v. United States.*

Much to their later regret, Justice Department prosecutors were chiefly responsible for publicizing the Schechter case and giving it momentum. Given their ideological worldview it is not difficult to understand why. The Schechters seemed ideally cast in the unsympathetic role as litigants who had knowingly endangered consumer health. In October 1934, a Brooklyn grand jury bolstered the government's confidence by issuing a sixty-count indictment for code violations, some of them felonies. It accused the brothers of requiring employees to work over the mandated forty-four to forty-eight hours, paying under the official minimum wage, undercutting the minimum price, and finally, piled on with the open-ended crime of "conspiracy" against the Code of Fair Practices for the Live Poultry Industry. Prosecutors emphasized that the Schechters had flouted the code's ban on "straight killing," a kosher practice where customers had free pick of any chicken in the coop for purchase. To the government, straight killing violated health rules and fostered cutthroat competition. To poultry sellers, such as the Schechters, by contrast, it represented a kind of "ghetto version of the Good Housekeeping Seal" which put the onus on customers to choose their birds and verify that "the product was as healthy as possible."[17]

The litigation pitted an expert legal team backed by federal might against a storefront lawyer working on a shoestring. Representing the NRA was Walter Lyman Rice, a graduate of Harvard Law School, then on the fast track to a successful career in the federal government. The Schechters hired a quintessential guy from the neighborhood, Joseph Heller, a graduate of Brooklyn Law School who, like them, was a Jewish immigrant. The pro-New Deal journalistic duo of Drew Pearson and Robert Allen depicted Heller as a "hawk nosed lawyer" with a "Brooklyn Hebrew accent." They also commented with some amusement on how he "labored over his lawbooks in Manhattan, determined to rank his name alongside that of Daniel Webster." Under the headline, "Joseph and His Brethren," they characterized the brothers as two of many of "the kosher butchers of the city" who work "in filth, blood and chicken feathers."[18]

The courtroom duels between Rice and Martin Schechter revealed a clash in attitudes both toward culture and the meaning of economic exchange. When Rice implied that the brothers had competed in too "keen" a way, the witness answered: "Chicken dealers will walk into my place and wouldn't like my price, and he would go out again . . . The market isn't stable. It might be 15 cents today, the market quotation, and tomorrow 18 cents." Rice persisted: "There is a lot of competition between you and your competitors is there not?" Schechter answered: "There is a lot of competition in every other business, the same thing." When in November 1934, a jury convicted the Schechters, Rice hailed the result as a "sweeping victory of immense importance." The brothers lost their first appeal but continued to push forward.[19]

"The Whole Code Must Fall"

The oral arguments at the Supreme Court began ominously for the administration and then went downhill. The questions to counsel from the justices expressed more curiosity about the nitty-gritty of the poultry industry than in abstract constitutional theory.

The accusations about straight killing, which had helped prosecutors in the lower courts, now redounded against them. Questioning from the anti-New Deal stalwart James Clark McReynolds playfully exposed the absurdities of the NRA poultry code. Heller's responses generated laughter in the courtroom. Under the governmental dictate, he pointed out, the "customer is not permitted to select the one he wants. He must put his hand in the coop . . . and take the first chicken that comes to hand." Once the laughter had subsided, Heller was adamant that his objections went far beyond the straight killing provision: "The whole Code must fall."

Fall it did. On May 27th, the Court unanimously struck down the National Industrial Recovery Act as an unconstitutional delegation of power to the executive branch. Even the two most progressive justices, Louis Brandeis and Benjamin Cardozo, signed on to the opinion. "Extraordinary conditions may call for extraordinary remedies," the Court concluded. "But the argument necessarily stops short of an attempt to justify action which lies outside the sphere of constitutional authority. Extraordinary conditions do not create or enlarge constitutional power." In a biting concurrence, Cardozo summarized the NRA as "delegation running riot."[20]

Soon after the ruling, Brandeis cornered two of Roosevelt's main advisors, the lawyers Thomas G. Corcoran and Benjamin Cohen, in the Supreme Court's robing room. He had a blunt message for them to pass on to their boss: "This is the end of this business of centralization, and I want you to go back and tell the president that we're not going to let this government centralize everything. It's come to an end."

Roosevelt was shocked at the sheer totality of his defeat. A few months earlier, he had confidently asked Congress for a two-year extension of the NRA, concluding that "the fundamental purpose and principle of the act are sound. To abandon them is unthinkable. It would spell the return of industrial and labor chaos." When informed of the vote lineup, the president wondered if "old Isaiah" (his nickname for Brandeis) had lost his good sense.[21]

Four days after the ruling, FDR famously castigated the Supreme Court for "the horse-and-buggy definition of interstate commerce." But Roosevelt's objections went beyond quibbles about constitutional interpretation. He belittled the Court for endorsing a theory "delightful in its naivete" of the ugly realities of the "voluntary processes on the part of business." Rather than abandon the idea of the NRA, Roosevelt still yearned to bring it back in a new form. He later conveyed to Morgenthau his dream to someday implement "an international cartel in different commodities" which would have the power to "tell England that she had too many people and she should move out ten million of her population. I would take a look at each country and, of course, when we made them disarm we would have to find new work for the munition workers in each country and that is where this international cartel would come in and your job would be to handle the finances."[22]

Monopoly Unionism through the Wagner Act

FDR's continuing nostalgia for the NRA put him in a distinct minority among New Dealers, most of whom considered that experience best left forgotten. A one-thousand-page report published by the Brookings Institution and co-authored by economists who had been "integral parts of the NRA," blamed it for creating "scarcity all around." An even harsher assessment appeared in 1937 by Charles F. Roos, the NRA's former chief economist, which declared that enforcement of the codes had "kept business in a churn, prevented re-employment, and consequently retarded American development."[23]

If bringing back a full-blown second NRA was impractical, Roosevelt set out for the next best thing, recreating as much as possible by piecemeal. He backed an existing bill by Senator Wagner (D-New York) to create a National Labor Relations Act. Through this legislation, FDR hoped to permanently institutionalize the NRA's agenda of boosting purchasing power. Section 9(a) of the Wagner bill codified collective bargaining as an approved legal doctrine in labor relations, but unlike the NRA, it laid out a clear definition of that term and a procedure to bring it about. If a majority of workers voted to unionize in an election supervised by the new National Labor Relations Board, a single union became the exclusive bargaining agent for all employees, whether members or not.[24]

A diverse, but hopelessly outnumbered, coalition fought an unsuccessful battle against the bill. Employers, not surprisingly, were firmly opposed. During the debate, Walter G. Merritt of the employer-funded League of Industrial Rights asserted that "this majority rule comes pretty nearly to the idea with which Mr. Mussolini originally started, in effect if you get a bare plurality the other party is rooted out. It would be almost like saying our Senate must be made up exclusively of Democrats." A record of past employer opportunism by business organizations, however, deflated the strength of these objections to collective bargaining.

Only two years earlier, many of the same groups had defended similar majority-rule systems controlled by business to impose price fixing under NRA codes.[25]

Also prominent in the coalition against the bill were the Communists and African American organizations. As Schlesinger points out, the "one group which exceeded the members of American business in their hatred of the bill was the American Communist Party." During the legislative debate, it promoted a variant of the system of "plural bargaining" which prevailed in most advanced industrial countries. For this reason, dissident unions, such as those controlled by the party, opposed the Wagner Act's enshrinement of monopoly unions selected by majority rule. The Communists unsuccessfully pushed for giving official recognition to any union representing at least 10 percent of the workers. The NAACP was suspicious of the collective bargaining provision of the bill because it empowered "organized labor to exclude from employment in any industry all workers who do not belong to a union. It is needless to point out the fact that thousands of Negro workers are barred from membership in American labor unions." Lester Granger of the Urban League later described the law as "the worst piece of legislation ever passed by Congress."[26]

When FDR signed the National Labor Relations Act (or Wagner Act) in July 1935 he put an official stamp, as Howard Dickman phrases it, on the theory that "individual laborers could not bargain equally with employers, that inadequate bargaining power led to inadequate purchasing power which in turn led to unemployment, and that, through organization and through collective bargaining, wages, purchasing power, and employment could be 'stabilized'." Through the Wagner Act, the United States also became one of the few advanced industrial countries to implement a variant of Fascist Italy's system of mandatory unionism imposed by majority rule.[27]

As many critics had predicted, the implementation of the Wagner Act inflicted great harm on black workers. An early warning sign was the lack of a non-discrimination clause due to opposition by the American Federation of Labor. The prohibition of replacement workers under the legislation removed a crucial means of leverage for black workers. In the past, African Americans had often first received work in that capacity when all-white unions went on strike. Just as fundamentally, as economic historian David E. Bernstein writes, "to the extent that the Wagner Act raised wages and labor standards beyond market levels, it had the same effect as a minimum wage in eliminating marginal African American jobs." In a broader sense, the Wagner Act, as economists

Thomas E. Hall and J. David Ferguson point out, gave more power to "insiders (those with jobs) who had an incentive and ability to exclude outsiders (those without jobs)."[28]

Few laws did more to eviscerate freedom of contract and freedom of association. The Wagner Act meant that millions of workers, whether they liked it or not, had to join a monopoly union and pay dues to that union. The National Labor Relations Board even interpreted the new law as prohibiting individual bargains outside of collective bargaining agreements as violating the employer's "duty to bargain." The special powers given to unions by the Wagner Act prompted a wave of unprecedented labor stoppages, peaking at more than four thousand in 1937, the highest up to that time.[29]

Despite his reputation as a champion of collective bargaining through organized labor, however, Roosevelt made a major exception. In a letter to Luther C. Steward, the president of the National Federation of Federal Employees, he warned that public sector workers "should realize that the process of collective bargaining, as usually understood, cannot be transplanted into the public service." Because, Roosevelt added, their services were essential to "the functioning of the Government, a strike by public employees" was "unthinkable and intolerable" since it would mean "the paralysis of Government by those who have sworn to support it."[30]

Tax Policy: Soaking the Poor

Few New Deal measures better demonstrated the gap between appearance and reality than the Revenue Act of 1935. FDR promoted it as a necessary reform to make the rich pay their fair share. "Wealth in the modern world," he proclaimed in pushing the legislation, "does not come merely from individual effort; it results from a combination of individual effort and the manifold uses to which the community puts that effort."

Continuing a trend started by Hoover in 1931, the Act raised the top marginal rate to 79 percent (the highest in history up to that time) on incomes over $5 million and imposed a 70 percent levy on large estates. It also substantially boosted the tax on corporate earnings.[31]

A political bonus of the Revenue Act of 1935 for FDR was to give him the upper hand against Huey "the Kingfish" Long in the "soak the rich" sweepstakes. Since 1934, Long had pushed a "Share Our Wealth" plan to tax great fortunes up to 100 percent for those worth over one hundred million. "I would sure like to have seen Huey's face," wrote humorist Will Rogers in reference to the Revenue Act of 1935, "when he was woke up in the middle of the night by the President who said: 'Lay over, Huey, I want to get in bed with you.'" But this time, Long, who had exclaimed "Amen" when listening to the speech, was gracious in sharing credit. The so-called insurgent progressives in the U.S. Senate, including Robert LaFollette Jr. (Progressive-Wisconsin) and George Norris, were equally enthusiastic about the tax bill.[32]

Despite its reputation, the Revenue Act of 1935 was harshly regressive in its application. The higher marginal tax rates motivated a scramble by the wealthy for tax shelters, such as tax-exempt bonds, or shifting money offshore. To make up for the shortfall, Roosevelt (as quietly as possible), like Hoover before him, turned to excise taxes including levies on theater admissions, gasoline, toiletries, and, later, alcoholic beverages. Unlike many well-off Americans, the mass of lower income consumers could not pass on the burden to others or hire the necessary legal talent to find loopholes.[33]

It's no exaggeration to characterize excise taxes as the lifeblood of the New Deal. In 1931, income taxes (personal and corporate) constituted 78 percent of federal revenue and excise taxes 22 percent. Hoover's, and then Roosevelt's, higher marginal rates put this in reverse. By 1935, excise taxes had spiked to 55 percent of federal revenue and in 1940 they were still 47 percent. Folsom sums up the irony: "When we think of various New Deal programs, we need to visualize their funding either largely or heavily coming from nickels and dimes paid weekly by tens of millions of smokers, car drivers, telephone callers, moviegoers, and cosmetics users." Yet Roosevelt's message to Congress on the Revenue Act of 1935 did not even allude to the centrality of excise taxes in the implementation of the Act.[34]

Dragnet Subpoenas and Political Retaliation

While Roosevelt experienced smooth sailing in tax policy, he soon ran into his first significant legislative defeat. The House rejected the so-called death sentence of the Wheeler-Rayburn Bill which FDR had seen as a weapon, much like the TVA and REA, to squeeze out private provision in power generation. The death sentence authorized the Securities and Exchange Commission to abolish utilities unable to prove they were part of a "geographically or economically integrated system." In arguing for the death sentence, Roosevelt characterized the utilities as "the most powerful, dangerous lobby . . . that has ever been created by any organization in this country." The unexpected resistance to the death sentence threw New Dealers off balance. By the end of June 1935, more than 800,000 letters and telegrams had poured into congressional offices condemning the bill as an assault on free enterprise.[35]

Hoping to revive the bill, Roosevelt sent his personal emissary, Thomas Corcoran, to Senator Burton K. Wheeler (D-Montana), one of the authors of the death sentence. Corcoran asked him to chair a probe into the opposition campaign. Wheeler begged off, fearing that he would be perceived "as a prosecutor and not an investigator," but recommended Senator Black, who proved eager to take the job. This arrangement made sense for both Black and Roosevelt. Widely dubbed "Chief Ferret" and "Chief Inquisitor" of the New Deal, Black had a reputation for both ruthlessness and tenacity. An explicit foe of big business, he regarded the utility companies with unbridled contempt. He did not want to regulate these entities but rather to "destroy them as holding companies with their network of chicanery, deceit, fraud, graft and racketeering." Another goal of Black (and Roosevelt) was to promote governmentally controlled alternatives to the power companies.[36]

With Black lined up, the Senate sped through a resolution establishing a committee "to make a full and complete investigation of all lobbying activities and all efforts to influence, encourage, promote or retard legislation, directly or indirectly, in connection with the so-called 'holding company bill,' *or any other matter or proposal affecting legislation*" (emphasis mine). While Roosevelt gave all the assistance that Black asked for, no direct evidence has surfaced of ongoing coordination. The two did not really have to work closely in tandem, however. Black and Roosevelt were of one mind in their zeal to protect the New Deal from its enemies. As Michael Stephen Czaplicki puts it, "Roosevelt gave critical support to Black, but it was a relationship of affiliation and shared ideology rather than of CEO to subordinate." Roosevelt knew that Black could be trusted to do the right thing, from the president's perspective. Later, he told his son James that if "you want something done in the Senate, give it to Black. He'll do it . . . Father said that the New Deal would have not been the same without Black."[37]

Making maximum use of a sweeping Senate authorization, Black moved with great haste. He leaned heavily on blanket *duces tecum* subpoenas ("under penalty bring with you"). Also known as dragnet subpoenas, they required the witness to bring to the hearing room all relevant (often defined in open-ended terms) papers, including correspondence and financial information. To make these subpoenas stick, Black made highly elastic use of the 'contempt' power. This allowed the affected chamber of Congress to cite recalcitrant witnesses and turn them over to prosecution in a federal court for potential jail time (a maximum of one year).[38]

Black's potent combination of *duces tecum* and the contempt power was, as Czaplicki notes, "designed to eliminate his target's capacity for choice and discussion through his presentation of constraining binaries: provide the information/go to Washington; swear under oath/go to Washington." Philip H. Gadsden, the chair of the Committee of Public Utility Executives, was the first to feel the full force of the dragnet subpoena. Black brought him in to testify only a day after the Senate had authorized the committee. Staffers presented the understandably bewildered Gadsden with a subpoena in his hotel room and whisked him off to the hearing room. As he testified, others ferried over boxes of evidence.[39]

"They All Claim That"

Under questioning, Gadsden depicted the Black Committee as an inquisition. He identified two kinds of lobbies: "One is a group that comes down here trying to get some selfish advantage out of the Government in preference to other taxpayers. I think the other group is a group like myself that come down here to do what they can to resist the effort of their Government to destroy their property." Black [interposing]: "They all claim that." Speaking later to reporters, Gadsden declared that "this isn't Russia" and complained that the committee had rifled through all his papers, including his personal checkbook. Although the members had the advantage of surprise, they had no luck in extracting damaging testimony.[40]

But four days later, on July 16th, they struck pay dirt, which transformed the investigation in Black's favor. After Representative Denis J. Driscoll (D-Pennsylvania) reported that a suspiciously high number of telegrams against the death sentence had poured in from the small town of Warren, Pennsylvania (many with last names starting with "B"), another witness identified a utility lobbyist who had copied names from the city directory as the source. The revelations uncovering thousands of "fake telegrams" from Warren and other locations injected tremendous momentum into the investigation. Although as utility company executive, and future GOP presidential candidate, Wendell Willkie pointed out, these were "an infinitesimal percentage of the total protests of utility stockholders," the sheer quantity was enough to put future witnesses on the defensive for quite some time.[41]

The fake telegrams controversy gave an opening wedge for a widened investigation. A few days later, Black asked the Bureau of Internal Revenue to issue a "general blanket order" for access to the tax returns of possible witnesses. The Bureau (quite likely with Roosevelt's approval) gave Black everything he wanted. While making the arrangements, Secretary Morgenthau privately observed that the senator was "in an awful hurry about it." Black had long dismissed philosophical or constitutional concerns about the privacy of tax returns as a false front for vested interests. The tax return request also illustrated Black's sweeping approach to obtaining evidence even when it seemed to compromise privacy. Many of the individuals on his list had no conceivable role in fake telegrams. Also, Black asked for returns from as early as 1925, predating the death sentence by a decade. The names included David Lawrence, an anti–New Deal columnist for the *U.S. News,* and those of two leading congressional opponents of the death sentence, US Representatives James W. Wadsworth Jr. (R-New York) and George Huddleston (D-Alabama).[42]

"From the Cradle to the Grave"

The Social Security Act of August 1935, which accurately ranks as FDR's most significant addition to the welfare state, was the fulfillment of his long-standing goals. "The principles of insurance," he had written in his 1932 book *Looking Forward,* "can be made to meet the basic problems of unemployment and old-age want. This is a sound business proposal." Rejecting "haphazard answers," the idea of a universal and centralized plan had a consistent appeal for him. In January 1935, FDR told Secretary of Labor Frances Perkins that he saw "no reason why every child from the day he is born, shouldn't be a member of the social security system . . . Cradle to the grave—from the cradle to the grave." In seeking universality, FDR hoped that the nation had repudiated an outmoded view of liberty "under which for many years a free people were being gradually regimented into the service of the privileged few. I prefer and I am sure you prefer that broader definition of Liberty under which we are moving forward to greater freedom, to greater security for the average man than he has ever known before in the history of America."

Roosevelt later elaborated on what that older system of liberty had to offer to the elderly: "Men and women too old and infirm to work either depended on those who had but little to share, or spent their remaining years within the walls of a poorhouse."[43]

The historical record contradicts Roosevelt's unremittingly bleak depiction of a pre-Social Security world dominated by deprivation. According to the most detailed study in 1923, the overall percentage of Americans over age sixty-five who were in almshouses ('poorhouses') was less than one percent. Moreover, the private role in providing retirement income was extensive and varied. One of the most significant examples was tontine, or deferred divided, insurance which represented a combination of life insurance, retirement income, and savings. Under tontine insurance, the annual dividends (or surplus) of the policy were "deferred" into a common savings fund shared by thousands of other Americans. Nine million of these policies were in force just after the beginning of the twentieth century.[44]

Tontine insurance became a victim of one of the most destructive binges of legislative overreach in American history. In 1905, many states, including the major life insurance company hub of New York, banned further sales of policies which permitted deferred dividends. The critics charged that the investment function of tontine insurance catered too much to the "gambling instinct." Economic historians Roger L. Ransom and Richard Sutch characterize the ban as "regulatory excess" against a form of insurance that was both actuarially sound and "an excellent investment, earning a rate of return substantially in excess of that generally available on other assets." By the time of the social security debate thirty years later, tontine insurance had become a distant memory.[45]

Deprived of purchasing this once widespread private alternative, Americans had to settle for a more limited menu for retirement income options. For many, the choice narrowed down to reliance on company pensions, a method which took off in popularity during the 1920s. By 1928, private pensions covered 6.4 million Americans, reaching about 15 percent of the workforce. The trend by the end of this period was for these plans to be underwritten by insurance companies, thus bringing greater solvency and less dependence on employer goodwill. Despite the stresses of the Great Depression, the failure rate of company plans remained low. They showed a capacity to survive, and even thrive, under all kinds of economic conditions. In fact, there were more pension plans in 1935 (750) than in 1930 (only 420).[46]

Americans showed little interest in governmental old age pensions in the first phase of the Great Depression. A leading advocate of compulsory insurance at the time lamented the lack of "clamor" among workers, pointing out that "in practically all of Europe, it was governmental authority that was behind social insurance measures." Not until 1934 did the first bills for old-age pensions get any serious consideration in Congress.[47]

The movement for governmental pensions eventually gained momentum from the combined failure of two U.S. presidents to find a solution to year-after-year double-digit unemployment. Over three million elderly Americans flocked to a network of clubs headed by Dr. Francis Townsend, an elderly physician from California who favored an "Old-Age Revolving Pension" plan. It proposed paying two hundred dollars per month to everyone over the age of sixty on condition that they spent everything. Funding was to come from a tax on all transactions. Huey Long's crankish Share Our Wealth plan, though only incidentally aimed at the elderly, had a similar panacea-like appeal. While FDR had no use for Townsend or Long, he was able to take advantage of the more favorable climate of opinion their efforts had created for his proposals.[48]

During the year-long period of study and debate on social security, Roosevelt never forgot political practicalities. Any saleable program, he emphasized, had to be couched in terms familiar to Americans such as "premiums," or "annuities," or "actuarial soundness." Of course, this verbiage, as FDR understood, did not strictly apply to social security which violated all basic insurance principles including premiums based on risk levels. To maintain the "self-supporting" idea, for example, he wanted to rely on payroll taxes, which were highly regressive, instead of general revenue. To Roosevelt this was the politically expedient course. "With those [payroll] taxes in there," he privately explained, "no damn politician can ever scrap my social security program."[49]

Derailing the Clark Amendment to protect Social Security

Everything seemed to be on track for FDR's social security plan until an amendment in May 1935 by Senator Bennett Champ Clark (D-Missouri). The Clark Amendment proposed allowing companies with existing retirement plans to opt out of social security on condition that their plans offered at least the same amount of benefit. This proposal was not just a flash in the pan. The Democratic Senate overwhelmingly approved the Clark Amendment by a vote of 55 to 35 despite determined opposition from administration allies.

Economic historian Carolyn L. Weaver states that "the Clark Amendment posed a very serious threat to the viability of the federal old-age insurance program. By subjecting the federal plan to competition, the government would have been forced, if only by default, to maintain a sound old-age insurance program. The voluntary flow of participants between competing suppliers would have dramatically reduced the potential monopolization of the old-age insurance industry."[50]

Proponents of the Clark Amendment asked a question that often stumped the president's allies: what was the justification for rejecting a retirement option which provided the same, or greater, benefits as social security? Even Paul H. Douglas, one of the drafters of the Social Security Act, conceded that in "view of all the safeguards, it seemed to the majority of the Senate and to a goodly section of the public, that there was really no legitimate objection against granting such an exemption." The Clark Amendment exposed the faulty basis and contradictions of FDR's universalist approach. As Weaver points out, in "less than ten sentences, the amendment cut through the insurance rhetoric of the debates and threatened the redistributive underpinnings of Social Security."[51]

Intent on derailing the Clark Amendment, FDR rounded up approved "experts" to lobby key senators. Senator Rober M. LaFollette, Jr. spoke for many critics when he warned that if the amendment was adopted "the Government having determined to set up a federal system of old-age [insurance], will provide in its own bill creating that system, for competition, which in the end may destroy the Federal system." In August, however, conferees compromised on terms favorable to the administration by both deleting the amendment and appointing a committee to study the issue. FDR signed the Social Security Act into law on August 14th and the Clark Amendment was never heard from again.[52]

"The Neutrality Blunder"

A defining characteristic of American public opinion during the 1930s was steadfast opposition to U.S. participation in another foreign war. This determination only grew more intense because of constant news coverage about saber rattling by Germany, Japan, and Italy. Novels and movies exposing the futility of World War I, such as *A Farewell to Arms* by Ernest Hemingway and *All Quiet on the Western Front* by Erich Maria Remarque, had a major impact on public thinking. Beginning in 1934, the Nye Committee of the U.S. Senate had popularized the belief that a cabal of bankers and arms manufacturers had hoodwinked the American people into supporting World War I.[53]

Although FDR cut his political teeth as a Wilsonian interventionist, he did not hesitate to play both sides of the street. Behind the scenes he was instrumental in crafting legislation to cater to popular antiwar feeling. At a White House meeting with members of the Nye Committee, the president recommended legislation to require "absolute neutrality in case of a foreign war." According to John T. Flynn, an investigator for the Committee, the "whole policy of the Neutrality Acts has been referred to as the 'neutrality blunder' as if it were the blunder of the President's critics instead of one in which he had not only shared but which he had actually initiated."[54]

Contrary to the president's original wishes, however, the final version of the bill required a sweeping arms embargo that included "implements of war," against all belligerents and permitting no discretion for the president. In August, Roosevelt compromised and signed the Neutrality Act of 1935 by getting an amendment to mandate a six-month time limit. Mussolini's invasion of Ethiopia in October became the first major test. Though hindered by the U.S. arms embargo, Italy was able to manufacture weapons or purchase them from other sources. The Ethiopians, who lacked the financial wherewithal to do the same, fought tenaciously but the invaders had overwhelming advantages in technology and resources. The war came to a de facto end in May when Italian forces occupied the Ethiopian capital.[55]

"Who Murdered the Vets?"

On Labor Day in September 1935, newspaper front pages were prominently reporting on the plight of American veterans but not in the way that anyone, least of all FDR, had intended. A hurricane blasted a camp full of World War I veterans in the Florida Keys, bringing an almost classic, and horrific, "chickens coming home to roost" moment for the administration after years of scattering bonus marchers and other veterans into assorted New-Deal-funded camps. By 1935, the federal government had sent more than two thousand veterans to work projects in Florida, including the construction of a road linking the Upper Keys to Key West. "If the U. S. had a Devil's Island," an article from *Time* opined, "the Florida Keys would be a good place to locate it . . . The veterans started kicking as soon as they got there, cursed the poor food, flimsy houses, inadequate medical care."[56]

The resulting controversy did not center on the hurricane itself, regarded as one of the worst in a century, but the bungled federal response. Despite much advance warning, the authorities failed to evacuate the camps and then compounded that blunder by not approving two waiting rescue trains. *Time* reported that when the "Red Cross, the American Legion, the National Guard, and the Coast Guard finally got into the devastated Keys over the broken bridges and wrecked roads they found signs of slaughter worse than war. Bodies were in the trees, floating in the creeks, bogged in the mud." When the grisly task of assembling the scattered human remains was over, the estimated body count came to 256 dead veterans.[57]

In the immediate aftermath, Harry Hopkins, in his capacity as FERA head and general New Deal troubleshooter, scrambled to minimize the political damage. In a public statement, he denied any government failure to heed advance warning: "I don't think anyone reading the weather reports . . . would necessarily have evacuated these people." Hopkins sent two top advisors to Key West to investigate: Aubrey Williams and Col. George E. Ijams. Their report disclaimed any federal responsibility and concluded that "the catastrophe must be characterized 'as an act of God' and was by its very nature beyond the power of man or instruments at his disposal to foresee sufficiently far enough in advance to permit the taking of adequate precautions capable of preventing the death and desolation which occurred." John J. Abt, an assistant to Williams, later admitted that the group was "on a political mission to defend the administration against charges of negligence."[58]

Press criticism of the federal response was brutal. *Newsweek* asked: "What were the veterans doing in the whirlwind's path? . . . Why didn't the FERA move them from the islands after the first hurricane warning? Why was the rescue train so late?" An editorial in the *Washington Post* blamed "gross negligence" which "seems to trace far back of the hurricane to the casual policy of assembling 'bonus marchers' in isolated and semi-concentration camps . . . Apparently the only reason for creating these special 'rehabilitation camps' in the South was to avoid the political embarrassment of further mass lobbying for the bonus." The editorial singled out Hopkins as a culprit. The *Chicago Daily Tribune* called the federal response "a piece of criminal folly committed by some one in Washington."[59]

Especially vehement in condemning the administration's handling of the hurricane was novelist and Key West resident Ernest Hemingway. After witnessing the disaster and the bungled federal response, he wrote an expose for the *New Masses*, "Who Murdered the Vets?" He asked: "Whom did they [the veterans] annoy and to

Ernest Hemingway indicts Hopkins and FDR for the deaths of 256 veterans.

whom was their possible presence a danger? Who sent them down to live in frame shacks on the Florida Keys and left them there in the hurricane months? Who is responsible for their deaths? . . . Who sent them down there? I hope he reads this—and how does he feel? . . . And what's the punishment for manslaughter now?" In his private correspondence, Hemingway even more specifically named names, writing that "Harry Hopkins and Roosevelt who sent those poor bonus march guys down there [to the Florida Keys] to get rid of them got rid of them all right.[60]

Looming Political Threats: Long and Coughlin

Embarrassment from the Key West tragedy, along with other reverses such as the Schechter decision, had left a mark. Roosevelt was facing stiffer winds as media and congressional critics grew more confident and assertive. Elisha Hanson, the counsel for the American Newspaper Publishers Association, observed that "whereas in 1933 practically all the columns read like pro-Administration propaganda, today the reverse is substantially true."

Beginning in February 1934, according to an analysis by the Democratic Party's leading internal pollster, Emil Hurja, Roosevelt's popular approval had eroded at a steady 1 percent each month from a high of 69 percent, bottoming out at 50 percent in September 1935 (the lowest since he took office). Administration insiders were already viewing the 1936 election prospects with some alarm.[61]

Since 1934, FDR had become increasingly worried about the potential political threat posed by Senator Long. An internal poll by Hurja in the spring of 1935 showed Long polling nearly 11 percent as a third candidate. Especially of concern was the Louisiana senator's broad national strength, including in the Rocky Mountain states where he had 13 percent, and his excellent polling among relief recipients, a key constituency for FDR. "It was easy to conceive a situation," wrote presidential advisor James Farley, "whereby Long . . . might have the balance in the 1936 election."[62]

FDR deployed every weapon at his disposal against the Kingfish including an extensive IRS probe in Louisiana of both Long and his top lieutenants. The president met regularly with Elmer Irey, the head of the IRS Intelligence Division, to narrow down possible names for prosecutors. Unintimidated, Long levelled a verbal counter blast from the Senate floor. "They did not attempt to provide any covering over this thing," he said of the investigators. "They just boasted that he [Long] and all his friends 'were all going away.'" A potential nightmare for the administration was that Huey Long and Father Charles E. Coughlin might link up their movements. While the radio priest still somewhat warily counted himself as FDR's ally, he had dissented on some key issues, including the bonus. To head off a possible alliance between the two rabble rousers, Roosevelt recruited Joseph P. Kennedy, a co-religionist of Coughlin, to intercede.[63]

Assassination in Baton Rouge

On September 7th, Coughlin answered the phone at his Detroit home and heard the voice of Kennedy, who was in Hyde Park visiting the president. After giving his greetings, Kennedy handed the phone over to FDR who greeted Coughlin: "Hiya Padre? Where have you been all the time? I'm lonesome. Come on down and see me." Coughlin promised to catch a train for Hyde Park after he had cleared up some unfinished business. Soon after Coughlin's conversation with FDR, Long was shot in Baton Rouge by the son of a political enemy. After he seemed to rally, the Louisiana Kingfish died in the early hours of September 10th while the radio priest, then en route to Hyde Park, was sleeping on the train. Coughlin read all about it in the morning papers at the Albany railroad station just before dawn. When Roosevelt rose from bed, it was Coughlin who told him that Long was dead. This news might well have dampened some of FDR's desire to appease Coughlin during the inconclusive meeting that followed.[64]

Despite Long's removal from the scene, a troubling electoral trend continued to haunt the administration. The GOP was starting to make noticeable inroads. While the slide in Roosevelt's approval in the polls had abated, his party lost two open House seats in 1935, including one in a traditionally Democratic district in Rhode Island. In November 1935, the Republicans captured the New York Assembly (FDR's home state), scored legislative gains in New Jersey, and won mayoral contests in Cleveland and Philadelphia.[65]

FDR responded by ramping up efforts to neutralize his enemies in preparation for the presidential election. The Black Committee became even more useful to the president by expanding its ostensible original mission to probe opposition to the "death sentence" to a more general investigation of anti-New Dealers. Senator Black, a committed champion of the president's policies, was eager, and more than able, to help in any way possible. By the fall of 1935, the Committee, working in close cooperation with the administration, had begun an all-out campaign to investigate, harass, and discredit FDR's opponents.

4

The Politics of Retaliation: The Black Inquisition

By the fall of 1935, several trends deepened Roosevelt's worries about the forthcoming presidential race, including disappointing polls, off-year election reversals, and legal rebukes from the Supreme Court.

The Black Committee, because of its highly malleable mandate, provided an almost ideal means for New Dealers to wage a counterattack. The authorizing law had empowered the Committee with maximum leeway "to make a full and complete investigation of all lobbying activities and all efforts to influence, encourage, promote or retard legislation, directly or indirectly, in connection with the so-called 'holding company bill,' *or any other matter or proposal affecting legislation*" (emphasis mine). At each stage, Roosevelt was a low-profile, but reliable enabler of the Committee's work.[1]

Examining Millions of Private Telegrams

With the president's full cooperation, Senator Black made unusually expansive use of a law which required telegraph companies to retain copies of all telegrams. He told Western Union, the leading company in that field, that he wanted carte blanche to search all telegrams sent through Washington, DC, from February 1st to September 1st, 1935. This wasn't just a dragnet subpoena. It was in a whole new category. Not surprisingly, company executives, who did not want to alienate customers fearful of losing privacy, refused to comply. They had long followed a general policy of resisting even limited subpoenas of this type. As with the earlier request for tax returns, however, the Roosevelt administration gave the Committee its full cooperation by arranging for the

Federal Communications Commission (FCC) to order Western Union to fully comply.[2]

In early October, staffers from the Black Committee and the FCC began poring over thousands of copies of incoming and outgoing telegrams. "We have at last worked out arrangements," wrote one of the representatives of the Black Committee on October 5th, "by which we can review all the telegrams in the offices of the telegraph companies." Paul C. Yates, the secretary of the Committee and a former FDR speechwriter, made the ultimate decisions on procedure as investigators scanned all telegrams sent to, and from, people on their lists. While Yates urged them to avert their gazes from content of a personal nature, he gave few other restrictions. Telegrams "in any way connected with lobbying activities" were fair game under the definition of indirect lobbying which encompassed just about every political reference.[3]

Because the Committee did not give notice to the senders or receivers, most of the targets found out, if they did at all, when confronted during a Senate hearing. In the context of a later time, the extent of the Committee's surveillance might be compared to a governmental body giving free rein at AT&T or Google to examine millions of text messages and emails. Over nearly a three-month period, staffers dug through great stacks of telegrams sent through Washington, DC, by sundry company employees, lobbyists, newspaper publishers, and political activists as well as every member of Congress. Finally finishing on January 3rd 1936, they had worked on an almost daily basis. One investigator stated that they had gone through "from 35,000 to 50,000 per day," making later total estimates of five million entirely plausible.[4]

Either because of a desire to keep potential targets in the dark or out of fear of questionable legality, the Black Committee cautioned the searchers to maintain secrecy. Yates confided that it was "Black's wish that we do everything possible to uncover all the facts . . . It would, of course, not be wise to mention the source of our information." Even as investigators culled through these telegrams, the Black Committee was using the contents as a basis for numerous targeted subpoenas.[5]

Controlling Radio through the FCC

The administration secured aid from the FCC in another realm as well. As most of the print press lined up against the president in the 1936 campaign, radio remained securely in his corner. A writer in *Broadcasting* even attributed "the perpetuation of the Roosevelt

Administration" to the "friendliness of radio." Because of FCC pressure, including the tense waiting for that six-month license renewal, broadcasters not only trod lightly but erred on the side of favoring the administration when in doubt. Republicans complained in vain.6

The major broadcast networks had a standard policy of carrying Roosevelt's speeches gratis as news or "civic affairs," thus avoiding the expensive equal time obligations of the Radio Act of 1927. That category encompassed such highly politicized utterances as the bare-knuckle State of the Union Address on January 6th blasting the "economic autocracy" who "steal the livery of great national constitutional ideals to serve discredited special interests" and "engage in vast propaganda to spread fear and discord among the people." When Henry P. Fletcher, the head of the Republican National Committee, tried to respond through a series of anti–New Deal skits, NBC president Lennox Lohr turned him down under the pretext that "such dramatic programs as you have offered would place the discussion of vital political and national issues on the basis of dramatic license rather than upon a basis of responsibly stated fact or opinion." Fletcher also met a rebuff from CBS President William S. Paley, who, overlooking the partisan tenor of some of Roosevelt's own speeches, explained that "appeals to the electorate should be intellectual and not based on emotion, passion or prejudice." A GOP official complained that the networks had "surrendered their independence to and joined the 'dictators of the New Deal'." In the end WGN (an independent station owned by the anti-Roosevelt *Chicago Daily Tribune*), carried the skits.[7]

The new year brought some discouraging developments for FDR and his allies. On January 6th the US Supreme Court demolished one of the mainstays of the First New Deal by striking down as unconstitutional the main powers of the Agricultural Adjustment Act. Moreover, confidential White House internal polls concluded that the president was likely to lose New York and Illinois and faced a close race in Iowa, Indiana, and Minnesota. As historian William E. Leuchtenburg frames it, Roosevelt's reelection as of January 1936 seemed "very much in doubt."[8]

"I Am Quite Sure I Could Not Keep My Hand Off the Rope"

Meanwhile, Black was pulling the noose tighter via more dragnet subpoenas on Western Union, although this time without the

FCC's direct help. He also expanded the probe of anti–New Deal organizations to include allied newspapers and law firms. The broad reach of the Black Committee's investigation alarmed Western Union's executives, who feared driving away privacy-conscious customers. In early February, the company began to automatically inform all subpoenaed individuals that the Black Committee had searched their telegrams. Before this time, it had done this work in secret, and most targets had no clue about what was happening. The change virtually guaranteed a lawsuit.[9]

The first legal action, brought on March 2nd by Silas Hardy Strawn on behalf of his law firm of Winston, Strawn, and Shaw, dramatically shifted the course of the investigation. He sued to prohibit any handover from Western Union to the Committee of copies of telegrams generated by "known officers, employees, and agents." Strawn's prominence made big headlines almost inevitable. He was a partner in a prestigious Chicago law firm, a past president of both the American Bar Association and the US Chamber of Commerce. To top it off, he was the former national finance chair of the Republican Party. Strawn's lawyer, Frank J. Hogan, blamed the Committee for conducting an inquisition into client information "of a private nature and which should not be subjected to public scrutiny."[10]

Of the many Americans informed that the Black Committee had examined their messages, few matched the red-hot anger of Newton D. Baker. Baker had served as Wilson's secretary of war and had made cautious criticism of some features of the New Deal. After Western Union told him that the Committee had looked through his telegrams for an entire year, he wrote, "Man of peace as I am, I am quite sure I could not keep my hand off the rope if I accidentally happened to stumble upon a party bent on hanging him [Black]." The new Western Union policy considerably weakened Black's advantage of surprise. It did not destroy it, however, since the Committee still had no obligation to share the actual contents of telegrams with witnesses.[11]

More than ever, leading American newspapers vigorously condemned the Committee's methods. The anti–New Deal *Chicago Daily Tribune* (published by FDR's old classmate at Groton, Robert "Bertie" McCormick) labeled the inquiry as "terroristic," but more establishment voices also joined in. The *Washington Post* detected a threat to representative government "when private messages are indiscriminately exposed to official scrutiny without the consent of the sender," while the *Baltimore Sun* observed that "resistance to New Deal policies" appeared to be the only criterion for investigation. Arthur Krock of the *New York Times* blasted the "snooping of Congressional bodies more interested in getting political ammunition against the enemies of the party in power than in contributing to the orderly consideration of legislation."[12]

The ranks of the opposition to the Black Committee grew steadily in Congress. Representatives James W. Wadsworth Jr. (R-New York), John J. Cochran (D-Missouri) and Andrew J. May (D-Kentucky) put the FCC's enabling role on center stage. Wadsworth was upset that the Committee had seized "tens of thousands of telegrams," including many "confidential or private in character . . . some of them passing between husband and wife." In the US House, a rare voice who spoke up for Black, and did it quite vigorously, was fellow New Deal zealot Rep. John E. Rankin (D-Mississippi), who brushed aside any objections as just so much "power propaganda."[13]

Resistance to Black came from some other unexpected quarters, including a leading spokesman of liberal reform: syndicated columnist Walter Lippmann. In prose just as strident as that of any Republican, he accused the Committee of "becoming an engine of tyranny in which men are denied the elementary legal protection that a confirmed criminal caught red-handed in the act can still count upon." Lippmann, who had impeccable civil liberties credentials (including defenses of Sacco and Vanzetti and John T. Scopes), saw similarities between Black's investigation and those of right-wing red hunters who "cared nothing [about] whom they slandered." Lippmann unsparingly challenged Black's motivations and abilities: the "Senator is an enthusiast for investigations but in the realm of justice he is an obvious illiterate." He closed by calling for an investigation of the investigators.[14]

The Courts and Congress Rebuke the Black Committee

On March 11th, Chief Justice Alfred A. Wheat of the Supreme Court of the District of Columbia (later renamed the District Court of D.C.) dealt another setback to Black by granting an injunction prohibiting the Committee from examining and seizing more telegrams from Winston, Strawn, and Shaw. Contra Black, Wheat asserted that he had jurisdiction to protect Strawn's Fourth Amendment rights against unreasonable search and seizure by Congress: "This subpoena goes way beyond any legitimate exerciseof the right of subpoena duces tecum." Wheat did not object to a more limited subpoena directed to specific telegrams or individuals but rather to a catch-all approach. Though Strawn had sued Western Union, not the Black Committee, the company preferred that the plaintiff prevail. The ruling, as Roger K. Newman observes, "was one of the few times in American history that a court had restrained a congressional investigating committee." Black responded that he was pondering a bill stripping the courts of power to issue injunctions in such cases.[15]

While the energized congressional opposition had dashed any hope of that happening, Black steered straight into a new controversy. At the center was William Randolph Hearst, the most famous newspaper publisher in American history. An exuberant nationalist and law-and-order advocate, Hearst had helped secure Roosevelt's nomination in 1932 but had since turned against his old ally. Roosevelt reciprocated this animus by instructing the Department of the Treasury to closely monitor his taxes. FDR's son Elliott remembers that his father had ordered a search "of every corner and crevice of Hearst's empire . . . My father may have been the originator of the concept of employing the IRS as a weapon of political retribution."[16]

On February 8th, the Black Committee served a direct subpoena on Hearst for a single telegram he had sent on April 5th 1935 to James T. Williams Jr., editorial writer for the Hearst papers. In that communication (marked "Confidential"), Hearst had instructed Williams to write editorials calling for the impeachment of Rep. John J. McSwain (D-South Carolina), the chair of the House Committee on Military Affairs: "He is the enemy within the gates of Congress . . . He is a Communist in spirit and a traitor in effect. He would leave the United States naked to its foreign and domestic enemies." It is rather odd that Black publicly subpoenaed the original from Hearst given that he already had a complete copy of it from the earlier search of the Western Union office. Perhaps he feared raising potentially embarrassing questions about the secretive nature and methods used in that search.[17]

On March 13th, Hearst petitioned the Supreme Court of the District of Columbia to prohibit Western Union from handing over the telegram to the Committee. His lawyer, Elisha Hanson, who doubled as a general counsel of the American Newspaper Publishers Association, charged that the Committee had violated the First, Fourth, and Fifth Amendments and stressed that the telegram had no reference to lobbying.[18]

Black's first instinct was to counterattack, but this time he did so in a most clumsy way. On March 18th, he sent on the Committee's behalf a copy of the Hearst telegram to both the press and McSwain. Black apparently hoped that his colleagues would be so offended by Hearst's inflammatory prose that they would rally to the Committee. Black unleashed his anger at Western Union for its uncooperative attitude toward the committee. In a public letter to the head of the company's Washington, DC, office, he implied that the owners were putting the needs of one particularly high-volume customer, William Randolph Hearst, ahead of the public good: "The Western Union Telegraph Co. would naturally not desire to bring out the fact that an effort had been made by its patron to intimidate and coerce in the performance of his legislative duty a Member of Congress [McSwain], whose reputation for loyalty and patriotic service is above criticism."[19]

Strange Bedfellows: Hearst and the ACLU

The release of the Hearst telegram backfired for Black in a major way, leading some to comment that it violated the Committee's pledge on March 8 to reveal only telegrams found to be relevant. His action, the *Washington Post* editorialized, showed [that the Black Committee had become "rather too smart for success." Instead of discrediting Hearst, the action had "sharply underlined the indefensible nature of its own dragnet tactics," which had revealed "a private wire from a citizen who has filed a charge of conspiracy against the committee."[20]

To fend off a possible injunction against it, the FCC announced that all previously seized telegrams were now "in the possession of the Special Committee of the United States Senate" and that it did not intend any "further investigation or examination" at Western Union. An editorial in the *Washington Post* attributed the FCC's decision to "public outcry against the OGPU [the Soviet Secret police] methods followed by Senator Black's investigators." Strapped for funds, and under fire, Black had no other choice but to announce that the Committee had completed its "field investigations."[21]

The FCC's decision forced the Black Committee to retreat on future searches but also shielded it from direct legal sanctions. Chief Justice Wheat made this clear, conceding his helplessness to intervene because the seizures had stopped and Black had withdrawn the Hearst telegram subpoena. At the same time, the Committee had acquired a vast store of material from a year of investigation. This led columnist and Republican pundit Alice Roosevelt Longworth (daughter of Theodore Roosevelt and, thus, Eleanor's first cousin) to quip that Black's "snoopers up to their eyebrows in their booty" had to be satisfied with "the millions of trophies of their acquisitiveness; engaged in the congenial occupation of ferreting out other people's business."[22]

Undeterred, Hearst both appealed the FCC's decision in the courts and demanded the return of all other seized telegrams. His newspapers continued to be as strident as ever. A representative editorial called Black the "symbol of the modern American Inquisition." One of several cartoons showed a giant black keyhole captioned "Will the People allow the Light of Liberty to be swallowed up by Black?" Hearst's newspapers did not limit their salvos to editorials or cartoons. Resident poet Berton Braley also took part. On April 11th he wrote:

You may have thoughts
But you must not speak
Or you'll be summoned
By a New
Deal Sneak![23]

"The End Justified the Means"

A most unfamiliar bedfellow for Hearst in the fight against the Black Committee was the American Civil Liberties Union (ACLU) which demanded that the Committee return "improperly seized" telegrams. As he had with Lippmann, Black found it perplexing that he had to worry about his left flank. Replying to the head of the Kansas state chapter, he wondered why a group claiming "to protect the masses of the people from loss of their economic and political liberty" had aligned itself with those who valued "property" over "human" rights.

The ACLU renewed its campaign against the Committee after news reports that the National Woman's Party, led by equal rights crusader Alice Paul, was on the target list. ACLU executive director Roger N. Baldwin asked Black why he was probing an organization that had nothing to do with utility legislation. Black evaded an answer, pleading that it was improper to share details in a case where subpoenas were pending. After emphasizing that he had not departed from time-worn American traditions, Black added, somewhat ominously, that he was "sure that upon mature consideration, you will wish to withdraw your request for information."[24]

The combined impact of the Strawn decision, the Hearst telegram, and the FCC's withdrawal of support even prompted some longtime New Dealers, notably US Representatives Emanuel

Celler (D-New York) and John McCormack (D-Massachusetts), a future speaker of the house, to break ranks with Black. Celler was relentless: "Commandeering private papers by the ton cannot be excused by the assertion that private wires are no longer private if they refer to public matters." To Celler, Black's release of the telegram to McSwain showed that wholesale subpoenas "can be made an instrument of oppression." The names or reputations of those targeted were beside the point, Celler argued. He did not care whether it was a Strawn or Hearst; the Committee had no right to examine five million telegrams. Celler went so far as to compare Black to Benito Mussolini and King George III in his use of espionage. Yet again, one of the few members to rise in Black's defense was administration loyalist Rep. Rankin, who lauded the Committee for doing "more for the American people than any other investigating committee I have ever known."[25]

The Committee's most powerful champion was Roosevelt himself, although he carefully avoided tipping his hand in public. On April 14th, Black's name figured prominently in a private discussion with Ickes about possible picks to chair a new Special Senate Committee to Investigate Campaign Expenditures of Presidential, Vice Presidential, and Senatorial Candidates. According to Ickes, Roosevelt laid out two options. The first was to "name a perfectly respectable Senator as chairman, one who stood pretty well in public opinion," and the second was to choose Black, backed by "a vigorous, aggressive chief investigator." Senate leaders apparently did not agree, and Augustine Lonergan (D-Connecticut), a conservative freshman who had voted against the death sentence, got the nod.[26]

Roosevelt referred more specifically to the Black Committee on May 3rd at a meeting with Raymond Moley. During a "nightmarish conversation [that] went on and on in circles for some two hours," Moley told the president that he preferred letting the guilty "go free than to establish the principle of dragnet investigations." He bluntly challenged Roosevelt to explain his lack of "moral indignation" when Black's committee had "ruthlessly invaded the privacy of citizens." Roosevelt responded with "a long discourse of how Black's invasion of privacy had ample precedent." The inference drawn by Moley was that Roosevelt believed that "the end justified the means." The conversation left Moley "with the harrowing intimation that the president was looking forward to nothing more than having the opposition of his 'enemies'—the newspapers, the bankers, the businessmen—reelect him." Only four days after this meeting, the *Chicago Daily Tribune* took its criticism to a new level by highlighting Black's (then only alleged)

Senator Hugo Black's Klan connections.

ties to the Ku Klux Klan. A front-page cartoon showed a group of hooded night riders. In the lead was "Senator Black of Alabama," carrying a banner titled "Black Inquisition."[27]

The Committee never met again under Black's chairmanship. His methods, while sometimes digging up dirt on anti–New Dealers, had proved too toxic. Moreover, even if the Committee had tried to continue, and had the necessary funds, Justice Wheat's ruling in the Strawn case had removed its main leverage over witnesses.[28]

The Stage-Managed 1936 Campaign

As the Black Committee was still in the headlines, another congressional committee was investigating the "veteran killer" Key West hurricane of the previous year. Twenty witnesses testified at hearings from March to May. Republican member Edith Nourse Rogers (R-Massachusetts) persistently tried to ask questions that might implicate either FDR or FERA director Harry Hopkins. Chair Rankin, who had so ardently defended Black, used his gavel to shut her down at every turn. Historian Christine Kay Seiler described the hearings as "a beautifully choreographed show by Rankin in response to the public's demand for an impartial investigation. The witnesses were hand selected and led through their testimonies to provide evidence that exonerated the Roosevelt Administration of any wrongdoing."[29]

The Republican and Democratic conventions in June mostly ignored these congressional investigations. An exception was the GOP platform's indirect reference to New Dealers who had bullied "witnesses and interfered with the right of petition" through "investigations to harass and intimidate American citizens." In the rest of the platform, the Republicans, who nominated Governor Alfred E. Landon of Kansas, conceded much to the New Deal including preservation of a more "workable" social security, and endorsed collective bargaining.[30]

Roosevelt's renomination speech forced the Republicans on the defensive and kept them there. The president's combative tone was totally unlike his moderate and vague phrasing at the 1932 convention. The most famous passage attacked the "economic royalists" who had fought the New Deal and falsely claimed "that we seek to overthrow the institutions of America. What they really complain of is that we seek to take away their power." The speech was also an affirmation of FDR's underlying, and sincerely held, political philosophy. He emphasized that the Democratic delegates did not want "merely to make Government a mechanical implement, but to give it the vibrant personal character that is the very embodiment of human charity." It was better, he suggested, to tolerate "the occasional faults of a Government that lives in a spirit of charity than the constant omissions of a Government frozen in the ice of indifference."[31]

A Close Presidential Race

As of the summer of 1936, Roosevelt had no guarantee of reelection. Credible polls predicted a close race and sometimes gave

Landon a slight edge. Two of them by Gallup in August showed the Republicans winning in the electoral college, as did an internal poll by Emil Hurja. Also, a surprisingly high 45 percent all Americans answered "yes" to a Gallup Poll question which asked, "Do you believe that acts and policies of the Roosevelt administration may lead to dictatorship?" Ickes complained in his diary that the "President smiles and sails and fishes and the rest of us worry and fume . . . the whole situation is incomprehensible to me."[32]

Although outwardly carefree, Roosevelt had deep concerns about the state of the campaign. His bitterness toward the leading metropolitan newspapers (radio was very much in his pocket) knew few bounds. A letter to William E. Dodd, the U.S. ambassador to Germany declared that if

> the Republicans should win or make enormous gains, it would prove that an 85 percent control of the Press and a very definite campaign of misinformation can be effective here just as it was in the early days of the Hitler rise to power. Democracy is verily on trial. I am inclined to say something a little later about the great need for freedom of the press in this country i.e., freedom to confine itself to actual facts in its news columns.[33]

"We Know What Is Expected of Us"

Meanwhile the FCC continued to bend its rules on radio to Roosevelt's advantage. Up to the official launch of the campaign in late September, the networks had carried twenty-two of his speeches for free and, of these, seven were obviously political in nature. All the while, the administration kept out an eagle-eye for outliers. When two Los Angeles stations refused to carry a fireside chat in September 1936, White House Press Secretary Stephen Early urged the Democratic National Committee to put them on a blacklist denying any further purchases of airtime.[34]

The FCC did not have to intervene, or even intend to intervene, to tip the scales for Roosevelt. The mere possibility of that happening was sufficient. A most revealing incident came in October after Senator Arthur Vandenberg (R-Michigan) used audio recordings of Roosevelt to stage a mock radio debate between himself, defending Landon, and the president. Half of the CBS affiliates cut the program off in response to mixed messages from the network about possible rules violations. After Republicans blamed "intimidation of all broadcasters by the New Deal administration," CBS refunded the money but refused all future ads based on the debate format as improper political dramatization. Over time, the Landon campaign shifted more of its ad-buying budget to the independent stations. Because those stations needed the money, they were more likely to take chances by carrying the ads, though these reached a much smaller audience.[35]

Various loopholes in the law and FCC interpretations of the rules, combined with the almost habitual network deference to the administration, gave Roosevelt a tremendous leg up. According to Becky M. Nicolaides, the "networks granted free time to at least 12 New Deal and federal agencies in the pre-convention period." Among these were three dramatic programs provided at taxpayer expense. Because they were governmental agencies, the normal network rule against dramatization in campaign ads did not apply to them.[36]

These one-sided bounties had almost incalculable value to the administration. While estimates for 1936 are not available, 375 stations in 1938 carried over eight thousand hours of the transcribed programs of the Federal Housing Administration, while the WPA had its own network radio show. When journalist Stanley High (who had also been a speechwriter for FDR) asked local station owners why they ran these programs for free, a typical reply was "We know what is expected of us." Bending over backward in this way was also an understandable strategy to curry favor at license-renewal time. According to High, "station owners, since they can never be sure that they are more than six months from the noose, are inclined to be on edge even in the best of times."[37]

Although neither candidate said much about foreign policy, FDR adeptly projected the image of a peace candidate. When right wing rebels in Spanish Morocco under General Francisco Franco, launched an invasion of Republican Spain (the Neutrality Act was not applicable because it was a civil war) Roosevelt, in accord with public opinion, pledged non-intervention. He also reached across the aisle by persuading Republican Senator Gerald Nye (R-North Dakota), who had chaired the Nye Committee to remain neutral in the race. Particularly memorable were FDR's comments in a speech in Chautauqua, N.Y. on August 14th.

The delivery was almost as effective as the content itself:

> I have seen war. I have seen war on land and sea. I have seen blood running from the wounded. I have seen men coughing out their gassed lungs. I have seen the dead in the mud. I have seen cities destroyed. I have seen two hundred limping, exhausted men come out of line—the survivors of a regiment of one thousand that went forward forty-eight hours before. I have seen children starving. I have seen the agony of mothers and wives. I hate war.[38]

As he so often did, FDR exaggerated. His exposure to the fighting in World War I was limited and sanitized. While the Navy had sent him on a guided inspection of American naval and marine bases in Europe, the main impression conveyed by his contemporaneous diary account was that of a sightseer. The passages alternate between accounts of official tours to the front, where he saw the fighting from a distance (though at his request he fired a 155 mm gun), and "congenial" dining interludes behind the lines with politicians, generals, and visiting relatives, such as his cousin Vincent Astor and his aunt Dora Delano Forbes. Other passages describe the after-effects of battle, such as burned out buildings, German prisoners of war being ferried south, the burial of "a number of dead Boche," but his encounters with the carnage of war were mainly of a second-hand nature.[39]

New Deal Money, Big-City Bosses, and Unions

FDR perfected the arts of targeting federal funds, including funds from the WPA, AAA, and REA, which had served him so well two years earlier. As before, he used Hurja's state-by-state tracking polls for guidance to target key states. Following FDR's lead, Hurja privately laid out the ground rules to those in charge of dispersal of funds: "Money, time and effort should not be wasted, but applied in those states close to the fifty percent line and carrying the largest possible electoral vote at the least expense." Once he had the necessary polling data, Hurja would elaborate: "We have this state for sure—waste no effort on it. We are certain to lose that state. Ignore it. Now here is a doubtful state that may be lost or won." Roosevelt gave a thumbs down to a previously scheduled plan to lay off thousands of WPA workers a month before the election. "I don't give a god dam[n] where he gets the money from," he told a subordinate, "but not one person is to be laid off on the first of October."[39]

The 1936 election was a classic illustration of the "political-electoral cycle." The flow of governmental funding increased significantly in the months before the election but then contracted in the aftermath. The WPA, in part of the great discretion it allowed the president, stood out in importance. In early 1935, for example, the program added 300,000 workers but in the period after the election 300,000 were almost immediately removed. Work relief spending rose by 268 percent from the fall of 1935 to the fall of

1936. The extent of the increase varied widely depending on the electoral prospects for the state, including a stunning 3,668 percent spike in Pennsylvania, a swing state carried by Hoover in 1932.[40]

Roosevelt's strategic reliance on federal resources also included the political manipulation of agricultural price supports. Taking extra precautions to keep doubtful farm states in the Democratic fold, he laid down an edict in February 1936 to Secretary of Agriculture Henry Wallace: "Henry, through July, August, September, October and up to the fifth of November 1st, I want cotton to sell at 12 cents [a pound]. I do not care how you do it. That is your problem. It can't go below 12 cents."[41]

Key recipients of New Deal campaign-related funds were big city mayors including Ed Flynn of New York City and Frank Hague of Jersey City, New Jersey (another crucial swing state). Hague, the chief gatekeeper of patronage in the whole state, demanded that WPA workers, as a condition of employment, "tithe" three percent of their salaries to the Democratic party and canvas for the party in elections. Sometimes, it was impossible to differentiate between the political apparatchik and the ordinary bureaucrat. One local WPA director forgot himself by answering the phone "Democratic headquarters!" In another case, a Democratic chairman in Pennsylvania demanded immediate payment of a required $28.08 campaign contribution or "it will be necessary to place your name on a list of those who will not be given consideration for any other appointment after the termination of the emergency relief work."[42]

During the election, FDR received powerful assistance from the Congress of Industrial Organizations (CIO), a union which owed its existence to such New Deal policies as collective bargaining rules. Empowered under Section 7(a) of the Wagner Act, John L. Lewis of the United Mine Workers (UMW) and other industry-wide unions had formed the CIO in late 1935 by splitting off from the more craft oriented, and conservative, American Federation of Labor (AFL). In the next six months, workers in the CIO-affiliated Steel Workers Organizing Committee, the United Mine Workers (UMW), the Amalgamated Clothing Workers, and the International Ladies Garment Workers Union launched successful organizing drives for Democrats at the block level. The UMW alone contributed $469,870 to Roosevelt's War chest. By the time of the election, FDR had the official backing of unions representing more than three million workers.[43]

A Double Game to Win Black Support

Noticeable African American defection from the GOP was rapidly underway in 1935 and 1936. The shift was occurring despite, not because of, FDR's abysmal record on civil rights. After both the 1932 and 1934 elections, he had repeatedly rebuffed NAACP proposals for a House vote on an anti-lynching bill. Walter White proved as susceptible as ever to the president's bewitching wiles. His meeting with FDR in early 1936 set the standard for the campaign. The president told White that there was "no chance" for a vote on the bill but then followed by dangling the possibility of a federal probe of "lawlessness in general, which would include lynching."[44]

White, still inclined to take FDR at his word, brought the idea up to several leading politicians and officials but had no success. Attorney General Homer Cummings was typical in being both "evasive and unresponsive." At White's request, the First Lady asked her husband on his behalf. When she returned with the answer, she broke the bad news, explaining that the president had asked Congress for "only three things" (spending, a tax bill, and a relief bill) and that if he "made an exception for legislation concerning lynching, he would have to do the same thing with other causes as well. The better rule was to make no exceptions at all." But Eleanor made sure to open a slight ray of hope. "Of course" she asserted, the president was "quite willing" that "Congress itself" should push an anti-lynching bill. Nothing more happened on the anti-lynching bill. White never came to terms with the overwhelming evidence that FDR did not remotely share his civil rights priorities. "You cannot name one thing he [FDR] ever did to solve the antilynching problem," remembered Thurgood Marshall who was the NAACP general counsel in 1936. "Roosevelt never said one word in favor of it . . . He was not the great friend of Negroes that some people think." Perhaps FDR didn't seem to care about civil rights because he didn't have to care. Internal polling and reports on the ground showed that African Americans, regardless of the president's stand on this issue, were already joining Democratic ranks in large numbers.[45]

Two main factors spurred African Americans to move into FDR's column: a steady flow of New Deal funds and a perception that they had a powerful friend in Eleanor. Republican efforts to win them back were too little and too late. While, as Republicans pointed out, African Americans received these New Deal funds under highly unequal conditions, the money still often mattered a great deal to them. Roosevelt, fearful of alienating Southern

Democrats, relied on surrogates to advertise these bounties, including in urban black neighborhoods. Just before the election, for example, Ickes gave a national radio speech dedicating a new federally financed chemistry building at Howard University, a leading black college. Ickes declared: "Not only has the Public Works Administration made grants to Howard University, it has also sought to increase the educational equipment available to Negroes in all sections of the nation from elementary schools to colleges."[46]

Thousands of African Americans showed gratitude for this funding in their naming practices, including the following newborns at Harlem hospital: Franklin Delano Wilford, Franklin Delano Kulscar, Donald Roosevelt Evans, Roosevelt Little, and many Eleanors. A black WPA worker from Springfield, Ohio gave his reasons: "I . . . don't think it is fair, to eat Roosevelt bread and meat and vote for Gov. Landon.'" This sentiment, of course, rested on a contradiction and an irony. Prominent in the ranks of the African American unemployed were victims of the New Deal's high price/high wage policies such as the NRA and AAA.[47]

Sinking Prospects for Landon

By October, faint signs of economic improvement, Landon's lackluster campaign, and funneling patronage to doubtful states bolstered the confidence of Roosevelt's advisers. While the Black Committee's methods produced some headaches for the administration and discontent among civil libertarians, it had still had success in fostering the impression that the main anti–New Deal organizations were part of a selfish cabal of big business interests.

Yet FDR had left nothing to chance. This was a far different campaign than in 1932. An illustration was the contrast between the two pre-election speeches in Pittsburgh. In 1932, Roosevelt put the blame on Hoover's deficits and big spending and called for governmental retrenchment but in 1936, he warned that "To balance the budget in 1933 and 1934 or 1935 would have been a crime against the American people. To do so we should either have had to make a capital levy that would have been confiscatory, or we should have had to set our face against human suffering with callous indifference."

Landon faced an almost impossible mission. He was trying to promote lower taxes and balanced budgets while, at the same time, appealing to voters who had become dependent on New Deal programs, including work relief. FDR gained great pleasure in exploiting these contradictions in his speeches. "You cannot promise to repeal taxes before one audience," he charged, "and promise to spend more of the taxpayers' money before another audience . . . You cannot make good on both promises at the same time."[48]

While FDR's advisors discounted the *Literary Digest*'s now infamous pre-election telephone poll showing a Landon victory, the major commercial polls, as well as those conducted internally, predicted a Roosevelt victory. In November, Roosevelt won a landslide of epic proportions, carrying every state except Maine and Vermont. He carried 60.8 percent of the popular vote and scored even higher among African Americans. The president garnered 71 percent of their vote compared to only 23 percent in 1932.[49]

New Deal spending proved instrumental in shifting the votes of a wide cross section of other geographical and demographic groups. Journalist David Lawrence wrote probably the most thorough study of the subject. Lawrence correlated the votes for each candidate with amounts of AAA and relief spending county-by-county outside of the solidly Democratic south. His findings revealed a consistent pattern. Counties which received more AAA and relief funds were significantly more likely to vote for the president. For example, Roosevelt won 60 percent in the highest funded AAA counties while Landon actually carried those counties (with 53 percent of the vote) which had no funding. In the swing state of Pennsylvania, FDR won 60 percent of the vote in the counties with the highest spending on relief but only 45 percent in those with the lowest spending. Although Vermont was one of only two states voting for Landon in 1936, Roosevelt carried the counties with the highest relief spending. "The following equation," historian Folsom sums up in reference to Lawrence's study, "seems to be true: FDR + $ in patronage = reelection."[50]

Just one day after the election, a decision of the United States Court of Appeals of the District of Columbia in the Hearst telegram case gave some limited solace to dispirited anti–New Dealers. The court blasted the FCC for sanctioning a "wholesale" examination of telegrams and then turning these over to the Black Committee "without authority of law and contrary to the very terms of the act under which the Commission was constituted." It declared that "telegraph messages do not lose their privacy and become public property when the sender communicates them confidentially to the telegraph company," elaborating that in many states it was a "penal offense" to violate this privacy. The decision, along with that in the Strawn case, stood as an important precedent against any future mass seizure of private telegrams.[51]

While there were obvious parallels between the Black Committee of the 1930s and the anti-Communist congressional investigations of the 1940s and 1950s, the distinctions in origins and purpose were equally significant. In contrast to the various congressional red hunts, the Black Committee was first and foremost a presidential creation stemming from Roosevelt's wish to establish a congressional committee to discredit opponents and he was instrumental in the selection of Black, a loyal political foot soldier, to lead it. The two most famous anti-Communist committee chairs, Martin Dies and Joseph McCarthy, by contrast, were quintessential independent actors. They were generally oblivious to, and contemptuous of, the priorities of presidents or other congressional leaders. Without McCarthy's notorious, and entirely self-generated, speech in Wheeling, West Virginia, he would have stayed an obscure junior senator. Black's investigation ended because the president no longer needed it, while McCarthy's ended because, in great part, President Eisenhower intervened in a hostile way. Shorn of power, McCarthy became irrelevant, while Black's patron rewarded him with a seat on the US Supreme Court.

For the time being at least, Roosevelt had no more need for "inquisitions." The 1936 election results seemed to guarantee him even more freedom of action than in the First New Deal. Naysayers appeared helpless to prevent a Third New Deal if Roosevelt wanted it, and want it he apparently did. Indicative of this was his election-eve proclamation at Madison Square Garden:

> I should like to have it said of my first Administration that in it the forces of selfishness and of lust for power met their match. I should like to have it said of my second Administration that in it these forces met their master.

Roosevelt had foreshadowed this attitude, however, months earlier when he confided to Morgenthau: "Wait until next year, Henry, I am going to be really radical . . . I am going to recommend a lot of radical legislation."[52]

But, beginning in 1937, nothing went according to plan. Roosevelt's second term brought some unexpected reverses. Just as importantly, these reverses prompted the president to revive, and in some ways expand, the retaliatory and investigative methods pioneered by the Black Committee.

5

Roosevelt Confronts a Right-Left Free Speech Coalition

Few periods in American history have coincided with a more vigorous rise in popular support for the Bill of Rights than the two years following Roosevelt's reelection, though he did not intend this to happen. FDR gave unwitting aid to the rise of pro-free speech sentiment by his responses to a series of unpredictable events.

The first two years of the president's second term began with three months of uninterrupted triumph followed by interludes of confusion, embattlement, false starts, several high-profile setbacks, an economic dip, and finally a determination to retaliate.

The Court-Packing Plan

The origins of the president's troubles began with his proposal in February 1937 to "pack" the Supreme Court. FDR had long regarded that institution as a barrier to protecting and expanding the New Deal. He asked for Senate authorization to appoint up to six new justices for each over the age of seventy, thus boosting the membership to as high as fifteen. He said that he wanted to relieve the workload of the elderly justices, a rationale that nobody took seriously. Like many others in the White House inner circle, Benjamin Cohen, an author of the bill to impose the "death sentence" on large public utilities, which had prompted the creation of the Black Committee, worried that the president's election victory had "gone to his head."

Democrats led the resistance while Republicans wisely stayed in the background. The diverse coalition which opposed Court

Packing turned to an almost ideal standard bearer, Senator Burton K. Wheeler (D-Montana), who had impeccable New Deal credentials and was the first significant national figure to have endorsed Roosevelt for president. FDR went all out to bring Wheeler back into the fold by sending a dinner invitation addressed to "dear Burt from his 'old friend' Franklin." Wheeler would have none of it. "I've been watching Roosevelt for a long time," the senator told Thomas Corcoran. "Once he was only one of us who made him. Now he means to make himself the boss of us all. Your Court plan doesn't matter: he's after us." Vice President Garner, when asked his true opinion about the plan, held his nose and turned his thumb downward.[2]

The National Committee to Uphold Constitutional Government (NCUCG), organized and financed by publisher Frank Gannett, became a major stumbling block to the court plan. Founded just after the president's announcement, it pioneered direct mail methods and had an impressive list of supporters, including the progressive reformer and civil libertarian Amos Pinchot, journalist Dorothy Thompson, Pulitzer-Prize-winning novelist Booth Tarkington, publisher S.S. McClure, and the Reverend Norman Vincent Peale.

White House mail ran nine to one against the plan, but FDR was undaunted. "All we have to do," he reassured Farley, "is to let the flood of mail settle on Congress. You just wait. All I have to do is to deliver a better speech and the opposition will be beating a path to the White House door." The first day of the hearings, however, brought the president bad news from which he never recovered, when Wheeler read a letter from Chief Justice Charles Evans Hughes denying any backlog in the Court's docket.[3]

Sacrificing Civil Rights (Again)

For the better part of 1937, FDR's obsession with Court Packing pushed aside nearly everything else. Left behind again was the long-delayed anti-lynching bill. It did not seem to matter to the president that the proposal had wide popular appeal. It had the backing of nearly all Republicans in Congress and most Northern Democrats, 70 percent of Americans (according to the Gallup poll), and a remarkably high 65 percent of white southerners. When asked to comment at a press conference in January, Roosevelt deflected: "I should say there was enough discussion going on in the Senate."

The proponents, lacking encouragement from the White House, found it impossible to overcome a Democratic filibuster, which included among its leaders Senator Hugo L. Black. Roosevelt's excuse for inaction to Walter White was the familiar refrain that an antilynching bill alienated "too many valuable people" needed for other legislation.[4]

Court Packing remained a key FDR priority despite considerable evidence that any threat to the New Deal had subsided. Justice Owen Roberts (joined later by Chief Justice Hughes) began to switch his vote to uphold New Deal initiatives. On March 29th, the Court sustained a state minimum wage law for women in *West Coast Hotel Co v. Parrish*, essentially reversing its earlier ruling in *Adkins v. Children's Hospital.* Subsequent decisions upheld the constitutionality of the Wagner Act and Social Security. Historians continue to debate why Roberts made his shift though a reaction to the president's February speech was not one of the reasons. He had voted the same way in December (two months before Roosevelt's speech) in an earlier 4 to 4 tie in the *West Coast* case (Justice Harlan F. Stone had been ill).[5]

Political Retaliation

If anything, Roosevelt's determination to push Court Packing stiffened after the switch by Roberts. In May, he retaliated ruthlessly against his old friend, law partner, and former political ally, Grenville Clark (who had supported him in 1936) when he formed the National Committee for Independent Courts (NCIC). "Under your hat," wrote Roosevelt to the NCIC in a missive intended for Clark, "within a few weeks quite a storm is going to break over the heads of individuals who have been cheating their own government. Watch and see how many lawyers condemn them and how many lawyers condone them." On July 2nd, a story in the *New York Times* announced that federal officials had accused Clark of improperly benefiting from a tax shelter.[6]

FDR's scheme to discredit the NCIC collapsed when Rep. Hamilton Fish (R-New York), who represented the president's home district, revealed that Eleanor Roosevelt had benefited from the same, perfectly legal, tax deduction. The controversy took on a second life when the IRS forced its chief counsel Morrison Shafroth and his assistant to resign because they objected to the targeting of Clark. Fish accused the president of operating "a kind of Soviet GPU or American spy system." For added measure, the *New York Times* praised the "Courageous Resignations."[7]

FDR's response after Governor Herbert Lehman of New York, a long-time Democratic ally, came out against Court Packing at almost the last minute, exposed some ugly thoughts lurking underneath an affable demeanor, as recorded by Walter Trohan of the anti-New Deal *Chicago Daily Tribune*. After getting assurances that any comments were off the record, Roosevelt snapped "What else could you expect from a Jew?" This statement did not surprise Trohan , because the same FDR who had championed the quota system at Harvard "had made similar remarks about some of his most devoted supporters before.[8]

Fearful that his court proposal was slipping away, Roosevelt redoubled the pressure on Senate Majority Leader Joe Robinson (D-Arkansas). Described as "Purple and trembling," the elderly and ailing Robinson soldiered on, but he finally reached the point of exhaustion. On July 12, he left the Senate floor complaining of chest pains. He was found dead two days later on his apartment floor clutching a copy of the *Congressional Record*. Roosevelt's decision to skip the funeral did no favors to the Court Packing cause. In a view shared by some in the Senate, national radio commentator Boake Carter (who had supported FDR in 1936) blamed the president for driving Robinson to an early grave. After returning on the funeral train with Democratic senators, Garner brought the latest bad news to the White House: "You're licked, Cap'n. You haven't got the votes."[9]

A Klansman on the Supreme Court

A new Supreme Court opening (the first in his administration) gave FDR some consolation. Seeking a "thumping, evangelical New Dealer," he nominated Senator Hugo L. Black. Black had an easy confirmation after the Judiciary Committee decided not to have an open hearing, perhaps because it did not want him to field embarrassing questions about the Black Committee or alleged past associations with the Ku Klux Klan. Harold Ickes triumphantly recorded in his diary: "So Hugo Black becomes a member of the Supreme Court of the United States while the economic royalists fume and squirm and the President rolls his tongue around in his cheek."[10]

But Black was not yet entirely safe. Soon after he took his seat on the bench, a series of major articles in the Pittsburgh *Post Gazette* chronicled his Klan background which included a life-time membership in that organization. Calls mounted for Black's resignation and several key senators said they would have voted against him if they had known. Black responded with an evasively crafted national radio address saying that he had "dropped" the Klan before becoming a senator. Privately there was more to the story.

Black later recalled that FDR (who had publicly denied any knowledge of the Klan connection) had reassured him that "there was no reason for my worrying about having been a member of the Ku Klux Klan. He said that some of the best friends and supporters he had in the state of Georgia [FDR's second home] were strong members of the organization. He never in any way by word or attitude, indicated any doubt about my having been in the Klan nor did he indicate any criticism of me for having been a member of that organization."[11]

Depression II and "Regime Anxiety"

During this period, the American people were suffering from the effects of the "Roosevelt Recession," sometimes known as "Depression II." In the ten months, beginning in the fall of 1937, industrial production plummeted by 30 percent and stock prices by 50 percent. The GDP shrank precipitously as joblessness spiked to over four million. In 1937, the national income was still only 85.8 percent of the 1929 level compared to the United Kingdom which had advanced to 124.3 percent. Countries such as Chile and Australia had growth rates about 20 percent while that of the U.S. was only -7 percent.

While unemployment had persisted everywhere, the U.S. recovery lagged comparatively behind in that category as well. It was not until 1941 that gross private investment in the U.S. finally reached the 1929 level. Secretary of the Treasury Morgenthau lamented. "We are spending more than we have ever spent before and it does not work." "The historical record is damning," charged Benjamin Anderson, professor of economics at the University of California at Los Angeles and formerly a chief economist of Chase National Bank. "The· New Deal, viewed as an economic policy designed to promote employment, is condemned by the historical and statistical record."[12]

The president's attacks on big business were intensifying in shrillness. According to historian William Leuchtenburg, these stemmed from Roosevelt's belief that "businessmen as a class were stupid, that newspapers were just as bad; nothing would win more votes than to have the press and the business community aligned against him." According to economic historian Robert Higgs, a combination of factors including anti-business attacks and Court Packing fostered "regime anxiety" fears that the U.S. was on the verge of dictatorship. In May 1939, a poll by *Fortune* of business executives found that 64.8 percent agreed with the statement that

"The policies of the administration have so affected the confidence of businessmen that recovery has been seriously held back."[13]

Further exacerbating regime anxiety was a wave of strikes in the aftermath of the Wagner Act. They took a militant turn in December 1936 when the CIO-affiliated United Auto Workers staged a sit-down strike at a General Motors plant in Flint, Michigan, and closed the doors to non-union workers. Although the strikers were clearly trespassers under the law, Democratic Governor Frank Murphy did not send in the national guard and Roosevelt refused to take sides. "Roosevelt's mere neutrality," writes H.W. Brands, "revealed the sea change that occurred in America." The strike grew to 136,000 workers and prevented 300,000 cars from being built. After six weeks, General Motors capitulated and recognized the union as the official bargaining agent for the workers.[14]

Roosevelt blamed that paucity of investment on a concerted business conspiracy (or "capital strike") against the New Deal. When Morgenthau suggested that the president make gestures to restore business confidence, FDR replied that he was "fully conscious of the situation which exists . . . Business, particularly the banking business, has ganged up on me." With Roosevelt's encouragement, top administration officials, including Secretary of Interior Ickes, publicly condemned the "capital strike." A measure of eroding business confidence was the widening gap between the yield in short and long-term corporate bonds. The average yield of longer-term bonds, Higgs reports, "remained at extraordinarily high levels from 1936 through the first quarter of 1941." What had happened was that the confidence of investors "in their ability to appropriate the longer-term interest payments and principal repayments promised by the country's most secure corporations plummeted between early 1934 and early 1936."[15]

The British economist John Maynard Keynes sent a letter of advice to Roosevelt in February 1938 on the "present slump." While he recommended "large-scale investment" via greater government spending to stimulate demand, Keynes especially stressed the importance of a more conciliatory attitude toward business. "If you work them [businesspeople] into the surly, obstinate, terrified mood, of which domestic animals, wrongly handled, are so capable," Keynes gently, and diplomatically, warned, "the nation's burdens will not get carried to market; and in the end public opinion will veer their way." If Roosevelt's dissembling reply is any indication, Keynes's letter had no impact on his thinking. It highlighted the minor points made by Keynes and ignored the substantive ones. "It was very pleasant and encouraging to know that you are in agreement," he answered, "with so much of the Administration's economic program. This confirmation coming from so eminent an economist is indeed welcome. Your analysis of the present business situation is very interesting.The emphasis you put upon the need for stimulating housing construction is well placed."[16]

Keynes might not have sufficiently appreciated just how much political expediency animated FDR's attacks on big business. When economist Jacob Viner, a longtime advisor, complained about the ongoing "warfare on business," the president, as sometimes happened with people he trusted, became more candid. "Viner," he asserted, "If I'm going to succeed and my administration is going to succeed, I have to maintain a strong hold on my public. In order to maintain a firm hold on the public, I have to do something startling once in a while. I mustn't let them take me for granted."[17]

Neutrality, "Fool's Gold," and the Quarantine Speech

FDR continued to treat foreign policy as a distraction from other priorities, and he tried to keep that distraction as fleeting as possible. The main exception was that he did not want to alienate widespread antiwar feeling. As the fighting in Spain continued to rage, for example, he prodded Senator Nye in 1937 to push an amendment to apply the Neutrality Act to civil wars. "Roosevelt was trying not only to assure quick passage of a Spanish arms embargo," historian Robert Dallek observes, "but also to avoid a congressional debate that could forestall action on judicial reform. His overriding concern in January 1937 was to legitimize New Deal achievements by curbing the Supreme Court." Other new revisions to the Neutrality Act included a "cash and carry" provision for combatants purchasing U.S. goods, thus giving advantage to countries with sufficient naval capacity, such as the United Kingdom and Japan. But, again, Roosevelt did not want to disturb U.S. trading revenue. He refused to use the embargo to sanction Germany and Italy for aiding Franco, in part because it might create pressure for him to extend it to France and Russia for aiding the Republicans[18]

FDR was similarly risk avoidant after Japanese and Chinese troops clashed at the Marco Polo Bridge in July 1937 (the official beginning of World War II in Asia). In refusing to apply the Neutrality Act to the war, he also rejected the option of embargoing such "implements of war" oil, and cotton, all of which Japan needed. As John T. Flynn observed, the "President defied the mandatory provisions of the Neutrality Act because his administration required that at this moment America should get a little of that 'fool's gold' [FDR's earlier term for tainted wartime profiteering] from Japan."[19]

If the truth be told, the morass in China, a country long enfeebled by foreign meddling and warlordism, defied a simple remedy. Moreover, from the beginning of the 1930s, U.S. policy had shown little consistency. The U.S. had vigorously protested after Japan had invaded northwest China, eventually creating the puppet regime of Manchukuo in 1931, for example, but was silent about Soviet intervention in Mongolia or in the Xinjiang region of northwestern China, including a military takeover in 1934 to install a pro-Communist government. More immediately, the Sino-Japanese War had put American troops, sent earlier to enforce (increasingly outmoded) treaties, in harm's way. On December 11th 1937, Japanese planes, during attacks on Nanjing, bombed the clearly marked American gunboat *Panay* on the Yangtze River, killing two crew members. Although the Japanese government cooled tensions with a full apology and compensation, U.S. forces in China had an untenable status and an impossible mission. "Had the President applied the Neutrality Act," John T. Flynn points out, "as he was duty-bound to do—this boat would not have been protecting American oil tankers delivering oil amidst two warring armies in China. The purpose of the Neutrality Act was to avoid precisely an incident like this."[20]

Roosevelt's most publicized response to the war between Japan and China, though he did not name those countries specifically, was the "Quarantine Speech" delivered in Chicago in October 1937. "We are determined to keep out of war," he warned, "yet we cannot insure ourselves against the disastrous effects of war and the dangers of involvement. We are adopting such measures as will minimize our risk of involvement, but we cannot have complete protection in a world of disorder in which confidence and security have broken down." He compared foreign aggression to "an epidemic of physical disease," that required peace-loving nations to impose "a quarantine of the patients in order to protect the health of the community." When pressed on how he intended to do this, however, he denied any intention of compromising American neutrality. FDR told Cardinal George Mundelein of Chicago that his plan did not "not contemplate either military or naval action against the unjust aggressor nation, nor does it involve 'sanctions' as generally understood, but rather a policy of isolation, severance of ordinary communication in a united manner by all the governments in the pact."[21]

Joseph Grew, U.S. ambassador to Japan, complained that the president's rhetoric in the Quarantine Speech had undermined his efforts to win over besieged moderates in Tokyo still resentful of earlier U.S. discrimination against immigrants. "There goes everything I have tried to accomplish in my entire mission in Japan," Grew lamented after reading the text. From another perspective, Rep. Hamilton Fish concluded that it "would be more beneficial to the country, if the President stopped passing moral judgements and attempting to police other nations, and instead sought to do justice in our own country, by urging the enactment of the Anti-lynching Bill."[22]

The president continued an erratic course toward the Spanish Civil War. After Franco's forces split the Spanish Republic in two in April 1938, Senator Nye (belying his reputation as a narrow "isolationist," and taking some political risk) proposed a bill to lift the embargo on the government but not the rebels. Roosevelt, who had once lectured the cabinet in favor of such a policy, refused to back it, fearful that he might lose electoral support from the more pro-Franco U.S. Catholic hierarchy.[23]

Coldness Toward the Plight of Europe's Jews

Multiple reports of antisemitic persecution in Europe carried little weight with the president. After Rabbi Stephen Wise, an ally and friend, reported that Poland was calling on Jews to pack up and leave, Roosevelt gave a shocking reply. He found the Polish government's position to be understandable because "the Jewish grain dealer and Jewish shoe dealer and Jewish shopkeeper" exercised disproportionate control over the economy. After the forced Anschluss of Austria into Germany in 1938 sparked more persecution, FDR rejected a promising proposal from the Dominican Republic to admit as many as 100,000 Jews. His motivation was a fear that it might create a stepping stone to evade U.S. immigration laws.[24]

A spate of news stories highlighting antisemitic outrages in Europe finally prompted Roosevelt to make a political gesture. In March 1938, he invited thirty-one countries to meet at the French resort town of Evian-Les-Bains to discuss refugee issues. One after another, however, delegates announced that it was impossible for their particular country to admit more Jews because it might foster a "racial problem" or worsen unemployment. The remarks of Myron Taylor, the U.S. representative, contained little more than self-congratulatory praise about the alleged liberality of U.S. immigration laws. The German government took propaganda advantage calling it "astounding" that the delegates had offered lip service against persecution yet none wanted to admit the victims of that persecution.[25]

"Beware! Libel Me at Your Peril"

After the defeat of Court Packing, FDR shifted his main priority to executive reorganization. The original scheme was sweeping and centered, in the words of historian Charles Schilke, on implementing "continuous central planning and program coordination." A friendly observer from the *New Republic* concluded that it gave the president the power to "do almost anything that came into his head." Reinforcing American fears of granting the executive branch this kind of discretion were daily reminders of Hitler's and Stalin's atrocities. An influential group of senators were so hostile to the proposal that the administration clumsily put it under wraps. A much watered-down reorganization bill still did not appease the skeptics.[26]

As the prospects for executive organization and other New Deal goals appeared to be receding, FDR's relations with the press reached a new low. Media scrutiny, observes historian Gary Dean Best, had "lifted the 'curtain' and exposed Roosevelt's hidden intentions through thousands of words in editorials and columns." According to Richard W. Steele, Roosevelt's "message seemed to be—recognize newspaper owners as your enemies and do not trust what you read in your papers." The New Deal's sometime friend Walter Lippmann said that Roosevelt wanted to "muzzle the press as he would like to pack the court. In the quest for power one thing leads to another and the incredible soon comes to be regarded as necessary and then accepted as inevitable." Roosevelt's contempt for the newspapers came more into the open. At a press conference in August 1937, he testily lectured the reporters: "I understand. You fellows are placed in such a position very often . . . I can appreciate what you are told to write . . . it does not take away, in any way, from my affection for the group of you." The pro-New Deal *Nation* warned that "when Mr. Roosevelt hates, he hates deeply and vengefully. The President never forgets an affront or injury."[27]

A prime target of Roosevelt's anger was the radio commentator Boake Carter. On behalf of the president, White House Press

Secretary Stephen Early made an appeal in November 1937 to his friend, Marjorie Merriweather Post, a director of General Foods, which sponsored Carter's commentaries. Like her husband Joseph Davies, recently appointed as ambassador to the Soviet Union, she was a veteran of Democratic causes. But Carter gave no hint of backing down. After the sinking of the *Panay*, in December 1937, he accused Roosevelt of stoking up prowar feeling.[28]

In response, General Foods cajoled the commentator into an agreement to be "constructive" and show "suitable restraint of language and without invective or criticism of the motives, character, and mental or moral attributes of personalities." In a triumphant "Dear Boss" letter, Davies informed FDR that Carter had pledged to eschew interpretation and "be confined exclusively to reporting the news." But Carter did not see the agreement that way and continued to be as strident as ever. According to Harold Ickes's diary in February 1938, the "President told Miss Perkins [Secretary of Labor Frances Perkins] that he would be happy if she could discover that Boake Carter, the columnist and radio commentator, who has been so unfair and pestiferous, was not entitled to be in this country. It appears that an investigation of his record is being made." It was indeed. The Department of the Treasury was scrutinizing Carter's background and his 1936 taxes, while the State Department searched (unsuccessfully) for a pretext to deport him back to the United Kingdom. When a noticeably rattled Carter got wind of these efforts, he wrote to the president: "Beware! Libel me at your peril."[29]

Roosevelt revealed his true feelings during a dinner conversation with Jerre Mangione, then working in the Federal Writers Project of the WPA. A committed FDR partisan at the time, Mangione recalled that as the evening wore on, the president volunteered that he was having Carter "thoroughly investigated" and that the results, when revealed, "would put an end to his career." Mangione was crestfallen: "That Roosevelt, the statesman I had admired, should admit to such vindictiveness came as the greatest jolt of all."[30]

As pressures from the administration bore down on him, Carter's commentary became much more tepid. "I pulled my punches," he later admitted, "and because of this and, contributing reasons, my radio rating, which had been at the top, began to drop." In August 1938, CBS discontinued the program. In a lecture tour later that year, Carter accused the "Great White Father in Washington" (Roosevelt) of bullying station owners worried about six-month license renewals and of intimidating CBS into firing him. Freedom of speech, to the extent it was genuine, he reported regretfully, applied only to the print press. "Despite the fact that newspapers also depend on advertising for their buns and coffee," Carter asserted, "newspaper . . . publishers can write what they want . . . The unhampered radio commentator is a thing of the past." By the end of 1938, not a single anti-New Deal radio commentator remained on the major networks.[31]

Turning on the Spending Spigots

A depressed economy continued to frustrate an increasingly rudderless Roosevelt. The stock market plunged again in March 1938 and resistance to the New Deal agenda intensified both within Congress and from below. If these trends continued, big GOP gains were likely in the 1938 election. Acting under this incentive, Roosevelt was receptive when a group of advisors met at Warm Springs in April to propose a "compensatory" spending program of $3.7 billion for public works and relief. They included three allies of WPA head Harry Hopkins, Lauchlin Currie, Aubrey Williams, and Leon Henderson.

Hopkins, according to his friend Robert Sherwood, regarded "money [his own as well as that of others] as something to be spent as quickly as possible." Not invited to the meeting at Warm Springs was the more fiscally conservative Secretary of Treasury Morgenthau, an advocate of balanced budgets. He knew the battle was lost when the president began "to outline the various schemes he had in mind for spending money."[32]

The meeting at Warm Springs is sometimes depicted, and dressed up, as a turning point in favor of Keynesian demand management but the result was consistent with the president's previous practice of boosting federal domestic spending in election years and lowering it in off years. WPA employment had declined in the first six months of 1936, for example, but increased in the last six months. It fell again in 1937 and early 1938 but spiked again in the last six months. AAA spending was four times higher in 1938 than in the previous year. In line with these trends, historian Gavin Wright concludes that "WPA employment reached peaks in the fall of election years. In states like Florida and Kentucky—where the New Deal's big fight was in the primary—the rise of WPA employment was hurried along in order to synchronize with the primaries."[33]

The biggest shift brought by the Warm Springs meeting was not the level of spending and deficits but Roosevelt's official rationale for them. He increasingly emphasized such generalized goals as "buying power" and putting "idle money and idle men to work." As Alan Brinkley puts it, government spending, "Roosevelt now implied was no longer a necessary evil, to be employed sparingly as a solution to specific problems. It was a positive good, to be used lavishly." Despite the perception of some, the amounts resulting from the 1938 spending program fell far short of the sums considered sufficient by Keynes. The deficit that year, for example, was about the same as that of 1936, as a percentage of GDP. According to George Selgin, "the New Deal considered as a program for ending the Great Depression, had relatively little in common with Keynesian economics."[34]

The Minton Committee

Creative targeting of patronage and political retaliation ran along parallel tracks as priorities in FDR's reelection strategy. Thus, it comes as no surprise that April 1938, the same month as the Warm Springs meeting, was also when the Minton Committee began its first hearings. The loyalty of Senator Sherman Minton (D-Indiana) to the president had a level of intensity that was "uncommon even among fellow true-believers" and included a "strong strain of populism, and belief that government must be powerful." Nobody in Congress had more energetically and enthusiastically pushed Court Packing. A grateful Roosevelt asked Minton to fill the first available Supreme Court slot but he demurred because he wanted to stay in the Senate, and the job went to Black. FDR gave his full blessing to the Minton Committee at a "council of war" with the members by chiming in, "We have just begun to fight."[35]

The National Committee to Uphold Constitutional Government (NCUCG), which had done so much to frustrate Court Packing and other New Deal measures, was the main target of the hearings. Just before they began, Minton committee staffers arrived at the NCUCG's New York offices to begin rifling through file cabinets. They came with an order demanding all documents "which in any way relate to efforts to influence or suppress or foment public sentiment, or to influence the passage or defeat of Federal legislation, or to influence public contracts, activities, or concessions." These aggressive methods, as well perceived badgering of witnesses at the hearings, unleashed a torrent of media criticism. The *Chicago Daily Tribune* charged that the Minton Committee had become "the GPU of this administration," while the *New York Herald Tribune* considered it guilty of "terrorism."[36]

"To Embarrass, Worry, Terrorize, and Destroy"

Behind the scenes, the administration extended essential aid to the Minton Committee, including access to the tax returns of witnesses. It relied for legal authority on the same 1935 executive order that had authorized the predecessor Black Committee to inspect returns "in connection with the so-called 'holding company bill,' or any other matter or proposal affecting legislation." But the administration's assistance to the investigation inspired even more press criticism, including a full-bore attack by columnist Walter Lippmann, a highly respected voice among many of the president's supporters. Lippmann, who had two years earlier expressed similar antagonism toward Black, condemned the probe as another effort by New Dealers "to embarrass, worry, terrorize and destroy . . . If this is not to be described as arbitrary government and capricious tyranny, what is the accurate way to describe it?" Lippmann closed his article by making a direct appeal to the American Civil Liberties Union to lead "the fight against the lawlessness of men like Black and Minton."[37]

Meanwhile, Roosevelt continued to escalate his war with the press. At a meeting with newspaper editors on April 21st, he complained again that publishers had routinely ordered reporters to slant their coverage. He also boasted that he was "more closely in touch with public opinion . . . than any individual in this room." If Minton and Roosevelt felt enveloped by enemies, Grenville Clark's lead address at the annual meeting of the American Newspaper Publishers Association (ANPA) in late April gave them even more to worry about. He charged that the Minton Committee's tactics were "designed to intimidate persons who dare, in a country supposed to be free, to oppose legislation desired by the administration in power." It was not Clark's speech, however, but a seemingly unrelated ANPA report that most drew Minton's ire. It questioned whether the current federal policy of granting six-month short-term licenses for stations had made "broadcasters unduly sensitive . . . if not subservient, to the administration in power."[38]

"You Boys Asked for It, You Know"

Incensed by the ANPA's implication of nefarious intentions by FDR, Minton proposed a bill imposing criminal penalties for newspapers which published "false" news. The short and unambiguous text made it a felony for newspapers or other periodicals to publish as "fact anything known to the publisher, or his, or its, responsible agents, to be false," punishable by up to a two-year prison sentence or a $10,000 fine. Through his bill, Minton hoped to force the "Tory" (a favored term of FDR as well) newspapers (90 percent of which by his estimate opposed the president) to curb their "false propaganda." His list of prime offenders included such anti–Roosevelt voices as the *Philadelphia Inquirer*, the *Washington Post*, the *New York Herald Tribune*, and "the unspeakable" *Chicago Daily Tribune*.[39]

Media pundits made the logical assumption that Minton was acting at the president's behest. As a longtime administration loyalist, entrusted to the position of assistant majority whip in his freshman term, he fit the profile of a disciplined team player rather than a person to go off half-cocked. Soon after the introduction of the bill, *Newsweek* said as much: "Those who know Senator Minton say he must have had Roosevelt's tacit approval before introducing a bill to make news distortion a felony." The pro-New Deal *Christian Science Monitor* found "little doubt" that Minton's proposal "reflected the views of Mr. Roosevelt." There was other evidence that Minton had encouragement from above. An unidentified "veteran Capitol Hill reporter," who was close to Minton, told historian David N. Atkinson that "someone in the administration" had put Minton up to introducing the 'gag law'." If true, this would have been consistent with Roosevelt's habit of floating trial balloons.[40]

But if FDR had any responsibility for the bill's origins, he was not about to tip his hand, at least not yet. Asked about it the day after Minton's speech, and just as an adverse reaction was starting to set in, he punted. Instead of answering directly, the president joked about the possibility of referring the proposal to the Federal Bureau of Prisons but added that it did not have sufficient funds to accommodate everyone that might be punished under such a law. Before moving on to the next question, and getting a good laugh, he quipped to the reporters, "You boys asked for it, you know."

If Roosevelt had floated a trial balloon, however, it deflated rapidly. Just about everyone, it seemed, either hated the bill or avoided comment. The *Washington Post* condemned "Minton's ridiculous bill," as based "on the Hitler-Mussolini technique." Hands down, the most stridently antagonistic voice was the *Philadelphia Inquirer*, which had backed Roosevelt's reelection but had rebelled after Court Packing. On a single day, the paper ran a cartoon of Minton waving a "press gag" flag and a special front-page editorial that blamed Roosevelt for pushing the bill to "punish, muzzle and coerce the press" and referred to Minton as "a perfect servant of an august master." Germany's official news service did Minton's cause no favors by volunteering that every "decent person will approve 100 percent of Senator Minton's proposal."[41]

"So This Is Jersey Justice"

Just as Minton was trying to restrict First Amendment rights in one realm, Mayor Frank Hague of Jersey City, New Jersey, was doing it in another. Beginning in 1937, Hague began a sustained effort to drive out CIO organizers, whom he regarded as Communist tools and disruptors of business conditions. The city denied speaking and meeting permits to the union and allied groups, such as the American Civil Liberties Union (ACLU). Hague also selectively enforced building codes, imposed discriminatory tax assessments, used intimidation to close off private meeting halls, and took steps to muzzle the dissident press.[42]

Hague's alliance with Roosevelt began even before there was a New Deal. Although he had backed Al Smith for the 1932 Democratic nomination, he had quickly won Roosevelt's favor by staging one of the largest Democratic campaign rallies in American history. Thereafter, the Jersey City boss had dependably put Roosevelt over the top in the swing state of New Jersey at election time, reaping as a reward a steady flow of federal money. He also served as vice chair of the Democratic National Committee (DNC). It was Hague, rather than the governor or a senator in New Jersey, who controlled the dispersal of all New Deal patronage funds and had a veto over the state's federal judicial and patronage appointments. Working in tandem with Harry Hopkins, he exerted control over nearly 100,000 federally funded jobs in the state. The stench of corruption was palpable, but Roosevelt and Hopkins chose to ignore it.[43]

Hague's antics posed a dilemma because they served to alienate key elements in the New Deal coalition, including labor unions. Roosevelt's initial reaction was to appear to be above the fray even as he quietly continued to run interference for the mayor. At the height of the CIO organizing drive, Postmaster General James A. Farley found out that a henchman of the mayor was reading the mail of one of Hague's political enemies. Pointing to hard evidence, Farley proposed prosecuting Hague for both mail tampering and tax evasion. Roosevelt wanted no part of it. He responded to Farley: "Forget prosecution. You go tell Frank to knock it off . . . But keep this quiet. We need Hague's support, and we want New Jersey."[44]

The Hague free speech controversy came to a head just two days after Minton proposed his controversial bill. At the center was the perennial, but well respected, Socialist Party presidential candidate, Norman Thomas. Thomas was pivotal in transforming just another labor-organizing controversy into a national test case for First Amendment protections. On April 30th, Thomas showed up in Jersey City to speak at an open-air rally even though the city had turned him down for a permit. Ready to spring, police immediately arrested him when he got out of his car to address a crowd of one thousand. Thomas barely had time to utter "So this is Jersey justice" before the officers whisked him away and expelled him from the city.[45]

"Squelch Minton Before Minton Smears the New Deal"

Americans across the ideological divide were beginning to pair Hague and Minton as common dangers to free speech. To Lippmann, for example, Minton's use of tax returns involved "as fundamental a question of civil liberty as Mayor Hague's recent performances." Lippmann soon secured reinforcement from a major Republican figure: Alfred M. Landon, the GOP standard-bearer in 1936. When Landon heard about Thomas's "deportation," he fired off a letter of support to his 1936 Socialist opponent blasting Hague's actions as a "gross violation of our sacred rights of free speech." The two men struck up a lifetime friendship and Landon pledged to join "shoulder to shoulder with you in this fight for free speech." To Landon, Minton's bill represented "a dire threat to the press" that "may reflect the president's attitude." At a minimum, Roosevelt's "views have, no doubt, encouraged Senator Minton and others."[46]

The bad publicity stung enough that Minton let his bill die in the Senate Committee on Interstate Commerce (chaired by one of his leading Democratic adversaries, Burton K. Wheeler). In response, anti–New Deal *Philadelphia Inquirer* responded with two cartoons. The first showed Minton in a tar barrel underneath the slogan, "Honest—I Was Only Kidding," while the other, "Franklin Discovers Lightning Again," featured a kite flown from the White House labeled "Sen. Minton's attack on the Free Press." The kite, titled as a "White House Feeler," carried a bolt of lightning that hit the executive mansion.[47]

More worrisome for the president was the unexpected opposition to the Minton Committee from publisher J. David Stern, perhaps the most important newspaper ally of the White House. Stern's chain of newspapers ran both an anti-Minton cartoon and an editorial warning that the Democratic Senate "should sit on Minton: Quick" because his "gag bill" was playing "into the hands of the reactionary newspapers of this country by trying to suppress them." The controversy had so threatened Roosevelt's agenda that it was time for Democrats to "squelch Minton before Minton Smears the New Deal." The president, an avid newspaper reader, almost certainly knew about the editorial, and, if so, the content was unlikely to instill more confidence in the Minton Committee's usefulness to the New Deal.[48]

The president's press conference on May 10th did nothing to reassure pro-New Deal civil libertarians. When asked about threats to "free speech and assembly in Jersey City," Roosevelt evasively dismissed the controversy as a "local police matter." As to removing Hague as DNC vice chairman, he deflected that the best person to comment was the Democratic national chairman, James A. Farley. The overall impression conveyed by the president served to further tarnish the New Deal's civil-liberties pretensions and, just as importantly, create an opportunity for conservatives to attack. The pro-FDR *New York Post* fretted that Republicans were "catching on" to Landon's efforts to tie together "Hagueism" and New Dealism and thus successfully rebranding the GOP as "the champion of liberty and enemy of repression."[49]

The Genesis of a Free Speech Coalition

Roosevelt's perceived complicity in attacks on the First Amendment by Minton and Hague motivated Grenville Clark to team up with the Republican Arthur T. Vanderbilt (the outgoing president of the American Bar Association) and Frank J. Hogan (the incoming president) to form the Bill of Rights Committee of the American Bar Association. Vanderbilt had represented Silas Strawn in the telegram case against the Black Committee two years earlier. As the conservatives and moderates took the initiative, anti-Hague New Dealers gave new vent to their anger about Roosevelt's passivity. In an open letter, the prominent liberal Oswald Garrison Villard questioned whether Roosevelt was a "true patriot" because he had not taken the first train to Jersey City, to "stand up in the public square there without asking for any permit." Similarly, the *New Republic* lamented that Hague was basking "in the continuing approval of President Roosevelt," while the *Nation* wanted to cut off Hague's control of state WPA projects.[50]

Pressed on all sides, as well as by a dismal economy, Roosevelt realized the necessity of solidifying his base, even while keeping in line the big city Democratic machines so essential for election turnout. On June 24th, he made his move by adding a passage in a fireside chat. It did not specifically mention Hague or Jersey City, but the message between the lines was hard not to miss. Roosevelt expressed concern "about the attitude of a candidate or his sponsors with respect to the rights of American citizens to assemble peaceably and to express publicly their views," adding that the "American people will not be deceived by anyone who attempts to suppress individual liberty under the pretense of patriotism." These admonishments enabled Roosevelt to protect his left flank when he made his far more controversial call in the same fireside chat for a purge of "Copperheads" in upcoming Democratic primaries and replacing them with more reliable "liberal" allies.[51]

If Roosevelt had intended to blunt negative commentary on his role in the Hague controversy, he more than succeeded. The press devoted far more space to the proposed purge of anti-Roosevelt Democrats than to the oblique, and comparatively short, passage that referred to Hague's abuses, but what commentary did appear was overwhelmingly positive. The *New York Times* concluded that "all thoughtful Americans, 'conservatives' and 'liberals', supporters and opponents of the Administration," could agree on the president's defense of free speech. But Roosevelt had no intention of toppling Hague from his perch. He kept him as the DNC's vice chairman and left his patronage intact.[52]

Although Roosevelt's preoccupation with Court Packing and reorganization had largely undermined any dream of a Third New Deal, he achieved one important victory: the Fair Labor Standards Act. It was the first law (with the partial exception of the chaotic NRA), which imposed a national minimum wage. Because it did not readjust for regional differentials, however, it served to depress employment in the low-wage South. The Labor Department estimated that as many fifty thousand workers (most of them African Americans) lost their jobs just weeks after the law went into effect.[53]

As the 1938 campaign heated up, Roosevelt stepped up his attacks on the press. At his presidential press conference, he declared that 85 percent of newspapers were "Tory." When a reporter pointed to a recent poll that three hundred out of eight hundred of them had praised the president's position on Hague, Roosevelt said that he did not believe it. In phrasing reminiscent of Minton, his election eve letter to the *St. Louis Post-Dispatch* proclaimed that "our newspapers cannot be edited in the interests of the general public, from the counting room." He mused on the possibility of "a national symposium on that question, particularly in relation to the freedom of the press. How many bogies are conjured up by invoking that greatly overworked phrase."[54]

More than ever, advocates of free speech on the left and right were grouping together Roosevelt, Hague, and Minton as joint offenders. The ever-persistent Norman Thomas charged that Roosevelt represented "the party of Frank Hague," while Albert Jay Nock, an individualist and civil libertarian, blamed New Deal policies of centralization:

> Given a Roosevelt who manipulates or disregards the law as he sees fit, and you immediately spawn a tribe of Murphys, Hagues, Ickeses, Wallaces, Blacks, Mintons, who may freely manipulate or disregard the law as *they* see fit. (emphasis Nock's)

The ACLU was less outspoken but, as historian Laura Weinrib observes, the "Roosevelt administration's tepid response to Mayor Hague pushed the ACLU, once more, toward the federal courts." Rising public support for the First Amendment and disdain toward Court Packing and executive reorganization, closely tracked daily headlines about the abuses of dictators including Hitler, Stalin, and Mussolini.[55]

The cooperative legal strategy of the ABA's Bill of Rights Committee and the American Civil Liberties Union brought results on October 27th. A district court issued a sweeping and precedent-setting final decree prohibiting any further "deportations" in Jersey City or interference with the right of citizens to picket and exercise free assembly in public parks and other open-air venues. The decision seemed anticlimactic in a time when views toward the First Amendment were rapidly shifting. According to Weinrib, "civil liberties had a popular salience that would have astounded dissenters during the First World War. Public approval of the outcome in Hague was a forgone conclusion. The dominant sentiment in press coverage of the decision was that the Supreme Court had not gone far enough."[56]

Quite reluctantly, it was beginning to dawn on Roosevelt himself that perceptions that he had a cavalier attitude toward the First Amendment was not serving him well. His association with Hague and Minton, combined with his much-publicized failed purge, had further encouraged suspicions among civil libertarians, who otherwise favored his New Deal agenda, that Roosevelt did not share their beliefs in the Bill of Rights. The ultimate costs at the ballot box could not be brushed aside. Nearly every member of Congress targeted for defeat in Roosevelt's purge had won their primary races.[57]

"Good Man!" 1938 as a Turning Point

While domestic issues dominated the 1938 campaign discourse, the crisis over Czechoslovakia was impossible to ignore. In 1919, the victorious Allies had extended official recognition to the multiethnic new country of Czechoslovakia (formerly part of the Austro-Hungarian Empire) as a centralized, democratic state. In the process, they barred the German minority in the so-called Sudetenland from joining the area with either Austria or Germany and, secondarily, rejected proposals to defuse ethnic and religious tensions by dividing Czechoslovakia into numerous self-governing cantons on the Swiss model.

More than decade later, Hitler stoked up lingering resentments by prodding local Nazis to agitate for more and more power. For a time, an invasion by Germany looked imminent. Europeans, as well as Roosevelt, had little appetite for the possibility of another world war. But British Prime Minister Neville Chamberlain and Hitler headed it off through the Munich Pact pressuring Czechoslovakia to cede the Sudetenland to Germany in exchange for a guarantee to the remaining Czech-Slovak remnant nation. Rather than fight alone, Czechoslovakia capitulated.

When he heard about the deal, FDR sent a wire to Chamberlain: "Good Man," and a week later told the U.S. ambassador to Italy that he was "not a bit upset" about the Munich agreement. Roosevelt even showed a tendency to claim credit for making it all possible. Press Secretary Steve Early told reporters that "all drafting was done by President Roosevelt who virtually assumed control of the State Department."[58]"

"We Will Tax and Tax, and Spend and Spend, and Elect and Elect"

As the election approached, the flow of federal money became more effusive. Hopkins of the WPA, appeared to be an ideal choice for the president as point man in matters of dispersal. According to reporter Arthur Krock, Hopkins allegedly told two companions at the racetrack during the height of the campaign: "We will tax and tax, and spend and spend, and elect and elect." Hopkins applied this strategy to the Kentucky primary campaign between FDR's preferred choice, Senate Majority Leader Alben Barkley, and popular challenger Kentucky governor Albert B. "Happy" Chandler.

Over three hundred WPA employees under the close supervision of Hopkins recruited relief recipients to support Barkley. Through a combination of real and implied threats, they induced many of those who were Republicans to register as Democrats so they could back Barkley. In some cases, WPA employees dispensed Barkley buttons to relief recipients and threatened to deny their checks if they did not wear them. A series of post-election Pulitzer Prize winning articles by journalist Thomas L. Stokes of Scripps-Howard revealed these and other unseemly details.[59]

In 1938, however, the strategic deployment of government funds proved insufficient to overcome voter discontent over the economy, Court Packing, government reorganization, political purges, and other evidence of executive overreach. The Republicans gained eighty-one seats in the House and eight in the Senate and won thirteen governorships. Even so, without the flow of federal money, it could have been far worse for FDR. Democrats maintained hefty majorities in the House (262 to 169) and Senate (69 to 23).

The election of 1938 also coincided with a turning point in popular attitudes toward the First Amendment and free expression in a broader sense. The diverse revulsion against perceived attacks on free expression by Hague and Minton came together to nurture the development of a broad cross-ideological coalition for civil liberties. Roosevelt was more an obstructer than an enabler in this shift. He worked in de facto partnership with the Minton Committee, and regardless of whether the senator's press bill reflected his exact views, he did nothing to stand in the way. It was Congress and the press that stopped the bill. Similarly, Roosevelt's default position on Hague's abuses was to ignore them. Pressure from journalists, government officials, and judges finally forced him to act, and then in a cautious and partial way. The evidence of widening popular support for the Bill of Rights also raised a question. In the event of another war, would Americans be more protective of these rights than it had been in World War I?

6

"Again, and Again, and Again": The Politics of War

FDR had squandered any prospect of a transformative domestic agenda after the 1936 elections because of his obsession with Court Packing. That opportunity never came again. Beginning in 1939, a fortified coalition of conservatives in both parties stood ready to block any hint of a Third New Deal. Just as importantly, events in Europe and Asia constantly intruded into the public discourse and the president's time.

The foreign-centric nature of the last two years of the second term was already apparent a week after the elections, due to events following the murder of Ernst vom Rath, a German embassy official in Paris, by Herschel Grynszpan, a seventeen-year-old Jew. Intending to kill the ambassador, Grynszpan was striking back because the Nazis had expelled his parents, along with thousands of others, to the eastern border. Because Poland was refusing to admit them, however, they were languishing in a no-man's land. Nazi officials responded to the assassination by staging a series of "spontaneous demonstrations." These culminated in the murder of scores of Jews and the confinement of twenty thousand others in concentration camps.

"By nightfall," wrote journalist Otto Tolischus, "there was scarcely a Jewish shop, café, office or synagogue in the country that was not either wrecked, burned severely or damaged." These atrocities came to be summarized as "Kristallnacht" (night of broken glass) because of the countless store windows shattered. The German cabinet also levied a collective fine on its Jewish community of one billion marks (the equivalent of over four hundred million dollars at the time) for complicity in vom Rath's murder. Although

Germany wanted to force a mass exodus, it reduced to almost nothing the amount that each Jew could take out of the country.[1]

FDR's Non-Response

Roosevelt's reaction to Kristallnacht was timid and lethargic. The quota system, which had not been updated since the 1920s, allowed the admission of a mere twenty-seven thousand immigrants from Germany (both Jewish and non-Jewish) per year. Always paltry, the quota became even more so after the annexations of the Sudetenland and Austria brought four hundred thousand additional Jews into the Reich. After Kristallnacht, the State Department rejected the United Kingdom's offer to donate the unused capacity of its quota so the U.S. could admit sixty thousand more German Jews. Moreover, unlike the comparatively stingy Americans, the British welcomed ten thousand Jewish children and fifteen thousand women to work as nannies and housekeepers.[2]

In contrast to Roosevelt, many others in the administration were eager to do something to help. Secretary of Labor Frances Perkins called on the president to immediately admit the maximum combined quota for the next three years (82,000 in all). Roosevelt rejected this proposal although 1939 was the first and only year in his tenure that the U.S. admitted the full quota from Germany. On November 18th, Governor Lawrence Cramer of the U.S. Virgin Islands persuaded the legislative assembly to open the doors to refugees as "temporary visitors." Secretary of the Interior Ickes backed the measure but Roosevelt was against it for the same reason he had rejected the Dominican Republic's earlier offer. He feared that the admittees might sneak onto the mainland and thus worsen the "social and economic problem[s]" of the Virgin Islands [3]

The Kennedy Plan

The most ambitious proposed rescue scheme was the Kennedy Plan, named after the U.S. Ambassador to the United Kingdom, Joseph P. Kennedy. After making a fortune in the stock market and other investments, he became both a major donor to FDR in 1932 and an important Democratic party player. The president, operating on the theory of "Set a thief to catch a thief," had tapped Kennedy to be the first head of the Securities and Exchange Commission. Five years later, Roosevelt must have appreciated the ironic spectacle of a wealthy Catholic Irishman arriving at the Court of St. James's in March 1938.[4]

The true author of the Kennedy Plan was George Rublee, the energetic septuagenarian chair of the London-based Intergovernmental Committee on Refugees. He envisioned a haven for Jews in thinly populated areas in Africa, North America, and South America and hoped to defray the enormous costs, including ships and temporary camps, through financing by governments and Jewish organizations. When Rublee first proposed the scheme to Kennedy, the ambassador dismissed it as hopeless but changed his mind after Kristallnacht. Once he lent his name to the project, interest suddenly picked up. Publicity about the Kennedy Plan netted a sympathetic front-page story in the *New York Times* and an article in *Life* which declared that if "his plan for settling the German Jews, already widely known as the 'Kennedy Plan', succeeds, it will add new luster to a reputation that may well carry Joseph Patrick Kennedy into the White House."[5]

Roosevelt quickly threw cold water on that enthusiasm by denying any knowledge of the plan. In private, he vented at Kennedy's "grandstanding," and rebuked him by announcing that henceforth Myron Taylor was to be the official spokesman on refugee issues. There is no indication that the president considered the plan on its merits. Rublee sloughed off this disappointment and pushed forward all on his own to find a means to save Germany's Jews. After an uphill battle, he negotiated a specific deal with the Nazis in late February 1939 to allow four hundred thousand to emigrate. Although the German government still exacted confiscatory levies on the property of each refugee, it agreed to put a portion of this money into a trust fund and cover transportation costs to the border, under the supervision of a new corporation based in London. After hearing about the deal, Kennedy phoned Rublee and "in an entirely new tone, expressed great surprise. How could this have happened? Why hadn't they done something like this before if they were willing to do such things?" Ahead lay the daunting logistical and financial tasks of setting up the corporation in London and, most importantly, finding resettlement locations.[6]

A Diverse Coalition Rallies to Help European Jews

The Kennedy Plan was rather late in the game but it, or something like it, had potential wide appeal. While seven out of ten Americans opposed loosening the quota system, an even larger majority wanted to help persecuted Jews in some way. When in February

1939 Senator Robert Wagner (D-New York) and Rep. Edith Nourse Rogers (R-Massachusetts) proposed to admit twenty-thousand Jewish children from Germany, the list of endorsers included former president Hoover, Alfred Landon, and his running mate, Frank Knox. Grace Coolidge, the widow of the late president, along with her neighbor in Northampton, Massachusetts, pledged to personally take care of twenty-five of the children. Despite favorable mentions by Eleanor, any momentum for the bill withered away, another victim of presidential indifference.[7]

Some indication of the breadth of cross-ideological support for helping besieged Europe's Jews was a proposal by the iconoclastic civil libertarian journalist and anti-New Deal social critic H.L. Mencken of the *Baltimore Sun*. Although some later derided the "sage of Baltimore" for allegedly antisemitic views, he proved far more compassionate about Jewish suffering than Roosevelt. To Mencken, plans of the Kennedy type to disperse "the refugees between the infernos of British Guiana and the remote wilds of Tanganyika" were both unrealistic and needlessly costly. Instead, it was "much more honest and much more humane" to immediately admit all the German Jews, which he estimated at four hundred thousand, to the U.S. There was "no reason whatsoever for believing it would be impossible to absorb them, or even difficult."

Mencken pointed out that "Almost as many Jews as that came into the United States during every year from 1903 to 1914, and yet the republic somehow survived." He considered it unfair to expect American Jews to carry the funding burden because it would only make them targets of the "Ku Kluxers." He challenged the "so-called Christians . . . who are now so free with weasel words of comfort and flattery, and so curiously stingy with practical aid" to take financial responsibility.[8]

The challenges to rescue plans multiplied after Germany violated its pledge at Munich by marching into Czechoslovakia, thus bringing some four hundred thousand additional Jews into the Reich. Chamberlain rapidly abandoned appeasement and pledged to come to the defense of Poland in case of attack. This "Polish guarantee," sometimes described as a "blank check," proved a stupendous miscalculation because geographically distant Britain and France did not have the wherewithal to back it up with troops. According to Kenneth Davis, "the hurried, ill-considered unilateral guarantee" was "an assurance that Britain's hands were now tied to Poland, with the latter as prime mover." A tragic byproduct of increased tensions in Europe was the total unraveling of the rescue plan negotiated by the London-based Rublee a month earlier.[9]

"No Loud Screaming Against the School Authorities"

For many African Americans, the big news of March 1939 was much closer to home: a controversy involving acclaimed black contralto, Marian Anderson, and the Daughters of the American Revolution (DAR). Sol Hurok, Anderson's manager, had applied for her to perform at the prestigious Constitution Hall in Washington, D.C., but the DAR, which was the owner, turned it down as contrary to a "white artists only" policy. Concurrently, Hurok had also applied to the DC Board of Education for Anderson to use the auditorium of the all-white Central High School. The Board refused and cited a 1906 federal segregation law for DC schools.

Although local civil rights activists protested both decisions, they put priority on fighting the Board of Education's rejection. The protest movement to defend Anderson, NAACP counsel Charles Houston declared, "at present will confine itself to how far colored people can be prevented from using public school facilities."[10]

Perhaps the first mention of the Roosevelt name in connection with this controversy appeared in an editorial on February 25th in the *Washington Tribune*, an African American newspaper: "Many colored citizens of Washington consider you a sincere friend of the race. [We] would appreciate an expression from you on the D.A.R.'s exclusion of Marian Anderson from Constitution hall or the local school board's refusal for her use of Central High School auditorium or an expression on both." One day later, Eleanor resigned in protest from the DAR. She elaborated: the "question is, if you belong to an organization and disapprove of an action which is typical of a policy, shall you resign or is it better to work for a changed point of view within the organization?"

Eleanor's statement focused exclusively on the DAR and omitted any mention of the DC school board. African American folklorist and novelist Zora Neale Hurston later observed that the First Lady had "rushed into the fray and gave with a howl against narrow-minded racial discrimination that could be heard in Addis Ababa. And probably was. But it was all directed against the DAR. No loud screaming against the school authorities." At the suggestion of Anderson's manager and the NAACP, Secretary Ickes of the Department of Interior allowed an open-air Easter Sunday performance at the Lincoln Memorial and millions listened on the radio.[12]

Although this issue was often linked to her, Eleanor Roosevelt had no apparent role in the outdoor concert and, quite discreetly, did not even attend. While that performance had lasting symbolic importance, it barely dented the segregationist status quo in Washington, D.C. An undeniable consequence of the First Lady's selectivity, however, was to lift all blame from the Democrats for Anderson's mistreatment and shift it exclusively to the DAR. "As far as the high-school auditorium is concerned," Hurston declared, "to jump the people responsible for racial bias would be to accuse and expose the accusers themselves. The District of Columbia has no home rule; it is controlled by congressional committees, and Congress at the time was overwhelmingly Democratic. It was controlled by the very people who were screaming so loudly against the DAR. To my way of thinking, both places should have been denounced, or neither."[13]

Nevertheless, Eleanor's resignation from the DAR brought FDR almost incalculable political benefits. African Americans hailed the outdoor concert as a "grand epoch making event" and a "demonstration in Democracy of which as Americans we may be justly proud." A black man in Brooklyn was representative: "If we had more leaders of the type that . . . our beloved President and Mrs. Roosevelt are what a grand and glorious country this really would be [for] the minority groups." It was a political win-win issue for the administration in every sense. As Weiss puts it, the affair "was different from an issue such as antilynching legislation in that it in no way threatened the established system of race relations in the South; it involved no federal encroachment on state rights; and it entailed no congressional action, hence no need to risk votes that the administration needed for other measures."[14]

"The Saddest Ship Afloat"

Soon after Anderson was striking a blow for racial justice through her rendition of "My Country, 'Tis of Thee" on Easter Sunday, the German liner, the *S.S. St. Louis*, "the saddest ship afloat," began its journey from Hamburg carrying some 937 Jewish refugees. Once it docked in Havana, a gut-wrenching series of events ensued. Unbeknownst to the passengers, just one week earlier, the Cuban president had invalidated all recent landing permits.[15]

Although the press publicized the suffering of the passengers, the administration did not reveal any discernible sympathy. Secretary of State Hull turned down a request to grant six-months visas to the refugees because none of them were able to prove a "definite home where they were coming from and in a situation to return to it." In desperation the sympathetic German captain took the ship to Florida where it lingered for three days. The only answer from the White House to a petition from the refugees was the arrival of a Coast Guard cutter which was tasked with keeping the ship far enough from shore to keep the passengers from breaking for freedom by swimming or taking small boats. The *S.S. St. Louis* returned to Europe, where many of the passengers eventually perished in the Holocaust.[16]

In contrast to his coldness and indifference toward these refugees during this period, the president often complained vociferously in private that Britain was not doing enough to oppose German territorial expansionism. By the summer, he was urging Kennedy to "put more iron up Chamberlain's backside" in his effort to enforce the guarantee to Poland. Kennedy responded that this would accomplish nothing unless the British had some iron to fight with. Simultaneously, FDR pushed to revise the Neutrality Act by repealing the arms embargo. In reference to his congressional opponents, the president sarcastically told Morgenthau that "we ought to introduce a bill for statues of [non-interventionist senators] Austin, Vandenberg, Lodge and Taft . . . to be erected in Berlin and put the swastika on them." Concurrently, Roosevelt was moving aggressively against Japan. In July, he gave the required six-month notice to suspend the Treaty of Commerce and Navigation of 1911. This action dealt a major blow to relations between the two countries. Tokyo condemned the decision as "unthinkable."[17]

During the same period, Roosevelt orchestrated a Machiavellian plot to surmount the two-term tradition which had held sway since George Washington. When Postmaster General and political advisor, James Farley began to test the presidential waters for him self, FDR asked Cardinal George William Mundelein of Chicago to meet with his potential challenger. During the conversation with Farley, Mundelein cited the ill-fated candidacy of Al Smith as evidence that the odds were stacked against a Catholic president. He opined that FDR was both a "truly a great man" and "extremely generous" toward Farley.[18]

When Farley came to call at Hyde Park on July 23rd, the president's prevarication skills were in peak form. "We must save democracy," FDR emphasized. "It's the only way to save the country . . . Jim, you and I have got to be together in 1940 to work for the good of the country and the party, just as we have in the past." After this cryptic preamble, he bent over and whispered, "Jim, I am going to tell you something I have never told another living soul. Of course, I will not run for a third term." The president went over a list of other possible candidates but omitted the most likely frontrunners including Hull, Hopkins, and Farley himself. He stressed the shortcomings of each man as a candidate. The conservative and increasingly estranged Garner was "just impossible," for example, while the much more pro-New Deal Henry Wallace just didn't have "It."[19]

World War II Begins in Europe

Meanwhile, Hitler and Stalin were conspiring to carve up Poland and the Baltics. The result on August 23 was a Treaty of Non-Aggression between Germany and the Union of the Soviet Socialist Republics, under which both countries pledged not to go to war against each other if either fought another country. Later added to the deal was a secret protocol, the German-Soviet Treaty of Friendship, which established a German sphere of influence in western Poland and a Soviet one in the east, including two (later three) of the Baltic republics and Finland.

The Germans moved first, marching into Poland at dawn on September 1st. Fulfilling the terms of their guarantee, both Britain and France declared war within the next two days. Stalin cannily held back his troops which minimized any pressure for a simultaneous declaration against the Soviet Union during this critical period.[20]

Poland gamely resisted but the blitzkrieg was overwhelming. Chamberlain's guarantee was little more than a scrap of paper, although it had fostered the illusion among the hapless defenders that relief was on the way. "Having supposedly gone to war over Poland," writes historian Lynne Olson, "Britain and France did nothing to help that tortured country except send a few token patrols across the Maginot line and fly a few reconnaissance flights over German territory." On September 17th, once Germany had crushed most of the Polish resistance, Stalin's troops marched in from the east and seized the remainder of the country. Ten days later, the capital of Warsaw surrendered.[21]

In response to the crisis in Poland, the president began to push for the outright repeal of the Neutrality Act, saying that he regretted "that the Congress passed that Act. I regret equally that I signed that Act." He did not mention, however, his centrality in conceiving of the original law. Even so, he assured Americans that the U.S. had no intention of joining as a belligerent: "Let no man or woman thoughtlessly or falsely talk of America sending its armies to European fields." Again, many in Congress fiercely resisted the president's call to repeal the arms embargo and the Neutrality Act. Americans overwhelmingly favored the Allies but they also wanted to keep the United States out.

Congress rejected full repeal but allowed arms sales on a cash and carry basis. Britain benefited especially because of its comparatively massive naval and merchant marine capacity. The new law prohibited American ships from carrying goods into belligerent ports or American passengers on belligerent ships. Key fears driving these restrictions were memories of the inflammatory consequences of the sinking of the British passenger liner *Lusitania* in 1915 by a German U-Boat, bringing the death of 128 Americans.[22]

A long lull ensued in the fighting between the Allies and Germany. Journalist William Shirer called it a "queer sort of war" after witnessing French and Germans building fortifications. Although they were in sight of each other, not a shot was fired. U.S. Senator William Borah (R-Idaho) aptly coined the term, "the Phony War." The main exception to the phoniness was the Soviet invasion of Finland in November. Ironically, the Soviet Union might well have become a full belligerent alongside Germany, had Britain and France followed through on a scheme to seize the port of Narvik in neutral Norway. The intended purpose was to create a conduit for military aid, and possibly troops, for the Finnish resistance which had successfully frustrated Soviet hopes for a quick victory. During the same period, the British and French governments gave serious consideration to striking directly against the German war machine by bombing oil fields in the Soviet Caucasus. "In February 1940," writes historian Sean McMeekin, "loose talk of Allied plans to go to war with the Soviet Union was all over London and Paris, and spreading through the bazaars of the Middle East too." Any chance of this ended in March 1940 when Stalin cut his losses and signed an armistice with Finland to end the war."[23]

"Roosevelt Threw Back His Head and Laughed"

Meanwhile FDR was running as a de facto candidate even while keeping up the pretense of being above the fray. In January, he delegated Ickes to put together "a little group" which included Attorney General Robert Jackson and Benjamin Cohen, to handle the details, including delegate recruitment. "If ultimately he [FDR] decided to accept the nomination for a third term," concludes historian Richard Moe, "he didn't want to be seen either then or later as having anything to do with it. He wanted to leave absolutely no fingerprints." His subterfuge relied on keeping possible rivals off balance, confused, and uncertain.[24]

A conversation recounted by Farley (still a candidate) in January 1940 both displayed FDR's jaded sense of humor and his true priorities: "'Jim, I have the grandest joke for you. I had Garner, Barkley, and Rayburn in this morning for the conference on the anti-lynching bill. And you'll never guess what Jack [Garner] said. Very seriously he said that he had given considerable thought to the legislation and that he felt that the colored race in the border states and in the northern cities was such that he thought the legislation had to be passed'. . . . Roosevelt threw back his head and laughed till tears came to his eyes . . . 'Don't you love it? Jack has done a complete about face on it now that he's looking for votes'." This sampling of Rooseveltian humor reveals much about the president's attitudes toward African American civil rights. Rather than seeing these second thoughts from his conservative Texan vice president as an opening to renew a long delayed anti-lynching bill, Roosevelt saw them as objects of mirth.[25]

Germany's occupation of Norway and Denmark (April 1940) and the Netherlands (May 1940) did nothing to shake FDR's indifference toward Europe's imperiled Jews. When Senator William H. King (D-Utah) and Rep. Franck Havenner (D-California) proposed a bill to open Alaska to Jewish refugees, Roosevelt expressed no opinion in public despite an impressive list of backers including the secretaries of labor and interior, actors Luise Rainer and Paul Muni, the Federal Council of Churches, and the American Friends Service Committee. Roosevelt privately told Ickes that it was impossible to admit more than ten thousand settlers to Alaska per year. He urged that if the bill were approved, "not more than ten percent would be Jews, so we would be able to avoid the undoubted criticism that we would be subjected to if they were an undue proportion of Jews." The King-Havenner bill died in committee soon after hearings in May. Had it gone into effect, the law might have saved Anne Frank, then living in Nazi occupied Holland. At the time, her father, Otto Frank was desperately writing U.S. officials for permission of the family to immigrate.[26]

The Hunt for a Fifth Column

Soon after Winston Churchill became Prime Minister in May, the new British Security Coordination (BSC), ensconced in Rockefeller Center, initiated a vast covert operation to spread pro-Allied propaganda and manipulate American politics by discrediting non-interventionists. The head of this effort was Canadian businessman and World War I hero the diminutive William "Little Bill" Stephenson, later used as a model by Ian Fleming for James Bond. FDR gave his secretive, but full, cooperation. Stephenson's American partner was William "Big Bill" Donovan, a member of FDR's law school class at Columbia, a multimillion-dollar Wall Street lawyer, and an assistant attorney general under President Hoover. *Washington Post* columnist David Ignatius calls the BSC operation "a virtual textbook in the art of manipulation" while British historian Nicholas Cull characterizes it as "one of the most diverse, extensive . . . undercover campaigns ever directed by one sovereign state at another."[27]

The BSC, which had nearly one thousand employees in New York City alone, benefited from an overwhelmingly compliant media. Stephenson repeatedly passed on disinformation and other negative stories about non-interventionists, usually via cutouts, to the press. Those who "rendered services of particular value" in this regard included columnists Dorothy Thompson, Walter Lippmann, and Drew Pearson, as well as publishers Arthur Sulzberger of the *New York Times*, Ralph Ingersoll of *PM*, and Helen Reid of the *New York Herald Tribune*. As Ignatius summarizes, "the British spymasters played this media network like a mighty Wurlitzer" (organ). Robert Sherwood, a close aide to FDR, observed that "If the isolationists had known the full extent of the secret alliance with a foreign power, their demands for impeachment of the President would have been a great deal louder."[28]

In tandem, FDR stepped up his reliance on surveillance and behind-the-scenes harassment. In May, he authorized his attorney general "to secure information by listening devices direct[ed] to the conversation or other communications of persons suspected of subversive activities against the Government of the United States." The same month, the president passed on to FBI Director J. Edgar Hoover hundreds of telegrams, many praising the famous aviator Charles Lindbergh, an emerging spokesman among the antiwar forces. FDR asked for a thorough scrutiny including of "the names and addresses." Eager to please, Hoover opened FBI files on each one and kept the president appraised. Without naming anyone directly, Roosevelt's Fireside Chat on May 26th declaimed against a "Trojan Horse. The Fifth Column that betrays a nation unprepared for treachery." These "dividing forces" must not be able to spread their "undiluted poison" in the "New World as they have in the Old." But, fortunately for the protection of American civil liberties, administration insiders provided a counterweight to some of the president's most repressive inclinations. Attorney General Jackson disdained the theory that "anyone you don't like is a member of the Fifth Column," while Solicitor General Francis Biddle asked "Why shouldn't Lindbergh say 'England is defeated, we must keep out,' if he wants to? Isn't that part of our theory of freedom of speech? Isn't that the thing that we must fight back with other ideas?"[29]

German Espionage Failures

In emphasizing the danger of a "Trojan Horse" or "Fifth Column," Roosevelt consistently, and quite intentionally, exaggerated the potency of German espionage. Contrary to the impression he left, pro-Nazi organizations in the U.S. never made important inroads. Illustrative of the Bund's inability to get traction was the fallout from a much-publicized rally at Madison Square in February 1939, two days before George Washington's birthday. Historian Lynne Olson describes it as a "public relations disaster" for Berlin because it "outraged Americans and made them think that the Bund was considerably better organized and more dangerous to America's security than it actually was." The number of Bund activists in the United States probably never exceeded eight thousand, along with about twenty thousand sympathizers. The harsh public reaction to the rally prompted the German government to cut ties with that organization, which soon receded to fewer than two thousand members, as well as largely abandon attempts to influence more mainstream non-interventionists.[30]

Berlin's professional U.S. spy network, if it can be called such, was miniscule by comparison. According to Attorney General Robert Jackson, "the Nazis never had an extensively organized espionage or sabotage ring in this country." Moreover, Hitler had flatly ordered Admiral Wilhelm Canaris, the chief of the Abwehr (German military intelligence), not to conduct sabotage of the United States. All organized espionage activities pretty much disappeared on a single day. On July 30th, the FBI put thirty-three Nazi agents behind bars, including the man who had stolen the plans for the Norden bombsight.[31]

"A Badly Managed Puppet Show"

As the presidential season approached, FDR continued to throttle potential Democratic rivals. After Farley told Garner over lunch that the president was going to run, the vice president responded: "It begins to look that way. Hell, he's fixed it so nobody else can run now." Farley related that Al Smith had once warned him never to take Roosevelt at his word. "I laughed at him [Smith]," Farley told Garner. 'Now, he's laughing at me."[32]

Events conspired against the GOP prior to its convention in June. In the immediate run up, Allied troops evacuated France from the harbor of Dunkirk which was followed by Churchill's rousing "We shall fight on the beaches" speech. Critically important to powering the Nazi war machine throughout this period were massive imports of Soviet oil and raw materials, such as cotton and nickel (courtesy of the Treaty of Non-Aggression of 1939). After Germany occupied Paris on June 15th, Stalin immediately responded by seizing and annexing Estonia, Latvia, and Lithuania, eventually also occupying a slice of eastern Romania. Just before the convention assembled on June 24th, France signed a humiliating surrender, bringing occupation and a collaborationist government under Marshal Henri Petain based in the city of Vichy. In a public relations coup, Roosevelt struck a chord of "national unity." He appointed two well-known pro-interventionist Republicans to his cabinet: publisher Frank Knox as secretary of the Navy, and Henry Stimson, Hoover's secretary of state, as secretary of war.[33]

The GOP convention chose an outsider and non-politician, the charismatic and politically moderate Wendell Willkie, a self-made utility executive who promptly ignored his party's mostly antiwar platform. Sensing a chance to finally defeat Roosevelt, however, the non-interventionists in the party, including Willkie's main GOP rival Robert A. Taft (R-Ohio), the son of President William Howard Taft, closed ranks around their new standard-bearer. Like Landon four years before, Willkie pledged fealty to most of the New Deal but promised to administer it more efficiently. At a cabinet meeting on June 28th, Roosevelt, either disingenuously or naively, characterized his entirely mainstream opponent as representing "a new concept in American politics—the concept of the 'corporate state' on the order of Fascist Italy."[34]

Roosevelt had still not announced as a candidate, even while he was maneuvering to derail potential challengers. Ever playing the double game, he told Farley on July 7th (only a week before the Democrats met): "Jim I don't want to run—and I'm going to tell the convention so." After a brief pause, however, he asked: "Jim, what would you do if you were in my place?" Farley, who had become familiar with Roosevelt's habit of disassembling, had a ready response: "I would do exactly what General Sherman did many years ago—issue a statement saying I would refuse to run if nominated and would not serve if elected." Farley had finally cornered him. "Jim," FDR replied, "if nominated and elected I could not in these times refuse to take the inaugural oath even if I knew I would be dead within thirty days." Although it seemed that Roosevelt wanted the nomination by acclamation, Farley was not going to give him that pleasure by withdrawing.[35]

Even before the delegates assembled, the columnists Joseph Alsop and Robert Kintner compared the convention to "a badly managed puppet show." The proceedings opened in confusion, doubt, and frustration. It was natural for the delegates to wonder what Roosevelt expected of them. In some panic, Ickes sent a telegram to the president on the second day that "the convention is bleeding to death" and that FDR's "reputation and prestige may bleed to death with it." But Roosevelt still wanted to keep up the play acting. He delegated Senate Majority Leader Alben Barkley (D-Kentucky) to read a statement which said that he did not have "any desire or purpose to continue in the office of President, to be a candidate for that office, or to be nominated by the Convention for that office. He wishes in all earnestness and sincerity to make it clear that all the delegates to this Convention are free to vote for any candidate."[36]

The first reaction of the delegates to this announcement was silent bewilderment, but this soon gave way to guidance from an invisible and apparently disembodied force. A "thundering" voice bellowed from the loudspeakers: "'We want Roosevelt! Chicago wants Roosevelt!' 'The party wants Roosevelt!' 'New York wants Roosevelt!' 'The world wants Roosevelt!'" The disembodied voice came from a microphone in the basement and was that of Thomas D. Garry, Chicago's superintendent of sewers. According to Farley, Mayor Edward J. Kelly, a key big city political ally of Roosevelt, had recruited Garry, later dubbed "the voice from the sewers."[37]

After the delegates responded by giving the president an overwhelming victory, the selection of a vice-presidential candidate was a comparative afterthought. FDR quickly settled on Secretary of Agriculture Henry A. Wallace, though he had belittled him as presidential timber in his meeting with Farley in 1939. Rexford Tugwell explained that "it grew on him that Henry Wallace could be counted on to the limit." But Wallace rubbed many the wrong way for his perceived radicalism, ascetic habits (he never drank or played poker with influential Democratic politicos in the Capital), and propensity for eastern mysticism. The delegates almost rebelled at the prospect but Roosevelt, in a rare show of loyalty, snapped: "Well damn it to hell they will go for Wallace or I won't run." Wallace prevailed but the ugly mood of those present so moved Wallace's wife to tears that she asked Eleanor Roosevelt, "Why are they booing my Henry?"[38]

Roosevelt's acceptance speech put the finishing touch on the charade of the unwilling public servant compelled by the popular will to serve the greater good. He began innocently: "Lying awake, as I have, on many nights, I have asked myself whether I have the right, as Commander-in-Chief of the Army and Navy, to call on men and women to serve their country or to train themselves to serve and, at the same time, decline to serve my country in my own personal capacity, if I am called upon to do so by the people of my country." While "Only the people themselves can draft a President," he concluded. "If such a draft should be made upon me, I say to you, in the utmost simplicity, I will, with God's help, continue to serve with the best of my ability and with the fullness of my strength."[39]

In the months after the convention, the New Deal electoral apparatus mustered the requisite federal resources with the greatest efficiency. The WPA, after laying off workers and cutting spending through much of 1940, ramped up the numbers dramatically in September. According to the Republicans, the AAA "was rushing out payments [in October] ordinarily made in November and December." The biggest single political bonus for the president, according to the historians Burton W. and Anita Folsom, was a naval base in Corpus Christi "that gave Brown & Root [a major construction company with close ties to the emerging military-industrial complex] the profits to give Lyndon Johnson the campaign money that he spent to capture House seats for Democrats across the country."[40]

Willkie's support for most of FDR's foreign policy both put him at a "me too" disadvantage and gave the president valuable political cover. The Republican candidate, for example, endorsed FDR's plan to send fifty old destroyers to Great Britain in exchange for a string of naval bases stretching from the Canadian coast to South America. Less than two weeks later, Willkie probably tipped the balance for the first peacetime national conscription in American history, the Selective Service Act, a measure widely condemned in the GOP. Senator Hiram Johnson (R-California) complained that the Republican nominee "broke the back" of the anti-draft forces in Congress.[41]

In his campaign rhetoric, Willkie also steered away from pointing out Roosevelt's inconsistent and selective use of his powers under the Neutrality Act. Although Stalin had ordered attacks on the same number of countries (seven) as had Hitler since August 1939, the president had refused to designate the Soviet Union as a belligerent under the terms of the Act. Privately Roosevelt's justification for this double standard was to keep the Soviets from going over completely to the German side but it made it difficult to argue that they had a higher moral ground. Just about the only protests the president mustered toward Soviet aggression in 1940 were symbolic, but empty, gestures of continuing to recognize the Baltic republics and maintaining their embassies in the United States.[42]

"A Stab in the Back of Democracy"

Prominent African Americans complained vociferously about federal discrimination in war mobilization. They had much to complain about. The armed forces were rigidly segregated and unequal. African Americans were completely excluded from the Marine Corps and the Army Air Corps and were often limited to menial tasks, such as latrine units. The Navy confined them to the messman's branch, a limitation officially reaffirmed by Secretary of the Navy Knox just after the passage of Selective Service who stipulated that all the officers must continue to be white.[43]

As Willkie pushed an increasingly pro-civil rights agenda, however Roosevelt took steps to shore up black support. In September, he, along with secretaries Knox and Stimson, met at the White House with A. Philip Randolph, the head of the Brotherhood of Sleeping Car Porters, Walter White of the NAACP, and T. Arnold Hill of the National Urban League. They pressed the government to end military segregation. Roosevelt soothingly parried that the U.S. was "not confining the Negro into the noncombat services" as it had in World War I. "We're putting 'em right *in*, proportionately, into the combat services." After the meeting, however, the administration released a statement that it was against any attempt to "intermingle colored and white enlisted personnel." To add insult to injury, the wording indicated that African Americans at the meeting shared that view. The normally compliant White accused Roosevelt of a "stab in the back of democracy." He vowed never to meet again with FDR unless the president retracted the statement but, as usual, failed to follow through on this promise.[44]

The same month brought a new threat to Roosevelt's foreign policy, the formation of the America First Committee (AFC). Initially the group drew primary strength from Ivy League universities, including such exemplars of the campus elite as Kingman

Brewster, the chairman of the *Yale Daily News* and Spencer Klaw, president of the *Harvard Crimson*. Other student members were such future notables as R. Sargent Shriver, who became head of the Peace Corps, Potter Stewart who was destined for the Supreme Court and future presidents John F. Kennedy and Gerald Ford. Gore Vidal, then fifteen, established a student chapter at Phillips Exeter. The AFC mobilized against the Selective Service bill which it argued was a threat to democracy. Soon the AFC expanded beyond campus to include R. Douglas Stuart, a founder of Quaker Oats, General Robert Wood of Sears-Roebuck, Theodore Roosevelt Jr., and his sister Alice Roosevelt Longworth. The membership encompassed both anti-New Dealers and New Dealers as well as socialists and pacifists, such as Norman Thomas and Oswald Garrison Villard. It tried to avoid any extremist taint by excluding both Communists and fascists.[45]

U.S. relations with Tokyo, already reeling from the repudiation of the Treaty of Commerce and Navigation in July, suffered another blow when Japan joined the Tripartite Pact along with Germany and Italy in September. What became known as the Axis Powers was a reformulation of the existing Pact of Steel between Germany and Italy. The members pledged to defend each other if attacked and recognized realms of domination including Japan's Greater East Asia Co-Prosperity Sphere. The Soviet Union was willing to join but Stalin imposed a long list of conditions which Hitler was unwilling to accept, such as Soviet hegemony over Bulgaria and withdrawal of German troops from Finland.[46]

Willkie Mounts a Political Offensive

While the first polls after the Democratic convention included a Willkie surge, this soon dissipated and, by October 6th, the Gallup poll showed Roosevelt leading in forty-two states. A fatal weakness for Willkie was that non-interventionist voters saw little difference between the two candidates. By early October, however, the rhetoric of the Republican standard bearer was almost like that of an America Firster. "If [Roosevelt's] promise to keep our boys out of foreign wars is no better than his promise to balance the budget," Willkie charged, "they're already almost on the transports." If FDR was re-elected, he predicted a war by April 1941 and, more provocatively, eventual dictatorship.

The Democrats counterattacked by implying that Willkie had Fifth Column inclinations. While Henry Wallace conceded that every Republican was "not an appeaser and not a friend of Hitler," he added that "you can be sure that every Nazi, every Hitlerite, and every appeaser is a Republican." Willkie had practical reasons for his more antiwar rhetorical shift. Evidence was mounting that Germany was losing the Battle of Britain and that a cross-channel invasion was no longer imminent. The Royal Air Force had become so effective, destroying three planes to each one it lost, that the Luftwaffe had to shift to nighttime bombing. Polls in late October put Willkie "within easy striking distance of victory."[47]

Policing Black Republicans in Memphis

In the month before the election, the president also faced discontent from his African American base. A prominent example was black entrepreneur, J.B. Martin the chair of Shelby County Republican party. Martin's South Memphis Drug Store was one of the largest of its kind owned by African Americans. He had later acquired the Memphis Red Sox and was the president of the Negro American [Baseball] League. In most of the solidly Democratic South, a local Republican chair for an African American was an empty honor, but not so in Memphis. In that city, black votes still mattered because of a long-term arrangement between Democratic Boss E.H. Crump, a loyal big-city ally of FDR, and the Shelby County GOP. Crump allowed and selectively encouraged some African American voting, contingent on them backing his political machine in crucial primaries.[48]

J.B. Martin (far left), in front of his South Memphis Drug Store.

But Martin, who dreamed of a credible and competitive opposition party, had other ideas. On October 21st, he staged a multiracial rally of over one thousand for Willkie. Even if the GOP presidential standard bearer lost statewide (the state had gone Republican as recently as 1928), a national victory might put a powerful protector in the White House. Crump, however, was not about to let an upstart black Republican imperil his alliance with the president. He had loyally supported FDR since 1932 and, in return, had netted Memphis millions in federal dollars. Crump demanded that Martin resign and shutter GOP headquarters or he would "police" his drugstore.

When Martin remained defiant, Crump's officers began searching patrons, including kindergarteners, running "their hands over little dresses and poked into the pockets of knickers." An isolated Martin lamented that "local influential persons are absolutely afraid to help me in my case" and that Crump was trying to put "me in the workhouse and I couldn't stand that." Roscoe Conkling Simmons, a black Republican leader and a nephew of Booker T. Washington, compared Crump to Hitler. In Memphis, he asserted, it was almost as easy to convict a black person with a trumped-up crime as "getting up 'charges' against Jews in Germany." He quipped, "Maybe Mr. Roosevelt will give less attention to Germany and more, at least briefly, to Memphis.."[49]

As Crump was contending with J.B. Martin, the national GOP was firing blasts against the president's civil rights record. On October 19th, the party ran a front-page ad in the *Baltimore-Afro American* pointing out that Roosevelt, who had just announced the promotion of one hundred white colonels to brigadier general, had skipped Colonel Benjamin O. Davis Sr., despite a distinguished record which dated back to the Philippine War. "What chance have colored draftees," the ad declared, "WHITE OFFICERS ONLY!" But Roosevelt, as in the past, was able to pull a rabbit out of the hat. One week after the Republican ad, he reversed course and promoted Davis to brigadier general. While this was an important "first," it was also true that the sixty-year-old Davis was nearing retirement. While the black press gave fulsome praise for the promotion, Secretary of War Stimson complained in his diary that "the Negroes are taking advantage of this period just before [the] election to try to get everything they can in the way of recognition from the Army."[50]

Roosevelt finished the election campaign with a devastating pronouncement. Speaking in Boston on October 30th, he declared matter-of-factly: "And while I am talking to you mothers and fathers, I give you one more assurance. I have said this before, but I shall say it again and again and again: Your boys are not going to be sent into any foreign wars." After hearing Roosevelt's vow over the radio, Willkie was livid: "That hypocritical son of a bitch! This is going to beat me." It may have made the difference. The president won comfortably but it was the closest presidential contest since 1916.[51]

Careening Toward War: Lend-Lease

In December 1940, FDR and Churchill were jointly working, mostly in secret, to deepen U.S. involvement. As part of this effort, FDR formulated the Lend-Lease scheme, a brilliant strategy to promote direct aid to Britain without calling it direct aid. He made the analogy to a good citizen lending a garden hose to a neighbor to put out a fire. He also indicated, though didn't exactly promise, that the "hose" would someday be returned or replaced: "'There were 150 feet of it,' the neighbor might say when the job was done. 'All right, I will replace it.' Now, if I get a nice garden hose back, I am in pretty good shape."

The specifics of how and when this would happen were, intentionally, never clear. As critics pointed out, it was impossible to "lend" an artillery shell or a torpedo. Senator Taft was one of many to point to the flaws in the analogy: "Lending arms is like lending chewing gum. You don't want it back." Senator Wheeler had his own analogy. He remarked that Lend-Lease was "the New Deal's triple A foreign policy, it will plow under every fourth American boy." FDR, who generally kept his cool during hot political debates, castigated the statement from a former political comrade as the "most untruthful, the most dastardly, unpatriotic thing that has ever been said." No one was more enthused about FDR's fight for Lend-Lease than Churchill who promised his son that "I shall drag the United States in."[52]

One of the most famous speeches of Roosevelt's career coincided with the Lend-Lease debate. When considered against the president's poor record in defending the First Amendment, the wording was laced with irony. In his annual message to Congress in January 1941, Roosevelt stated that all individuals in the world deserved "four essential human freedoms. The first two of the four, "freedom of speech and expression, . . . freedom of every person to worship God in his own way" were completely in line with familiar American traditions. The third freedom, "freedom from want" represented a major break from that tradition, and begged the question of who would fund the financial costs of guaranteeing this freedom, and how. He ended with a rhetorical, but ultimately amorphous, flourish with "freedom from fear—which, translated into world terms, means economic understandings which will secure to every nation a healthy peacetime life for its inhabitants—everywhere in the world."[53]

The politically exiled J.B. Martin, then living in Chicago, must have had mixed feelings if he listened to the president's speech. The Crump machine, after "policing" his drug store, had driven him out of Memphis. In March, the head of the Civil Rights Section of the Department of Justice, after taking Martin's deposition, had pondered in his presence the timing of grand jury testimony into the "open, notorious, public and continuing search of all patrons of a business establishment." Unfortunately for Martin, the Department of Justice, presumably on orders from federal higher-ups, decided not to take action on his behalf. A consequence was to empower the Crump organization with an ever greater sense of invincibility.[54]

Meanwhile, the president's strategy for pushing through direct aid to Britain in the guise of Lend-Lease, had paid off. The bill passed overwhelmingly in both the House (in February) and the Senate. The Senate majority (62: 32) was nearly filibuster proof. No single piece of legislation did more to speed the march toward U.S. belligerency. "What I think it means," wrote Assistant Secretary of State Adolf Berle, "is a steady drift into a deep gray stage in which the precise difference between war and peace is impossible to discern."[55]

During the Lend-Lease debates, Roosevelt treated events in the Pacific as comparative distractions. When naval commanders in Hawaii asked for more aircraft under a new law to conduct reconnaissance, arguing that Pearl Harbor was vulnerable to attack, he sent the planes instead to Great Britain. The U.S. was underestimating Japan, in part, because its success in breaking that country's supposedly impregnable diplomatic code in September 1940 had fostered a false sense of security. In honor of the almost magician-like feat of deciphering that code, these communications came to be known as the "MAGIC intercepts." As historian Joseph E. Persico put it, "the Tokyo foreign office might as well have placed FDR on its distribution list, since he could read what Japanese diplomats were telling each other almost as soon as they could."[56]

The Search for an Incident

During the spring and summer, U.S. naval commanders, with Roosevelt's encouragement, were becoming ever more reckless in aiding the British fight in the North Atlantic. In April 1941, Stimson recorded in his diary that FDR had decided that it was "too dangerous" to ask Congress for authorization to convoy British ships to home from U.S. ports. Polls showed that about half of Americans opposed convoys, especially if the German subs sank U.S. ships.

Multiple sources attest that FDR was seeking nearly any kind of "incident" to justify direct involvement on the British side. On May 23, Stimson wrote that the "President shows evidence of waiting for the accidental shot of some irresponsible captain on either side to an occasion of his going to war." During the same month, Roosevelt told Morgenthau that he was "waiting to be pushed into this situation."[57]

Hitler, who already had his hands full, did not want to also fight the U.S. Spurning the demands of the German High Command which depicted Lend-Lease as a "declaration of war on Germany," he issued a complete ban of any aggressive action toward American ships. "Under no circumstances," Admiral Erich Raeder, the head of the German Navy High Command wrote in his diary on May 22nd, "does he [Hitler] wish to cause incidents which would result in U.S. entry into the war." The Fuehrer also rejected proposals to occupy Iceland and the Azores for similar reasons.[58]

To nudge public opinion toward wider involvement, Roosevelt stressed the specter of a Nazis plan for "world domination," including a direct threat to Americans. Unless stopped now, he declared in a May 27th radio address, "the Western Hemisphere will be within range of the Nazi weapons of destruction" and "Germany would literally parcel out the world—hoisting the swastika itself over vast territories and populations, and setting up puppet governments." FDR, of course, was playing on well-documented popular fears about a possible foreign invasion. In early June, polls showed that two thirds of Americans believed that if Hitler defeated Britain, his next targets would be Latin America and the United States.59

Despite FDR's reliance on sensationalism, presidential insiders did not take seriously scenarios of Nazi invasions of the Americas. Berle dismissed the possibility out of hand after the British sank the German battleship, *Bismarck* in late May. "The fact that the Bismarck was sunk [substantially] by air power," he wrote in his diary,

> seems to make it plain that if there is anything like an effective air force, a naval invasion of the Western Hemisphere is out of the question. Even if Germany conquered Europe, and if they outbuilt us navally and with merchant marine, it would still be a question whether these ships could live long enough to reach the United States.

The Magazine of Wall Street pointedly asked: "If Hitler can't cross the English Channel, how can he cross the Atlantic Ocean?" Historian Joseph E. Persico boils it down: "Hitler had not the slightest intention of invading the Western Hemisphere."[60]

Germany's surprise invasion of the Soviet Union in early June 1941 made it more difficult to argue that Britain was in imminent peril. Stimson concluded that the widening of the war had rendered nearly impossible a German invasion of the British Isles as well as any occupation of Iceland. While many interventionists wanted to bolster the Soviets as a common foe of Germany, others viewed the new conflict as a kind of "plague on both their houses." Rep. Hamilton Fish spoke for many describing it as "preposterous to think of America being aligned with Joe Stalin as our pal and comrade with his hands dripping with blood of murdered priests and nuns and the same dagger in his hand which he plunged into the backs of Poland, Latvia, Estonia, Lithuania and our friend the little honest Republic of Finland."[61]

By the end of June, however, Roosevelt, who had done almost nothing to counter Stalin's aggression in 1939 and 1940, was going all-out to help the besieged Soviet forces. He approved Stalin's request (which was the first of many) for 1.8 billion dollars in military supplies under Lend Lease. On a special mission to Moscow in late July, Harry Hopkins, acting as Roosevelt's special emissary, gave the Soviet dictator a virtual blank check. He reassured Stalin that FDR was "confident in Soviet victory and is prepared to do whatever is required to get the necessary aid to the Soviet Union."[62]

Most Americans did not share Roosevelt's enthusiasm for aiding the Soviets. Gallup polls showed majorities, including in FDR's home state of New York, opposing the extension of Lend Lease to the USSR. The critics included both non-interventionists in Congress (who had just come one vote shy in the U.S. House of defeating an extension of the draft) and American Catholics, long a mainstay of the New Deal coalition. Working with the Soviet government, Roosevelt launched a well coordinated public relations campaign. He told the Soviet ambassador that it was essential for Moscow to "get some information back to this country regarding the freedom of religion . . . it might have a very fine educational effect before the next lend-lease bill comes up in Congress."

The president also tasked prominent Catholics in his administration to use their influence to soften American attitudes. More stunningly, he emphasized at a press conference in September that Article 124 of the Soviet Constitution protected "Freedom of conscience" which, according to FDR, meant "Freedom of religion. Freedom equally to use propaganda against religion which is essentially what is the rule in this country, only we don't put it quite the same way."[63]

Mobilizing the Dollar-a-Year Men

The first stage of domestic mobilization exposed the tensions between FDR's New Deal inclinations, on the one hand, and practical and political considerations on the other. He began by creating the Office of Production Management (OPM) in January, the Office of Civil Defense (OCD) in April and the Office of Price Administration and Civilian Supply (OPACS) in August. At first these agencies functioned primarily as bully pulpits and there was little coordination between them. The head of the OPM was William Knudsen, the president of General Motors, who, like about a thousand other such businessmen, served under a government salary of one dollar per year, and was assisted by labor leader Sidney Hillman, a New Deal partisan.[64]

At the helm of the OCD was New York's pugnacious and quirkily charismatic Mayor Fiorello LaGuardia, who settled into an uneasy partnership with his deputy director, Eleanor Roosevelt. LaGuardia, David Brinkley remembers, often turned up "flying around town in OCD cars with sirens screaming and being photographed in funny hats." In contrast to LaGuardia's more traditional stress on recruiting volunteer air raid wardens and fire brigades, Eleanor envisioned the OCD as a "social defense organization." OPACS's director was the acerbic New Dealer, Leon Henderson. His repeated exhortations for sacrifice often backfired. Instead of heeding his urgings to "cheerfully forgo the luxury of new automobiles," for example, Americans rushed to car showrooms.[65]

"Somebody Might Be Killed"

A. Philip Randolph was especially vocal among black leaders in complaining that wartime mobilization was leaving African Americans behind. The administration, despite promises to the contrary, had done nothing to counter discrimination and Jim

Crow since his meeting with the president in 1940. Running out of patience, Randolph began organizing a grass-roots movement to demand equal treatment in wartime mobilization by staging a March on Washington.

These efforts so alarmed FDR that he asked his wife to serve as a troubleshooter. She wrote to Randolph urging cancellation of the march because, in her words, it might lead to a tragic "incident" which would unravel all civil rights gains. Eleanor felt "very strongly that your group is making a grave mistake . . . I am afraid it will set back the progress which is being made, in the Army at least, toward better opportunities and less segregation."[66]

But Randolph pressed ahead. In some alarm, FDR and Eleanor arranged for the labor leader to come to the White House. During the meeting, Randolph, still smarting from the presidential duplicity of 1940, reaffirmed his demand for a strong executive order outlawing discrimination in war industries. Roosevelt's first response was to brush it off. He said if he did this that "there'll be no end to other groups coming in here and asking me to issue executive orders." When told that one hundred thousand might show up, the president's affability fell away. "Somebody might be killed," he exclaimed, adding that he had no intention of negotiating with a gun to his head. He softened this, however, with a hint of undetermined possible future action if Randolph played ball. "Call it off,' he told the labor leader, "and we'll talk again."[67]

But Roosevelt was coming to realize that he had to bend, or at least make an appearance of bending. Randolph extracted a promise from him that the Department of Justice would draft an executive order for his consideration. After rejecting several versions, Randolph, almost at the last minute, cancelled the march. Executive Order 8802 proved half-hearted, despite improvement from earlier drafts. Among African Americans, the criticism of Zora Neale Hurston was especially harsh: "Poor Randolph was tricked and trapped by that committee that FDR sent into a backroom of the White House to come back with some device that would save the face of the Administration and that was all that happened." Although promising to counter discrimination in war industries, it said nothing about discrimination, including segregation, in the armed forces. The enforcement was also weak because the predominantly white officials in the FEPC did not want to rock the boat as the U.S. careened toward war. According to a federal study in the fall of 1941, more than half of all defense jobs still barred black workers and, even when not officially excluded, rejections were alarmingly high.[68]

Evidence Mounts Revealing Nazi Atrocities

The first evidence of Nazi mass genocide against Jews dates from this period. In October, reports from the Jewish Telegraphic Agency, encapsulated later that month in an article in the *New York Times,* described Nazi machine gun massacres of thousands of Polish Jews, some of them while praying in synagogues. There were additional reports of widespread killings in Odessa and Kiev. Despite convincing proof of a horrific turn in the persecution, the administration's stance toward refugees showed no sign of shifting. While FDR and his advisors certainly viewed the Nazis as international gangsters, the plight of the Jews was never a priority.[69]

In the Far East, the main accomplishment of FDR's economic sanctions was to undermine the more moderate factions in the Japanese government. After Tokyo strong-armed Vichy into allowing more bases in Indochina in July, the administration retaliated by freezing assets. The more truculent Ickes complained that the president "was still unwilling to draw the noose tight. He thought that it might be better to slip the noose around Japan's neck and give it a jerk now and then." Roosevelt followed up in early August with an oil embargo which he had intended to be partial but became total because of confusion by both Japan and U.S. bureaucrats.[70]

By this time, Roosevelt, his gaze fixed on the North Atlantic, redoubled the search for a pretext. When he met with Churchill at the Atlantic Conference in Newfoundland, he bemoaned that any attempt to formally declare war on Germany would drag on for months. As an alternative, he told the prime minister that he planned to "wage war, but not declare it, and that he would become more and more provocative . . . Everything was to be done to force an 'incident'." Seeking to provoke an altercation, FDR fully committed the U.S. Navy to escort British ships all the way to Iceland.[71]

Missed Opportunities for Peace with Japan

A corollary to Roosevelt's "Europe first" strategy was to stall off Japan as long as possible. "The President's idea," Churchill observed "is to negotiate about these unacceptable conditions and thus procure a moratorium of say thirty days, during which we may improve our position in the Singapore area and the Japanese would have to stand still."

This preoccupation with stalling came at the cost of any seriousness about finding a middle ground. An example was the administration's deleterious response to a direct proposal in August from Japanese Premier Fumimaro Konoe for a summit meeting with Roosevelt in the mid-Pacific. The proposal partly reflected the emperor's worries about the drift toward war. Some indication of Konoe's seriousness was his intention to bring several admirals and generals to "share responsibility" for the result. Konoe also agreed to negotiate a withdrawal from Indochina and pledged to refrain from further attacks outside the area.[72]

Rather than leap at the chance for a summit, a dramatic ploy that had the support of U.S. Ambassador in Tokyo Joseph Grew, FDR, after some prevarication, responded on September 3 with disabling and unrealistic conditions, including a demand for immediate withdrawal from China and reducing trade barriers. The U.S. position served to undermine Konoe and embolden the hawks in his country's army who warned that oil supplies during the winter monsoons might no longer be sufficient. James MacGregor Burns comments that Japanese leaders in these and other negotiations found Roosevelt to be

> the most baffling of Western leaders. He appeared to shift overnight from conciliation to threats to high-blown preaching to invitations to parley. But item by item—so gradually as to rob Tokyo of a dramatic issue—he was restricting the export of war materials to Japan.

Navy Chief of Staff Prince Hiroyasu Fushimi, a cousin of the emperor, summed up the emerging consensus in his government that "In the end, we will need to get oil from the Netherlands East Indies."[73]

The administration was also laggard in taking advantage of a stunning sign of flexibility on the China withdrawal issue. It was first put forward at a meeting on October 13th between Assistant Secretary Welles and Kaname Wakasugi, a minister at the Japanese embassy who had recently returned from consultations with the prime minister and the emperor's brother. After repeating the proposal for a Konoe-Roosevelt summit, which the U.S. had already rebuffed, Wakasugi said that "the Japanese Government was willing to evacuate all of its troops from China." He also asked if FDR was willing to mediate between China and Japan. According to Undersecretary Welles, the meeting ended with Wakasugi's warning that the agreement must "be reached before it was too late [and that] the control of the Army and of the Navy under present conditions was such as to make it sure that the Government would be able to carry out and implement the terms of such agreement."[74]

The Japanese proposals for a summit and China evacuation merited bold and rapid responses but neither was forthcoming. "By insisting that Japan promise in black and white, then and there, to conform to every American requirement," writes historian Herbert Feis, the U.S. had made the premier's task "impossible." Roosevelt showed little curiosity about these openings which, in any case, were closed off five days later when the hardliner Hideki Tojo replaced Konoe and Japan began to set the machinery for an attack into motion.[75]

The Greer, a Secret Map, and the Kearny

Roosevelt continued to grope in vain for a sufficiently provocative pretext in the North Atlantic. Lord Halifax reported to Churchill on October 10th that the president had admitted "that if he asked for a declaration of war he wouldn't get it and opinion would swing against him." The best known of these incidents centered on the U.S. destroyer, the *Greer*. At the time, it was working in close collaboration with a British plane in stalking a German U-boat. Several hours later, the submarine fired (and missed) at its pursuer and the *Greer* responded by firing several depth charges (all missed). Although the Navy reported to FDR "no positive evidence that [the] submarine knew [the] nationality of [the] ship at which it was firing," Roosevelt jumped on the incident as a cause célèbre and a basis for adopting a policy to "shoot on sight.[76]

In a Fireside Chat, the president rattled the saber with new vigor: "when you see a rattlesnake poised to strike, you do not wait until he has struck before you crush him. These Nazi submarines and raiders are the rattlesnakes of the Atlantic." H.W. Brands observes: "What Roosevelt had portrayed as an unprovoked attack by the German submarine upon the *Greer*, had in fact been provoked by the *Greer's* assisting the British plane depth-charging the German submarine. And the *Greer's* actions had been in keeping with existing orders that Roosevelt had not revealed to the American public."[77]

Later, FDR ratcheted up again in both rhetoric and substance after an incident involving another U.S. destroyer, the *Kearny*. After coming to the aid of a British convoy, and dropping several depth charges against a German submarine, that ship had suffered torpedo damage, leaving seven Americans dead. "We have wished to avoid shooting," FDR declared in a Navy Day address on October 27. "But the shooting has started. And history has recorded who fired the first shot." Most dramatically, Roosevelt revealed the existence of a captured "secret map," which showed that the Nazis planned to divide South and Central America into "five vassal states" including "our great life line—the Panama Canal." A second captured document revealed a Nazi plan to "abolish all existing religions-Protestant, Catholic, Mohammedan, Hindu, Buddhist and Jewish alike" in favor of one "International Nazi Church."[78]

Both of FDR's bombshell documents were fakes, courtesy of William Stephenson's BSC. The clandestine unit of that organization, for example, had sent the map from Toronto to William Donovan who then shared it with the president. It is unclear whether Roosevelt had any personal knowledge of this dubious background, but Berle and other advisors had warned him previously that the BSC had a history of manufacturing or transmitting fake documents. Regardless, FDR, like many presidents before and after him, was not quibbling about the provenance of a document that furthered his agenda, especially one that fed into widespread public fears of a direct Nazi threat to the Americas.[79]

"I Will Go Down in Disgrace"

Japan pursued a two-pronged approach through most of November. Even as Tojo's new government was formulating plans for an attack, it extended the timeline for talks from November 25th to November 29th. "After that," according to a MAGIC intercept, "things are automatically going to happen." By this time, Japan had dropped the earlier consideration of evacuating China. On November 20th, it proposed instead to withdraw troops from southern to northern Indochina in preparation for pulling them out completely "after the establishment of an equitable Pacific Peace" and to refrain from further attacks outside the area.[80]

FDR's "War Memorandum" responded to the Japanese proposal with inflexible counter demands on November 26th: immediate total withdrawal from Indochina and China, abandonment of the Asia Co-Prosperity Sphere, recognition of the Nationalist government in Chungking, and withdrawal from the Tripartite Pact. These were nonstarters and Roosevelt knew it. The president had accepted the inevitability, and to some extent the desirability, of war with Japan. A day earlier, he told his top advisors that the main "question was how we should maneuver them into the position of firing the first shot without allowing too much danger to ourselves." FDR was now ready to go to war, incident or no incident. On November 29th, he told British ambassador Lord Halifax that if Japan attacked British or Dutch possessions, "we should obviously be all together."[81]

The big mystery was not the certainty of a Japanese attack but the location. The president, and most of his advisors, guessed Thailand, Singapore, the Dutch East Indies, or, less likely, the Philippines. Almost nobody imagined Pearl Harbor, though the Japanese diplomatic code gave a significant pre-attack clue on the timing when it ordered the destruction of all code machines at 1:00 p.m. Washington time. This was 7:30 a.m. in Hawaii, ideal for catching the defenders off guard. As the Japanese fleet steamed toward the target, it maintained strict radio silence, even as the Imperial Navy was sending deceptive code and radio messages that it was still stationed in "home waters." When Roosevelt heard the first reports of the havoc wreaked by some 351 enemy planes at Pearl Harbor, killing over two thousand Americans, destroying nearly 200 planes, and sinking or damaging twenty ships, a White House butler later reported: "I heard him remark as further details continued to come in about the destruction of the fleet. 'My God! How did it happen? I will go down in disgrace'."[82]

FDR had vastly underestimated Japanese capabilities, but he was not alone. The operative battle plan of Admiral Husband Kimmel in Hawaii, as approved by his superiors, had discounted a naval attack on Pearl Harbor because of perceptions that the Japanese lacked sufficient resources and that their pilots were inferior in training and skill compared to their American counterparts. This thinking was also consistent with a 1940 assessment by Ickes in his diary that it was well understood that "the Japanese are naturally poor air men." Instead, Kimmel's plan emphasized the danger of internal sabotage and took for granted that the likely response would be for the U.S. fleet to steam from secure bases in Pearl Harbor in a mission of retaliation.[83]

Did Roosevelt Know?

Did Roosevelt know all along that the attack was going to be at Pearl Harbor? The best-known advocate of this view is Robert B. Stinnett who contends that the president, looking for a "back door" to a war against Hitler, intentionally left Pearl Harbor vulnerable to a Japanese attack. Stinnett's thesis cannot withstand close examination. Contrary to his claims, for example, there is no evidence that the U.S. broke the crucial Japanese naval code (much less passed those intercepts to FDR) nor is there any evidence that the attack fleet ever broke radio silence. As documented by multiple, and highly diverse, critics, there's no good reason to believe that these communications came from the fleet itself. Another serious flaw in Stinnett's thesis was that keeping such a vast enterprise secret entailed almost inevitable, and insurmountable, logistical problems because of the necessary participation of multiple co-conspirators.[84]

Absence of direct foreknowledge of the Pearl Harbor attack, however, does not excuse or mitigate FDR's other derelictions.[85] He kept the two main local commanders, Admiral Kimmel and General Walter C. Short, in the dark about the near certainty of an attack at some location after the "War Memorandum" and intercepts showing Japanese orders to destroy code machinery and systems. Prior to this, of course, the president, because of his fixation on the North Atlantic, had starved both Pearl Harbor and other U.S. forces in the Pacific of needed resources, such as observation planes.

Even the rushed post Pearl Harbor investigation by the Roberts Commission, which carefully avoided pinning blame on FDR, concluded that "due to the enormous demand on the Nation's capacity to produce munitions and war supplies, there was a deficiency in the provision of material for the Hawaii area" and that local commanders were repeatedly turned down when they "made numerous recommendations to the War and Navy Departments for additional forces, equipment and funds which they deemed necessary to insure the defense of the Hawaii coastal frontier under any eventuality."[85]

More fundamentally, the president repeatedly fumbled on pursuing prospects for peace in negotiations with Japan. The main consequence of abrogating the Treaty of Commerce and Navigation, for example, was to push Tokyo further into the hands of the Axis. This was followed by FDR's failure to aggressively pursue Japan's proposals for a summit or, more fleetingly, to evacuate China. While the president did not exactly seek a "back door to war" in Europe via Japan, he was responsible, both through inattention and inflexibility, for needlessly heightening the likelihood of a Pacific war. State Department legend George F. Kennan sums it up well: "surely it cannot be denied that had FDR been determined to avoid war with the Japanese, he would have conducted American policy quite differently . . . He would not have tried to starve the Japanese Navy for oil. And he would have settled down to some hard and realistic doings with the Japanese, instead of letting them be deluged and frustrated by the cloudy and unintelligible moralisms of Cordell Hull."[86]

7

FDR's Wartime State and the Poisoned Fruit of Unconditional Surrender

If Roosevelt had not served a third term, historians would have had a compelling case for assigning him to the category of failed presidents. The list on the debit side of the ledger as of 1940 was formidable.

Most obviously, his administration had failed to deliver recovery from the depression, including persistent unemployment. The stock market had still not reached 1929 levels and would not do so until 1954. Roosevelt's woeful civil rights record was one of perpetual inaction on lynching, voting rights, and Jim Crow in the military. More tragic still was the president's refusal to throw a lifeline to Jewish refugees, including his turning away of the *S.S. St. Louis.*

Because he did, in fact, seek and secure reelection, and ended his life as a triumphant commander in chief against the Axis, historians have shied away from such a harsh accounting. They have also skirted over the underside of the president's wartime record: stepped up civil liberties violations, an intrusive command economy, inability to bring recovery from the depression, needless bloodletting from a policy of unconditional surrender and destruction, and finally, abandonment of Europe's imperiled Jews.

After Pearl Harbor, Roosevelt was more popular than ever. In the hours after the attack, a parade of leading non-interventionists rallied behind the administration. Even Rep. Hamilton Fish, a past arch-nemesis of FDR, urged Americans "to present a united front in support of the President." Robert McCormick's *Chicago Daily Tribune* declared in a front-page editorial: "All of us, from this day forth, have only one task. That is to strike with all our might to protect and preserve the American freedom that we all hold dear."

Senator Wheeler put it more concisely: "Let's lick the hell out of them." The America First Committee disbanded. Only one member of Congress voted against declaring war on Japan, Rep. Jeannette Rankin (R-Montana).[1]

Japan speedily followed up Pearl Harbor by striking hard at Hong Kong, Malaya, Guam, and Wake Island. General Douglas MacArthur, the U.S. commander in the Philippines, proved stunningly negligent. Despite considerable advance warning after Pearl Harbor, and an urgent request from Major General Lewis H. Brereton, the commander of the Far East Air Force in the Philippines, he tarried for six crucial hours before greenlighting a counter strike. As U.S. planes at Clark Field fueled on the ground in preparation for that mission, a Japanese attack from the air decimated them. The same Congress and administration which eventually subjected the commanders in Hawaii and the Pacific to intensive and repeated scrutiny, never investigated MacArthur's actions that day.[2]

The War within a War

A simultaneous triple declaration of war against Japan, Germany, and Italy was FDR's for the asking, but he decided not to pursue it. He well understood the possibility of prominent objectors and the risk of a lengthy and contentious debate. Another possible factor in deterring him was that MAGIC intercepts indicated a probable declaration of war by Germany against the United States. But Roosevelt also made sure to give Hitler an extra push, just in case. In a now little remembered Fireside Chat on December 9th, he declared: "We know also that Germany and Japan are conducting their military and naval operations in accordance with a joint plan . . . Remember always that Germany and Italy, regardless of any formal declaration of war, consider themselves at war with the United States at this moment."

FDR was trying, as historian Thomas Fleming puts it, to "bait Hitler into declaring war or, failing that, to persuade the American people to support an American declaration of war on the two European fascist powers." If the goal was to bait, the ploy worked. The Fuehrer was hot with outrage the next day. He characterized the speech as proof that the U.S. was a de facto belligerent and, on December 11th, Germany and Italy, following Hitler's lead, declared war.[3]

FDR's Fireside Chat on December 9th was also an ideological call to arms reminiscent of Wilson's "wartime collectivism." The president declared:

> It is not a sacrifice for any man, old or young, to be in the Army or the Navy of the United States. Rather it is a privilege . . . It is not a sacrifice for the industrialist or the wage earner, the farmer or the shopkeeper, the trainman or the doctor, to pay more taxes, to buy more bonds, to forego extra profits, to work longer or harder at the task for which he is best fitted. Rather it is a privilege.

This rhetoric probably pleased such advisors as Henry Wallace, the head of the Economic Defense Board (renamed the Bureau of Economic Warfare (BEW) on December 17th), who were intent on making war mobilization into a New Deal demonstration project. Wallace wanted to weave together the production of strategic commodities, most notably rubber, with such progressive goals as improved labor and health conditions. The BEW's pursuit of this agenda was so fervent that it paid above-market prices and dispensed massive subsidies to stimulate production of natural rubber in Haiti and Brazil.[4]

Wallace's New Deal approach almost immediately ran afoul of the conservative Jesse Jones, a wealthy businessman, and major donor to the president's campaigns, who headed the cash-rich Reconstruction Finance Corporation (RFC). Unlike Wallace, Jones wanted to give incentives to profit-oriented companies to manufacture synthetic rubber from oil. He regarded the BEW's "social minded uplifters" as a drag on the war effort. Rather than choosing between the methods of Wallace and Jones, FDR straddled by allowing both to proceed along separate tracks. When it became apparent, however, that domestically produced rubber was far more cost effective, FDR finally came down the side of Jones. He did this, however, in a most prevaricating way which kept alive the hopes of his vice president. He authorized Wallace to make all major purchases but then undercut that authority by stipulating that the cash had to come from Jones.[5]

The ideological "war within the war" between New Dealers and the "dollar-a-year men" also consumed, and eventually unraveled, the Office of Production Management (OPM), headed by William S. Knudsen. After Pearl Harbor, Knudsen's outwardly cordial relationship with the president began to sour. The first public sign of trouble was a speech by Eleanor Roosevelt in January 1942 which gave her rendition of a conversation with the OPM head. She said that Knudsen had responded to her complaint about insufficient retraining programs for lost jobs in the auto industry by looking at her "like a great big benevolent bear as if to say, 'Now Mrs. Roosevelt don't let's get excited.'" Her reply, according to the speech, was: "I wonder if you know what hunger is? Has any member of your family ever gone hungry."

The irony was that Danish-born Knudsen was far more likely than most, including Eleanor, to have had a bout with hunger. The OPM head had come from very humble origins, arriving in the U.S. at age twenty with thirty dollars in his pocket. Barely speaking English, Knudsen had worked as a reamer and riveter at $1.75 per day while living in a boarding house. Only days after Eleanor's speech, Knudsen, who had little discretion over retraining or anything else, was out of a job. He found out at an official meeting when his secretary handed him a page torn from the news ticker. It said that Roosevelt had abolished the OPM and replaced it with a new War Production Board (WPB), to be headed by another "dollar-a-year man," Donald Nelson.[6]

At first, Nelson, a former vice president of Sears, was popular with both the business world and the New Dealers. "His [Nelson's] powers over procurement and production are absolute," declared the *New York Times Magazine*. "Every Federal department, establishment and agency must take orders from him." His authority even extended to determining the quantity of fabric per garment for women's clothing so as to discourage "wasteful" styles such as long dresses. One of his first acts at the WPB was to shut down production of civilian vehicles.

But Nelson, despite having vast powers on paper, proved helpless in fending off more experienced powerbrokers, such as Under Secretary of War Robert Patterson. Patterson, who headed procurement for the Army, was single-minded in promoting public sacrifice to the war effort. An example was his unsuccessful call to ban comic newspaper strips, which he regarded as a waste of paper and detracting from the serious business of war. For the same reason, he took offense at Seven-Up delivery trucks on the streets of Washington, D.C. "So long as gas and tires and equipment are being wasted on that kind of damn foolishness," he charged, "the civilian economy doesn't deserve *anything*."[7]

The most intrusive wartime mobilization agency was the Office of Price Administration (OPA), which rejected the whole basis of the market economy. With New Deal ideologue Leon Henderson as its head, the OPA prohibited any price or rent above the "maximum" "regardless of any contract, agreement, lease or other obligations heretofore or hereafter entered into." Fleming comments: "Not a few Americans found OPA's bureaucrats arrogant and heavy handed and Henderson himself abrasive." *Time* predicted that "OPA is likely to be the most unpopular of agencies, a sort of kitchen Gestapo." It was the author of many perverse consequences, including chronic shortages. Under the rule of the OPA, it became commonplace for landlords to convert their apartment units into storage for commercial use, require larger deposits, add extra charges for furniture, or deny permission to have pets. Because FDR feared offending his labor allies, however, he did not initially propose similar ceilings on wages.[8]

"When Are You Going to Indict the Seditionists?"

If free contract and property rights took a beating during World War II, so too did the protections of the Bill of Rights. Even before Pearl Harbor, FDR repeatedly prodded his more pro-civil-liberties-minded Attorney General Francis Biddle to muzzle free speech. In November 1941, for example, he urged "a Grand Jury investigation of the money sources behind the America First Committee" because it "certainly ought to be looked into and I cannot get any action out of Congress." But Biddle resisted. More boldly, he promised not to prosecute alleged subversives because "free speech as such ought not to be restricted."[9]

Roosevelt had never much cared for Biddle's gestures toward tolerance and liked them still less after December 7th. He stepped up the pressure "to clean up a number of these vile [right-wing] publications" and to move "against publishers of seditious matter." He made it a regular practice to send Biddle news clippings as examples. In each case, he appended notes with comments like "What about this?" or "What are you doing to stop this?" Eventually, the president's frustration spilled over into cabinet meetings. "His technique was always the same," Biddle remembered. "When my turn came, as he went around the table, his habitual affability dropped . . . He looked at me, his face pulled tightly together. 'When are you going to indict the seditionists?' He continued to do this "the next week, and every week after that." Roosevelt also ordered a new round of wiretaps covering both political adversaries and members of his own cabinet. "Hell, my father just about invented bugging. [He] had them spread all over, and thought nothing of it," wrote John Roosevelt, the president's son.[10]

While no mass roundups of dissidents occurred on Roosevelt's watch, he had nothing against mass roundups as such. The numbers of Japanese Americans interned, which exceeded several fold all arrests of suspected dissidents in World War I, shows as much. Instead, a mass roundup of dissenters, and other limits on free speech, were never in the cards for one simple reason: the "mass," if defined as vocal opponents of the war, had almost evaporated after Pearl Harbor. "If one looks at the paucity of opposition to the war," writes Richard W. Steele, a specialist on this subject, "and the extraordinary efforts to suppress what little radical dissent there was, the administration's record is less restrained than the figures suggest."[11]

If Roosevelt, or others around him, had wanted to prosecute pre-war noninterventionists, that too was not feasible, albeit for different reasons. Unquestionably Roosevelt desired more vigorous action on that front, but resistance from below repeatedly got in the way. The unhappy experiences of Americans with governmental excesses over more than two decades had nurtured a widespread civil-liberties consciousness. Examples included repression of dissent during World War I, Prohibition enforcement abuses, the Black Committee, and Hague's deportations. Roadblocks against executive branch overreach came not only from judges but also from lawyers on the federal payroll. Even when egged on from above, more than a few gummed up the legal works by quibbling over technicalities and using methods of delay. Would-be prosecutors were also aware that support for civil liberties had filtered down to ordinary Americans, including potential jury pools. These legal and popular constraints on centralized federal power were highly imperfect but, taken together, provided a significant brake on administration discretion.[12]

Roosevelt's public persona as an amiable champion of democracy and liberalism coexisted with a considerable private vindictive streak. If anything, he outdid Wilson in vindictiveness by pestering subordinates to crack down harder than they may have otherwise wanted. The comparatively passive Wilson more often acted as a rubber stamp for zealous underlings. But FDR tirelessly probed the limits of his own power through such diverse methods as sedition trials, tax audits, and allied congressional investigations. Principle did not appear to impede him. "He was not much interested in the theory of sedition," recalls Biddle, "or in the constitutional right to criticize the government in wartime. He wanted this anti-war talk stopped." Echoing this, Steele concludes that although Roosevelt gave lip service to the principle of free speech, "he rarely interpreted it as preventing the executive branch from doing what was necessary to ensure his broadly conceived view of national security."[13]

"F.B.I., Naval Intelligence and Army Intelligence All Disapproved of It"

At first, FDR expressed relatively few concerns about Japanese Americans and even these might have been discounted had he listened to John Franklin Carter, who headed his personal secret intelligence unit. In a report to the president shortly after Pearl Harbor, Carter characterized the Nisei as no "more disloyal than any other racial group in the United States with whom we went to war." But Carter had underestimated his boss's readiness to cherry-pick when it suited his needs. Roosevelt invariably latched onto any wording that conveyed a less favorable impression. Commenting on one of Carter's reports, for example, FDR fixated on a passage that "Dams, bridges, harbors, power stations, etc. are wholly unguarded. The harbor of San Pedro [Los Angeles port] could be razed completely by four men with hand grenades and a little study at night." This so alarmed the president that he made sure to call it to the attention of Secretary of War Stimson even as he glossed over the report's general conclusion that 90 percent of the (American born) Nisei "were completely loyal to the United States."[14]

Compared to what came later, Japanese Americans on the West Coast experienced relative calm in the two months after Pearl Harbor. The press seemed more inclined to defuse rather than to fire up racist fears. The *San Francisco Daily News* declared that to "subject these people to illegal search and seizure, then arrest them without warrant to confinement without trial, is to violate the principles of Democracy as set forth in our Constitution." As late as January 23rd, the *Los Angeles Times* characterized the Nisei as good Americans who "deserve sympathy rather than suspicion" and Carter continued to suggest that the president defend Japanese Americans through his bully pulpit. But Roosevelt did nothing at this crucial turning point. Had he deployed his famous charm and eloquence, perhaps citing the four freedoms, he might have prevented much suffering. He did not behave like a president who was trapped by conditions or distracted by other issues, but rather like a man who really did not care.[15]

Roosvelt's silence enabled political and military officials to move into the breach and set policy by default. Illustrative of this was Secretary of War Stimson's reaction to a proposal from Rep. Leland M. Ford (R-California) that "all Japanese, whether citizens or not, be placed in inland concentration camps." Although Stimson did not endorse the idea outright, his response was just reckless enough to give it more momentum. He volunteered that "the Army is prepared to provide internment facilities in the interior to the extent necessary." The man who came to be identified as the public face of internment, Lieutenant General John L. DeWitt of the Western Defense Command, initially, unlike the president, went on record against sending the Nisei to camps, calling it "damned nonsense." DeWitt's ultimate endorsement of internment in late January was not too surprising, however. For the cautious and indecisive commander, it was the easiest route to take.[16]

One of the highest placed officials who opposed internment was Attorney General Biddle. He was also inept in the political power game. Biddle confessed later that he felt overawed and intimidated by the imposing Stimson, a fellow blue blood who was nearly twenty years his senior. A cabinet meeting on January 20th revealed his shortcomings as a bureaucratic infighter. After Stimson immediately steered the discussion into a possible evacuation of Japanese Americans, Biddle failed to challenge the premise and then meekly suggested "that the time might come that there would be certain areas where the president might suspend the writ of Habeas Corpus." Like John Franklin Carter before him, he did not realize that temporizing with FDR only opened the way to undercut his own case. "Biddle's reassurance that the legal obstacles to removing citizens from restricted areas could be evaded in an emergency," historian Greg Robinson comments, "was an invitation to the President to ignore constitutional issues entirely."[17]

Although Biddle did not act like he knew it, he came from a position of potential negotiating strength. He might have had an important ally in J. Edgar Hoover had he chosen to mobilize him. "The necessity for mass evacuation," the FBI director had advised Biddle, "is based primarily upon public and political pressure rather than on factual data." The best argument that Biddle could have made to his politically attuned boss was the lack of any public groundswell for tougher measures. A survey by the Office of Facts and Figures on February 4th reported general satisfaction with existing governmental controls on Japanese Americans. Many years later Biddle even considered it doubtful that "political and special group pressure aside, public opinion even on the West Coast supported evacuation."[18]

Finally, when it was probably too late, the Attorney General presented his case directly to the president on February 7. He opened strongly, stating that "mass evacuation at this time [is] inadvisable, that the F.B.I. was not staffed to perform it." However, after this fairly resolute preamble, he attached disabling qualifiers that "the army should be directed to prepare a detailed plan of evacuation in case of an emergency caused by an air raid or attempted landing on the West Coast." Predictably, Roosevelt saw what he wanted to see and gave a characteristically diversionary and cryptic response. "Generally he approved," Biddle remembers, "being fully aware of the dreadful risk of Fifth Column retaliation in case of a raid."[19]

Had Biddle chosen to more strenuously resist he might have successfully combined forces with possible allies scattered throughout the federal bureaucracy. In August 1942, an ACLU internal report explained that "Practically all of the officials who commented on the evacuations" agreed that it was done "without the approval of the government agencies most directly concerned. The statement was made repeatedly by one official or another that the F.B.I., Naval Intelligence and Army Intelligence all disapproved of it." The list opposing internment also included Secretary of Interior Ickes, who had jurisdiction over the lands where many of the camps were built. It was Roosevelt himself who was, in the words of George W. Bush, the "decider." Robinson puts it well: "the President was willingly misled. He had access to reliable information, which he ignored, from sources he trusted, notably the FBI, that the Japanese Americans did not represent a danger. By contrast, the President lent credence to the wildest and most unsubstantiated anti-Japanese rumors."[20]

Dr. Seuss (Theodor Geisel) depicts Japanese Americans as dangerous Fifth Columnists.

"It Was the Wrong Thing to Do"

The wording of Roosevelt's Executive Order 9066 of February 19th was deceptively bland. It authorized the secretary of war to prescribe "military areas" and "determine, from which any or all persons may be excluded" and "to provide for residents of any such area who are excluded therefrom, such transportation, food, shelter, and other accommodations as may be necessary, in the judgment of the Secretary of War or the said Military Commander." The text did not mention any specific group or place but featured such code words as "any and all persons excluded" to describe those to be evacuated. In this respect, the wording had parallels to the Constitution's well-known coded euphemism "other persons" to refer to slavery. As with the "Three Fifths" and fugitive slave clauses, a probable purpose of the code words in Executive Order 9066 was to obscure the true nature of what was taking place.[21]

Claims that assert or imply that Executive Order 9066 was an unavoidable response to the neutral dictates of military necessity cannot withstand scrutiny. Roosevelt did not consider military necessity to be a sacrosanct doctrine when it did not suit his needs. He always reserved the right of discernment to accept or reject policy proposals recommended on that basis. For example, the president vetoed DeWitt's request to remove Italian and German aliens from the West Coast under Executive Order 9066. He also gave a thumbs-down to a plan to remove all Japanese Americans from the East Coast. When listening to advisers on this issue, he was often highly selective. While he chose to take advice from DeWitt and Stimson, he did not bother to seek out credible military sources who might have contradicted them, such as George Marshall, US Army chief of staff. As someone who considered himself an "old navy man," Roosevelt was singularly uncurious about the views of such well-informed naval officers as Lieutenant Commander Kenneth Ringle, who regarded internment as unnecessary.[22]

The wording which Roosevelt approved for Executive Order 9066 was so broad that it could potentially also cover Japanese Americans in Hawaii. At one-third of the population of the islands, however, their mass incarceration presented enormous logistical and financial obstacles; yet even after he signed Executive Order 9066, Roosevelt still wanted to do it. On February 26th 1942 he informed Secretary of the Navy Knox that he had "long felt that most of the Japanese should be removed from Oahu to one of the other Islands." While Roosevelt conceded that such an undertaking involved "much planning, much temporary construction, and careful supervision of them when they get to the new location," he did not "worry about the constitutional question—first, because of my recent order and, second, because Hawaii is under martial law." But the Hawaiian internment scheme soon collapsed of its own weight, including the possible expense of diverting so many ships and personnel from fighting Japan in the Pacific as well as indirect opposition from the commander on the ground in the islands.[23]

While Executive Order 9066 did not mention race, nationality, or a specific place, the Army's various public proclamations that followed it most certainly did by stipulating "any person of Japan-ese ancestry." If the "slave codes" of the states served to translate or define the "other persons" code phrase in the Constitution, DeWitt's proclamations did the same through the "any and all persons" wording in Executive Order 9066. Moreover, because only DeWitt's name appeared at the bottom of all the enforcement orders, he, not FDR, became the public face of internment. Purging any mention of race or ancestry from the text of the executive order could, and did, help insulate the administration from perceived culpability. That omission may have also contributed in subtle ways to the failure of historians to hold Roosevelt more accountable.[24]

Somewhat belatedly, Stimson drafted and sent to Congress a bill specifying legal punishments for violations of the new rules. It had the same coded wording as Executive Order 9066: "whoever shall enter, remain in, leave, or commit any act in any military area or military zone prescribed, under the authority of an Executive order of the President [shall] . . . be guilty of a misdemeanor and upon conviction shall be liable to a fine not to exceed $5,000 or to imprisonment for not more than one year, or both, for each offense." A faint glimmer of dissent that quickly died came from Senator Robert A. Taft, who called the proposal "probably the 'sloppiest' criminal law I have ever read." Taft understood, however, as did everyone else in Congress, the true meaning of the coded language and was not going to object "because I understand the pressing character of this kind of legislation for the Pacific coast today."[25]

At least some others in Congress had private misgivings. Senator Wheeler later stated that he had "protested to various high-level government officials" that internment violated the "principles of the Four Freedoms." He warned that if the government "can get away with such treatment of citizens of Japanese descent, it can do the same to any minority." Even more noteworthy in retrospect, Wheeler's good friend, Senator Truman, said in 1961 that "They called it relocation, but we put them in concentration camps, and I was against it. It was the wrong thing to do." If Senators Wheeler and Truman had these objections at the time, however, they did not express them during the discussion and vote on Public Law 503.

The dozens of subsequent specific exclusion orders issued by DeWitt followed the same template. Handbills appeared in such high-visibility spots as telephone poles, giving "Instructions to All Japanese" living in the area. Those who failed to comply within a week were liable for criminal prosecution. The Army only allowed the internees to take what they could carry, not including pets which often had to be destroyed. The attendant racism took on a life of its own. When asked about the fate of American-born kids in orphanages, a chief aide of DeWitt replied that "if they have one drop of Japanese blood in them, they must go to camp."[27]

The New Deal welfare state, as represented by the Works Progress Administration (WPA), played an unheralded, but essential, role in implementing internment. From March to the end of November 1942, that agency spent $4.47 million on removal and internment, slightly more than the $4.43 million spent by the Army for that purpose during that period. In terms of scale, this endeavor ranked perhaps as the most gigantic single "WPA project" of all time. Jason Scott Smith observes that "the eagerness of many WPA administrators to place their organization in the forefront of this wartime enterprise is striking." That iconic New Deal agency installed such signature concentration camp trappings as guard towers and spotlights. Harry Hopkins, the father of the WPA, expressed pride in his agency's accomplishments in the "building of those camps for the War Department for the Japanese evacuees on the West Coast."[28]

Trying to Quash Major Press Outlets

Through it all, Roosevelt continued to push for legal action against major non-interventionist voices in the so-called "Patterson-McCormick Axis" (the *New York Daily News*, *Washington Times-Herald*, and the *Chicago Daily Tribune*). He became increasingly impatient with Biddle's response that he did not have sufficient evidence for a prosecution. A turning point was a cabinet meeting in March 1942. After the president unleashed another verbal tirade against "subversive sheets," Biddle was finally ready to appease him by revoking the second-class mailing status of selected publications under the Espionage Act. Roosevelt liked that approach but wanted to go further, and quickly. At a press conference soon after the cabinet meeting, he revealed his mindset when he stated that several unnamed journalists present were "sixth columnists" who were, "wittingly or unwittingly," dupes of the Axis. Subversives of this type never prevailed, he added, unless they had "a vehicle to distribute their poison."[29]

Contrary to Roosevelt's wishes, Biddle focused on the smaller fry rather than the major metropolitan publishers. The most important of these was Father Coughlin's *Social Justice*, which had a distribution of about two hundred thousand. The main accusation was that it had violated the Espionage Act because of a "substantial contribution to a systematic and unscrupulous attack on the war effort of our nation, both civilian and military." Many civil libertarians, including Roger Baldwin, the head of the ACLU, regarded the government's case as untenable. The government avoided an embarrassing trial, however, when Coughlin's Catholic superiors ordered him to shut down the publication.[30]

Not content with the Radio Priest's relatively puny scalp, Roosevelt kept pressing for harsher measures. On April 22, 1942, he cautioned Biddle about the "subversive mind of Cissy Patterson." Six days later, his Fireside Chat underscored that "this great war effort . . . must not be impeded by a few bogus patriots who use the sacred freedom of the press to echo sentiments of the propagandists in Tokyo and Berlin." Much more than Biddle, the president regarded the suppression of *Social Justice* as a small opener rather than the final act. As a possible basis for sedition prosecutions, he sent Biddle clippings from the *Chicago Daily Tribune*, the *New York Daily News*, and the Hearst newspapers, so as "to let the whole country know the truth about these papers. The tie-in between the attitude of these papers and the Rome-Berlin broadcasts is something far greater than mere coincidence." After some more prodding, Biddle conducted an analysis which concluded, quite likely to the president's dismay, that the articles did not reflect or follow German propaganda.[31]

"A Very Useful Preventive Effect"

Much more quietly, the administration carried on with the official harassment of black newspapers. Historian Patrick S. Washburn, the leading authority on this topic, concludes that "the black press was in extreme danger of being suppressed until June 1942." The basis of FDR's animus was no mystery. Quite a few black newspapers had tirelessly documented Jim Crow conditions in the military, federal medical facilities, and defense industries as well as selective and hypocritical enforcement of the Four Freedoms. These were the stories their readers wanted. When fifty-six black leaders were asked only a month after Pearl Harbor to assess the popular climate, a stunning thirty-six said that most African Americans did not completely support the war effort.[32]

After Pearl Harbor, black journalists and activists kept up their fight for equal treatment and civil rights. They wanted to avoid the uncritical "Close Ranks" strategy that W.E.B. DuBois had advocated in World War I. This strategy found its most concrete application a month later in the Double V campaign (fighting for democracy simultaneously at home and abroad) popularized by the *Pittsburgh Courier*.

The tenor of this reporting was almost guaranteed to get under the skin of top administration officials. On April 27th 1942, Archibald MacLeish, who a few months earlier as the Librarian of Congress had presided over commemoration of the first "Bill of Rights Day," forwarded to Biddle articles from the Washington (DC) *Afro American* that in his view had "seditious implications." He suggested "a very useful preventive effect, if your department could somehow call attention to the fact that the Negro press enjoys no immunity." A month later, Roosevelt urged both Biddle and Walker to personally admonish black editors to cease "their subversive language."[33]

Matters came to a head when Biddle summoned to his office John H. Sengstacke, the publisher of the *Chicago Defender* and the president of the National Newspaper Publishers Association (NNPA), an African American group. Placed on the table were copies of several leading black papers, including the *Chicago Defender*, the *Baltimore Afro-American*, and the *Pittsburgh Courier*. Characterizing these as seditious, Biddle warned that the government was "going to shut them all up." The conversation continued to heat up, but Sengstacke calmly held his ground. He then suggested a compromise. He promised that black publishers would tone down criticism if the government would forgo indictments and give black journalists more access.[34]

Biddle verbally assented to Sengstacke's proposal and black publishers promptly fulfilled their part of the bargain. A federal study of the *Pittsburgh Courier*, for example, devoted considerably less space to the Double V campaign in April 1943 when compared to August 1942. Moreover, the main targets of negative coverage shifted to local government and private business and away from the federal government. The application of the Biddle–Sengstacke compromise proved one-sided in the government's favor, however, and federal access for the black press did not improve. In late 1942, Sengstacke complained that the attitude of "administrative officials in Washington to date is far from being encouraging."[35]

Moreover, federal authorities did not shift to a cooperative or hands-off approach after the Sengstacke-Biddle meeting but instead ratcheted up monitoring and informal pressure. In the first half of 1942 alone, FBI agents visited leading black newspapers that had critical stories about the federal government. In the end, however, informal pressure was a win-win for the government. A Department of Justice analysis concluded that the likely result of declaring unmailable "a paper as prominent and as respected by the Negro population as the *Pittsburgh Courier*" would be "further unrest and possibly [arousing] a spirit of defeatism among the Negro population." A public prosecution of one of these publications posed risks of alienating black voters in key Northern swing states. Because the *Courier* had the highest circulation of all black newspapers and had provided valuable past support for Roosevelt, the potential political risks of revoking its mailing status were much higher compared to *Social Justice*.[36]

Creating a Command Economy

By mid-1942, the OPA's clamp down on prices, which now encompassed an array of products, had nurtured a culture of evasion, favoritism, and dishonesty. As Higgs points out, "selling the available products to friends—to whites, to pretty girls, to those first in line—popped up everywhere, threatening to make many commodities unavailable to persons unfavored by the sellers." In the case of gas, for example, the OPA issued A cards to most drivers which allowed them five gallons per week. B cards, allowing more gas, went to war workers, doctors, and others deemed deserving because of their vocations. The X cards, which allowed unlimited mileage, represented the final, and most privileged category. People with political pull were often able to get X or B cards. The most obvious example was the automatic granting of X cards to every member of Congress. Rationing soon encompassed an array of goods including cheese, sugar, cotton, fish, and shoes. Draconian beef and pork rationing pushed many Americans to resort to black markets and substitutes, such as horse, rabbit, and muskrats. Criminals proved inventive in finding new ways to counterfeit ration books.[37]

FDR was not immune to the political abuses of wartime mobilization. According to Henry Wallace's diary, the president had suggested in May that Isador Lubin, the head of the Bureau of Labor Statistics "doctor up the cost of living figures by leaving out some item so as to make it appear that the cost of living was not really rising so much as it is really is." Wallace objected and FDR did not pursue it. Roosevelt also used wartime mobilization to target critics in the press. While the WPB allowed an increase in printing and other supplies to the *Chicago Sun*, a very pro-New Deal paper, it denied them to the *Chicago Daily Tribune*.[38]

Midway Repercussions

Meanwhile, the tide of the war was beginning to shift. On June 4th, the combined fleet of the Japanese Navy fell into an American trap while advancing on Midway Islands. Admiral Chester Nimitz, the commander of the Pacific Fleet, knew they were coming based on MAGIC intercepts. "Midway was Nimitz's greatest battle," writes military historian Eric Larrabee. "He planned it, he picked its commander, he ordered it into execution. He proceeded thus because he had decided to accept as valid an intelligence estimate that forecast the time, location, and strength of a Japanese attack." Japanese army units were so overconfident that they began listing Midway as their next mailing address. When it was all over, Nimitz's forces had sent four carriers to the bottom of the Pacific and destroyed over 200 planes. Admiral Isoroku Yamamoto, who knew he was beaten, ordered a withdrawal.[39]

The fallout from the Battle of Midway brought a partial exception to Biddle's reticence about prosecuting the "big fish" in the press. In June 1942, the Department of Justice began investigating the *Chicago Daily Tribune* for possible violations of the Espionage Act. These centered on a front-page story on June 7th 1942 by reporter Stanley Johnson that had also appeared in the Patterson-owned *Washington Times Herald* and the *New York Daily News* on the Battle of Midway. It revealed that American military authorities had advance knowledge of the size of the Japanese attack force. While the story did not report that the United States had broken the Japanese naval code (nor did the reporters know this fact), that was a natural inference for an enemy agent.

Before submitting the story, Johnson had asked the managing editor, James Loy "Pat" Maloney, and Washington Bureau Chief Arthur Sears Henning if the content violated the Code of Wartime Practices, which governed censorship decisions. Henning, who was thoroughly familiar with the rules, gave assurance that it did not, as did Maloney. At the time, the Code said nothing about the movement of enemy ships in enemy waters.[40]

Administration officials were not about to give publisher Robert R. McCormick the benefit of the doubt, however. Roosevelt even wanted to deploy the Marines to occupy the Tribune Tower. At his suggestion, the Department of Justice empaneled a grand jury and selected a respected veteran prosecutor. The case imploded when the navy failed to provide promised evidence that Johnson's story had exposed "confidential information concerning the Battle of Midway." Biddle confessed years later that he "felt like a fool" as a result. Even had the case moved forward, prosecutors faced a high bar of proving willful intent.[41]

New Evidence about the Holocaust

Shocking new information became available in June 1942 that the Nazis had a master plan for the gradual extermination of Europe's Jews. The Jewish Socialist Bund in Poland reported the use of vans to gas Jews in portable gas chambers. Two months later, Gerhart Riegner of the World Jewish Congress passed on to Rabbi Stephen S. Wise (a key FDR ally and confidant) a report "that in the Fuehrer's Headquarters, a plan has been discussed, and is under consideration, according to which all Jews in countries occupied or controlled by German numbering 3½ to 4 millions should, after deportation and concentration in the East, be at one blow exterminated in order to resolve once and for all the Jewish question."

Similar reports (several attested to by Assistant Secretary of State Sumner Welles) provided, as Medoff points out, "credible evidence that the Germans had already carried out a deliberate slaughter of hundreds of thousands of European Jews."[42]

Americans Chafe at Wartime Controls

The intrusions of the federal bureaucracy, large and small, bore down especially hard on Americans in the month before the 1942 elections. A much-publicized example was the passage of a revolutionary bill which took a gigantic leap toward converting the income tax from a "class tax" (centered on the wealthy) into a "mass tax" paid by ordinary Americans through withholding. As a result, the number of people required to file skyrocketed from seven million to forty-two million in a single year. Also in October, the Selective Service announced a lowering of the draft age to eighteen and the OPA cut the daily coffee ration portion to one cup per day (Americans drank an average of three).

If voters were seeking a culprit for the shortcomings of war mobilization in a broader sense, an election eve article by Senator Truman, the chair of the Special Committee to Investigate the War Program gave them one. Without naming names, he pointedly blamed a "lack of courageous unified leadership and centralized direction at the top."[43]

The 1942 elections brought severe reverses to the Democrats and strengthened the working bi-partisan conservative majority. The president's party lost forty-seven house seats (leaving the GOP just shy of a majority) and nine senate seats. In a poll conducted by Ed Pauley, a wealthy donor to FDR, Democratic congressional candidates singled out for blame alleged "coddling" of labor unions and regulatory overreach by federal bureaucrats. According to Pauley, "the most universal and serious complaint of all" centered on the acerbic OPA head Henderson. "It appears from the letters that the complaint is directed rather at Mr. Henderson and his attitude and methods than at the abstract question of . . . rationing and price control." The election results also strengthened the hand of Jesse Jones, and weakened those of New Dealers, such as Wallace and Henderson. By this time, as Alan Brinkley observes, "over ten thousand business executives (most of them Republicans) had moved into offices, cubicles, and even converted bathrooms in the hopelessly overcrowded headquarters of the war agencies."[44]

FDR responded pragmatically to the election by sacrificing the WPA, then beset by accusations of boondoggling. In his termination statement, he praised the WPA for a "job well done" in the development of New Deal public works projects but, significantly, left out its then still ongoing role in the building and management of concentration camps for Japanese Americans. Although the WPA wound down final operations in February 1943, former employees of the agency formed the backbone of the new War Relocation Agency, tasked with administering the camps.[45]

The "Unconditional Surrender" Meeting

Despite some political setbacks, a major bright spot for Roosevelt was the successful Allied landing in North Africa in Operation Torch. General Dwight D. Eisenhower was able to avoid much potential bloodshed by negotiating, with presidential authorization, an agreement with Admiral Francois Darlan, a senior Vichy commander in French North Africa. Under the deal, Darlan ordered his troops to cease fire in exchange for a guarantee that he could keep his position as the designated French authority in North Africa. New Dealers blasted the agreement as a shameless compromise with fascism and Roosevelt himself showed mounting discomfort. Given the initial intensity of the French Vichy resistance to the Allies, however, he did not have much of a choice. The deal became increasingly moot in December after Darlan was struck down by an assassin.

The Casablanca Conference of January, which included meetings with Churchill and Free French leader Charles De Gaulle, showed contradictory presidential impulses. FDR proved amenable, for example, to continuing the old Vichy's restrictions on Jews during the slow transition to Free French control of North Africa in the months after Darlan's assassination) including quotas and disfranchisement. Also, the slave labor camps, which held thousands of Jews, remained open. In a conversation with French General Charles Noguès, FDR agreed that Jews, if left unrestricted, might "overcrowd the professions." The president also stressed "the specific and understandable complaints which the Germans bore towards the Jews in Germany, namely, that while they represented a small part of the population, over fifty percent of the lawyers, doctors, school teachers, college professors, etc. in Germany were Jews." This characterization was a far cry from the historical facts. Jews at the time Hitler took power constituted only about 11 percent of doctors, 16 percent of lawyers, 3 percent of the college professors and less than 1 percent of the schoolteachers in Germany.[46]

One of the most important decisions made at Casablanca was to put first priority on using North Africa as a base of operations for a landing in Sicily later in the year (though further advances on the Italian peninsula were only implied). A result of this was to put off any invasion across the English Channel, perhaps until mid-1944. This was a victory, although a temporary one, for Churchill who wanted to downplay a cross-channel attack and strike the Axis through its "soft underbelly" by launching operations in the Balkans.[47]

FDR shocked Churchill in a negative way, however, at the final press conference by saying that "we had a General called U.S. Grant. His name was Ulysses Simpson Grant, but in my, and the Prime Minister's, early days, he was called 'Unconditional Surrender' Grant. The elimination of German, Japanese, and Italian war power means the unconditional surrender by Germany, Italy, or Japan." FDR's underlying premise had no genuine historical basis. Grant's demand for unconditional surrender only applied at the battle of Fort Donelson in 1862, not to the entire Confederacy. Nor did he require unconditional surrender at Appomattox three years later. Grant gave generous terms to Robert E. Lee's Army of Northern Virginia. These included allowing Confederate troops to keep their horses, receive federal rations, and be sent home with a parole contingent on a promise to never again take up arms against the Union. Lincoln himself never made a demand for unconditional surrender.[48]

FDR's unconditional surrender policy not only broke with tradition but with the views of the best-known political and military figures of his time. Although he loyally backed the president's position in public, for example, Churchill was never comfortable with it. At the outset, he complained in his diary that unconditional surrender might fuse the Axis "together in a solid desperate block." Eisenhower had even greater disdain for that doctrine: "If you were given two choices—one to mount the scaffold and the other to charge twenty-bayonets—you might as well charge twenty bayonets."[49]

While FDR later claimed that the idea of unconditional surrender had just "popped into my mind" at the press conference, he had given it careful thought beforehand. The night before the press conference he had shared his thinking with advisor Harry Hopkins. "Of course," it's just the thing for the Russians. They couldn't want anything better. Unconditional surrender. Uncle Joe [FDR's nickname for Stalin] might have made it up himself." If this was the motivation, FDR had misunderstood Stalin. Counterbalancing the Soviet dictator's call for harsh treatment toward Germany was a fear that the demand for unconditional surrender would stiffen resistance. Another motivation for FDR was probable regret for the Darlan deal and the consequent criticism from so many of his supporters. So proud was FDR of his proclamation that he even suggested naming Casablanca as the "unconditional surrender meeting."[50]

The Nazis, then reeling from setbacks, regarded unconditional surrender as a propaganda windfall. Joseph Goebbels exulted: "I should never have been able to think up so rousing a slogan. If our Western enemies tell us, we won't deal with you, our only aim is to destroy you . . . how can any German, whether he likes it or not, do anything but fight on with all his strength?"

By contrast, dissident German political and military leaders of the clandestine "Front of Decent People," who were plotting to exploit recent battlefield reverses to stage an anti-Hitler coup, were despondent. Admiral Canaris, who as the chief of the Abwehr (the German military-intelligence service) was the most prestigious of the plotters, lamented that "other side have now disarmed us of the last weapon which we could have ended it [the war]. Now, I cannot see any solution."[51]

Europe's Jews Abandoned Again

Yet again, opportunity knocked to help Europe's Jews, and yet again, nobody answered. In January, the Romanian government, perhaps seeking some distance from its earlier shotgun marriage with the Axis, offered to transport 72,000 Jews to an Allied port on Romanian ships with the only requirement that transportation costs (about $130 per refugee) be paid. The Catholic bishop of Bucharest even added a sweetener by offering to fly the Vatican flag on the ships. After word of the proposal started to leak out, playwright, screenwriter, and militant Jewish activist, Ben Hecht, decided to exert some pressure from below through an ad: "The Doors of Roumania [sic] are Open! Act now!" The British government immediately dismissed the proposal as "blackmail," however, and the State Department showed apparent agreement by taking no action.[52]

The Bermuda Conference in April 1943, which the U.S. and the U.K. had called to address the issue of Jewish refugees, similarly accomplished nothing of substance. The American delegate repeated the official rationale for inaction by announcing that "The true and final solution to the refugee problem [is] complete and final victory." The U.S. also rejected using its still unfilled quota to admit more Jews, much less to transport those refugees on empty returning Liberty Ships. The British delegate rejected any talk of negotiations with Axis elements to release Jews, arguing quite coldly that "many of the potential refugees are empty mouths for which Hitler has no use" and that any deal would relieve him "of an obligation to take care of these useless people." The conference refused to endorse economic aid to Jews behind Axis lines because this might violate the blockade, even though there was a precedent. Beginning in 1942, the Allies had secured Germany's permission to provide relief to starving Greeks from ships chartered from neutral Sweden.[53]

Baruch's Failed Comeback

Some of FDR's advisors tried to introduce some order and consistency into wartime mobilization, but they were never able to make headway. In 1943, James Byrnes, then director of the Office of Economic Mobilization, had briefly persuaded FDR to convert the War Production Board into a superagency modelled after the old War Industries Board and to bring Bernard Baruch out of retirement to head it. But Roosevelt changed his mind after Hopkins advised that it might make him look weak.

Nobody, however, told Baruch who came to the White House to "report for duty." FDR sent him away after some chit-chat about the Middle East and neither mentioned any job offer. To Roosevelt, a status quo with Nelson was politically preferable to a new regime, with the legendary, and overshadowing Baruch at the center. FDR kept Nelson in place, as politically enfeebled as ever. As Alan Brinkley notes, the president was "probably swayed by his belief that such an ingratiating and palpably unambitious man [Nelson] would not likely challenge the President's own political and administrative pre-eminence."[54]

Red Star Over Washington, D.C., and Hollywood?

The Allies were advancing on all fronts. In the Pacific, the U.S. prevailed at Guadalcanal and in subsequent months the Aleutian Islands and Solomon Islands. In North Africa, Axis forces surrendered in May and Germany abandoned the naval war by ceasing operations in the North Atlantic. Soon thereafter, the British initiated bombing raids on the Ruhr, the main center of German industry. The war exploits of the Soviet Union, especially its hard-won victory at Stalingrad, received wide praise. "Scarcely a negative book about the Soviet Union," Thomas Fleming observed, "was published throughout 1943." The same situation prevailed in Hollywood.[55]

Administration insiders were beginning to see signs that FDR's health was not all that it should be. Some of his bad habits, such as smoking forty Camels per day, were starting to take a toll. He complained to Churchill at Casablanca that he had caught a "bug" and that he was unable to focus after 2:00 P.M. William Allen White also noticed a slowdown in the later hours. "As his speech went on," he observed, "his voice seemed to lose its fire . . . In the final sentences his voice dropped and I could not hear his last three words. But I could see then that the steam in the old boiler . . . had taken its toll of rust." In May 1943, Churchill asked his personal physician: "Have you noticed that the president is a very tired man? His mind seems closed; he seems to have lost his wonderful elasticity." Wendell Willkie, who often visited the White House, was sure that he would be the next president.[56]

The popularity of all things Soviet further escalated after the film *Mission to Moscow* (based on the bestselling book of the same name by former ambassador Joseph E. Davies) premiered in May 1943. Five years earlier, Davies, along with his wife Marjorie Meriweather Post, had spearheaded the campaign to silence anti-FDR radio commentator Boake Carter. Roosevelt was so exuberant about *Mission to Moscow* that he had both provided a blurb ("This book will last") and personally interceded with Jack Warner to adapt it to film. Old Soviet hands at the State Department, by contrast, privately called the book and the movie, "Submission to Moscow."[57]

The lavish movie dramatization was a love letter, even more so than the book, to both the Soviet Union and Roosevelt. An early scene of the movie, *Mission to Moscow*, is a White House meeting in 1936 between Davies (played by Walter Huston) and the president (played by an experienced FDR voice imitator, Jack Young and shot from behind). The two of them break the ice by reminiscing reverently over a signed photo of Woodrow Wilson on Roosevelt's desk. FDR persuades Davies to accept an appointment as ambassador to the Soviet Union to be his eyes and ears there and to help prevent looming war.

On arrival at the Kremlin, Davies finds to his relief the Russian people are much like everyday Americans and that their pragmatic and public-spirited leaders want peace and progress. He meets Stalin, a reassuring, benign, pipe smoking "easy boss." The workers in collective farms and factories are hard-working, dedicated, and happy.

Davies is an eyewitness to the infamous purge trials of 1937. Instead of seeing the defendants as innocent victims who go to their deaths after forced confessions (as many at the time understood), he tells reporters that he is convinced of their guilt. After returning to the U.S., Davies meets again with FDR who suggests that he campaign against America Firsters who are hindering preparedness for war. In public debate sparrings with "isolationists and defeatists," the former ambassador vigorously defends both the Berlin-Moscow Pact, which he praises as an example of wise Soviet "stalling" to allow time to rearm. More stunningly, he blames Finland for the Soviet invasion of that country. Davies predicts a bright future international partnership and discounts fears that the Soviet Union will ever "promote dissension in the internal affairs of other nations."

The widespread pro-Soviet feeling which dominated in 1943 tended to crowd out consideration of much less flattering reports. On April 12th, German radio had announced the discovery of mass graves of murdered Polish soldiers in the Katyn Forest of western Russia. The Nazis and Soviets blamed each other but more objective British and American governmental studies indicated Stalin's guilt. After the fall of the Soviet Union in 1989, documents revealed that in April 1940, the Soviet dictator had ordered the execution and burial of as many as nineteen thousand captured Polish officers, government officials, intellectuals, and landowners.[58]

While Roosevelt never made a public statement, he privately said that he "didn't want to believe it" and, if necessary, would "pretend not to." Meanwhile, Elmer Davis of the Office of War Information, an agency formed to promote the war effort, belittled these reports as "fishy" and "phony propaganda." In media commentary for newsreels, he also cited the Katyn accusations as a nefarious illustration of the Nazi "big lie" technique intended to create divisions among the Allies. When broadcasts from local Polish American radio stations in Detroit and Buffalo began reporting the true facts, the FCC and the Office of War Information silenced them.[59]

The First Bitter Fruit of Unconditional Surrender

The Allied landing at Sicily on July 9th gave Italy an irresistible incentive to defect from the Axis. It also created a most delicate situation in terms of timing and perception. On July 16th, Churchill and FDR issued a "joint message to the people of Italy" which, at the Prime Minister's urging, did not stress unconditional surrender, stating that "the sole hope for Italy's survival lies in honorable capitulation to the overwhelming power of the military forces of the United Nations." Nine days later, the Fascist Grand Council, working with the king, deposed, and then arrested, Mussolini and appointed retired Field Marshal Pietro Badoglio as prime minister. On the next day, Badoglio, even while trying to reassure Germany, distanced Italy from fascism by abolishing the Grand Council.[60]

The prospect for a quick surrender after the fall of Mussolini gave new momentum to Churchill's effort to downplay a cross-Channel invasion and to strike Germany instead from the south. More specifically, he favored a campaign through the Balkans and then onward to Vienna so as to crush "the retreating right flank of German armies" thus saving "middle Europe from the Russians." For this reason, Churchill regarded the imposition of unconditional surrender on Italy as a "grave mistake" which would "break down the whole structure and expression of the Italian state." On July 27th, Eisenhower, who was also leery of the doctrine of unconditional surrender, made a broadcast to the Italian people which called for surrender but did not include the unconditional qualifier.[61]

But FDR had other ideas. In a Fireside Chat on July 23rd, he was resolute "that our terms to Italy are still the same as our terms to Germany and Japan—'Unconditional surrender.' We will have no truck with Fascism in any shape or manner. We will permit no vestige of Fascism to remain." In this one speech, FDR almost completely precluded the possibility of a relatively bloodless surrender. Subsequently, when American officials met Badoglio's emissaries in Lisbon, the Italians balked after Eisenhower (taking his cues from the recent statement of the commander in chief) sent word that any surrender had to be unconditional. The interminable negotiations between the Allies and Italy gave Germany precious time to entrench itself on the Italian peninsula.[62]

Finally on September 3rd, Badoglio, still trying to hide his intentions from Hitler, agreed to an armistice with the Allies which did not include the "unconditional" proviso. To coincide with the official announcement, U.S. General Maxwell Taylor made a clandestine flight to Rome to coordinate a quick seizure of nearby airfields by U.S. airborne troops. But he was too late. He had to hastily cancel the mission because German troops had gotten there first. Badoglio and the king made a hasty escape from Rome and German parachutists rescued Mussolini from confinement at a mountain resort (and he soon headed a puppet government in the north). German troops poured in and took over nearly every part of the peninsula not then under Allied control. On September 20th, the U.S. handed Badoglio a document entitled, "The Unconditional Surrender of Italy." He balked again, pushing for elimination of that phrase, but finally signed nine days later.[63]

The dragged-out negotiations and resultant uncertainty enabled German troops to position themselves to make the Allies pay dearly as they fought their way northward in a war of attrition.

The capture of Rome, which many credible observers had originally projected as a matter of weeks, did not occur until June 1944. When the Italian campaign had finally drawn to a close, the Allies had lost as many as seventy thousand troops and Italy had suffered massive devastation. If Roosevelt had moved swiftly to get flexible surrender terms, the Allies might well have avoided, or at least mitigated, what proved to be a costly northward slog. This "was the first taste," writes historian Thomas Fleming, "of the bitter fruit of unconditional surrender."[64]

In contrast to his stubborn emphasis on unconditional surrender, conditions forced FDR to be more flexible in domestic policy. Wallace's policies on rubber, which had included the squandering of five million dollars on Haitian rubber, had proved an unmitigated disaster. The cost per pound on one of the BEW plantations there was $546! By contrast, plantations owned by Firestone Tire & Company in Liberia, working in tandem with Jesse Jones of the RFC, produced 65,000 tons of natural rubber at a cost of thirty cents a pound. Wallace also proposed spending $400 million in the Amazon Valley, including free food and health care. For FDR, the final straw was a news story and accompanying editorial cartoon in Cissy Patterson's *Washington Times-Herald* which documented Wallace's close ties to mystic Nicholas Roerich, whom he addressed in his letters as "Dear Guru." Roosevelt, his hand finally forced, fired Wallace as BEW head. While the Vice President accepted this humiliation with outward grace, he privately griped that FDR had "betrayed the cause of liberalism."[65]

But the "war within a war" over the control of domestic mobilization was not completely through yet. The New Dealers had lost several consecutive rounds, but they had the advantage of high-placed friends. As long as Wallace was Vice President, and as FDR's health came more into the question, he remained a key player. In foreign policy, perhaps the most important expression of New Dealism was the doctrine of unconditional surrender.

Roosevelt saw total victory as essential to annihilate the old order in Germany and Japan and then build totally anew under close Allied supervision. But unconditional surrender was exacting a devastating toll in blood and destruction by increasing the resolve of Axis troops to fight to the bitter end. Refusal to engage in negotiations, a central premise of FDR's interpretation of that doctrine, also dashed hopes for millions of Europe's Jews.

8

The Culmination of a Failed Presidency

At first glance, the final months of 1943 represented a high-water mark for FDR. The alliance he was leading was beating the Axis on all fronts and a new postwar world order based on international cooperation and democracy appeared imminent. Moreover, American factories were overwhelming the enemy by churning out endless supplies of new weapons.

Judged by other standards, however, this period was a low-water mark for FDR. The president's refusal to negotiate with Axis countries, which also applied to dissident elements or coup leaders, closed off both a possible early end to the war and torpedoed any serious effort to rescue Jews who were behind Axis lines.

Roosevelt looked the other way when key Democratic party allies blatantly violated the Four Freedoms in the United States. One of the most egregious examples was Boss Crump's systematic harassment of black Republican leader, J.B. Martin. In 1943, when Martin briefly returned from exile in Chicago to throw out the first ball at an All-Star Game of the Negro American League, policemen entered his box, put him in a holding cell, and ordered him to leave town. Later recounting his plight to Attorney General Biddle, Martin tentatively asked for help so he could return to settle his business affairs, but "knowing the situation as I do, I am afraid to return." The only official response he received was a statement that Crump's actions did not constitute "any violation of federal law."[1]

Less than a month after Martin's second expulsion, a powerful new champion for free speech in Memphis entered the fray: A. Philip Randolph. Unlike Martin, Randolph had the necessary organizational muscle and immunity from local pressure for a war of attrition. That didn't stop Crump from trying. He ordered County Sheriff Oliver Perry to head off Randolph's scheduled talk at a local Baptist church. Perry brought in twelve local black leaders, took them to a cell, and threatened to arrest them. "If you don't want to meet him at the train and tell him," he specified, "I will." They did as Perry asked.[2]

Undaunted, Randolph redoubled his crusade for free speech by returning a few days later to speak at a black church and college. He unleashed a verbal torrent: "If American soldiers of both races fight for the right of free expression and free assembly, it is our duty on the home front to keep . . . those democratic principles." He took a parting shot at the "spineless Negro stooges" who had met him at the train station. Randolph pointedly asked how it was possible for the Tennessee-born Secretary of State Cordell Hull to spread the Four Freedoms to other countries "when there is no right to freedom of speech and assembly in Memphis, a city of his own state?"[3]

As he fought toe-to-toe with Crump, Randolph was privately urging Eleanor Roosevelt

> to speak out against this species of fascism in our Country. Memphis, it appears to me, is the head front of a native variety of fascism. If we can expose this unamerican and undemocratic rule of Boss Crump, it will help democracy at home and abroad. If Boss Crump can get away with this attack upon one of our Four Freedoms in Memphis, it may become epidemic in America.

The much-delayed reply of the First Lady (who had longtime friendly relations with Crump) was uncharacteristically abrupt: "I referred your letter to a friend of mine when I received it and I am sorry it has not been answered before. I was advised not to do anything, as it might do more harm than good."[4]

"Rescue through Victory"

An ideological first cousin of "Unconditional Surrender" was "Rescue through Victory." Both doctrines shunned any dealings with Axis elements for purposes other than unconditional surrender. As Roosevelt explained in early 1943, "the only terms on which we shall deal with any Axis government, or any Axis factions, are the terms proclaimed at Casablanca: 'Unconditional Surrender'."

There were also more unsavory motivations for "rescue through victory." As R. Borden Reams of the State Department's

Division of European Affairs confided to his colleagues in early 1943: "There was always the danger that the German government might agree to turn over to the United States and to Great Britain a large number of Jewish refugees. In the event of our admission of inability to take care of these people, the onus for the continued persecution would have been largely transferred from the German government to the Allied nations."[5]

By 1943, the ongoing carnage occurring under the policy of "rescue through victory" was severely testing the patience of activists. The American Jewish Congress complained that "if action is delayed until 'the final defeat of Hitler', there may be no Jews left in Europe to save." The most vociferous opponent of "rescue through victory" was Peter Bergson (a pseudonym for Hillel Kook). His Emergency Conference to Save the Jewish People in Europe rejected more staid approaches and pressed for greater flexibility in finding ways to rescue Jews trapped behind Axis lines. It urged the president, for example, to promote the use of neutral countries as havens and to include Jews in prisoner exchange programs and International Red Cross monitoring.[6]

The Emergency Committee won praise from across the ideological spectrum including Harold Ickes, former president Hoover, and publisher baron William Randolph Hearst. Hearst's newspapers featured front-page editorials which proclaimed: "REMEMBER, Americans, THIS IS NOT A JEWISH PROBLEM. It is a HUMAN PROBLEM." Eleanor Roosevelt endorsed the Emergency Committee's proposal for a special governmental agency to help refugees. When she informed her husband, however, his reaction was true to form: "I do not think this needs any answer at this time. F.D.R." The Emergency Committee's most publicized direct-action event was the "We Will Never Die" dramatization, which featured celebrities such as Paul Muni and Edward G. Robinson. When Eleanor sent praise for the Washington, D.C. performance, she appended a restatement of the administration's official policy: "we hope that ways may be found to save as many people as possible, but the best way to do that is to win the war as rapidly as possible and that the allied armies throughout the world are achieving."[7]

Following "We Will Never Die," Bergson arranged for four hundred Orthodox Rabbis to make a pilgrimage to the Capitol for a personal plea to the president. The media gave the scheduled event considerable publicity, but Roosevelt left the White House rather than endure the discomfort. Instead, the bearded rabbis met with Vice President Wallace who, according to *Time*, "squirmed through a diplomatically minimum answer," emphasizing that a rapid victory in the war was the best remedy. The capstone of Bergson's campaign was a full-page advertisement written by Ben Hecht in the *New York Times* on November 5. He said that the ghost of his "Uncle Abraham," who was "sitting on the windowsill two feet away from Mr. Roosevelt," was waiting in vain for the president to act. "The Germans will think that when they kill Jews," Hecht warned, "Stalin, Roosevelt, and Churchill pretend nothing is happening." Two days later, Bernard Baruch complained to Hecht that Roosevelt was "very upset" and wanted a moratorium on this kind of criticism.[8]

Although FDR turned a cold shoulder to the Emergency Committee, Congress was much more receptive. In November, Senator Guy M. Gillette (D-Iowa) proposed a bill for a committee of experts to "effectuate a plan of immediate action designed to save the surviving Jewish people of Europe from extinction at the hands of Nazi Germany." The ideologically diverse cosponsors included Senators Taft and Edwin Johnson (D-Colorado) and the pro-New Deal Rep. Will Rogers (D-California). To forestall "certain action in Congress," however, including potentially embarrassing hearings, FDR issued an executive order in January 1944 creating a War Refugee Board (WRB). Gillette, quite prematurely, declared victory and withdrew his bill.[9]

By this time, Bergson had already gotten under Roosevelt's skin. The administration ordered an FBI investigation, eavesdropped on his phone calls, and scrutinized his financial records. While the ostensible purpose was to uncover evidence of wrongdoing, an internal FBI memo came closer to the truth. It stated that Bergson had "been in the hair of Cordell Hull." The federal investigation lasted for several years but never uncovered any financial irregularities.[10]

An illustration of FDR's inflexibility on unconditional surrender was his response to a series of anti-Hitler plots in 1943 and 1944. One of the early ringleaders was Admiral Wilhelm Canaris, the head of both the Abwehr (military intelligence for the Wehrmacht) and the informal clandestine Front of Decent People. Only weeks after the Casablanca Conference, Canaris travelled to Istanbul to meet with George H. Earle, the president's Special Emissary for Balkan Affairs. He stressed that the best hope for a successful plot was to modify unconditional surrender. FDR's only response to this proposal was to order Earle to cease all contact with Canaris.[11]

Undaunted, the Abwehr head continued through the rest of 1943 to send emissaries to neutral capitals, including Sweden,

Spain, and Switzerland to try to initiate talks with the British and Americans. To prove his good will, he offered to fly a member of the German general staff to London to facilitate any allied landing after modification of unconditional surrender. The offer sufficiently impressed O.S.S. head William Donovan that he made a separate appeal to Roosevelt. In the meantime, Allen Dulles, the OSS station head in Berne, was reporting to Washington that whole streets in Germany were plastered with posters: "Down with Hitler and Stop the War!" None of this impressed Roosevelt who had no intention of negotiating with people whom he regarded as "the East German Junkers."[12]

In his message to Congress on September 17th 1943, the president reaffirmed opposition to any revision of unconditional surrender: "But there is one thing I want to make perfectly clear: When Hitler and the Nazis go out, the Prussian military clique must go with them. The war-breeding gangs of militarists must be rooted out of Germany—and out of Japan—if we are to have any real assurance of future peace." FDR's dedication to unconditional surrender, however, was not restricted to Germany. He applied it with almost equal enthusiasm to Italy and Japan, two countries that had been U.S. allies in World War I.[13]

The Tehran Conference

Even before the president arrived in Tehran for his first meeting with both Stalin and Churchill, he had abandoned any pretense of preserving Polish territorial integrity (the cause célèbres for Britain and France in 1939). In a pre-conference conversation with a visitor at Hyde Park, he endorsed keeping the Molotov-Ribbentrop line drawn by Hitler and Stalin in 1939 as the western Soviet border: "I'm not sure that a fair plebiscite if there ever was such a thing would not show that these eastern provinces would not prefer to go back to Russia."

Stalin assumed control of the negotiating terrain from the outset. He persuaded the president to forgo staying at the American legation in favor of the (heavily bugged) residential quarters of the Soviet embassy. The Americans observed that "more than few Soviet servants" (including hotel maids) were wearing NKVD (secret police) uniforms underneath their outer garments.[14]

A key issue on the agenda was setting a date for a cross-channel invasion (Operation Overlord). which was slated for Normandy. As before, Churchill pushed instead for a campaign in the Balkans while admitting that it might delay Overlord by a month or two.

In a conversation with Eisenhower days earlier, he had "dwelt at length on one of his favorite subjects—the importance of assailing Germany though the 'soft underbelly,' of keeping up the tempo of our Italian attack and extending its scope to include much of the northern shore of the Mediterranean . . . while the project of invasion across the English Channel left him cold." He envisioned Allied forces (perhaps using naval landings on the Adriatic coast) striking through Yugoslavia and on to Vienna to attack German forces retreating from the Russian front.[15]

Stalin was dead set against allowing a second front so uncomfortably close to what he regarded as his special sphere of influence. Instead, he urged the cessation of offensive operations in Italy, though Rome was still in the hands of the enemy, and putting all emphasis on Overlord. As a supplement for that operation, but purely a supplement, he suggested a simultaneous naval landing (diverting forces from Italy) on the southern coast of France. In opposition to Churchill's proposal, Stalin emphasized that "the Balkans are far from Germany" though, as Churchill could have pointed out, Trieste, a likely landing point in the Adriatic, was only 275 miles from Munich, more than three times closer than the distance between the Normandy coast and the Rhine. The Soviet dictator's most compelling counter to Churchill, however, was to point out the difficulties of crossing the Alps.[16]

FDR, not surprisingly, backed Stalin's proposal for a landing in southern France to supplement Overlord, and rejected Churchill's plan for an independent campaign in the Balkans. Those decisions not only transformed the character of the war but also helped to reshape the postwar world. Mark Clark, the commander of American forces in Italy, later lamented that the "weakening of the campaign in Italy in order to invade Southern France, instead of pushing on into the Balkans, was one of the outstanding mistakes of the war...Stalin knew exactly what he wanted...and the thing he wanted most was to keep us out of the Balkans." In fairness, the best window of opportunity for such a campaign may have already closed. The bungled and drawn-out negotiations over the surrender after the fall of Mussolini had given the Germans precious months to reinforce their troops in Italy as well as to fortify the narrow Ljubljana Gap, the main attack pathway through the Alps. By late November 1943, these changed conditions made a successful campaign through the Balkans much less feasible.[17]

Throughout the Tehran Conference, FDR tried to "get at" the Soviet dictator, often at Churchill's expense. With Stalin looking on, he joked at dinner about the Prime Minister's brandy habit and archaic imperial pretensions. As Churchill's face reddened with anger, Roosevelt was happy to see a broad smile appear on Stalin's face which finally brought "a deep heavy guffaw." In continuation of the charm offensive, he asked Stalin if he minded being called "Uncle Joe." This question prompted such delight (at least in the president's retelling) that the Soviet dictator walked from the other side of the table to shake FDR's hand. At another point, Stalin led a toast proposing the summary execution of one hundred thousand German officers but then indicated a willingness to lower this to fifty thousand. In front of an outraged Churchill, who was well aware of the Katyn Forest massacre, Roosevelt made his own toast: "Suppose we compromise and make it 40,000."[18]

FDR was sympathetic to Stalin's drive for a punitive peace (though the two men parted ways on unconditional surrender). They agreed on the goal of breaking up Germany into several separate states even as Churchill expressed discomfort. As he had planned in advance, FDR also quietly assented to the Molotov-Ribbentrop border line though with the proviso that Poland be given "compensation" from German territory up to the Oder River line. The three negotiators expressed little concern that this plan necessitated vast ethnic cleansing of long-established communities (both German and Polish). FDR also assented to Stalin's conquest and annexation of the Baltic republics. Roosevelt, who had long since soured on the Darlan agreement, said that the French ruling class was so irredeemable that it was best to exclude anyone over age forty from a future government. Stalin was leery of Roosvelt's emphasis on the shaky Republic of China as one of the "four policemen" (along with the U.S., the Soviet Union, and the United Kingdom) to maintain peace in the postwar world.[19]

Roosevelt returned home in an upbeat mood. In his first Fireside Chat after Tehran, he exulted that "Marshal Stalin . . . is truly representative of the heart and soul of Russia; and I believe that we are going to get along very well with him and the Russian people—very well indeed."[20]

"God-Awful" Health

The Tehran Conference was also a major turning point in the president's health decline. At the first dinner, for example, Roosevelt had to be wheeled out of the room after "suddenly in the flick of an eye" he "turned green" and started to perspire. He later complained of a high fever and persistent cough which he nicknamed the "Tehran flu." In the coming weeks, Farley commented that "hundreds of persons, high and low, reported to me that he looked bad, his mind wandered, his hands shook, his jaw sagged, and he tired easily."[21]

Obstructing more than helping was Admiral Ross T. McIntire, the president's official physician. An ear, nose, and throat specialist, he won FDR's confidence, and friendship, through treatments of his sinus problem. The grateful patient appointed him as official presidential physician which, in turn, eventually led to promotions to Admiral and Surgeon General of the navy. "McIntire over the years," observes historian David M. Jordan, "took care of Roosevelt's sinuses, and FDR took care of McIntire." Credibly described as a "medical ignoramus" or as "more courtier than doctor," his first inclination was to minimize any problem.[22]

At the insistence of FDR's daughter, Anna Roosevelt Boettiger, who did not trust McIntire's reassurances, a team of specialists conducted an examination at Bethesda Naval Hospital on March 28th. Their report revealed severe hypertension, serious enlargement in the heart, and alarming indicators of congestive heart failure. The head of the team, cardiologist Howard Bruenn heard a "blowing sound" in the president's heart which evidenced severe pressure on the aortic valve. Bruenn concluded that the patient's condition was "God-awful" and that he could die any minute. According to journalist David Brinkley, FDR clearly "did not have the strength and stamina to preside for another four years over the end of a world war and the complexities and dangers to follow it. It is probably not too much to say that he was already dying."[23]

McIntire shamelessly stepped forward as the public face of a coverup with the press. On April 4th, he told reporters that the Bethesda examination had revealed nothing to worry about and implied, quite wrongly, that he spoke for Bruenn. McIntire declared that "we decided for a man of sixty-two-plus, we had very little to argue about." He continued: "About all he needed" was "some sunshine and more exercise."[24]

But McIntire's mendacities aside, the patient's condition did not improve. A Secret Service officer later recalled finding the president laying on the floor beside his wheelchair six times in 1944 and 1945. Also, FDR's hands shook so much that he could no longer shave himself. In late May, Turner Catledge, the *New York Times* political reporter "was shocked and horrified" when he visited the White House. His first impulse on seeing the president "was to turn around and leave . . . I knew I was looking at a terribly sick man . . . Repeatedly he would lose his train of thought, stop and stare blankly at me. It was an agonizing experience for me."[25]

Dr. New Deal Prescribes an Economic Bill of Rights

In December 1943, FDR made a very public show of adopting a new wartime persona. He gave a speech indicating that he intended to shelve the New Deal for the duration of the war. He used the analogy, quite ironic given his own considerable health ailments, of physician and patient.

Many years ago, that "old Dr. New Deal," who specialized in "internal medicine" had treated an "awfully sick patient called the United States of America." The search for a cure took a "number of years" and finally succeeded. But two years ago, the needs of the patient changed after a "bad accident . . . on the seventh of December." This new medical challenge required the services of an "orthopedic surgeon, Dr. Win-the-War." His expert treatment had finally led the patient to throw away his crutches. Though on the mend, full recovery was contingent on complete victory in the war.[26]

Roosevelt's "Dr. New Deal" returned from retirement with a vengeance less than two weeks later in the State of the Union Address. Described by James MacGregor Burns as his most "radical speech in his life," it proposed an "Economic Bill of Rights." The starting premise was that the Bill of Rights of 1791, with its focus on such rights as free speech and trial by jury, had "proved inadequate to assure us equality in the pursuit of happiness." Hence, Congress had an obligation to implement a charter of additional "self-evident" rights. FDR's open-ended list to assure the new "basis of security," included the "right to a useful and remunerative job . . . to a good education . . . to earn enough to provide adequate food and clothing and recreation . . . to a decent home . . . to adequate medical care . . . to adequate protection from the economic fears of old age, sickness, accident, and unemployment." It would also guarantee "every farmer" the right "to raise and sell his products at a return which will give him and his family a decent living and "every businessman . . . freedom from unfair competition."[27]

The "economic rights" advocated by Roosevelt (unlike the more "negative rights" in the original bill of rights) required significant tax increases for even minimal implementation. But Americans, already weighted down with sky-high marginal rates, balked at that prospect. Americans earning $4,000 dollars (about $71,000 in 2025) paid a marginal rate of 26 percent while those with incomes over $500,000 paid 98.7 percent. That paid by those with incomes of more than a million dollars was over 100 percent!

A barometer of public anger about these burdens was the popularity of a proposed constitutional amendment to limit federal taxes to 25 percent on incomes, gifts, and inheritance. In 1944, seventeen of the necessary thirty-two states had approved a call for a constitutional convention to ratify it.[28]

Much to the president's dismay, the Revenue Bill that landed on his desk in February took a status quo approach and did not raise any rates. His stinging veto message characterized it as "not a tax bill but a tax relief bill providing relief not for the needy but for the greedy." The veto message sparked rebellion in Congress. The normally loyal Senator Alben Barkley (D-Kentucky) resigned as majority leader in protest. Both houses overwhelmingly voted to override. According to Senator Claude Pepper (D-Florida), who was very much in the New Deal camp, the "senators, with three or four exceptions, rose and applauded. Then they filed by Barkley's seat to shake his hand while the packed galleries cheered." The Democrats then defiantly reelected him as majority leader.[29]

Japanese Americans had particular reason to regard the Economic Bill of Rights as a cruel joke. For them, a "decent home" often meant a desert dormitory with Army-issued cots. Any "remunerative job" in the camps paid considerably less than if performed by a white counterpart. The freedom from "unfair competition" meant nothing to people shorn of their businesses because of confinement in the camps. If the 1791 Bill of Rights was "inadequate" to assure "equality in the pursuit of happiness" that shortcoming applied with double force to the loss of the First through Tenth Amendment rights of Japanese Americans.

By this time, however, top administration officials were pressing Roosevelt to shut down the internment camps. They pointed out that any purported "military necessity" or dangers to the West Coast because Japan was in retreat on all fronts. At the same time, the exploits in the European theater of Nisei volunteers in the 442nd Regimental Combat Team had created a positive impression among Americans. In December 1943, Biddle warned the president that the "present practice of keeping loyal American citizens in concentration camps on the basis of race for longer than is absolutely necessary is dangerous and repugnant to the principles of our Government." But Roosevelt did not want to rock the boat on the eve of the 1944 campaign.[30]

Moreover, the president's private comments did not indicate a softening of his own racial animus. His assistant, William D. Hassett, said that he had "related an old Chinese myth about the origin of the Japanese. A wayward daughter of an ancient Chinese emperor left her native land in a sampan and finally reached Japan, then inhabited by baboons. The inevitable happened and in due course the Japanese made their appearance." Roosevelt also speculated that Japanese skulls were less developed and that this had accentuated "devious and treacherous" traits. That idea so fascinated him that he asked the eminent anthropologist Aleš Hrdlička, "Could that be dealt with surgically?"[31]

When Ickes suggested again in June that the president close the camps, the response he received immediately focused on the possible political cost. "The more I think...of suddenly ending the orders excluding Japanese Americans from the West Coast," he told Ickes, "the more I think it would be a mistake to do anything too drastic or sudden." Seemingly reading the president's mind after reporting to him that Stimson and Assistant Secretary of War John J. McCloy also wanted to end internment, Under Secretary of State Edward R. Stettinius Jr. (who agreed with Stimson and McCloy) interjected: "The question appears to be largely a political one, the reaction in California, on which I am sure you will probably wish to reach your own decision."[32]

If the Economic Bill of Rights included the taint of racial double standard so too did the Servicemen's Readjustment Act of 1944 (better known as the GI Bill of Rights). The genesis was Roosevelt's call in October 1943 for a massive program to educate and retrain returning soldiers. The bill began to work its way through Congress in January 1944 and reached the Oval Office in June. A key drafter was Rep. John Rankin (D-Mississippi), the chair of the Committee on World War II Legislation who, during the New Deal, had run interference for FDR on the Death Sentence and the Key West scandal. Rankin ensured, as Ira Katznelson puts it, that the final product made "Jim Crow safe," by giving local district committees control over benefit eligibility and dispersal.[33]

Because of that provision, many Southern blacks did not even fill out applications. Although African Americans were nearly half of Mississippi's population, only 2,600 (compared to 16,000 whites from the state) had applied by 1946 for unemployment benefits under the bill. There was also evidence of widespread disparities outside of the South, however. Of seven thousand mortgages insured under the GI Bill in New York and the northern New Jersey suburbs during this period African Americans held fewer than one hundred.

The Veterans Editor of the *Pittsburgh Courier* concluded that the "the veterans' program had completely failed veterans of minority races." One year later, a study by the racially integrated American Veterans Committee concluded that it was "as though the G.I. Bill has been earmarked 'For White Veterans Only'." While many blacks in subsequent decades were able to benefit from the GI Bill after the breakdown of Jim Crow at the local level, the wartime and immediate postwar period presents a much more bleak picture[34]

The 1791 Bill of Rights Under Siege

Even as FDR was proclaiming a menu of new rights, his other actions were systemically undermining those listed in the Bill of Rights of 1791. In January 1944 the Justice Department announced indictments of thirty defendants in *U.S. v. McWilliams* under the Smith Act of 1940 making it a felony to cause insubordination in the armed forces. With the notable exception of Japanese American internment, no legal action better summarized the president's attitudes toward constitutional rights during this period. In relying on the highly malleable standard of "sedition," the government followed such discredited anti-free speech precedents as the prosecution of Eugene Debs in World War 1.

Ironically, Attorney General Biddle had mostly intended the case as a sop to his boss. Roosevelt had wanted a far more ambitious prosecution of leading pre-war noninterventionists, including publishers in the so-called Patterson-McCormick Axis. Assembled in Washington, D.C., from all over the United States, the defendants were a bizarre and diverse amalgam of ex-Bundists, anti-Semites, Roosevelt haters, and obscure right-wing cranks. They included Elizabeth Dilling, the author of hyperbolic red-baiting books, Joseph McWilliams, who had run for Congress in 1940 under the banner of the American Destiny Party, and Lawrence Dennis, a Harvard-educated veteran of the American foreign service.[35]

More obscure, but probably more representative of the defendants, was Elmer J. Garner (age 78), proprietor of *Publicity*, a small weekly in Wichita, Kansas, and one of the publications that had lost its second-class mailing status under the Espionage Act. While Garner, like most other defendants, was antisemitic and Anglophobic, he did not derive these views from Nazi influence but from his much earlier activism in the Farmers' Alliance. But even Garner was typical of most alleged seditionists in offering support for the current war. After Pearl Harbor, in fact, he pledged support for "OUR PRESIDENT and our leader in this extraordinary emergency."[36]

Prosecutors had originally named in the indictment, but then wisely dropped, the more mainstream William Griffin, the publisher of the Hearst-affiliated *New York Enquirer*, later renamed the *National Enquirer*. Like Garner, he had pledged support for the president after Pearl Harbor. But Griffin was able to produce numerous past testimonials from politicians and Jewish leaders. More dramatically, he had a 1932 letter from then-Governor Roosevelt, asking him to give a seconding speech for his presidential nomination at the Democratic convention in Chicago and praising his "fine spirit of fair play and good citizenship."[37]

The most sensationalistic allegation was participation in a worldwide conspiracy to "destroy democracy" in favor of a "national socialist or fascist" regime. A problem with the picture drawn by the prosecution of a more generalized conspiracy is that many of the defendants did not even know, much less particularly like, each other. The judge, Edward C. Eicher, a Roosevelt loyalist, gaveled the trial to order on April 17th 1944, in the US District Court of the District of Columbia, to much media fanfare. Twenty-five reporters and twenty-two defense lawyers (plus prosecutors) crowded into the courtroom, leaving only twenty seats for spectators.[38]

Initial press coverage, especially on the political left, was overwhelmingly favorable to the prosecution. The *New Masses,* similar to other leftwing publications, however, tempered its praise by complaining that the government was too fixated on the "small fry" and needed to "lay hands on the main culprits." No wonder, the Communist Party's *Daily Worker* commented, that "this trial makes the [*New York*] *Daily News* nervous. After all, the defendants are being tried for publishing the kind of material in which the *Daily News* specializes." The pro-New Deal *Chicago Sun* rejected out of hand any possibility that the defendants were on trial for "entertaining certain social or political beliefs."[39]

George S. Schuyler, recently under FBI scrutiny for his hard-hitting articles in the *Pittsburgh Courier*, was a rarity in depicting the plights of the sedition trial defendants, Japanese Americans, and African Americans as analogous and interdependent. The Roosevelt administration, according to Schuyler, was persecuting the defendants for what they "said and wrote," and had presented no evidence of collusion or participation in a conspiracy. If these individuals were culpable for opposing the policies of Roosevelt or his subordinates, he asked (following the same approach as his defense of Japanese Americans), "then who is safe? I may be nabbed for speaking harshly about Brother Stimson's treatment of Negro lads in the Army."[40]

In the first weeks of the proceedings, the sometimes jaw-dropping antics of the defendants gave reporters good copy. As a movie camera captured the moment on film, a photographer snapped pictures of Lois de Lafayette Washburn (who claimed to be descended from the famous Frenchman) thumbing her nose at the Capitol building and giving a stiff-armed fascist salute. She also slapped a photographer and proclaimed, on hearing her name called in court, "Lafayette we are here to defend what you gave us—our freedom from tyranny."[41]

The novelty of all this soon wore off, however, as thirty often vulgarly rambunctious defendants, most represented by separate counsel, competed for the limelight. When prosecutors said the defendants had "picked out" a fuehrer to rule them, their chanted response was "Who? Who?" They appeared amused when they named retired General George Van Horn Moseley, former second in command in the army, though no evidence was presented that any defendant had contact with him after 1939.

Howls of laughter greeted the prosecutors' characterization of Lawrence Dennis as "The Alfred Rosenberg of the movement in this country." Although Judge Eicher's rulings reflexively favored the prosecution, he never got control of the courtroom. The disorder became ever more tedious for all concerned. The ex-prosecutor Kenesaw M. Landis II of the pro-New Deal *Chicago Sun*, who gradually lost faith in the prosecution, confessed that he felt like he was "in a zoo, with the Judge a rather careless keeper."[42]

In April, the same month that the sedition trial began, Americans were picking sides over the most dramatic case of individual civil disobedience during World War II. At the center was Sewell Avery, the president of Montgomery Ward, a leading department store chain. Federal regulators accused Avery of violating a federal "maintenance of membership" rule that companies fire any employee who failed to join a union. Avery had rejected a union contract for Montgomery Ward containing the rule which he argued only applied to defense industries. The union called on the War Labor Board for help and Attorney General Biddle demanded access to the company's books. To this, Avery answered: "To hell with the government." Obeying Biddle's orders to "Take him out!" the two soldiers, offering profuse apologies to Avery, linked hands and carried the sixty-nine-year-old corporate executive, clad in his business suit, from the building. As they took him away, he glowered at Biddle: "You—you New Dealer." A Gallup poll showed that six out of ten Americans agreed with Avery, not the government.[43]

At about this time, Roosevelt's friend George Earle arrived at the Oval Office after returning from Istanbul. He brought with him compelling evidence of Stalin's guilt in the Katyn Massacre including horrific photos of the mass execution scene as well as testimony from eyewitnesses. The president did not want to entertain doubts which contradicted his "Uncle Joe" conception of Stalin. He testily told his old friend that "this is entirely German propaganda and a German plot. I am absolutely convinced the Russians did not do this."[44]

The "Dump Wallace" Movement

In contrast to 1940, FDR, while repeatedly stating his reluctance to do so, indicated in the months before the convention a willingness to run. The main question was the fate of Henry A. Wallace on the ticket. Democratic National Committee Chair Bob Hannegan had assembled an anti-Wallace cabal of big city bosses, top party officials, and major donors. They argued that the vice president's unorthodox inclinations, including a fascination with eastern religion and horoscopes, and advocacy of leftist views turned off too many voters. An invaluable member of the group was Roosevelt's appointment secretary General Edwin "Pa" Watson, who controlled the president's schedule.

While FDR the New Dealer liked Wallace, and wanted to keep him, FDR the candidate recognized the political liabilities of doing so. But Wallace also had powerful friends. Early on, when the president still had not decided to seek a third term, Eleanor had encouraged Wallace to consider running as Roosevelt's natural heir should her husband retire from the race.[45]

Instead of making an up or down decision about his choice for vice presidential candidate, FDR procrastinated through a divide and conquer strategy. While he promised not to "dictate" to the delegates, he offered both subtle and open encouragement to several potential candidates. The possibilities under consideration at various points were James Byrnes, the Director of the Office of War Mobilization, sometimes dubbed "assistant president," Speaker Sam Rayburn of Texas, Supreme Court Justice William O. Douglas, Senator Barkley, and Cordell Hull (who did not want to run for health reasons). Barely on the radar for Roosevelt was Senator Harry S Truman of Missouri. When Wallace began a lengthy good-will tour to Russia and China, the vice president seemed unaware that he was leaving the country exactly when the campaign against him was gathering steam.[46]

Meanwhile, Wallace's supporters pled his case in his absence. In June, FDR told Secretary Morgenthau that Eleanor was tirelessly hounding him to "insist" (as he had in 1940), that the delegates nominate Wallace. Morgenthau, a backer of removing Wallace, pointed out that delegates at a recent party conference in Kentucky had ripped the vice president's picture off the wall as onlookers cheered. Wallace had measurable popular support, however. A Gallup poll in March put him as the clear preference at 46 percent, followed by Hull at a distant second of 21 percent. Wallace was still out of the country, and thus unable to share the credit, when the Allies made the much-delayed capture of Rome on June 4th and, two days later, successfully landed at Normandy in Operation Overlord and by the end of August, the Allies were in Paris.[47]

Despite this continued progress on the battlefield, dangers loomed on the horizon for the president. The Republicans had rallied behind the youthful New York Governor Thomas E. Dewey, a former star prosecutor of gangland figures. While Dewey, like Landon and Willkie, pulled his punches on the New Deal, he subtly raised Roosevelt's chief vulnerabilities. Democrats, he declared in his acceptance speech, "tell us is that in its [the New Deal's] young days it did some good things. That we freely grant. But now it has grown old in office. It has become tired and quarrelsome. It seems that the great men who founded this nation really did know what they were talking about when they said that three terms were too many." The anti-Wallace forces repeatedly emphasized to Roosevelt that any running mate needed to add votes beyond the already secure New Deal base.[48]

Soon after Wallace returned to U.S. soil in early July, he met with the president who was still playing his double game. FDR confessed that he was under great pressure to replace him on the ticket. He also dangled the prospect of a prominent place in "world economic affairs" in his "very progressive" next term and specified an intent after the election to remove Wallace's nemesis Jesse ("Jesus H.") Jones. On the other side, however, FDR rejected point blank Wallace's offer to withdraw from the vice-presidential contest and agreed to draft a message saying he would vote for Wallace if he were a delegate.[49]

If any mystery remained about Roosevelt's candidacy, he removed it on July 11th in a statement to the *New York Herald Tribune*. As in 1940, he depicted himself as an unwilling candidate compelled to public service. "If the convention should carry this out, and nominate me for the Presidency, I shall accept. If the people elect me I will serve . . . I do not want to run . . . reluctantly, but as a good soldier, I repeat that I will accept and serve in this office, if I am ordered by the Commander in Chief of us all—the sovereign people of the United States."[50]

July 11th was a turning point in the veepstakes. Roosevelt met after dinner at the White House with Hannegan and other members of the anti-Wallace cabal. Those present, including big donor Ed Pauley, New York Democratic boss Ed Flynn, Postmaster General Frank Walker, and Chicago Mayor Ed Kelly, assessed the pros and cons of each possibility. Although Byrnes was a favorite for the president, Sidney Hillman of the powerful CIO-PAC, strongly objected. His main sticking points were Byrnes's past white supremacist statements on race and enforcement of the "little steel formula" wage limits as a wartime administrator. In exchange for keeping Byrnes off the ticket, however, Hillman agreed to back away from Wallace. When the group recommended Truman, FDR went along but with no enthusiasm. Unbeknownst to everyone else in the room, he was still egging on Byrnes, telling him, for example, that he was "the best qualified man in the whole outfit." Byrnes was so certain of success that he asked Truman to nominate him but Truman, after initially agreeing, begged off after finding out about the decision of the meeting on July 11th. On hearing that Barkley was going to give a speech to nominate FDR, Byrnes told him: "If I were you, I wouldn't say anything too complimentary about him."[51]

Wallace was not about to go quietly. He took hope from FDR's final statement (made at Wallace's earlier request) on July 14th that he would "personally would vote for his [Wallace's] renomination if I were a delegate to the convention," while promising not to dictate to the delegates. Even at this late date, Wallace still had a chance. A key obstacle was that the "enemy" (namely DNC Chair Hannegan) controlled the convention machinery. But Wallace's commitment to principle also worked against him. Over the objections of his more politic backers, his convention speech called for repeal of the poll tax, thus alienating a wide swath of potential Southern support.[52]

Roosevelt's acceptance speech emphasized that he had felt compelled to accept a nomination "offered me—in spite of my desire to retire to the quiet of private life." He said that it was not "fitting" for him to campaign in the normal sense; he made sure to get in a dig against his opponent. "The people of the United States will decide this fall whether they wish to turn over this 1944 job—this worldwide job—to inexperienced or immature hands . . . or whether they wish to leave it to those who saw the danger from abroad, who met it head-on, and who now have seized the offensive and carried the war to its present stages of success."[53]

By this time, FDR had resumed his relationship with the recently widowed Lucy Mercer Rutherford, his mistress from the Wilson era. With the reluctant cooperation of his daughter Anna, and behind Eleanor's back, the couple had several clandestine meetings at the White House, FDR's Hyde Park home, and, sometimes, Lucy's New Jersey estate. Anna justified the deception as necessary to buoy the president's spirits in a time of failing health.[54]

Untried Rescues, "Junker Plots"

Despite FDR's continued absolutist statements about "rescue through victory," the creation of the War Refugee Board (WRB) in January 1944 opened a small sliver of flexibility. The WRB helped arrange escape routes for Jews through neutral countries, such as Spain and Turkey, and facilitated an active underground behind Axis lines. According to Wyman, "Roosevelt took little interest [in the WRB] except as a source of occasional favorable publicity." Although voluntary contributions (mostly from Jews) funded more than 90 percent of the WRB's slim budget, it made the most of these meager resources. It cooperated with diplomat Raoul Wallenberg who, while in Budapest, single handedly saved twenty thousand Hungarian Jews by issuing them Swedish passports. "What we did was little enough," the WRB's director later recalled, "Late and little, I would say."[55]

The WRB was a positive step but more substantial opportunities were slipping away, most notably a failure to exploit the widening fissure between the Hungarian strongman Admiral Nicholas Horthy and the Axis. Horthy offered to allow the immigration of all Jewish children under age ten who had foreign visas and all other Jews who had Palestine certificates (granted by the British government). For a full month after this proposal, the British and Americans bickered about details. When they finally agreed to find havens for the refugees, it was too late. Hitler had closed off any further movement across Hungary's borders, leading to almost certain death for the vast majority of Hungary's two hundred thousand Jews. Wyman laments that "no matter what the outcome might have been, the month's delay in responding remains unconscionable."[56]

Meanwhile, the Roosevelt administration was tragically uninterested in the potential use of American bombers to destroy either the Nazi killing machines or transport lines to them. Such raids had become quite feasible by 1944 because of Allied control of the skies. On June 18th, the president of the Brooklyn-based Agudath Israel urged bombing the railways into Auschwitz, using detailed sketches from escapees of the layout of the camp and location of the gas chambers. The War Department answered with the familiar objection that it would entail a wasteful "diversion of considerable air support essential to the success of our forces" and that the "most effective relief which can be given to victims of enemy persecution is to insure the speedy defeat of the Axis."[57]

Contradicting the "diversion" excuse, Allied planes had flown repeatedly in close proximity. On August 20th, for example, a fleet of over one hundred U.S. bombers hit oil factories less than five miles from Auschwitz. A foray to also hit the gas chambers would have delayed that mission by mere minutes. While the Germans were usually able to quickly repair damaged tracks, it could take weeks (especially late in the war) for them to do the same for tunnels, viaducts, and bridges. Despite additional proposals to bomb Auschwitz, the War Department never bothered to conduct a feasibility study or consult the Air Force. The most serious attempt to destroy the death camps was a suicidal uprising of prisoners in Auschwitz in October 1944, who successfully blew up one of the crematorium buildings.[58]

Just before D-Day, Admiral Canaris of the Front of Decent People pressed again for a conditional surrender formula in an appeal to British security head, Stewart Menzies. In another show of good faith, he had leaked valuable intelligence about the German Army's anti-invasion defenses, including its order of battle, and had secured the cooperation of General Erwin Rommel. When the British restated it was impossible to modify unconditional surrender, the Admiral exclaimed in desperation: "Finis Germaniae."[59]

By this point, leadership in the Front of Decent People was already shifting to the thirty-seven-year-old Colonel Claus von Stauffenberg. Von Stauffenberg's background ran completely counter to FDR's stereotype of an atavistic East Prussian junker. He was a Catholic and came from a noble family in the principality of Wurttemberg, historically one of the most liberal parts of Germany. Von Stauffenberg brought two powerful bombs (both provided by the Abwehr) in a briefcase to a meeting at Hitler's headquarters in eastern Germany. In the restroom, he successfully set one of the timers, a major challenge for a man with only two fingers. After leaving on a pretext, he heard an explosion and boarded a plane, thinking that Hitler was dead. The plot came apart after confirmation that the Fuehrer had survived and von Stauffenberg, and most of those around him, were executed.[60]

Instead of citing the plot as a beacon to inspire greater German resistance to Hitler, Roosevelt reacted with total silence. The only kind words, ironically, came from the Soviet Union. Stalin's Free Germans Committee declared: "Generals, officers, soldiers . . . turn your arms against Hitler. Do not fail these courageous men!"[61]

"We Either Have to Castrate the German People Or . . ."

The Morgenthau Plan was a rare case when FDR suffered political blowback from his Carthaginian approach to the Axis. Roosevelt had given the inspiration in a conversation he had with Morgenthau on August 18th. "We have got to be tough with Germany," Roosevelt had told him, "and I mean the German people, not just the Nazis. We either have to castrate the German people or you have to go to treat them in such manner so they can't just go on reproducing people who want to continue the way they have in the past." The main point of the Morgenthau Plan was to strip Germany of all industry and subdivide the land into small agricultural plots. It also prohibited the wearing of "any military uniform or any uniform of any quasi-military organization." For good measure, it banned all military parades and, since a nation of subsistence farmers did not need planes, prohibited all aircraft.[62]

FDR had more than sufficient warning that the Morgenthau Plan might backfire against him. Stimson argued that it "will tend through bitterness and suffering to breed another war." Determined to press ahead anyway, FDR stressed that "every person in Germany should realize that this time Germany is a defeated nation . . . if they need food to keep body and soul together beyond what they have, they should be fed three times a day with soup from Army soup . . . they will remember that experience all their lives." Churchill's first reaction on hearing about the plan at the Second Quebec Conference in August compared it to "chaining himself to a dead German." But this resistance was fleeing. Churchill shifted ground after it became apparent that his "cooperation" was necessary for Britain to get an additional $6.5 billion ($110 billion in current dollars) in Lend-Lease assistance. What do you want me to do," the Prime Minister asked in consternation, "stand up and beg like Fala [Roosevelt's dog]?" Churchill finally backed down and co-signed a memorandum (adding some softened, but meaningless, verbiage) to convert Germany "into a country primarily agricultural and pastoral in its character." According to Hull, the British "had joined in on this extreme starvation plan in order to get Morgenthau's help in obtaining six and a half billion dollars credit proposed by the Secretary of the Treasury."[63]

As more details leaked out, however, it became obvious that just about everybody hated the Morgenthau Plan. It may have been the final straw which led Secretary Hull to resign. Dewey charged that the plan would only stiffen German resistance while propaganda chief Joseph Goebbels called it a plot to convert Germany into a giant potato patch. General George Marshall was so upset that he complained to Morgenthau that "Just as the army placed loudspeakers at the front urging Germans to surrender," the news of his plan had "stiffened the will of the Germans to resist."

FDR, the political realist, moved to cut his losses, by casting Morgenthau in the role of scapegoat. When the Treasury Secretary came to his office, the president kept him waiting at the door. He also reassured Stimson that he never contemplated turning Germany into an agricultural state, innocently quipping that "Henry Morgenthau pulled a boner." As the persistent Morgenthau seems to have suspected, however, FDR's reversal rested on political considerations, not an ideological shift. "I never heard my husband say that he had changed his attitude on the plan," Eleanor recalled. "I think the repercussions brought about by the press stories made him feel it was wise to abandon [it] at that time."[64]

Even as he looked forward to a punitive peace, Roosevelt's response to the Warsaw Uprising showed his continuing deference to Stalin. In late July, local units of the underground "Home Army" affiliated with the anti-Communist Polish government in exile in London, had struck back against the occupiers after the German governor of Poland had ordered the conscription of an additional one hundred thousand Polish men for forced labor. Using arms that had been stowed away since 1939, the Poles marched on the Jewish Warsaw Ghetto, liberating hundreds of Jewish prisoners who took up arms alongside them. Although radio broadcasts from Moscow had previously encouraged the city to rise up against the Nazis, the Soviets stood back. An exasperated Churchill entreated Stalin to allow RAF pilots to provide airdrops from Soviet airfields, but to no avail. Stalin, who had just authorized a Polish puppet government in Lublin, condemned the Home Army's struggle as a "reckless and terrible adventure." Despite appeals from both Churchill and the U.S. ambassador, W. Averell Harriman, the president approved a telegram which instructed the embassy not to press the Soviet dictator on the issue. "There is a tendency on the part of the British," it elaborated, "to go considerably farther than the president is prepared to go." Meanwhile, the Nazis were rushing in reinforcements. Starved from a lack of outside support, the Warsaw Uprising collapsed after a month of fighting.[65]

The Fala Speech and War Victories

Despite FDR's Morgenthau Plan blunder and other missteps, Dewey was unable to make any headway. Part of the problem was the Republican candidate himself. "In public Dewey came across as pompous and cold," David Brinkley observes. "And for good reason." Roosevelt's handlers proved adept at keeping their sick and enfeebled boss insulated from prying eyes. Moreover, though much diminished in capacity, the president's reservoirs of charm and biting humor had still not completely run dry.[66]

Proof of this was the iconic "Fala speech" in late September delivered for a dinner organized by the Teamsters. Using an idea first suggested by actor Orson Welles, Roosevelt brought the house down with his retort to accusations that he had sent a destroyer to pick up his dog from the Aleutians: "These Republican leaders have not been content with attacks on me, or my wife, or on my sons. No, not content with that, they now include my little dog, Fala. Well, of course, I don't resent attacks, and my family doesn't resent attacks, but Fala does resent them . . . He has not been the same dog since." Eight years later, Richard Nixon used it as a model for his equally successful "Checkers Speech." The Fala speech was a defining moment in the campaign and Dewey, who had tried to sell himself as a champion of youthful initiative, fumbled a response. Instead of letting it slide or playing along, he acted as a killjoy by condemning the speech as "snide." The whispering about a tired and ailing president temporarily fell by the wayside. "Even the stoniest of Republican faces around U.S. radios," *Time* commented, "cracked into a smile over the Fala story." Events in the war were also breaking in Roosevelt's favor. The Allies entered Germany from the west and MacArthur fulfilled his pledge to "return" to the Philippines.[67]

Safety First

But to Roosevelt this was not the time to take any political risks. He remained adamantly against an early release of Japanese Americans from concentration camps. Ickes lamented that it was "the President himself who has insisted that the ban not be lifted until after the election." FDR's icy cynicism of intentionally leaving Japanese Americans to languish behind barbed wire during this period is impossible to explain away. Despite appeals from cabinet members and officials such as the head of the War Relocation Authority, Roosevelt clung to the status quo because of electoral motivations. His decision to keep Japanese Americans in the camps, writes Peter Irons, so as "to gain partisan advantage in the 1944 elections—provides a final count in the indictment of his political leadership."[68]

In the November election, Roosevelt prevailed comfortably by 53 to 45 percent in the popular vote and 412 to 99 in the electoral college. It was the closest presidential margin since 1916. Turnout was high and Sidney Hillman's CIO-PAC was instrumental in registering union members (the CIO alone had grown to four million members) and getting them to the polls. For Democratic insiders, any celebration was tempered by the realities of the president's health. On returning from a victory party, Truman told a friend that "The last time that he saw Mr. Roosevelt the pallor of death was on his face and he knew he would be president before the term was out."[69]

The Final Act for the Sedition Trial and Japanese Internment

The Sedition Trial, still grinding along after six months, had descended into chaos. The extended lectures by prosecutors on the history of worldwide National Socialism presented all-too-inviting opportunities for twenty-two defense lawyers to challenge any claims. And, indeed, in the seven months of the trial prosecutors gave them plenty to object to. The mound of evidentiary paper rose so high that the government was unable to supply enough copies for the defense counsel. Even many of the hardened "New Deal lawyers" appointed by the court had become disdainful of the prosecution's case and acted accordingly.

Long before this, the daily "dreary farce," as Biddle privately called it, had dropped from the front pages. The ranks of newspapers covering the trial, once as high as twenty-five, thinned to only leave a few stalwarts, including the *Daily Worker*. The most monumental of the dropouts was the *Washington Post*, which had played a major role as an instigator. In a complete turnabout, the paper compared the proceedings to the Moscow purge trials engineered by Stalin in the late 1930s and as "a black mark against American justice for many years to come."[70]

The end (or de facto end) was dramatic. On November 30th 1944, Judge Eicher, "worn out and unhappy," died of a heart attack in his sleep. No wonder. Prosecutors had barely begun to present their case and had some two hundred witnesses lined up. The *Saturday Evening Post* spoke for many when it editorialized that "only the death of Judge Eicher availed to release American justice from an exhibition far more appropriate to the court rooms of Berlin and Moscow than to those of the United States."[71]

Earlier in November, the president had privately decided to wind down Japanese internment but decided to keep the plan secret until two pending Supreme Court rulings. Through his contacts on the Court, Roosevelt had advance knowledge of the general outcome of *Korematsu* (which upheld the constitutionality of Executive Order 9066) and *Endo* (which convolutedly both called for the release of current internees and upheld the executive order). In the meantime, however, a news conference on November 21st offered a typically Rooseveltian hint that something was afoot. When asked about the continuing incarceration of Japanese Americans, Roosevelt mused, "It is felt by a great many lawyers that under the Constitution they can't be locked up in concentration camps." The president's use of the term "concentration camps" stands in contrast to those who now use less sinister labels such as internment or relocation camps. When a reporter asked if the lack of espionage by Japanese Americans had made the orders unnecessary, the president answered in feigned innocence, "That I couldn't tell you because I don't know." He did know. He had secretly decided the issue long before he spoke.[72]

On December 17th, just one day before the Court handed down *Korematsu* and *Endo*, the War Department publicly announced what Roosevelt had already decided in early November. It said that Japanese Americans who had passed loyalty screenings would, after January 2nd 1945, be "permitted the same freedom of movement throughout the United States as other loyal and law-abiding citizens." The effect of this decision was to render both *Endo* and *Korematsu* almost entirely moot. By early 1946, the federal government had completely emptied the camps.[73]

Concentration camps for Japanese Americans constituted Roosevelt's greatest violation of the Bill of Rights but they were also part of a pattern. Even if he had never signed Executive Order 9066, his overall record in protecting the Bill of Rights ranks worst, or nearly the worst, of any president. If considered as a puzzle piece on the board, internment was an outsized piece, but it was still one among many.

Only ten days after the announced end of internment, Roosevelt ordered the War Department to seize Montgomery Ward because of Avery's refusal to carry out the maintenance of membership rule. "We cannot allow Montgomery Ward to set aside the wartime policies of the United States Government," he wrote to Stimson, "just because Mr. Sewell Avery does not approve of the Government's procedure for handling labor disputes."[74]

The ever more enfeebled FDR began his fourth term on January 20th with the shortest inauguration speech in American history, clocking in at just over six minutes. Rather than personally greeting his guests, he had himself wheeled back to his room. On seeing him, Wilson's widow commented that he looked "exactly as my husband did when he went into his decline." FDR's big plans for a "very progressive" fourth term began to immediately unravel. He had intended to appoint Joseph Davies, of *Mission to Moscow* fame, to undersecretary of state but Davies had to beg off on orders from his doctor. While the president gained narrow Senate approval of Henry Wallace as Secretary of Commerce, the deposed Jesse Jones and his allies successfully defeated a plan to also give Wallace authority over the massive loan authority of the Reconstruction Finance Corporation and the Foreign Economic Administration.[75]

FDR, Stalin, and Churchill meet at Yalta, February 1945, to plan the postwar world.

The Yalta Conference

Only two weeks after he began his fourth term, the sick and weary chief executive journeyed seven thousand miles to the resort community of Yalta in the Crimean Peninsula of the Soviet Union. As in Tehran, Stalin had insisted on a meeting close to home and under conditions he controlled. The president's health was faltering but his determination to exact vengeance was not. After observing the destruction in Crimea, he told his host: "I'm more blood thirsty than a year ago. I hope you make another toast proposing the execution of fifty thousand German officers." On seeing FDR, Churchill's physician wrote that the "the President appears a very sick man. He has all the symptoms of hardening of the arteries of the brain in an advanced stage so that I give him only a few months to live."[76]

Roosevelt's main preoccupation at Yalta was a new international organization (the United Nations) to preserve the postwar peace. In an empty gesture, Stalin gave a vague pledge to increase democratic participation in the Soviet-dominated Polish government. Because his troops were entrenched, the Soviet dictator had a strong negotiating hand, but Roosevelt had some potential leverage, though there is no evidence that he ever contemplated applying it. In February 1945, he might have pushed for Soviet concessions, as he seems to have done earlier with Churchill, by threatening to reduce forthcoming Lend Lease aid (about $1.8 billion for February to September 1945).[77]

A key negotiating advantage for Stalin, fully revealed in 1995 with the official release of the Venona documents, was his access to a Soviet spy network in the U.S. According to these decrypts of Soviet diplomatic communications from the period, the Soviets had over three hundred agents in the United States. The State Department's delegation to Yalta, for example, included the highly placed Alger Hiss (code-named by the Soviets as Ales), a former clerk of Supreme Court Justice Frankfurter. According to a telegram sent by the American embassy in Washington, D.C. to Moscow, "Ales has been working with the Neighbors [Soviet military intelligence] continuously since 1935." Hiss participated in the drafting of the "Declaration of Liberated Europe" at Yalta which set official policy on such issues as the composition of the Polish government. After the conference, Hiss shared his Yalta intelligence with Andrei Vyshinsky, Soviet Commissar of International Affairs, the infamous prosecutor in the Moscow show trials nearly a decade earlier.[78]

While Hiss's involvement in Soviet espionage did not become public knowledge until after Roosevelt's death, administration insiders had some warnings. Most notably, in 1939, journalist Whittaker Chambers, a former fellow member of Hiss's spy ring, had revealed the details of his espionage to Assistant Secretary of State Adolf Berle. Sometime after the Berle meeting (which apparently did nothing to impede Hiss's rise) Walter Winchell told FDR that Hiss was a Soviet spy. The president's reaction, according to the columnist, was one of outrage: "Leaning closer and pointing a finger in my face, he [Roosevelt] angrily said, 'I don't want to hear another thing about it! It isn't true'." FDR did not invite Winchell to the White House again for several months.[79]

Another top spy mentioned prominently in these documents was the economist Lauchlin Currie. Because of his direct access to the president, he was able to transmit valuable intelligence to the KGB during the war. Currie was instrumental in convincing FDR that the Chinese Communists were relatively harmless "agrarian democrats." Also well placed was Lawrence Duggan, a top advisor in the state department who passed on to the Soviets highly secretive information about the invasion of Italy and relations between the U.S. and the U.K. in the Middle East. Most powerful of all in this spy network, however, was Harry Dexter White, the number two man in the Treasury Department, an expert in tax and foreign policy who sent at least fifteen messages to the KGB late in the war.[80]

White had used his position as Morgenthau's right-hand man on several occasions to advance Soviet goals. In 1941, for example, Vitaly Pavlov, a high ranking official in the NKVD (Soviet secret police), entreated White on behalf of his government to push a hardline toward Japan in negotiations. Ultimately, the views he expressed found their way into the fateful "War Memorandum" of November 26th to Japan which, according to Rear Admiral Edwin T. Layton, had been drafted by "Morgenthau's adroit young aide, Harry Dexter White." Three years later, White was instrumental in writing the "Military Handbook" which had first laid out in detail the Morgenthau Plan, a measure that very much coincided with Soviet goals.[81]

In their book *Stalin's Secret Agents*, M. Stanton Evans and Herbert Romerstein make the startling claim that the reach of the Soviet espionage network extended all the way up to Harry Hopkins himself. They identify him as the American spy described as" Agent 19" in the Venona documents. The best known specialists in the history of Soviet espionage, however, including John Earl Haynes, Harvey Klehr and Alexander Vassiliev, disagree. They provide a more compelling case, citing the notebooks of Alexander Vassilev who was given access to the KGB archives, that Agent 19 was, in fact, Lawrence Duggan. If Hopkins were not taking instructions from the Soviet government, what were his motivations? Perhaps the best explanation comes from historian Sean McMeekin, who aptly uses the term "pro-Soviet whisperer" (rather than a spy) to describe Hopkins. Rather than taking marching orders from the Kremlin, he more closely fit the profile of a naive leftist ideologically predisposed to give Stalin the benefit of the doubt as a relative force for good and social justice in the world.[82]

For related reasons, the study of Soviet espionage in the United States during World War II can only take us so far in explaining the conduct of American foreign policy. While administration initiatives, such as the effort to scuttle meaningful peace negotiations with Japan in 1941, the Morgenthau Plan, and at Yalta often aligned with Soviet goals, the chief architects of U.S. foreign policy from the president on down had their own reasons for acting as they did. Even if Hiss, White, Currie, and Duggan had never served in the administration, it is doubtful that the course of American policy would have been fundamentally different.

The Final Month

After Roosevelt's return from Yalta, he delivered a listless and rambling speech to Congress. Apparently unable to use his right hand, he turned the pages awkwardly with his left. Contrary to the obvious impression conveyed by the news cameras, he denied any problem with his health: "I was well the entire time. I was not ill for a second, until I arrived back in Washington, and there I heard all of the rumors which had occurred in my absence. I returned from the trip refreshed and inspired. The Roosevelts are not, as you may suspect, averse to travel. We seem to thrive on it!"[83]

One of the most tragic illustrations of the same absolutist mindset, which had also birthed "unconditional surrender" and "rescue through victory," was the mass bombing of civilians in early 1945. Some months earlier, FDR had endorsed a study probing the effect of strategic bombing on Germany and Japan, including "the psychological and morale effect on an interior community, which had hitherto been free from attack, a large influx of evacuees." Strategic bombing brought the death of nearly six hundred thousand German civilians. "In some towns," wrote Hans Rumpf in his overview, *The Bombing of Germany*, "the casualties amongst those who stayed at home were greater than amongst the men who went to the front." More notoriously, the U.S. and the U.K. had dropped nearly three hundred tons of incendiaries on Dresden (a city with almost no war industries) from February 13th–15th which wiped out thousands of residents, seven thousand public buildings and thirty thousand houses.[84]

Tokyo had its turn to endure this terror less than a month later. To maximum effect, General Curtis LeMay had removed most of the machine guns from planes to increase bomb load capacity. American B-29s dropped over one thousand tons of incendiaries on a city that had a population density of 135,000 per square mile. Japanese civilians erupted like kindling and those in bomb shelters dropped like flies from carbon monoxide poisoning. The United States Strategic Bombing Survey estimated that more than eighty thousand Japanese died on a single day and more than a million saw their homes destroyed.[85]

Other victims of the policy of unconditional surrender, of course, were members of the anti-Hitler resistance who had reached out in vain for the president's support. As Allied troops drew near, the Nazis shipped the few remaining survivors of the Front of Decent People, including Canaris and his second in command at the Abwehr, to a concentration camp in Bavaria where they awaited their fates. Expecting imminent execution, Canaris tapped out a message to a Danish secret agent in the next cell: "I die for my country and with a clear conscience." On April 9th, with American forces only fifty miles away, their captors stripped them naked and hanged them.[86]

During the last month of his life, FDR said nary an unkind word about Stalin. He was downright nasty to his old friend George Earle for expressing a contrary opinion. After FDR failed to reply to his many warnings about Stalin, Earle wrote to the president's daughter Anna that "Russia today is a far greater menace than Germany ever was." Although "your father resents the fact that I told him the truth," he pledged to keep silent if FDR insisted. If the president said nothing, however, he promised to share his views about Stalin and Katyn in one week. That statement finally roused Roosevelt. "I specifically forbid you," he wrote to Earle on March 24th, "to publish any information or opinion about an ally that you have acquired."[87]

In response to compelling evidence that Poland was on the verge of losing its freedom, FDR began to waver somewhat. In a letter to Stalin on April 1st, he rejected as unacceptable any solution which resulted "in a thinly disguised continuance of the present Warsaw regime . . . and would cause the people of the United States to regard the Yalta agreement as having failed." On April 11th, however, he sounded again like his old self. "I would minimize the general Soviet problem as much as possible because these problems," he wrote to Churchill, "in one form or another, seem to arise every day and most of them straighten out as in the case of the Bern meeting."[88]

On the same day, Secretary Morgenthau came to call at Warm Springs and found a man who seemed dazed and confused. He had to hold the drink glasses as Roosevelt poured, lest his shaking hands topple them. Morgenthau's pled once again for a harsh policy toward Germany. The president answered him: "Henry, I am with you 100 percent." One day later, FDR was sitting in his armchair for a portrait which Lucy wanted to give to her daughter. After complaining of a terrible headache, he slumped forward and lost consciousness. He died less than three hours later. In the meantime, Lucy, warning that the Roosevelt family was on the way "and the rooms must be vacant," left the premises with the portrait artist.[89]

"Inside He Was the Coldest Man I Ever Met"

Roosevelt had done nothing to prepare his successor, Harry S. Truman. Although Wallace, because of his background in science, had knowledge of the atomic bomb project, FDR had kept Truman completely in the dark. While Truman repeatedly praised FDR in subsequent years, there was also an undercurrent of resentment. In an unguarded movement, the eighty-six-year-old former president shared what he "really thought" of Roosevelt: "Inside he was the coldest man I ever met. He didn't care about you or me or anyone else in the world on a personal level, as far as I can see. But he was a great president. He brought the country into the twentieth century."[90]

Roosevelt was dead but his policies to varying degrees survived. Truman, despite some private misgivings, felt obligated to apply unconditional surrender against Japan. The logical culmination of that rigid policy was the atomic bombings of Hiroshima and Nagasaki. The president's son, James, was almost certainly right when he said that his father "was prepared to drop an atomic bomb on Japan." Ironically, though the final surrender was labelled "unconditional," it only came after Truman assented after the bombs to a condition that the weary Japanese had insisted for months: keeping the emperor.[91]

Many historians assume, often as a matter of course, that FDR's wartime economic mobilization brought recovery from the depression. Seymour Melman asserts that "the economy [was] producing more guns and more butter . . .Americans had never had it so good." Doris Kearns Goodwin even hails World War II mobilization as an economic model applicable to modern times: the expanded productivity" brought by wartime mobilization, she argues, "ensured a remarkable supply of consumer goods to the people as well . . . Government was a source of full employment, macroeconomic recovery, technological breakthrough, worker training, reindustrialization, and a good deal of incidental social progress."[92]

Robert Higgs, however, casts serious doubt on the reputation of World War II as a spur to economic advance. Unemployment almost disappeared, to be sure, but primarily because of a direct transfer of men into military jobs, rather than a net gain for the civilian economy. These "military 'jobs' differed categorically," Higgs points out. "Often, they entailed substantial risks of death, dismemberment, and other physical and psychological injuries. Military service yielded little pay under harsh conditions . . . Sustained exposure to combat drove many men insane."[93]

The long list of wartime privations endured by civilians included depleted housing caused by rent control disincentives, and unavailable or poor-quality goods because of rationing. Moreover, length of the work week climbed from 38.1 hours to 45.2 in 1944, reaching 50 in bituminous coal mining. The rate of disabling injuries per hour worked rose by 30 percent between 1940 and 1943. "It is difficult to understand," Higgs concludes, "how working harder, longer, more inconveniently and dangerously in return for a diminished flow of consumer goods, comports with the description that 'economically speaking, Americans had never had it so good'."[94]

Sustainable recovery came despite, not because of, federal actions and, in the words of economic historians Richard K. Vedder and Lowell E. Gallaway, under an "extraordinarily contractionary fiscal policy." The size of the federal budget plummeted some $54 billion in 1944 (with a deficit equaling 25 percent of GDP) to only $15 billion in 1947 (with a surplus equaling 5.7 percent of GDP). The federal government also steadily paid down the overall public debt. Meanwhile, unemployment remained at 4.1 percent or lower. The key drivers of economic recovery were supply side factors, such as rising profits and a fall in wage costs, rather than spurt in overall consumption. In fact, governmental spending fell at a far steeper rate than any rise in consumer purchases.[95]

The main contribution of World War II to economic growth was a shift in psychological attitudes. The success of the U.S. in prosecuting victory against two major powers spurred the rise from the bottom up of a "can do" attitude. Hence, even before the war ended, Americans rejected the pessimistic predictions from leading New Dealers and economists who favored big spending programs, such as Alvin Hansen, Paul Samuelson, and Leon Henderson, of mass unemployment and possibly depression. Higgs notes that by early 1945, the "prospect of a peacetime economy electrified investors. Stock prices surged in 1945 and again in 1946."[96]

While Roosevelt deserves credit for easing the New Dealers out of leadership in wartime mobilization agencies, the hegemony of the "dollar-a-year men" and big private contractors was a mixed blessing. Particularly problematic was that it helped lay the foundation for the modern military-industrial complex. John Morton Blum points to the example of industrialist Henry J. Kaiser, one of the leading dollar-a-year men. According to Blum "government supplied his capital, furnished his market, and guaranteed his solvency on the cost-plus formula—and so spared him from the need of cost efficiency, rewarded speed at any price, and came close to guaranteeing his profits." In 1941 and 1942, FDR apparently gave no thought to another possible mobilization model: the comparatively light-handed approach of the Union during the Civil War. Despite many flaws, including inflation and localized corruption, as Richard F. Bensel observes, it "relied almost as exclusively on market forces and open competition for military contracts for the provision and pricing of goods and services." The Union mobilization was not nearly as plagued by the negative consequences of price and wage controls, rationing, and seizure or micromanagement of businesses. But Roosevelt, enamored by the example of his mentor Woodrow Wilson, who had, in turn, borrowed from German "War Socialism," probably did not give his choice a second thought.[97]

Franklin D. Roosevelt was not a great president nor even a good one. The list of reasons for making this assessment is long. During the 1930s, his economic policies needlessly prolonged the worst economic downturn in American history. Even after the completion of two terms, unemployment remained in double digits.

His record on civil liberties was dismal by any measure. As president, he egged on the inquisitorial Black Committee's surveillance, without cause or warrant, of millions of private telegrams.

Despite repeated pleas from both black and white allies, he was consistently passive throughout his presidency toward lynching and other forms of racial oppression. The darkest stain on his civil liberties legacy was the confinement of more than one hundred thousand Japanese Americans (most of them native-born citizens) into concentration camps. He simply did not have to do it. FDR imposed this policy over the objections of many key advisors including his attorney general, director of the FBI, and secretary of the interior.

His failures in foreign policy began in his first year in office with his disastrous decision to scuttle the London Economic Conference. In doing so, he also dashed one of the best hopes to stem rising protectionism and other forms of economic autarky. The collapse of the conference brought a tragic cycle of economic warfare which eventually extended to the battlefields of Europe. In the period before Pearl Harbor, FDR showed little interest in possible openings for compromise on the issue of China or for serious negotiation, such as Japanese proposals for a summit.

After the U.S. entered the war, the president's rigid stand for unconditional surrender worsened the destructive nature of the conflict. All the while Roosevelt was chronically insensitive toward the suffering of Europe's Jews, the victims of Allied terror bombing, and German anti-Hitler plotters. In domestic policy, his wholesale violations of the Bill of Rights both before and during World War II, such as sedition prosecutions, provided precedents for similar abuses during the McCarthy Era and beyond.

Describing Roosevelt as a failed president does not imply that he lacked talents in the arts of politics and persuasion. To the contrary. By those standards, FDR often excelled as an "effective" chief executive. The basis of failure ran deeper than that. It can best be assessed by studying the consequences of his actions. FDR was a failed president primarily because he repeatedly put his considerable abilities at the service of far less laudable goals including a ruthless preoccupation with personal and political advancement, self-defeating economic policies, and the erection of a vast and unaccountable centralized federal bureaucracy.

Endnotes

1 From Country Squire to President

1 Sherry Zane, "'I Did It for the Uplift of Humanity and the Navy': Same Sex Acts on the Origins of the National Security State, 1919–1921," *The New England Quarterly* 91:2 (June 2018), 303.
2 James MacGregor Burns, *Roosevelt: The Lion and the Fox* (1956; reprinted San Diego: Harcourt Brace Jovanovich, 1984), 7–8.
3 Burns, *Roosevelt: The Lion and the Fox*, 8.
4 Burns, *Roosevelt: The Lion and the Fox*, 7–8.
5 Burns, *Roosevelt: The Lion and the Fox*, 15.
6 Daniel T. Rodgers, *Atlantic Crossings: Social Politics in a Progressive Age* (The Belknap Press of Harvard University Press, 1998), 76–108; Thomas C. Leonard, *Illiberal Reformers: Race, Eugenics, and American Economics in the Progressive Era* (Princeton: Princeton University Press, 2016), 17.
7 Leonard, *Illiberal Reformers*, 11–16; Richard M. Gamble, *The War for Righteousness: Progressive Christianity, the Great War, and the Rise of the Messianic Nation* (Wilmington: ISI, 2003), 64; American Economic Association, Report of the Organization of the American Economic Association, 1:1, March 1886 ([Baltimore]: Publications of the American Economic Association, 1886), 6–7; Sidney Fine, *Laissez-Faire and the General Welfare State* (Ann Arbor: University of Michigan Press, 1956), 239–240.
8 Burns, *Roosevelt: The Lion and the Fox*, 25–26; Jean Edward Smith, *FDR*, 31–32.
9 David Michaelis, *Eleanor* (Simon and Schuster, 2020) 34–42, 74–75; Mary Grabar, *Debunking FDR: The Man and the Myths* (New York: Regnery, 2025), 87–92; Jean Edward Smith, *FDR*, 45–47.
10 Michaelis, *Eleanor*, 106, 108.
11 Grabar, *Debunking FDR*, 93, 102; Jean Edward Smith, *FDR*, 57, 59, 63–64; Michaelis, *Eleanor*, 114.
12 Jean Edward Smith, *FDR*, 60.
13 Jean Edward Smith, *FDR*, 84; Burns, *Roosevelt: The Lion and the Fox*, 38–41; Franklin D. Roosevelt, "Liberty of the Individual versus Liberty of the Community," https://www.cooperative-individualism.org/roosevelt-

franklin_liberty-of-the-individual-1912-mar.htm, accessed July 22nd 2024.

14 Robert McElvaine, *The Great Depression, America, 1929–1941* (New York: Times Books, 1984), 95–97; John T. Flynn, *Country Squire in the White House* (Doubleday, 1940), 117.

15 Jean Edward Smith, *FDR*, 93.

16 Frank Freidel, *Franklin D. Roosevelt: The Apprenticeship* (Boston: Little, Brown and Company, 1952), 135; Burns, *The Lion and the Fox*, 30.

17 Burns, *Roosevelt: The Lion and the Fox*, 47–53; Grabar, *Debunking FDR*, 143–44; Michaelis, *Eleanor*, 126–132.

18 Davis, *FDR: The Beckoning of Destiny: 1882–1928: A History* (New York: G.P. Putnam's Sons, 1972), 305; Michaelis, *Eleanor*, 127–139.

19 Glenda E. Gilmore, *Gender and Jim Crow: Women and the Politics of White Supremacy in North Carolina, 1896–1920* (Chapel Hill: University of North Carolina Press, 1996), 66, 83, 88, 92, 103–05; Michaelis, *Eleanor*, 127–136.

20 Woodrow Wilson, *A History of the American People*, vol. 9 (New York: Harper and Brothers, 1918, reprint of the 1910 edition), 58.

21 Kathleen L. Wolgemuth, "Woodrow Wilson and Federal Segregation," *The Journal of Negro History* 44:2 (April 1959), 158, 173; "Roosevelt Appoints a Negro," *Chicago Daily Tribune*, April 11th 1907, 5; Ralph W. Tyler, "Against Segregation," *Washington Post,* April 25th 1913, 1.

22 "Roosevelt's Jim Crow Order Is Revealed Here," *New York Amsterdam News*, October 29th 1930, 1; "Segregation Order Has Been Revoked," *New York Age*, September 14th 1916, 1; August Meier and Elliott Rudwick, "The Rise of Segregation in the Federal Bureaucracy, 1900–1930, *Phylon* 28:2 (2nd Qtr., 1967), 181.

23 Flynn, *Country Squire in the White House*, 18–19; Burns, *Roosevelt: The Lion and the Fox*, 51.

24 Burns, *Roosevelt: The Lion and the Fox*, 61; Davis, *FDR: The Beckoning of Destiny*, 385, 394.

25 H.W. Brands, *Traitor to His Class: The Privileged Life and Radical Presidency of Franklin Delano* Roosevelt (Random House, 2009), 104; Jean Edward Smith, *FDR*, 140; Michaelis, *Eleanor*, 150, 162.

26 Brands, *Traitor to His Class*, 89; Michaelis, *Eleanor*, 155–59.

27 Jean Edward Smith, *FDR*, 158–161; and Michaelis, *Eleanor,* 171, 283–84.

28 Davis, *FDR: The Beckoning of Destiny*, 512; Frank Friedel, *Franklin D. Roosevelt: The Apprenticeship* (Little, Brown, 1952), 333–34.

29 Michaelis, *Eleanor*, 185–86.

30 Joseph E. Persico, *Roosevelt's Secret War: FDR and World War II Espionage* (Random House, 2002), 8–9, 97; Geoffrey C. Ward, *A First-Class Temperament: The Emergence of Franklin D. Roosevelt* (New York: Harper and Row, 1989), 198, 290, 350.

31 Zane, "'I Did It for the Uplift of Humanity and the Navy'," 279–284, 299; Lawrence R. Murphy, *Perverts by Official Order: The Campaign Against Homosexuals by the United States Navy* (New York: Harrington Park Press, 1988), 63–64, 71–73, 253.

32 Irwin F. Gellman, *Secret Affairs: FDR, Cordell Hull, and Sumner Welles* (New York: Enigma, 1995), 235; Zane, "'I Did It for the Uplift of Humanity and the Navy,'" 279–283, 291; Murphy, *Perverts by Official Order*, 110.

33 Zane, "The Newport Sex Scandal and the Early-Twentieth-Century Origins of the U.S. National Security State," (Ph.D. diss., University of

Connecticut, 2012), 3–4, 9–10, 121–22, 218–221; Murphy, *Perverts by Order*, 109.

34 Jean Edward Smith, *FDR*, 177.

35 Murphy, *Perverts by Order*, 255.

36 Zane, "The Newport Sex Scandal," 226–27.

37 Blanche Wiesen Cook, *Eleanor Roosevelt, 1884–1933*, Volume 1 (New York: Viking, 1992), 279–280; Davis, *FDR: The Beckoning of Destiny*, 621; Friedel, *Franklin D. Roosevelt: The Ordeal*, 81–83; Michaelis, *Eleanor*, 198–99, 201–02; "The Conquest of Haiti," *The Appeal* (St. Paul, Minnesota), September 25th 1920, 2.

38 Friedel, *Franklin D. Roosevelt: The Ordeal*, 92; Michaelis, *Eleanor*, 201–02.

39 Zane, "The Newport Sex Scandal," 242–43.

40 Zane, "The Newport Sex Scandal," 243–45.

41 Zane, "'I Did It for the Uplift of Humanity and the Navy'," 302–03; "Lay Navy Scandal to F.D. Roosevelt," *New York Times* (July 20th 1921), 4.

42 "Lay Navy Scandal to F.D. Roosevelt," 1–2; Michaelis, *Eleanor*, 206–07; Zane, "'I Did It for the Uplift of Humanity and the Navy'," 279–280, 305.

43 Davis, *FDR: The Beckoning of Destiny*, 676; Michaelis, *Eleanor*, 207, 209; Fulton Oursler, *Behold This Dreamer! An Autobiography* (Little, Brown, 1964), 375–76.

44 Davis, *FDR: The Beckoning of Destiny*, 704–05; Folsom, *New Deal or Raw Deal?* 25.

45 Rafael Medoff, *The Jews Should Keep Quiet: Franklin D. Roosevelt, Rabbi Stephen S. Wise, and the Holocaust* (Philadelphia: Jewish Publication Society, 2019), 285–86, 293.

46 Davis, *FDR: The Beckoning of Destiny*, 700–02; (Cover) *Time Magazine* 1:13, May 28th 1923; Roosevelt to John D. Rockefeller, Jr., April 10th 1926, https://historical.ha.com/itm/autographs/u.s.-presidents/franklin-d-roosevelt-typed-letter-signed-as-president-of-the-american-construction-council/a/6001-53372.s?ic16=ViewItem-BrowseTabs-Auction-Archive-ThisAuction-120115, accessed January 18th 2025.

47 Flynn, *Country Squire in the White House*, 35; Davis, *FDR: The Beckoning of Destiny*, 700-03; Fred A. Bjornstad, "A Revolution in Ideas and Methods": The Construction Industry and Socioeconomic Planning in the United States, 1915–1933, PhD. Diss., The University of Iowa, 201, 208.

48 Davis, *FDR: The Beckoning of Destiny*, 756; Grabar, *Debunking FDR*, 224; Burns, *Roosevelt: The Lion and the Fox*, 94–95.

49 Davis, *FDR: The Beckoning of Destiny*, 762–63, 786–87; Grabar, *Debunking FDR*, 143–44, 219.

50 "Roosevelt Says," *Macon Telegraph*, April 30th 1925, 4.

51 Burns, *Roosevelt: The Lion and the Fox*, 98.

52 Burns, *Roosevelt: The Lion and the Fox*, 124; Jonathan Hughes, *American Economic History* (Glenview, Illinois: Scott, Foresman/Little, Brown Higher Education, 1990), 460.

53 Hughes, *American Economic History*, 467, 472; Mark J. Perry, "Real GDP Fell by 29% from 1929 to 1933," AEIdeas, November 23rd 2008, https://www.aei.org/carpe-diem/real-gdp-fell-by-29-3-from-1930-to-1933/, accessed April 11th 2025; David T. Beito, *Taxpayers in Revolt: Tax Resistance during the Great Depression* (Chapel Hill: University of North Carolina Press, 1989), 6.

54 David T. Beito, *From Mutual Aid to the Welfare State: Fraternal Societies and Social Services, 1890–1967* (Chapel Hill: University of North Carolina Press, 2000), 222–23.

55 Jim Powell, *FDR's Folly: How Roosevelt and His New Deal Prolonged the Great Depression* (New York: Three Rivers Press, 2003), 58.

56 James Grant, The *Forgotten Depression: 1921: The Crash that Cured Itself* (Simon and Shuster, 2014), 68; Bryan, L. Boulier, H.O. Stekler, and Jeremy Dutra, "Measuring the Onset of the Great Depression: Then and Now," *Indian Economic Review* 36:1 (January–June 2001), 141; Vedder and Gallaway, *Out of Work*, 61.

57 Robert L. Hetzel, *Monetary Policy of the Federal Reserve: A History* (Cambridge University Press, 2008), 34.

58 Joan Hoff Wilson, *Herbert Hoover: Forgotten Progressive* (Long Grove, Illinois: Waveland, 1992 [1975]), 155–57, 163; Murray N. Rothbard, *American's Great Depression* (New York: Van Nostrand, 1963), 285–319; Vedder and Gallaway, *Out of Work*, 137; Herbert Hoover, "Address Accepting the Republican Presidential Nomination," August 11th 1912, https://www.presidency.ucsb.edu/documents/address-accepting-the-republican-presidential-nomination, accessed June 23rd 2024; Selgin, *False Dawn*, 68.

59 James Grant, *The Forgotten Depression*, 213–15; Folsom, *New Deal or Raw Deal?* 31–32; Herbert Hoover, Message Regarding the Smoot-Hawley Act, June 16th 1930, https://millercenter.org/the-presidency/presidential-speeches/june-16-1930-message-regarding-smoot-hawley-tariff-act#:~:text=June%2016%2C%201930%3A%20Message%20regarding%20the%20Smoot%2DHawley%20Tariff%20Act, accessed January 21st 2025.

60 Franklin D. Roosevelt to A.N. Mathers, March 11th 1930, in Elliot Roosevelt, ed., *FDR: His Personal Letters, 1928–1945* (New York: Duell, Sloan, and Pearce, 1950), 108.

61 Richard K. Vedder and Lowell E. Gallaway, *Out of Work: Unemployment and Government in Twentieth-Century America* (New York University Press, 1997), 67, 92–93, 103.

62 Gene Smiley, *Rethinking the Great Depression* (Chicago: Ivan R. Dee, 2002), 22.

63 George Selgin, *False Dawn: The New Deal and the Promise of Recovery, 1933–1947* (University of Chicago Press, 2025), 68; Powell, *FDR's Folly*, ix, 32.

64 Susan Estabrook Kennedy, *The Banking Crisis in 1933* (Lexington: University Press of Kentucky, 1973), 51–53, 203–04.

65 Flynn, *Country Squire in the White House*, 37; Burns, *Roosevelt: The Lion and the Fox*, 124; Rebecca Kobrin, "Too Big to Fail in 1930: The Failed Bank of United States and The Long Shadow of East European Jewish Immigrant Banking, *American Jewish History* 103:4 (October 2019), 458–59; Kenneth S. Davis, *FDR: The New York Years, 1928–1933* (Random House, 1985), 223; Anthony Gregory, *New Deal Law and Order: How the War on Crime Built the Modern Liberal State* (Harvard University Press, 2024), 65–66.

66 Davis, *FDR: The New York Years*, 60; Flynn, *Country Squire at the White House*, 30–31.

67 Flynn, *Country Squire in the White House*, 39; Davis, *FDR: The New York Years*, 223–24; John E. Moser, *Right Turn: John T. Flynn and the Transformation of American Liberalism* (New York University Press, 2005), 17–18.

68 Flynn, *Country Squire in the White House*, 39–40; Davis, *FDR: The New York Years*, 225–27; Milton Friedman and Anna Jacobson Schwartz, *A Monetary History of the United States, 1857–1960* (Princeton University

Press, 1963), 357; Richard Hofstadter, *The American Political Tradition* (New York: Vintage Books, 1948), 425–26.

69 Brands, *Traitor to His Class*, 232–33; Jean Edward Smith, *FDR*, 249.

70 Sebastian Edwards, "Gold, the Brains Trust, and Roosevelt," *History of Political Economy* 49:1 (2017), 3–4, 6; Burns, *Roosevelt: The Lion and the Fox*, 130, 154; Jim Powell, *FDR's Folly*, 12–13.

71 Powell, *FDR's Folly*, 15; Burns, *Roosevelt: The Lion and the Fox*, 153–54.

72 Powell, *FDR's Folly*, 13–14; Burns, *Roosevelt: The Lion and the Fox*, 154; Edwards, "Gold, the Brains Trust, and Roosevelt," 4, 13.

73 Davis, *FDR: The New York Years*, 320–26.

74 Stuart Chase, "A New Deal for America," *The New Republic* 71:917, June 29th 1932, 169–170; Franklin D. Roosevelt, "Address Accepting the Presidential Nomination at the Democratic National Convention in Chicago," https://www.presidency.ucsb.edu/documents/address-accepting-the-presidential-nomination-the-democratic-national-convention-chicago-1, accessed June 18th 2024.

75 Franklin D. Roosevelt, "Radio Address on the National Democratic Platform From Albany, New York," July 30th 1932, https://www.presidency.ucsb.edu/documents/radio-address-the-national-democratic-platform-from-albany-new-york, accessed June 16th 2024; Franklin D. Roosevelt, Campaign Address on Agriculture and Tariffs at Sioux City, Iowa, September 29th 1932, https://www.presidency.ucsb.edu/documents/campaign-address-agriculture-and-tariffs-sioux-city-iowa, accessed January 22nd 2025.

76 Selgin, *False Dawn*, 26; Burns, *Roosevelt: The Lion and the Fox*, 141, 143; Davis, *FDR: The New York Years*, 165; Franklin D. Roosevelt, "Campaign Address on Progressive Government at the Commonwealth Club in San Francisco, California," September 23rd 1932, https://www.presidency.ucsb.edu/documents/campaign-address-progressive-government-the-commonwealth-club-san-francisco-california, accessed June 18th 2024.

77 Oursler, *Behold This Dreamer!* 369–370; "Hoover's Fortune Shows Big Shrinkage Since 1914," *Washington Post*, July 25th 1932, 1; "Broad Street Gossip: Revising Fortunes Upward," *Wall Street Journal*, July 22nd 1929, 2.

78 Jean Edward Smith, *FDR*, 282–84; Gregory, *New Deal Law and Order*, 70.

79 Frank R. Kent, "The Great Game of Politics," *The Sun* (Baltimore), September 20th 1932, 1–2.

80 Franklin D. Roosevelt, "Campaign Address on the Federal Budget at Pittsburgh, Pennsylvania," October 19th 1932, https://www.presidency.ucsb.edu/documents/campaign-address-the-federal-budget-pittsburgh-pennsylvania accessed June 16th 2024; Edwards, "Gold, the Brains Trust, and Roosevelt," 14–16.

81 Nancy J. Weiss, *Farewell to the Party of Lincoln: Black Politics in the Age of FDR* (Princeton University Press, 1983), 20, 29–33; Timothy J Hoffman, "The Civil Rights Realignment: How Race Dominates Presidential Elections" (2015), https://scholarship.shu.edu/cgi/viewcontent.cgi?article=1006&context=pa, accessed July 20th 2024.

82 Beito, *Taxpayers in Revolt*, 8–9.

83 Eugene Lyons, *Herbert Hoover: A Biography* (New York: Doubleday, 1964, reprint of the 1948 edition), 312.

84 Lyons, *Herbert Hoover*, 309–310, 316–17; Smiley, *Rethinking the Great Depression*, 77; Letter from Herbert Hoover to Franklin D. Roosevelt,

February 18th 1933, https://teachingamericanhistory.org/document/letter-to-franklin-d-roosevelt/, accessed January 22nd 2025.

84 John T. Flynn, *The Roosevelt Myth* (New York: Devin Adair, 1948), 16–18; Raymond Moley, *After Seven Years* (New York: Harper and Brothers, 1939), 140; Lyons, *Herbert Hoover*, 316–17; Smiley, *Rethinking the Great Depression*, 27–30.

86 Kennedy, *The Banking Crisis of 1933*, 73–74; "Democrats in Disagreement on Bank Bill," *Stockton Evening and Sunday Record* (Stockton, California), January 10th 1933, 1; "Foes of the Bank Bill Set up Blockade in Senate Again," *Okmulgee Daily Times* (Okmulgee, Oklahoma), January 21st 1933, 1.

87 Brands, *Traitor to His Class*, 287; Herbert Hoover, *The Memoirs of Herbert Hoover, 1929–1941, The Great Depression* (New York: Macmillan, 1952), 210–12.

88 Lyons, *Herbert Hoover*, 312–313, 318; Kennedy, *The Banking Crisis of 1933*, 143; Jonathan Alter, *The Defining Moment: FDR's Hundred Days and the Triumph of Hope* (New York: Simon and Shuster, 2006), 181; Selgin, *False Dawn*, 45–46.

89 Brands, *Traitor to His Class*, 274–75; Jean Edward Smith, *FDR*, 290; Alter, *The Defining Moment*, 182.

90 Kennedy, *The Banking Crisis of 1933*, 136, 141; George Selgin, *False Dawn*, 36–37.

91 Kenneth S. Davis, *FDR: The New Deal Years, 1933–1937: A History* (Random House, 1986), 210.

2 Fear and Emergency: The First New Deal

1 American Rhetoric, "Top 100 Speeches of the 20th Century," https://www.americanrhetoric.com/top100speechesall.html, accessed August 1st 2024; "Top 100 American Speeches of the 20th Century," https://news.wisc.edu/archive/misc/speeches/accessed August 1st 2024; "Looking at 10 great speeches in American History," August 27, 2017, https://constitutioncenter.org/blog/looking-at-10-great-speeches-in-american-history, accessed August 1, 2024.

2 Cass R. Sunstein, "Trump Should Have Learned From FDR's 'Fear Itself' Speech," Bloomberg, March 12th 2020, https://www.bloomberg.com/view/articles/2020-03-12/trump-should-have-learned-from-fdr-s-fear-itself-speech, accessed August 1st 2024; Ira Katznelson, *Fear Itself: The New Deal and the Origins of Our Time* (New York: Norton, 2013), 522; Raymond Moley, *The First New Deal* (Harcourt, Brace and World, 1966), 115.
The database search was in ProQuest, geneology.com, and newspapers .com. See, for example, "Wise Words," *The Enterprise and Vermonter* (Vergennes, Vermont) July 29th 1932, 3.

3 Katznelson, *Fear Itself*, 98–99; unpublished manuscript by Mary Grabar; First Inaugural Address of Franklin D. Roosevelt, March 4th 1933, https://avalon.law.yale.edu/20th_century/froos1.asp, accessed August 1st 2024; Newsreel of Franklin D. Roosevelt 1933 Inauguration [Universal News Service], March 4th 1933, https://www.c-span.org/video/?421875-1/newsreel-franklin-d-roosevelt-1933-inauguration, accessed August 1st 2024; The Inauguration of President Roosevelt, March 8th 1933 [Hearst Movietone News], https://hearst.newsreels.net/v/3652a72, accessed August 1st 2024;

Arthur M. Schlesinger Jr., *The Age of Roosevelt: The Coming of the New Deal* (Houghton Mifflin, 1959), 1; William E. Leuchtenburg, *The FDR Years: On Roosevelt and His Legacy* (Columbia University Press, 1995), 50.

4 First Inaugural Address of Franklin D. Roosevelt, March 4th 1933; Davis W. Houck, *FDR and Fear Itself: The First Inaugural Address* (College Station: Texas A&M University Press, 2002), 140; Grabar, unpublished manuscript.

5 Kennedy, The *Banking Crisis of 1933*, 159; Selgin, *False Dawn*, 47–48; Powell, *FDR's Folly*, 53; Franklin Delano Roosevelt, Proclamation 2039, March 6th 1933, https://www.lawandfreedom.com/site/executive/execorders/Roosevelt.pdf?88;a79e, accessed August 1st 2024; Emergency Banking Act of 1933, March 9th 1933, https://www.federalreservehistory.org/essays/emergency-banking-act-of-1933, accessed August 1st 2024; Amity Shlaes, *The Forgotten Man: A New History of the Great Depression* (Harper Perennial, 2007), 157–58.

6 Jean Edward Smith, *FDR*, 328; Shlaes, *The Forgotten Man*, 159; Powell, *FDR's Folly*, 68.

7 Schlesinger, *The Age of Roosevelt: The Coming of the New Deal*, 337–341; Burns, *Roosevelt: The Lion and the Fox*, 169; Powell, *FDR's Folly*, 91.

8 Folsom, *New Deal or Raw Deal?* 82; Shlaes, *The Forgotten Man*, 264.

9 Christine Kay Seiler, "The Veteran Killer: The Florida Emergency Relief Administration and the Labor Day Hurricane of 1935," Ph.D. diss., Florida State University, 2003, 43–46; Grabar, *Debunking FDR*, 281; Jerome Tuccille, *The War Against the Vets: The World War I Bonus Army during the Great Depression* (Lincoln: University of Nebraska Press, 2018), 137–140.

10 Schlesinger, *The Age of Roosevelt: The Coming of the New Deal*, 294.

11 Powell, *FDR's Folly*, ix, 57; Susan Kennedy, *The Banking Crisis of 1933*, 204–210, 215, 220–22; Selgin, *False Dawn*, 57–58, 62–63.

12 Selgin, *False Dawn*, 136–37; Leuchtenburg, *Franklin D. Roosevelt and the New Deal, 1932–1940* (Harper and Row, 1963), 53; Beito, *Taxpayers in Revolt*, 144.

13 Kenneth S. Davis, *FDR: The New Deal Years, 1933–1937: A History* (New York: Random House, 1979), 92–94; Shlaes, *The Forgotten Man*, 45, 141–42, 174–76; Schlesinger, *The Age of Roosevelt: The Coming of the New Deal*, 324; Shlaes, *The Forgotten Man*, 45, 174–76; Message to Congress Suggesting the Tennessee Valley Authority, April 10th 1933, http://docs.fdrlibrary.marist.edu/odtvacon.html, accessed August 1st 2024.

14 Katznelson, *Fear Itself*, 254–55; Gregory, *New Deal Law and Order*, 195.

15 Smiley, *Rethinking the Great Depression*, 78–79; Shlaes, *The Forgotten Man*, 7, 9, 12; Powell, *FDR's Folly*, viii.

16 Shlaes, *The Forgotten Man*, 10, 153; Folsom, *New Deal or Raw Deal?* 60, 66.

17 Kari Frederickson, *Depression Dynasty: The Bankheads of Alabama* (Tuscaloosa: University of Alabama Press, 2022), 227–28; Folsom, *New Deal or Raw Deal?* 65–66; Selgin, *False Dawn*, 99; Powell, *FDR's Folly*, 135–36.

18 Shlaes, *The Forgotten Man*, 168; Folsom, *New Deal or Raw Deal?* 52, 60, 67; Davis, *FDR: The New Deal Years*, 274–75, 280; Leuchtenburg, *Franklin D. Roosevelt and the New Deal*, 78

19 Franklin D. Roosevelt, Press Conference, April 12th 1933, http://www.fdrlibrary.marist.edu/_resources/images/pc/pc0185.pdf, accessed January 26th 2025.

20 Franklin D. Roosevelt, Statement on N.I.R.A., June 16th 1933, https://www.presidency.ucsb.edu/documents/statement-nira, accessed August 9th 2024; National Industrial Recovery Act (1933), https://www.archives.gov/milestone-documents/national-industrial-recovery-act, accessed August 1st 2024; Schlesinger, *The Age of Roosevelt: The Coming of the New Deal*, 103–06.
21 Smiley, *Rethinking the Great Depression*, 91; Wolfgang Schivelbusch, *Three New Deals: Reflections on Roosevelt's America, Mussolini's Italy, and Hitler's Germany, 1933–1939* (New York: Henry Holt, 2006), 91–92; Schlesinger, *The Age of Roosevelt: The Coming of the New Deal*, 124.
22 Howard Dickman, *Industrial Democracy in America: Ideological Origins of National Labor Relations Policy* (La Salle: Open Court, 1987), 205–06, 422; Paul D. Moreno, *Black Americans and Organized Labor: A New History* (Baton Rouge: Louisiana State University Press, 2006), 165–67; Joseph A. Schumpeter, *Business Cycles: A Theoretical, Historical and Statistical Analysis of the Capitalist Process* (New York: McGraw-Hill, 1939), 1037; Lionel Robbins, *The Great Depression* (London: Macmillan, 1934, 127.
23 Franklin D. Roosevelt Statement on N.I.R.A.; and National Industrial Recovery Act (1933); Davis, *FDR: The New Deal Years, 1933–1937: A History*, 132, 260; Smiley, *Rethinking the Great Depression*, 90.
24 Katznelson, *Fear Itself*, 236; July 24th 1933: Franklin D. Roosevelt, Fireside Chat 3: On the National Recovery Administration, https://millercenter.org/the-presidency/presidential-speeches/july-24-1933-fireside-chat-3-national-recovery-administration, accessed January 26th 2025.
25 Elliott Roosevelt and James Bough, *A Rendezvous with Destiny: The Roosevelts of the White House* (New York: Putnam's, 1975), 79–80; Brands, *Traitor to His Class*, 384; Schlesinger, *The Age of Roosevelt: The Coming of the New Deal*, 115.
26 Schivelbusch, *Three New Deals: Reflections on Roosevelt's America, Mussolini's Italy and Hitler's Germany, 1933–1939* (Holt, 2006) 88; Folsom, *New Deal or Raw Deal?* 530; Schlesinger, *The Age of Roosevelt: The Coming of the New Deal*, 108, 110, 120.
27 Smiley, *Rethinking the New Deal*, 91; Flynn, *The Roosevelt Myth*, 45; Shlaes, *The Forgotten Man*, 151; and Leuchtenburg, *Franklin D. Roosevelt and the New Deal*, 68.
28 "Give a Man a Job!": National Recovery Administration Promotion, 1933, https://view.officeapps.live.com/op/view.aspx?src=https%3A%2F%2Fbcs.bedfordstmartins.com%2Fwebpub%2Fhistory%2FAmerica_in_Motion_videos%2Fnew%25207_29%2FAMMO_GiveaManaJob.doc&wdOrigin=BROWSELINK, accessed January 27th 2025.
29 Selgin, *False Dawn*, 24–25.
30 Gellman, *Secret Affairs*, 38–40; Davis, *FDR: The New Deal Years*, 131; Shlaes, *The Forgotten Man*, 161–62.
31 Moley, *The First New Deal*, 464, 494; Schlesinger, *The Age of Roosevelt: The Coming of the New Deal*, 229; Shlaes, *The Forgotten Man*, 161–62; Davis, *FDR: The New Deal Years*, 192–93, 198; Cordell Hull, *The Memoirs of Cordell Hull*, Volume 1 (New York: Macmillan, 1948), 253.
32 Brands, *Traitor to His Class*, 369; Davis, *FDR: The New Deal Years*, 128, 163, 190; First Inaugural Address of Franklin D. Roosevelt; Shlaes, *The Forgotten Man*, 162–63.
33 Shlaes, *The Forgotten Man*, 166–67; Selgin, *False Dawn*, 83–84, 215–16; Hull, *The Memoirs of Cordell Hull*, 198.
34 Schlesinger, *The Age of Roosevelt: The Coming of the New Deal*, 241;

Folsom, *New Deal or Raw Deal?* 26; Powell, *FDR's Folly*, 71–73; Executive Order 6261—Relating to the Sale and Export of Gold Recovered from Natural Deposits, August 29th 1933, https://www.presidency.ucsb.edu/documents/executive-order-6261-relating-the-sale-and-export-gold-recovered-from-natural-deposits, accessed August 1st 2024.

35 James Q. Whitman, "Of Corporatism, Fascism, and the First New Deal," *American Journal of Comparative Law* 747 (1991), 776; Dickman, *Industrial Democracy in America*, 214.

36 Schivelbusch, *Three New Deals*, 31–32; Elliott Roosevelt, *A Rendezvous with Destiny*, 106.

37 Schivelbusch, *Three New Deals*, 23; Whitman, "Of Corporatism, Fascism, and the First New Deal," 766; Davis, *FDR: The New Deal Years*, 37.

38 Schivelbusch, *Three New Deals*, 19–20; Burns, *Roosevelt: The Lion and the Fox*, 184.

38 Becky M. Nicolaides, "Radio Electioneering in the American Presidential Campaigns of 1932 and 1936," *Historical Journal of Film, Radio and Television* 8:2 (1988), 116, 121.

40 Robert J. Brown, *Manipulating the Ether: The Power of Broadcast Radio in Thirties America* (McFarland, 1998), 14; Robert W. McChesney, *Telecommunications, Mass Media, and Democracy: The Battle for the Control of U.S. Broadcasting, 1928–1935* (Oxford University Press, 1993), 182; Ruth Brindze, *Not to Be Broadcast: The Truth about Radio* (Vanguard Press, 1937), 134.

41 Leon Seymour Stein, "Editorializing by Broadcast Licensees: A Developmental Analysis of the Problem of Federal Regulation of Editorializing by Broadcast Licensees" (PhD diss., New York University, 1965), 99; Orrin B. Dunlap Jr., "Talking to the People: Radio Devices in White House Give President Quick Contact with Populace from Coast to Coast," *New York Times*, March 19th 1933, XB; Minna F. Kassner, "Radio Censorship," *Air Law Review* 8:97 (April 1937), 104; Richard W. Steele, *Propaganda in an Open Society: The Roosevelt Administration and the Media, 1933–1941* (Greenwood, 1985), 18–20.

42 McChesney, *Telecommunications*, 182; Steele, *Propaganda in an Open Society*, 19; Brown, *Manipulating the Ether*, 14.

43 Gary Dean Best, *The Critical Press and the New Deal: The Press Versus Presidential Power, 1933–1938* (Praeger, 1993), 25; Robert J. Brown, *Manipulating the Ether*, 14; James Ragland, "Merchandisers of the First Amendment: Freedom and Responsibility of the Press in the Age of Roosevelt, 1933–1940," *Georgia Review* 16 (Winter 1962), 382; Steele, *Propaganda in an Open Society*, 18–19.

44 "Lafount Urges NRA Cooperation," *NAB Reports* 1:26 (August 19th 1933), 118–19; Brindze, *Not to Be Broadcast*, 118–19.

45 Alan Brinkley, *Voices of Protest: Huey Long, Father Coughlin, and the Great Depression* (Vintage Books, 1982), 98, 108–111, 114.

46 Folsom, *New Deal or Raw Deal?* 94–97; Scott Berg, *Lindbergh* (New York: Putnam's, 1998), 292.

47 Elliott Roosevelt, *A Rendezvous with Destiny*, 101; Folsom, *New Deal or Raw Deal?* 96–97.

48 Folsom, *New Deal or Raw Deal?* 97; Berg, *Lindbergh*, 295; Schlesinger, *The Age of Roosevelt: The Coming of the New Deal*, 455.

49 Schlesinger, *The Age of Roosevelt: The Coming of the New Deal*, 120; Folsom, *New Deal or Raw Deal?* 49; James T. Patterson, *Congressional Conservatism and the New Deal: The Growth of the Conservative Coalition in Congress, 1933–1939* (University of Kentucky Press, 1967), 19–20;

Hull, *The Memoirs of Cordell Hull*, 318; Harold B. Hinton, *Cordell Hull: A Biography* (Doubleday, 1942), 314.

50 Folsom, *New Deal or Raw Deal?* 51.

51 Powell, *FDR's Folly*, 124; Schlesinger, *The Age of Roosevelt: The Coming of the New Deal*, 134.

52 Powell, *New Deal or Raw Deal?* 118; "How the South Interprets the New Deal," editorial cartoon, *Chicago Defender* (January 27th, 1934), 14; David E. Bernstein, *Only One Place of Redress: African Americans, and the Courts from Reconstruction to the New Deal* (Duke University Press, 2001), 85–89.

53 Moreno, *Black Americans and Organized Labor: A New History*, 167; Bernstein, *Only One Place of Redress*, 93, 94.

54 Richard Rothstein, *The Color of Law: The Forgotten History of How Our Government Segregated America* (Norton, 2017), 64–65.

55 Nancy J. Weiss, *Farewell to the Party of Lincoln: Black Politics in the Age of FDR* (Princeton University Press, 1983), 99–106; Neal R. McMillen, *Dark Journey: Black Mississippians in the Age of Jim Crow* (University of Illinois Press, 1990), 249; Davis, *FDR: The New Deal Years, 1933–1937*, 483.

56 Gregory, *New Deal War Law and Order*, 179–180; Weiss, *Farewell to the Party of Lincoln*, 108–09; Katzelson, *Fear Itself*, 159.

57 Weiss, *Farewell to the Party of Lincoln*, 136–140. For an early use of the term, see "The Black Cabinet Likely to Stay," *The Afro-American* (Baltimore), December 5th 1908, 1.

58 Eugene Davidson, "The Black Cabinet in the New Deal," *New York Age* (April 7th 1934), 2; and Weiss, *Farewell to the Party of Lincoln*, 156.

59 Hull, *The Memoirs of Cordell Hull*, 353–54, 370–71; Schlesinger, *The Age of Roosevelt: The Coming of the New Deal*, 254–58; Harold B, Hinton, *Cordell Hull: A Biography* (Doubleday, 1942), 288.

60 Schlesinger, *The Age of Roosevelt: The Coming of the New Deal*, 255–56, 260; Shlaes, *The Forgotten Man*, 198; Gellman, *Secret Affairs*, 96; Phil Magness, "The Problem of the Tariff in American Economic History, 1787–1934." Cato Publications, September 26th 2023, https://www.cato.org/publications/problem-tariff-american-economic-history-1787-1934#protectionism-income-tax-era, accessed February 3rd 2025.

61 Schlesinger, *The Age of Roosevelt: The Coming of the New Deal*, 359–360; Hull, *The Memoirs of Cordell Hull*, 357–59; A.M. Fox, "Quantitative and Qualitative Changes in International Trade during the Depression," *American Economic Review* 27:1 (March 1937), 20; Shlaes, *The Forgotten Man*, 198–99.

62 Hull, The Memoirs of Cordell Hull, 354; Fox, "Quantitative and Qualitative Changes in International Trade during the Depression," 20; Shlaes, *The Forgotten Man*, 171; Powell, *FDR's Folly*, 233; Selgin, *False Dawn*, 193–94, 299; Barry Eichengreen, *Golden Fetters: The Gold Standard and the Great Depression, 1919–1939* (Oxford University Press, 1995), 345–46; Smiley, *Rethinking the Great Depression*, 78.

63 Folsom, *New Deal or Raw Deal?* 169–171.

64 Folsom, *New Deal or Raw Deal?* 170–75; Davis, *FDR: The New Deal Years, 1933–1937*, 421.

3 The Second New Deal: Free Markets Plowed Under

1 Davis, *FDR: The New Deal Years*, 434–35.

2 Weiss, *Farewell to the Party of Lincoln*, 109–114; Robert L. Zanagrando, *The NAACP Crusade Against Lynching, 1909–1950* (Philadelphia: Temple University Press, 1980), 6.

3 Weiss, *Farewell to the Party of Lincoln*, 114.

4 Weiss, *Farewell to the Party of Lincoln,* 113–114; Gregory, *New Deal Law and Order*, 177.

5 Patrick J. Hearden, *Roosevelt Confronts Hitler: America's Entry into World War II* (DeKalb, Illinois: Northern Illinois University Press, 1987, 44.

6 Davis, *FDR: The New York Years*, 423; Hearden, *Roosevelt Confronts Hitler*, 44–46; Cordell Hull, *The Memoirs of Cordell Hull*, vol. 1 (New York: Macmillan, 1948), 373–74; Schlesinger, *The Age of Roosevelt: The Coming of the New Deal*, 258; Franklin D. Roosevelt to Jesse Jones, July 18th 1935, in Elliot Roosevelt, ed., *FDR: His Personal Letters*, 493–94; Douglas A. Irwin, "From Smoot-Hawley to Reciprocal Trade Agreements: Changing the Course of U.S. Trade Policy in the 1930s," in Michael D. Bordo, Claudia Goldin, and Eugene N. White, eds., *The Defining Moment: The Great Depression and the American Economy in the Twentieth Century* (University of Chicago Press, 1998), 343–44.

7 Powell, *FDR's Folly*, 96-97; Folsom, *New Deal or Raw Deal?* 84–86.

8 Barry B. Witham, *The Federal Theater Project: A Case Study* (Cambridge University Press, 2003), 4–5; Susan Quinn, *Furious Improvisation: How the WPA and a Cast of Thousand Made High Art in Desperate Times* (New York: Walker and Company, 2008), 76–77, 107–111; Garet Garrett, "Federal Theater for the Masses," in Amity Shlaes, ed., *New Deal Rebels* (Great Barrington: American Institute for Economic Research, 2023), 133–36.

9 Franklin D. Roosevelt, Executive Order 7037, Establishing the Rural Electrification Administration, May 11th 1935, https://en.wikisource.org/wiki/Executive_Order_7037, accessed August 25th 2024; Richard F. Hirsh, *Powering American Farms: The Overlooked Origins of Rural Electrification* (Johns Hopkins University Press, 2022), 17, 230;

10 Franklin D. Roosevelt, Address at Barnesville, Georgia, August 11th 1938, https://www.presidency.ucsb.edu/documents/address-barnesville-georgia, accessed August 21st 2024; Quinn, *Furious Improvisation,* 149–152; Hirsh, *Powering American Farms*, 20.

11 Quinn, *Furious Improvisation,* 151–52.

12 Hirsh, *Powering American Farms*, 23, 205–06.

13 Hirsh, *Powering American Farms*, 108, 187–88.

14 Carol Lee, "Wired Help for the Farm: Individual Electric Generating Sets for Farms, 1880–1930," Pennsylvania State University, Ph.D. diss., 1989), iii, 204–05; Hirsh, *Powering American Farms*, 76; Robert E. Wright, *FDR's Long New Deal: A Public Choice Perspective*, 174–75.

15 Hirsh, *Powering American Farms*, 212, 215–16, 227–28; Lee, "Wired Help for the Farm," 1.

16 Hirsh, *Powering American Farms*, 91.

17 Shlaes, *The Forgotten Man*, 204–05, 216–17.

18 Shlaes, *The Forgotten Man*, 220, 239–240; "New Names in *Who's Who*," *The Brooklyn Daily Eagle*, October 27th 1936, 30.

19 Shlaes, *The Forgotten Man,* 221, 224.

20 Shlaes, *The Forgotten Man*, 242.

21 Schlesinger, *The Age of Roosevelt: The Coming of the New Deal,* 161; Shlaes, *The Forgotten Man,* 243–44; Moley, *The First New Deal,* 296.
22 Folsom, *New Deal or Raw Deal,* 58–59, 69; Franklin D. Roosevelt, Press Conference, May 31st 1935, https://www.presidency.ucsb.edu/documents/press-conference-23, accessed August 17th 2024.
23 Selgin, *False Dawn,* 124–130; Davis, *FDR: The New Deal Years,* 529.
24 Davis, *FDR: The New Deal Years,* 528–29; Dickman, *Industrial Democracy in America,* 271; Folsom, *New Deal or Raw Deal?* 120.
25 Dickman, *Industrial Democracy in America,* 274.
26 Schlesinger, *The Age of Roosevelt: The Coming of the New Deal,* 405; Moreno, *Black Americans and Organized Labor,* 171–73; Dickman, *Industrial Democracy in America,* 214–16.
27 Dickman, *Industrial Democracy in America,* 214–15, 266.
28 Bernstein, *Only One Place of Redress,* 94–95; Moreno, *Black Americans and Organized Labor,* 102–04; Thomas E. Hall and J. David Ferguson, *The Great Depression: An International Disaster of Perverse Economic Policies* (Ann Arbor: University of Michigan Press, 1998), 144.
29 Dickman, *Industrial Democracy in America,* 279; Powell, *FDR's Folly,* 204.
30 Roosevelt to Luther C. Steward, August 16th 1937, https://www.presidency.ucsb.edu/documents/letter-the-resolution-federation-federal-employees-against-strikes-federal-service, accessed August 17th 2025.
31 Davis, *FDR: The New Deal Years,* 544; Folsom, *New Deal or Raw Deal?* 131–32; Franklin D. Roosevelt, Message to Congress on Tax Revision, June 19th 1935, https://www.presidency.ucsb.edu/documents/message-congress-tax-revision, accessed August 19th 2024.
32 Davis, *FDR: The New Deal Years,* 545.
33 Folsom, *New Deal or Raw Deal?* 127, 136–141.
34 Folsom, *New Deal or Raw Deal?* 126–27; Franklin D. Roosevelt, Message to Congress on Tax Revision.
35 Michael Stephen Czaplicki, "The Corruption of Hope: Political Scandal, Congressional Investigations, and New Deal Moral Authority, 1932–1952" (PhD diss., University of Chicago, 2010), 56–58; Arnold Markoe, "The Black Committee: A Study of the Senate Investigation of the Public Utility Holding Company Lobby" (PhD diss., New York University, 1972), 37–47. Czaplicki, "Corruption of Hope," 39, 57; Markoe, "Black Committee," 92; David D. Lee, "Senator Black's Investigation of the Airmail, 1933–1934," *Historian* 53:3 (Spring 1991), 439–441; Shlaes, *The Forgotten Man,* 254–55, 268, 280–82.
36 74 *Cong. Rec.*, S11003 (Daily ed., July 11th 1935); Czaplicki, "Corruption of Hope," 58, 253; Roger K. Newman, *Hugo Black: A Biography* (New York: Fordham University Press, 1994), 228.
37 Czaplicki, "Corruption of Hope," 43–47, 79, 83; Carl Beck, *Contempt of Congress: A Study of the Prosecutions Initiated by the Committee on Un-American Activities, 1945–1957* (New Orleans: Hauser Press, 1959), 6–9, 212–14; Donald A. Ritchie, "What Makes a Successful Congressional Investigation?" *OAH Magazine of History* 12:4 (Summer 1998), 21.
38 Newman, *Hugo Black,* 178–180; Czaplicki, "Corruption of Hope," 79;
39 Markoe, "Black Committee," 95–96.
40 Markoe, "Black Committee," 100; Jamie C. Euken, "Evil, Greed, Treachery, Deception, and Fraud: The World of Lobbying According to Senator Hugo Black," *Federal History* 6 (January 2014), 73–74.
41 Markoe, "Black Committee," 105–06; Euken, "Evil, Greed, Treachery," 74; "Executive Defends His Utility," *New York Times,* August 13th, 1935, 1.

42 Diaries of Henry Morgenthau Jr., July 24th 1935, 122C, Franklin D. Roosevelt Presidential Library and Museum; and Czaplicki, "Corruption of Hope," 96–99.

43 Franklin D. Roosevelt, *Looking Forward* (London: William Heinemann, 1933), 121; Schlesinger, *The Age of Roosevelt: The Coming of the New Deal*, 308-09; Franklin D. Roosevelt, Message to Congress on Social Security, January 17th 1935, https://www.presidency.ucsb.edu/documents/message-congress-social-security, accessed August 19th 2024; Franklin D Roosevelt, Fireside Chat, September 31st 1934, https://www.presidency.ucsb.edu/documents/fireside-chat-20, accessed January 31st 2025; Franklin D. Roosevelt, "A Social Security Program Must Include All Those Who Need Its Protection, August 15th 1938, https://www.ssa.gov/history/fdrstmts.html#message1, accessed February 2nd 2025.

44 Carolyn L. Weaver, *The Crisis in Social Security: Economic and Political Origins* (Durham: North Carolina: Duke University Press, 1982), 42, 47–49; Roger L. Ransom and Richard Sutch, "Tontine Insurance and the Armstrong Investigation: A Case of Stifled Innovation, 1868–1905," *Journal of Economic History* 47:2 (June 1987), 381–82, 385.

45 Ransom and Sutch, "Tontine Insurance and the Armstrong Investigation," 381; William J. Bernstein, "King William's Tontine: Why the Retirement Annuity of the Future Should Resemble Its Past (a review)," *Financial Analysts Journal*, Book Review, September 8th 2017, https://rpc.cfainstitute.org/research/financial-analysts-journal/2015/king-williams-tontine, accessed January 31st 2025.

46 Weaver, *The Crisis in Social Security*, 48–49, 62–64.

47 Weaver, *The Crisis in Social Security*, 64.

48 Weaver, *The Crisis in Social Security*, 70–71; Davis, *FDR: The New Deal Years*, 449, 459.

49 Schlesinger, *The Age of Roosevelt: The Coming of the New Deal*, 308–09; Franklin D. Roosevelt, Message to Congress on Social Security, January 17th 1935,https://www.presidency.ucsb.edu/documents/message-congress-social-security, accessed August 19th 2024.

50 Weaver, *The Crisis in Social Security*, 90–91.

51 Weaver, *The Crisis in Social Security*, 90–91.

52 Weaver, *The Crisis in Social Security*, 92; Carolyn L. Weaver, "Birth of an Entitlement, "May 1st 1996, AEI, https://www.aei.org/articles/birth-of-an-entitlement/, accessed August 19th 2024.

53 Hearden, *Roosevelt Confronts Hitler*, 79–80.

54 Flynn, *The Roosevelt Myth*, 168–170; Lynne Olson, *Those Angry Days: Roosevelt, Lindbergh, and America's Fight Over World War II, 1939–1941* (Random House, 2013, 28.

55 Hearden, *Roosevelt Confronts Hitler*, 79–80; Franklin D. Roosevelt, "Statement on Neutrality Legislation," August 31st 1935, https://www.presidency.ucsb.edu/documents/statement-neutrality-legislation, accessed August 19th 2024.

56 Jerome Tuccille, *The War Against the Vets: The World War I Bonus Army during the Great Depression* (University of Nebraska Press, 2018), 144–47; Christine Kay Seiler, "The Veteran Killer: The Florida Emergency Relief Administration and the Labor Day Hurricane of 1935," *The Florida State University*, 46; and "Catastrophe: Wind, Water, and Woe," *Time*, September 16th 1935, https://time.com/archive/6896231/catastrophe-wind-water-woe/, accessed August 19th 2024.

57 Seiler, "The Veteran Killer," 110, 114, 123–134; Tuccille, *The War Against*

the Vets, 163, 176–180; and "Catastrophe: Wind, Water, and Woe," *Time*.

58 Seiler, "The Veteran Killer," 429; Folsom, *New Deal or Raw Deal?* 100; "Hurricane Death Toll 'Act of God Probers Declare," *The Evansville Courier and Press*, September 9th, 1935, 1; Tuccille, *The War Against the Vets*, 190, 193.

59 Tuccille, *The War Against the Vets*, 189, 193; "An Act of God," *Chicago Daily Tribune*, September 12th 1935, 10.

60 Tuccille, *The War Against the Vets*, 172–74; Dan Monroe, "Hemingway, the Left, and Key West," in Kirk Cornutt and Gail D. Sinclair, eds., *Key West Hemingway: A Reassessment* (Gainesville: University Press of Florida, 2009), 96.

61 Betty Houchin Winfield, *FDR and the News Media* (Urbana: University of Illinois Press, 1993), 40–42; White, *FDR and the Press*, 35; Best, *Critical Press*, 17; Melvin G. Holli, *The Wizard of Washington: Emil Hurja, Franklin Roosevelt, and the Birth of Public Opinion Polling* (New York: Palgrave, 2002), 66.

62 Brinkley, *Voices of Protest*, 207–08

63 Folsom, *New Deal or Raw Deal?* 150; and Davis, *FDR: The New Deal Years*, 574.

64 Davis, *FDR: The New Deal Years*, 575–76.

65 Brinkley, *Voices of Protest*, 249–250; Holli, *Wizard of Washington*, 67–68; Folsom, *New Deal or Raw Deal?* 178–79.

4 The Politics of Retaliation: The Black Inquisition

1 74 *Cong. Rec.*, S11003 (Daily ed., July 11, 1935); and Czaplicki, "Corruption of Hope," 58, 253.

2 Jamie C. Euken, "Evil, Greed, Treachery, Deception, and Fraud: The World of Lobbying According to Senator Hugo Black," *Federal History* 6 (2014), 74–75; U.S. Senate, 74th Cong., 2nd sess., *Alleged Seizures of Telegrams and Records and Telephone Communications*, Document No. 188 (Washington, DC: Government Printing Office, 1936), 3–5; *Hearst v. Black et al.*, 87 F. 2d 68 (1936); Francis R. Stark to Black, March 16, 1936, Box 181, Folder 2, Senatorial File (Lobbying) Correspondence, Hugo L. Black Papers, Library of Congress, Washington, DC.

3 Special Committee to Investigate Lobbying Activities, Records, US Senate, 75th Cong., Telegram Files, 1935–38, National Archives; Czaplicki, "Corruption of Hope," 98; Harry Y. Saint to Black, March 13, 1936, Folder 6, Box 181 Senatorial File (Lobbying) Correspondence, Hugo L. Black Papers, Library of Congress, Washington, DC; and 74 Cong. Rec., S4495–96 (Daily ed., March 26, 1936).

4 74 Cong. Rec., H3265 (Daily ed., March 4, 1936); Felix Bruner, "Lobby Group Seeks to Find Wire Seizure Justification," *Washington Post*, March 5, 1936, 1; William Doherty, "Court's Power Challenged by Black Group," *New York American*, March 27, 1936, 4; Paul C. Yates to Black, September 25, 1935, Box 181, Folder 2, Senatorial File (Lobbying), Correspondence, Hugo L. Black Papers, Library of Congress, Washington, DC; and Saint to Black, March 13, 1936, Folder 6, Box 181 Senatorial File (Lobbying) Correspondence, Hugo L. Black Papers.

5 Czaplicki, "Corruption of Hope," 98–99; William Randolph Hearst v. Black; Hugo L. Black et al., In the Supreme Court of the District of Columbia, "Brief of Plaintiff in Support of Motion for Injunction Pendente Lite and

in Opposition to Motion to Dismiss for Want of Jurisdiction" [c. April 1936], 52, Folder: District of Columbia, Hearst vs. United States Senate Special Committee, 1935, Box B-48, Western Union Telegraph Company Records, Archives Center, National Museum of American History, Washington, DC.

6 Robert J. Brown, Manipulating the Ether: The Power of Broadcast Radio in Thirties *America* (Jefferson, NC: McFarland and Company, 1998), 14.

7 Becky M. Nicolaides, "Radio Electioneering in the American Presidential Campaigns of 1932 and 1936," *Historical Journal of Film, Radio and Television* 8, no. 2 (1988): 125–26; "Widespread Support for Radio in Political Broadcast Fracas," *Broadcasting* 10, no. 3, February 1, 1936, 8; and Franklin Delano Roosevelt, "Annual Message to Congress," January 3, 1936, https://www.presidency.ucsb.edu/documents/annual-message-congress-2, accessed September 7, 2024.

8 Holli, *Wizard of Washington,* 67–68; Folsom, *New Deal or Raw Deal?* 178–79; and William E. Leuchtenburg, *The FDR Years: On Roosevelt and His Legacy* (New York: Columbia University Press, 1995), 101–2.

9 Mark Sullivan, "Stories Clash on Seizure of Telegrams," *Hartford Courant* (Hartford, CT), March 9, 1936, 18; Hearst v. Black et al., "Brief for Plaintiff," 52; "Crusaders Tell Tactics in Black Inquisition Here," *Chicago Daily Tribune,* March 8, 1936, 17; and "Utility Inquirers Seize Files Here," *New York Times,* March 3, 1936, 7.

10 Silas H. Strawn v. The Western Union Telegraph Company, In the Supreme Court of the District of Columbia "Brief for Plaintiffs" [March 1936], 1–3, Folder: District of Columbia, Strawn v. Western Union, Western Union Telegraph Company Records, 1936, Archives Center, National Museum of American History, Washington, DC; "Silas Hardy Strawn, 1866–1946," *American Bar Association Journal* 32, no. 3 (March 1946): 164; Jeff Shesol, *Supreme Power: Franklin Roosevelt vs. the Supreme Court* (New York: W. W. Norton, 2010), 10; and Arthur Sears Henning, "Strawn Asks Court to Halt Lobby Snooping," *Chicago Daily Tribune,* March 3, 1936, 4.

11 William E. Leuchtenburg, "A Klansman Joins the Court: The Appointment of Hugo L. Black," *University of Chicago Law* Review 41, no. 1 (Fall 1973): 6–7.

12 "Washington: Black Inquisition," *Chicago Daily Tribune,* March 8, 1936, B7; Czaplicki, "Corruption of Hope," 87; "A Damaging Attitude," *New York Times,* March 22, 1936, E8; White, *FDR and the Press,* 31; Mark Sullivan, "Capitol Comment," *Centralia Sentinel* (Centralia, IL), March 6, 1936, 1; "Black Booty," Time 27, no. 11, March 16, 1936, 18; and Arthur Krock, "In Washington: Seizure of Telegrams May Be Campaign Issue," *New York Times,* March 6, 1936, 20.

13 "Black Group Gets Wires by the Millions," *Chicago Daily Tribune,* March 5, 1936, 1, 8; 74 *Cong. Rec.,* S3328, S3331 (Daily ed., March 5, 1936); and 74 *Cong. Rec.,* H3266 (Daily ed., March 4, 1936); and Kenneth W. Vickers, "John Rankin: Democrat and Demagogue" (MA thesis, Mississippi State University, 1993), 50–55.

14 Walter Lippmann, "Today and Tomorrow: Legislative Inquisition," *Los Angeles Times,* March 7, 1936, A4; and Ronald Steel, *Walter Lippmann and the American Century* (Boston: Little, Brown and Company, 1980), 167, 216–19, 227–33.

15 Newman, *Hugo Black,* 187–88; "Report of the Standing Committee on Communications to the American Bar Association," *Annual Report of the American Bar* Association 61 (1936): 644; "Senate Accepts Curb on

Activity of Lobby Inquiry," *Christian Science Monitor*, March 12, 1936, 2; Black to Western Union Telegram Company and T. B. Kingsbury, 18 March 1936, Folder 7, Box 181, Senatorial File (Lobbying), Correspondence, Hugo L. Black Papers, Library of Congress, Washington, DC; and Arthur Sears Henning, "Halt Senate Wire Seizures," *Chicago Daily Tribune*, March 12, 1936, 8.

16 Ben Procter, *William Randolph Hearst: The Later Years, 1911–1951* (New York: Oxford University Press, 2007), 170–71, 190–91, 206; Elliott Roosevelt and James Bough, *The Roosevelts of the White House*, 102.

17 "Increased Fund Asked to Push Lobby," *Washington Post,* March 13, 1936, 2; 74 *Cong. Rec.,* H3950 (Daily ed., March 18, 1936); and Arthur Sears Henning, "Black 'Terror' Acts Fought in New Court Acts," *Chicago Daily Tribune*, March 13, 1936, 1

18 Arthur Sears Henning, "New Suit Filed to Halt Black Wire Seizures," *Chicago Daily Tribune,* March 14, 1936, 1, 8; and "Hearst Files Suit on Lobby Inquiry," *New York Times,* March 13, 1936, 6.

19 Black to Western Union Telegraph Company and T. B. Kingsbury, March 18, 1936, Folder 7, Box 181, Senatorial File (Lobbying), Correspondence, Hugo L. Black Papers, Library of Congress, Washington, DC; "Hearst Telegram Given Out in House," New York Times, March 19, 1936, 1; 74 Cong. Rec., H3950 (Daily ed., March 18, 1936); and Black to Western Union Telegraph Company and Kingsbury.

20 "An Obvious Red Herring," editorial, *Washington Post,* March 21, 1936, 8.

21 "Court's Power Challenged by Black Group," *New York American*, March 27, 1936, 4; "Partial Retreat from Moscow," editorial, *Washington Post,* April 1, 1936, 8; and Czaplicki, "Corruption of Hope," 95. Even after the FCC ceased cooperation, however, Stanley Morse, executive president of the Farmers' Independence Council, alleged that a telegram sent on April 10 to E. V. Wilcox, the council's secretary who also testified that day, "apparently was in the hands of the Committee a few hours later." Stanley Morse to Member, 20 April 1936, Folder: I-60 NRA-Black, Hugo, Committee, 1936, Robert R. McCormick Papers, Robert R. McCormick Papers, Colonel Robert R. McCormick Research Center, Wheaton, IL.

22 "Report of the Standing Committee [American Bar Association]," 645; William A. Gregory and Rennard Strickland, "Hugo Black's Congressional Investigation of Lobbying and the Public Utility Holding Company Act: A Historical View of the Power Trust, New Deal Politics, and Regulatory Propaganda," *Oklahoma Law Review* 29, no. 3 (1976): 569; and Alice Roosevelt Longworth, "What Alice Thinks," *Los Angeles Times,* April 1, 1936, 5.

23 Newman, *Hugo Black*, 188; White, FDR and the Press, 95–96; "Senator Black Feeds on Poisoned Meet," editorial, *New York American*, April 28, 1936, 14; Cartoon, *New York American,* April 17, 1936, 22; and Berton Braley, "Sh-h-h-Sh-Shish," *New York American*, April 11, 1936, 10.

24 Czaplicki, "Corruption of Hope," 88–89; Newman, *Hugo Black*, 190; Black to Seba Eldridge, March 23, 1936, Box 181, Folder 6, Senatorial File (Lobbying) Correspondence, Hugo L. Black Papers, Library of Congress, Washington, DC; Roger N. Baldwin to Black, April 18, 1936, Hugo L. Black, Box 181, Folder 8, Senatorial File (Lobbying) Correspondence, Hugo L. Black Papers, Library of Congress, Washington, DC; and Black to Baldwin, April 29, 1936, Folder: American Civil Liberties Union, Box 11, Special Committee to Investigate Lobbying Activities, Records, U.S. Senate, 75th Cong., National Archives.

25 74 *Cong. Rec.,* H5543–5545 (Daily ed., April 15, 1936).

26 David T. Beito, *The New Deal's War on the Bill of Rights: The Untold Story of FDR's Concentration Camps, Censorship, and Mass Surveillance* (Oakland: The Independent Institute, 2023), 32.
27 Raymond Moley, *After Seven Years* (New York: Harper and Brothers, 1939), 336–39; "The Night Riders: An Old Southern Custom," cartoon, *Chicago Daily Tribune*, May 7th 1936, 1.
28 "Court Rebukes the FCC," *New York Times*, November 10th 1936, 5; "Senator Black Maps Course with Liberals," *Washington Post*, September 6th 1936, 2.
29 Seiler "The Veteran Killer," 161–62, 461–65.
30 "The Republican Party Platform of 1936," June 9th 1936, accessed May 24th 2017, http://www.presidency.ucsb.edu/ws/?pid=29639, accessed February 3rd 2025; Alfred E. Landon Address Accepting the Republican Presidential Nomination in Topeka, July 23rd 1936, Address Accepting the Republican Presidential Nomination in Topeka, Kansas, July 23, 1936, https://www.presidency.ucsb.edu/documents/address-accepting-the-republican-presidential-nomination-topeka-kansas, accessed September 6th 2024.
31 Franklin D. Roosevelt, Acceptance Speech for the Renomination for the Presidency, Philadelphia, June 27th 1936; https://www.presidency.ucsb.edu/documents/acceptance-speech-for-the-renomination-for-the-presidency-philadelphia-pa, accessed September 6th 2024.
32 Folsom, *New Deal or Raw Deal?* 180; Davis, *FDR: The New Deal Years*, 638.
33 Franklin D. Roosevelt to William E. Dodd, August 5th 1936, in Elliott Roosevelt, ed., *FDR: His Personal Letters, 1928–1945*, 606–07.
34 Nicolaides, "Radio Electioneering," 125–26, 133; Lynn D. Gordon, "Why Dorothy Thompson Lost Her Job: Political Columnists and the Press Wars of the 1930s and 1940s," *History of Education Quarterly* 34:3 (Fall 1994), 293.
35 Nicolaides, "Radio Electioneering," 127, 136.
36 Nicolaides, "Radio Electioneering," 125.
37 Stanley High, "No-So-Free Air," *Saturday Evening Post* 211:33 (February 11th 1939), 8–9; "Broadcasters Memorize This!" *Variety*, February 15th 1939, 1.
38 Robert Dallek, *Franklin D. Roosevelt and American Foreign Policy, 1932–1945* (Oxford University Press, 1979), 129; Franklin D. Roosevelt, Address at Chautauqua, N.Y., August 14th 1936, https://www.presidency.ucsb.edu/documents/address-chautauqua-ny, accessed September 7th 2024; Grabar, *Debunking Roosevelt*, 182–85; Franklin D. Roosevelt, "European Inspection Trip, Summer 1918," in Elliot Roosevelt, ed., *FDR: His Personal Letters, 1905–1928* (New York: Duell, Sloan, and Pearce, 1950), 396–439.
39 Folsom, *New Deal or Raw Deal?* 181, 183.
40 Folsom, *New Deal or Raw Deal?* 181–83.
41 Folsom, *New Deal or Raw Deal?* 183.
42 Folsom, *New Deal or Raw Deal?* 86–87, 97, 154–55, 182, 190.
43 Davis, *FDR: The New Deal Years*, 630–31.
44 Weiss, *Farewell to the Party of Lincoln*, 114–16; Timothy J Hoffman, "The Civil Rights Realignment: How Race Dominates Presidential Elections," 2 (2015),

https://scholarship.shu.edu/cgi/viewcontent.cgi?article=1006&context=pa, accessed July 20th 2024.

45 Weiss, *Farewell to the Party of Lincoln*, 116–18, 199–205; Michaelis, *Eleanor*, 327.

46 Folsom, *New Deal or Raw Deal?* 185.

47 Weiss, *Farewell to the Party of Lincoln*, 214, 219.

48 Davis, *FDR: The New Deal Years*, 641; Folsom, *New Deal or Raw Deal?* 186.

49 Gregory, *New Deal Law and Order*, 184; Davis, *FDR: The New Deal Years*, 643, 647; Hoffman, "The Civil Rights Realignment," 2.

50 Folsom, *New Deal or Raw Deal?* 187-91.

51 *Hearst v. Black et al.*, 87 F.2d 68 (1936), 69–70, 72; "Court Rebukes the FCC," *New York Times*, November 10th 1936, 5.

52 Franklin D. Roosevelt, Address at Madison Square Garden, New York City https://www.presidency.ucsb.edu/documents/address-madison-square-garden-new-york-city-1, accessed February 3rd 2025; Schlesinger, *The Age of Roosevelt: Politics of Upheaval*, 513.

5 Roosevelt Confronts a Right-Left Free Speech Coalition

1 Kenneth S. Davis, *FDR: Into the Storm*, Random House, 1993, 5; Brands,
2 *A Traitor to His Class*, 467–470.
Davis, *FDR: Into the Storm*, 70–71; Lynne Olson, *Those Angry Days: Roosevelt, Lindbergh and America's Fight Over World War II, 1939–1941*
3 (Random House, 2013), 59–62.
Davis, *FDR: Into the Storm*, 70–73; Flynn, *The Roosevelt Myth*, 108–09; Richard Polenberg, "The National Committee to Uphold Constitutional Government, 1937–1941," *Journal of American History* 52:3 (December 1965), 583; Joanne Dunnebecke, "The Crusade for Individual Liberty: The Committee for Constitutional Government, 1937–1958" (master's thesis, University of Wyoming, 1987), 46–47.

4 Gregory, *New Deal Law and Order*, 194; George C. Rable, "The South and the Politics of Antilynching Legislation, 1920–1940," *The Journal of Southern History* 51:2 (May 1985), 210–11; Weiss, *Farewell to the Party of Lincoln*, 245; Davis, *FDR: Into the Storm*, 203, 205, 240–43.

5 Jean Edward Smith, *FDR*, 387; David E. Bernstein, *Rehabilitating Lochner: Defending Individual Rights Against Progressive Reform* (University of Chicago Press, 2011), 70–71, 103; Jamie L Carson and Benjamin A Kleinerman, "A Switch in Time Saves Nine: Institutions, Strategic Actors, and FDR's Court Plan," *Public Choice* 113 (December 2002), 318.

6 Nancy Peterson Hill, *A Very Private Public Citizen: The Life of Grenville Clark* (University of Missouri Press, 2014), 81, 109, 113, 117.

7 Hill, *A Very Private Public Citizen*, 118; "'Evaders' of Taxes Not to be Called," *New York Times* (July 16th 1937), 7; Willard Edwards, "Slaps Revenue Bureau War on Roosevelt Foes," *Chicago Daily Tribune* (September 21st 1937), 13; "Shafroth Quits Revenue Bureau," *New York Times*, (September 17th 1937), 1; "Courageous Resignations," *New York Times* (September 18th 1937), 18.

8 "Lehman Against Court Plan," *Wall Street Journal*, (July 20th 1937), 4; and Walter Trohan, *Political Animals: Memoirs of A Sentimental Cynic* (Doubleday, 1975), 99.

9 Alben Barkley, *That Reminds Me* (Doubleday, 1954), 154; Davis, *FDR: Into the Storm,* 92–95; David H. Culbert "'Croak' Carter: Radio's Voice of Doom," *Pennsylvania Magazine of History and Biography* 97:3 (July 1973), 306–07.

10 Howard Ball, *Hugo L. Black: Cold Steel Warrior* (Oxford University Press, 1996), 90; "Senators Near Fist Fight Over Black," *St. Louis Globe Democrat* (August 17th 1937), 1; Davis, *FDR: Into the Storm,* 109–110.

11 Davis, *FDR: Into the Storm,* 110–12; Ball, *Hugo L. Black: Cold Steel Warrior*, 98–99.

12 Richard Polenberg, *Reorganizing Roosevelt's Government: The Controversy Over Executive Reorganization, 1936–1939* (Harvard University Press, 1966), 149–151; Thomas Fleming, The *New Dealers' War: FDR and the War within World War II* (Basic 2001) 63; Robert Higgs, "Regime Uncertainty: Why the Great Depression Lasted So Long and Why Prosperity Resumed After the War" in Higgs, *Depression, War, and Cold War: Challenging the Myths of Conflict and Prosperity* (Independent Institute, 2006), 5–7; Folsom, *New Deal or Raw Deal?* 248; Anderson, *Economics and the Public Welfare: Financial and Economic History of the United States, 1914–1946* (Van Nostrand, 1949), 490.

13 Leuchtenburg, *Franklin D. Roosevelt and the New Deal*, 183; Higgs, "Regime Uncertainty," 20.

14 Brands, *Traitor to His Class*, 463–66; Selgin, *False Dawn,* 204-05, 244.

15 Flynn, *The Roosevelt Myth*, 117; Brinkley, *The End of Reform: New Deal Liberalism in Recession and War* (New York: Vintage, 1995), 56–57; Robert Higgs, "Regime Uncertainty," 29.

16 Davis, *FDR: Into the Storm,* 210; John Maynard Keynes's Private Letter to Franklin Delano Roosevelt of February 1st 1938, https://delong.typepad.com/egregious_moderation/2008/12/john-maynard-ke.html, accessed October 7th 2024; and Roosevelt to Keynes, March 3rd 1938, https://www.fdrlibrary.org/documents/356632/390886/smFDR-Keynes_1938.pdf/e6a5bbc6-db07-4d65-8576-e4ea058c5641, accessed October 7th 2024.

17 Selgin, *False Dawn*, 237.

18 Lynne Olson, *Those Angry Days*, 28; Dallek, *Franklin D. Roosevelt and American Foreign Policy*, 136, 140–43, 249; Davis, *FDR: Into the Storm*, 154–55; Flynn, *The Roosevelt Myth*, 196; The Neutrality Act of 1937, May 1st 1937, https://www.digitalhistory.uh.edu/disp_textbook.cfm?smtID=3&psid=4072, accessed October 1st 2024.

19 Flynn, *The Roosevelt Myth*, 172; Dallek, *Franklin D. Roosevelt and American Foreign Policy*, 146–47.

20 Dallek, Franklin D. Roosevelt and American Foreign Policy, 146; Arthur C. Hasiotis, *Soviet Political, Economic, and Military Involvement in Sinkiang from 1928 to 1949* (Garland, 1987). 66–77, 87–88, 115; Davis, *FDR: Into the Storm,* 237, 154–56; Hearden, *Roosevelt Confronts Hitler*, 104; Flynn, *The Roosevelt Myth*, 172–73.

21 Quarantine Speech, October 5th 1937, https://millercenter.org/the-presidency/presidential-speeches/october-5-1937-quarantine-speech, accessed October 12th 2024; Dallek, *Franklin D. Roosevelt and American Foreign Policy*, 148–49.

22 Burton W. Folsom Jr. and Anita Folsom, *FDR Goes to War: How Expanded Executive Power, Spiraling National Debt, and Restricted Civil Liberties Shaped Wartime America* (Simon and Schuster, 2011), 14, 83; "Fish

Urges View On Lynching By FDR," *Atlanta Daily World*, November 9th 1937, 1.

23 Davis, *FDR: Into the Storm*, 154–56, 398–99.

24 Medoff, *The Jews Should Keep Quiet*, 73–74, 80–81.

25 Davis, *FDR: Into the Storm*, 269; "The Evian Conference" in *Holocaust Encyclopedia* https://encyclopedia.ushmm.org/content/en/article/the-evian-conference, accessed November 12th 2024; Medoff, *The Jews Should Keep Quiet*, 76–80.

26 Higgs, "Regime Uncertainty," 9; "Great Caesar Fell," *New Republic*, 95:1236 (April 13th 1938), 303; Polenberg, *Reorganizing Roosevelt's Government*, 41–42, 148–51, 169.

27 Gary Dean Best, *The Critical Press and the New Deal: The Press Versus Presidential Power, 1933–1938* (Westport: Praeger, 1993), 18, 115, 124; Richard W. Steele, *Propaganda in an Open Society: The Roosevelt Administration and the Media, 1933–1941* (Greenwood Press, 1985), 49; Robert S. Allen, "Roosevelt Fights Back," *Nation* 145:140 (August 21st 1937), 188; Graham J. White, *FDR and the Press* (University of Chicago Press, 1979), 40.

28 Steele, *Propaganda in an Open Society*, 129–130; "'Boss' Agrees Marvin McIntyre Can Accept Degree Here," 13A; Stanley High, "Not-So-Free Air," *Saturday Evening Post* 211:33 (February 11th 1939), 76.

29 Joseph E. Davies to Stephen Early, February 8th 1938, C.M. Chester to Joseph E. Davies, January 25th 1938 (Enclosure: "Proposal for Method of Operation with Mr. Boake Carter"), Folder: President Roosevelt, 1938, Stephen Early Papers, Franklin D. Roosevelt Presidential Library, Hyde Park, NY; and Culbert, "'Croak' Carter," 307–310; Harold L. Ickes, *The Secret Diary of Harold L. Ickes: The Inside Struggle, 1936–1939*, vol. II (Simon and Schuster, 1954), 313.

30 Jerre Mangione, *An Ethnic at Large: A Memoir of America in the Thirties and Forties* (Putnam's, 1978), 248.

31 Stanley High, "No-So-Free Air," *Saturday Evening* Post 211:33 (February 11th 1939), 76; "Carter, Quitting Air Reads Freedom Essay," *Editor and Publisher* 71 (September 3rd 1938), 10; Newman, *Radio Active*, 91; "Hampered on Radio, Says Boake," *Hartford Courant* (Hartford), October 19th 1938, 12.

32 Selgin, *False Dawn*, 224–25; Alan Brinkley, *The End of Reform: New Deal Liberalism in Recession and War* (Vintage, 1995), 98–100.

33 Folsom, *New Deal or Raw Deal?*, 92, 180–88; Davis, *FDR: Into the Storm*, 231; Gavin Wright, "The Political Economy of New Deal Spending: An Econometric Analysis," *The Review of Economics and Statistics* 56:1 (February, 1974), 35.

34 Brinkley, *The End of Reform*, 104; Julian E. Zelizer, "The Forgotten Legacy of the New Deal: Fiscal Conservatism and the Roosevelt Administration, 1933–1938," *Presidential Studies Quarterly* 30:2 (June 2000), 352–53; Selgin, *False Dawn*, 226.

35 Elizabeth Anne Hull, "Sherman Minton and the Cold War Court" (PhD diss., New School for Social Research, 1976), 16–17; Linda C. Gugin and James E. St. Clair, *Sherman Minton: New Deal Senator, Cold War Justice* (Indianapolis: Indiana Historical Society, 1987), 102; Bargeron, "New Senate Prosecutors," 119; David H. Corcoran, "Sherman Minton: New Deal Senator," PhD diss., University of Kentucky, 1977), np, 77, 115, 130, 156, 176; Drew Pearson and Robert S. Allen, "Washington Merry-Go-Round, Roosevelt Holds Fighting Conference with Eight Senators," *Seattle Daily Times*, (December 28th 1937), 6.

36 Dunnebecke, "The Crusade for Individual Liberty," 12–13; Isaac William Martin, *Rich People's Movements: Grassroots Campaigns to Untax the One Percent* (Oxford University Press, 2013), 92–93; Polenberg, *Reorganizing Roosevelt's Government*, 76; "The Black Inquisition Revived," editorial, *Chicago Daily Tribune* (March 24th 1938), 12; "Terrorism and the Senate," *New York Herald-Tribune*, March 24th 1938, vol. 1089, American Civil Liberties Cases, 1938, Federal Legislation, Clippings 2, American Civil Liberties Union Papers, Mudd Library, Princeton University, Princeton; Frederic Nelson, "Pressure by 'Inquiry'," *Baltimore Sun* (March 27th 1938), 8.

37 Minton to Henry Morgenthau, Jr., March 26th 1938, U.S. Senate, 75th Congress, Special Committee to Investigate Lobbying Activities, General Files, 1-32 to 1-45, Box 2; U.S. Bureau of Internal Revenue, *Treasury Decisions Under Internal-Revenue Laws* 34 (Washington, DC: United States Government Printing Office, 1939), 254–55; Walter Lippmann, "Today and Tomorrow," *Los Angeles Times* (April 30th 1938), A4; "Lobby Probers Can Use Income Tax Records," *Baltimore Sun* (April 22nd 1938), 1; Walter Lippmann, "Today and Tomorrow," *Canton Repository* (Canton, Ohio), April 26th 1938, 4.

38 Grenville Clark, "The Relation of the Press to the Maintenance of Civil Liberty" (address, American Newspaper Publishers Association, New York City, April 27th 1938), Correspondence–Federal Legislation, vol. 1092, American Civil Liberties Union Papers, Mudd Library, Princeton, NJ; "Press Affirms Freedom; Minton Asks Press Curb," *Chicago Daily Tribune*, April 29th 1938, 1.

39 "Here's Minton's Plan," *Progressive* 2:20, May 14th 1938, 4; "Minton Offers Bill to Censor Hostile Press," *Philadelphia Inquirer*, April 29th 1938, 34; "Senator Hits Publishers for Combining Demand for Free Press with a Blow at President's Use of Air to State Views," *Washington Post*, April 29th 1938, 30; "New Dealer Blasts Publishers, Want to Put Editors in Jail if They Print Untruths," *Dallas Morning News*, April 29th 1938, 4; "Minton Bill Asks Falsifying News Be Made Penalty," *Atlanta Constitution*, April 29th 1938, 9.

40 "The Periscope," *Newsweek* 11:19 (May 9th 1938), 7; Paul Y. Anderson, "Senator Minton Delivers Bitter Attack on Press," *St. Louis Star-Times*, April 29th 1938, 21; "Senator Minton and American Journalism," *Christian Science Monitor*, May 6th 1938, 3; and David N. Atkinson, "From New Deal Liberal to Supreme Court Conservative: The Metamorphosis of Justice Sherman Minton," *Washington University Law Quarterly* 361 (1975), 382.

41 Press Conferences of President Franklin D. Roosevelt, 1933–1945, Series 1: Press Conference Transcripts, April 29th 1938, 399–400, Franklin D. Roosevelt Presidential Library & Museum, http://www.fdrlibrary.marist.edu/archives/collections/franklin/?p=collections/findingaid&id=508, accessed October 7th 2024;"To Undermine the Press," editorial, *Washington Post*, April 20th 1938, X8; "Now the Gag," editorial, *Milwaukee Journal*, April 30th 1938, 4; M. L. Annenberg, "The New Dealers Can't Muzzle the Inquirer: A Statement by M.L. Annenberg," *Philadelphia Inquirer*, April 30th 1938, 1; "Another 'Great Liberal' Hoists His Standard," cartoon, *Philadelphia Inquirer*, April 30th 1938, 6; "German News Agency Praises Minton's Plan," *Chicago Daily Tribune*, May 1st 1938, 9; "Heil Minton!" editorial, *Philadelphia Inquirer*, May 3rd 1938, 8; German News Agency Praises Minton's Plan, *Chicago Daily Tribune*, May 1st 1938, 9.

42 Nelson Johnson, *Battleground New Jersey: Vanderbilt, Hague, and Their Fight for Justice* (New Brunswick: Rutgers University Press, 2014), 94–95.
43 Lyle W. Dorsett, *Franklin D. Roosevelt and the City Bosses* (Port Washington, NY: National University Publications, 1977), 101–05.
44 Laura Weinrib, *The Taming of Free Speech: America's Civil Liberties Compromise* (Harvard University Press, 2006), 229, 231, 236–37; Dayton David McKean, *The Boss: The Hague Machine in Action* (Houghton Mifflin, 1940), 191; Dorsett, *City Bosses*, 103–05.
45 Weinrib, *Taming of Free Speech*, 236–37; "Socialist Chief Manhandled, Wife Struck," *Philadelphia Record*, May 1st 1938, 1; McKean, *The Boss*, 236; "The Shape of Things," *Nation* 146:19 (May 7th 1938), 518.
46 Weinrib, *The Taming of Free Speech*, 229, 231, 236–37; Dayton David McKean, *The Boss: The Hague Machine in Action* (Houghton Mifflin, 1940), 191; Johnson, *Battleground New Jersey*, 107; Dorsett, *City Bosses*, 103–05.
47 Richard L. Harkness, "Minton Abandons Bill to Gag Press; Wanted Publicity," *Philadelphia Inquirer*, May 3rd 1938, 1; "Honest—I Was Only Kidding," cartoon, *Philadelphia Inquirer*, May 4th 1938, 11; "Franklin Discovers Lightning Again," cartoon, *Philadelphia Inquirer*, May 4th 1938, 10.
48 "Spare the President from Such Friends," editorial, *Philadelphia Record*, May 7th 1938, 8.
49 Press Conferences of President Franklin D. Roosevelt, 1933–1945, Series 1: Press Conference Transcripts, May 10th 1938, 407–08, Franklin D. Roosevelt Presidential Library and Museum, accessed August 23rd 2022, http://www.fdrlibrary.marist.edu/_resources/ images/pc/pc0066.pdf; and "Will Hague Be a National Issue?" editorial, *New York Post*, May 31st 1938, 10.
50 "Bar Urged to Fight for Civil Liberties," *New York Times*, June 12th 1938, 2; Nancy Peterson Hill, *A Very Private Public Citizen: The Life of Grenville Clark* (University of Missouri Press, 2014), 126; Oswald Garrison Villard, "Issues and Men," *Nation* 146:21, May 21st 1938, 589; "Mayor Hague's Long Shadow," *New Republic* 95:1228, June 15th 1938, 144; "The Shape of Things," *Nation* 146:23, June 4th 1938, 631.
51 Fireside Chat, June 24th 1938, http://www.presidency.ucsb.edu/ws/index.php?pid=15662, accessed October 7th 2024.
52 Weinrib, *Taming of Free Speech*, 239; "Editorial," *Baltimore Sun*, June 26th 1938, 1; Beito, *The New Deal's War on the Bill of Rights*, 87.
53 Bernstein, *Only One Place of Redress*, 101–02.
54 Graham J. White, *FDR and the Press* (University of Chicago Press, 1979), 35, 138; Franklin D. Roosevelt: "Letter of Congratulations to the St. Louis Post-Dispatch," *St. Louis Post-Dispatch*, November 2nd 1938, The American Presidency Project, https://www.presidency.ucsb.edu/ documents/letter-congratulationsthe-st-louis-post-dispatch, accessed October 7th 2024.
55 Weinrib, *Taming of Free Speech*, 239–240; "Cummings Drops Inquiry on Hague; Mayor Is Cleared," *Washington Post*, September 8th 1938, X1; "Hague Under Inquiry," *New York Times*, September 13th 1938, X8; "Thomas Belittles Inquiry on Hague," *New York Times*, September 13th 1938, 14; "Thomas Continues Drive on Democrats," *New York Times*, October 9th 1938, 33; Albert Jay Nock, "State of the Union: Job-holders' Paradise," *American Mercury* 45:177 (September 1938), 90–91.
56 "Federal Judge Restrains Hague on Deportations," *Chicago Daily Tribune*, October 28th 1938, 6; Weinrib, *Taming of Free Speech*, 242–44, 265.

57 John W. Jeffries, *A Third Term for FDR: The Election of 1940* (Lawrence: University Press of Kansas, 2017), 33; 92.
58 Davis, *FDR: Into the Storm*, 344; Mathew Vink, "The Competition for Self-Determination in Czechoslovakia, 1918–1919," *New Zealand Slavonic Journal* 46 (2012), 65–68; "To Regain Place," *The Topeka State Journal,* January 6th 1919, 4; Dallek, *Franklin D. Roosevelt and American Foreign Policy*, 166; Arnold A. Offner, "Appeasement Revisited: The United States, Great Britain, and Germany, 1933–1940," *The Journal of American* History 64:2 (September, 1977), 382; Richard Whalen, *The Founding Father: The Story of Joseph P. Kennedy* (Regnery Gateway, 1993 [1964]), 247–48.
59 Davis, *FDR: Into the Storm*, 262, 379; Powell, *FDR's Folly*, 98; Flynn, *The Roosevelt Myth*, 134–35.
60 Brands, *A Traitor to His Class*, 500.

6 "Again, and Again, and Again": The Politics of War

1 Michael R. Marrus, "The Strange Story of Herschel Grynszpan," *The American Scholar* 57:1 (Winter 1988), 70–73; Davis, *FDR: Into the Storm*, 364–65; H.W. Brands, *America First: Roosevelt vs. Lindbergh in the Shadow of War* (Doubleday, 2016), 45–46; Sheldon Spear, "The United States and the Persecution of the Jews in Germany, 1933–1939," *Jewish Social Studies* 30:4 (October 1968), 233.
2 Medoff, *The Jews Should Keep Quiet*, 84.
3 Davis, *FDR: Into the Storm*, 367; Medoff, *The Jews Should Keep Quiet*, 86, 94.
4 Richard Moe, *Roosevelt's Second Act: The Election of 1940 and the Politics of War* (Oxford University Press, 2013), 78.
5 Richard J. Whalen, *The Founding Father: The Story of Joseph P. Kennedy* (Regnery Gateway, 1993 [1964]), 230, 253–55, 268.
6 Whalen, *The Founding Father*, 255–56; Jane Karoline Vieth, "Joseph P. Kennedy: Ambassador to the Court of St. James's, 1938–1940," PhD diss., The Ohio State University, 1975, 210; Marc Eric McClure, *Earnest Endeavors: The Life and Public Work of George Rublee* (Praeger, 2003), 273–75.
7 Davis, *FDR: Into the Storm*, 370; Medoff, *The Jews Should Keep Quiet*, 82, 84–85.
8 H.L. Mencken, "The Problem of the Refugees," *The Sun* (Baltimore), January 1st 1939, 6.
9 Davis, *FDR: Into the Storm*, 425.
10 Allan Keiler, *Marian Anderson: A Singer's Journey* (University of Illinois Press, 2002), 181–191; "Board of Education is Denounced by Pickets," *Pittsburgh Courier*, February 25th 1939, 4.
11 Tikia K. Hamilton, "Making a 'Model' System: Race, Education and Politics in the Nation's Capital Before *Brown*, 1930–1950," Princeton University, Ph.D. diss., 2015, 109–110; Keiler, *Marian Anderson*, 202.
12 Jean Edward Smith, *FDR*, 401–02; Keiler, *Marian Anderson*, 199–201; Zora Neale Hurston, "A Negro Voter Sizes Up Taft," *Saturday Evening Post* 224:23 (December 8th, 1951), 152; Weiss, *Farewell to the Party of Lincoln*, 258; Hamilton, "Making a 'Model' System," 109–110.
13 Weiss, *Farewell to the Party of Lincoln*, 258–267; and Hurston, "A Negro Voter Sizes Up Taft," 152.

14 Weiss, *Farewell to the Party of Lincoln,* 205.
15 "Refugee Ship," *New York Times,* June 8th 1939, 24; Davis, *FDR: Into the Storm,* 370; Medoff, *The Jews Should Keep Quiet*, 87.
16 Medoff, *The Jews Should Keep Quiet*, 87–88.
17 Whalen, *The Founding Father*, 264; Dallek, *Franklin D. Roosevelt and American Foreign Policy*, 188–195; Folsom and Folsom, *FDR Goes to War*, 83.
18 Jeffries, *A Third Term for FDR*, 90.
19 Moe, *Roosevelt's Second Act,* 90–92; and Davis, *FDR: Into the Storm,* 531.
20 Dallek, *Franklin D. Roosevelt and American Foreign Policy,* 196–98; Davis, *FDR: Into the Storm,* 489.
21 Olson, *Those Angry Days*, 94; Davis, *FDR: Into the Storm,* 505.
22 Franklin D. Roosevelt, Message to Congress Urging Repeal of the Embargo Provisions of the Neutrality Act, September 21st 1939, https://www.presidency.ucsb.edu/documents/message-congress-urging-repeal-the-embargo-provisions-the-neutrality-law, accessed November 23, 2024; Roosevelt, Fireside Chat, September 3rd 1939, https://www.presidency.ucsb.edu/documents/fireside-chat-13, accessed November 23rd 2024; Dallek, *Franklin D. Roosevelt and American Foreign Policy*, 201, 204–05; and "Radio Address to the *New York Herald Tribune* Forum," October 26th 1939, https://www.presidency.ucsb.edu/documents/radio-address-the-new-york-herald-tribune-forum-0, accessed November 23rd, 2024.
23 Davis, *FDR: Into the Storm,* 508, 519; Brands, *America First*, 94, 115; Hearden, *Roosevelt Confronts Hitler,* 140; Sean McMeekin, *Stalin's War: A New History of World War II* (Basic Books, 2021), 134–35.
24 Moe, *Roosevelt's Second Act,* 117–18; Gellman, *Secret Affairs,* 204; Davis, *FDR: Into the Storm,* 531.
25 Folsom, *New Deal or Raw Deal,* 208–09.
26 Dallek, *Franklin D. Roosevelt and American Foreign Policy,* 218, 221; Medoff, *The Jews Should Keep Quiet*, 94–96; Medoff, "Op-Ed: Recalling a Mormon senator who tried to save Anne Frank's life," *Jewish Telegraphic Agency*, February 26th 2012, https://www.jta.org/2012/02/26/ideas/op-ed-recalling-a-mormon-senator-who-tried-to-save-anne-franks-life, accessed November 17th 2024.
27 Persico, *Roosevelt's Secret War*, 64, 77–78; and Olson, *Those Angry Days*, 116–18, 338.
28 Olson, *Those Angry Days*, 116–21, 131–32.
29 Olson, *Those Angry Days,* 105, 108, 112–13; Dallek, *Franklin D. Roosevelt and American Foreign Policy,* 225; Fireside Chat, May 26th 1940, https://www.presidency.ucsb.edu/documents/fireside-chat-10, accessed November 28th 2024.
30 Olson, *Those Angry Days*, 122–24.
31 Olson, *Those Angry Days*, 337; Persico, *Roosevelt's Secret War*, 43, 113–15.
32 Brands, *America First,* 179, 182.
33 Davis, *FDR: Into the Storm,* 553, 575; Hearden, *Roosevelt Confronts Hitler*, 148; McMeekin, *Stalin's War*, 165, 171–72, 208.
34 Davis, *FDR: Into the Storm*, 577–583.
35 Davis, *FDR: Into the Storm*, 589–591.
36 Jeffries, *A Third Term for Roosevelt*, 111–12; "Statement on Candidacy for a Third Term", July 16th 1940, https://www.presidency.ucsb.edu/documents/statement-candidacy-for-third-term, accessed November 28th 2024.
37 Moe, *Roosevelt's Second Act*, 224.
38 Olson, *Those Angry Days*, 187–89.
39 Radio Address to the Democratic National Convention Accepting the

Nomination, July 19th 1940, https://www.presidency.ucsb.edu/documents/radio-address-the-democratic-national-convention-accepting-the-nomination, accessed November 28th 2024.

40 Folsom and Folsom, *FDR Goes to War*, 43–45, 50.

41 Moe, *Roosevelt's Second Act*, 254; Fleming, *The New Dealers' War*, 76–77.

42 Dallek, *Franklin D. Roosevelt and American Foreign Policy*, 208; McMeekin, *Stalin's War*, 177, 234

43 Weiss, *Farewell to the Party of Lincoln*, 274; Delmont, *Half American*, 37–38.

44 Weiss, *Farewell to the Party of Lincoln*, 277–78; Folsom and Folsom, *FDR Goes to War*, 56; and Delmont, *Half American*, 37–38.

45 Olson, *Those Angry Days*, 221–27, 234

46 Brands, *America First*, 261; Olson, *Those Angry Days*, 409; Alexandr M. Nekrich, *Pariahs, Partners, Predators: German-Soviet Relations, 1922–1941* (Columbia University Press, 1997), 216; McMeekin, *Stalin's War*, 206–07.

47 Olson, *Those Angry Days*, 190; Moe, *Roosevelt's Second Act*, 283; Burns, *Roosevelt: The Soldier of Freedom*, 6; Davis, *FDR: Into the Storm*, 613–14; Jeffries, *A Third Term for FDR*, 147.

48 Beito, *The New Deal's War on the Bill of Rights*, 136–145.

49 Beito, *The New Deal's War on the Bill of Rights*, 143–49.

50 Delmont, *Half American*, 25–26, 41–42.

51 Brands, *America First*, 237; Jeffries, *A Third Term for FDR*, 160; and "Campaign Address at Boston, Massachusetts," October 30th 1940, https://www.presidency.ucsb.edu/documents/campaign-address-boston-massachusetts, accessed November 28th 2024.

52 Franklin Roosevelt's Press Conference, December 17th 1940, http://docs.fdrlibrary.marist.edu/odllpc2.html, accessed November 29th 2024; Olson, *Those Angry Days*, 276; Folsom and Folsom, *FDR Goes to War*, 59–60.

53 Folsom and Folsom, *FDR Goes to War*, 59–60; Franklin Roosevelt's Press Conference, December 17th 1940, http://docs.fdrlibrary.marist.edu/odllpc2, accessed November 29th 2024; President Franklin Roosevelt's Annual Message. Four Freedoms to Congress (1941), January 6th 1941, https://www.archives.gov/milestone-documents/president-franklin-roosevelts-annual-message-to-congress, accessed November 29th 2024.

54 Beito, *The New Deal's War on the Bill of Rights*, 154–55

55 Hearden, *Roosevelt Confronts Hitler*, 193–94.

56 Folsom and Folsom, *FDR Goes to War*, 79; Persico, *Roosevelt's Secret War*, 102.

57 Hearden, *Roosevelt Confronts Hitler*, 195–96; Dallek, *Franklin D. Roosevelt and American Foreign Policy*, 261, 265.

58 Olson, *Those Angry Days*, 295; Hearden, *Roosevelt Confronts Hitler*, 203; and Gellman, *Secret Affairs*, 257.

59 Radio Address Announcing an Unlimited National Emergency, May 27th 1941, https://www.presidency.ucsb.edu/documents/radio-address-announcing-unlimited-national-emergency, accessed November 29th 2024; Hearden, *Roosevelt Confronts Hitler*, 158.

60 Gellman, *Secret Affairs*, 255; Dallek, *Franklin D. Roosevelt and American Foreign Policy*, 276; Hearden, *Roosevelt Confronts Hitler*, 183–85; and Persico, *Roosevelt's Secret War*, 128.

61 Gellman, *Secret Affairs*, 256; Olson, *Those Angry Days*, 346; and Sean McMeekin, *Stalin's War*, 349–350.

62 McMeekin, *Stalin's War*, 351–54, 359.

63 McMeekin, *Stalin's War*, 354–55; Dallek, *Franklin D. Roosevelt and American Foreign Policy*, 277, 297; Franklin D. Roosevelt, Press

Conference, September 30th 1941, http://www.fdrlibrary.marist.edu/_resources/images/pc/pc0123.pdf, accessed May 16th 2025.

64 Doris Kearns Goodwin, *No Ordinary Time: Franklin and Eleanor Roosevelt: The Home Front in World War II* (Simon and Schuster, 1994), 54-56; David Brinkley, *Washington Goes to War* (Knopf, 1988), 64–65.

65 Goodwin, *No Ordinary Time*, 232–33, 281–82; Brinkley, *Washington Goes to War*, 101; Fleming, *The New Dealers' War*, 136; Davis, *FDR: The War President*, 77–79, 195–98, 254.

66 Delmont, *Half American,* 51–54; Davis, *FDR: The War President*, 203.

67 Davis, *FDR: The War President,* 204–05; Delmont, *Half American*, 57–58.
Delmont, *Half American,* 59–60; Carla Kaplan, ed., *Zora Neale Hurston: A*
68 *Life in Letters* (New York: Anchor Books, 2002), 543–44; Davis, *FDR: The War President*, 205.

69 Medoff, *The Jews Should Keep Quiet,* 97–102.

70 Gellman, *Secret Affairs*, 265; Dallek, *Franklin D. Roosevelt and American Foreign Policy,* 274–75.

71 Dallek, *Franklin D. Roosevelt and American Foreign Policy,* 285–86.

72 Brands, *America First*, 347; Burns, *Roosevelt: The Soldier of Freedom,* 135–37.

73 Burns, Roosevelt: *The Soldier of Freedom*, 79, 146; Hearden, *Roosevelt Confronts Hitler*, 213–15; Gellman, *Secret Affairs,* 265; Eric Larrabee, *Commander In Chief*, 77, 85.

74 Memorandum by the Under Secretary of State (Welles) [Washington,] October 13th 1941, https://history.state.gov/historicaldocuments/frus1931-41v02/d370, accessed November 29th 2024; Dallek, *Franklin D. Roosevelt and American Foreign Policy,* 303.

75 Davis, *FDR: The War President,* 315; Dallek, *Franklin D. Roosevelt and American Foreign Policy*, 303.

76 Hearden, *Roosevelt Confront Hitler*, 206; Dallek, *Franklin D. Roosevelt and American Foreign Policy,* 287–88.

77 Roosevelt, Fireside Chat, September 11th 1941 https://www.presidency.ucsb.edu/documents/fireside-chat-11, accessed November 29th 2024; Brands, *America First*, 354.

78 Brands, *America First*, 382; Franklin D. Roosevelt Administration: Navy Day Address on the Attack on the Destroyer *Kearny*, October 27th 1941, https://www.jewishvirtuallibrary.org/president-roosevelt-ldquo-navy-day-address-rdquo-on-the-attack-on-the-destroyer-kearney-october-1941, accessed November 30th 2024.

79 Olson, *Those Angry Days*, 402–03; Persico, *Roosevelt's Secret War*, 125–28; Gellman, *Secret Affairs,* 252; Hearden, *Roosevelt Confronts Hitler*, 207–08.

80 Dallek, *Franklin D. Roosevelt and American Foreign Policy,* 306–07; Burns, *Roosevelt: The Soldier of Freedom*, 155.

81 Hearden, *Roosevelt Confronts Hitler*, 219–220; Dallek, *Franklin D. Roosevelt and American Foreign Policy*, 307; Hull Note (War Memorandum], November 26th 1941, https://worldjpn.net/documents/texts/pw/19411126.O1E.html, accessed November 30, 2024.

82 Dallek, *Franklin D. Roosevelt and American Foreign Policy*, 308, 311; Burns, *Roosevelt: The Soldier of Freedom*, 160; Folsom and Folsom, *FDR Goes to War*, 89; Persico, *Roosevelt's Secret War*, 144–48; Robert J. Hanyok, "'Catching the Fox Unaware,': Japanese Radio Denial and Deception and the Attack on Pearl Harbor," *Naval War College Review* 61:4 (Autumn 2008), 108–111.

83 Persico, *Roosevelt's Secret War*, 147–153; Fleming, *The New Dealers' War*, 45; Folsom and Folsom, *FDR Goes to War*, 81, 86, 92–93.

84 Robert B. Stinnett, *Day of Deceit: The Truth About FDR and Pearl Harbor* (Simon and Schuster, 2000), 5, 21–22, 45–48, 52, 83, 123–27, 203. Challenges to Stinnett's thesis, and the evidence behind it, include Persico, *Roosevelt's Secret War*, 153; Philip H. Jacobsen, "Pearl Harbor: Who Deceived Whom?" *Naval History* 17:6, December 2003, https://www.usni.org/magazines/naval-history-magazine/2003/december/pearl-harbor-who-deceived-whom, accessed November 30th 2024; "The Truth about Pearl Harbor: A Debate," Presentation by Stephen Budiansky, January 30th 2003, Independent Institute, https://www.independent.org/issues/article.asp?id=445, accessed November 30, 2024; Justus D. Doenecke, Review, *Day of Deceit: The Truth about FDR and Pearl Harbor*, *Journal of American History* 89:1, June 2002, 281–82; Richard Bernstein, "'Day of Deceit',: On Dec. 7, Did We Know We Knew?" *New York Times*, December 15, 1999, https://archive.nytimes.com/www.nytimes.com/books/99/12/12/daily/121599stinnett-book review.html?scp=98&sq=idea%20of%20the%20day&st=cse, accessed December 2nd 2024.Folsom and Folsom, *FDR Goes to War*, 88–89; David Kahn, *The Codebreakers: The Comprehensive History of Secret Communications from Ancient Times to the Internet* (Simon and Schuster, 1996), 38–43.

85 U.S. Senate, 77th Congress, Second Session, Document 159, "Report of the Commission Appointed by the President of the United States to Investigation and Report the Facts Relating to the Attack Upon Pearl Harbor in the Territory of Hawaii on December 7th 1941 (Washington, D.C.: GPA, 1942), 2, 4–5.

86 Burns, *Roosevelt: The Soldier of Freedom,* 151; and Fleming, *The New Dealers War*, 47-48.

7 FDR's Wartime State and the Poisoned Fruit of Unconditional Surrender

1 Olson, *Those Angry Days*, 427; Goodwin, *No Ordinary Time,* 295; Brands, *America First*, 399.

2 Larrabee, *Commander In Chief,* 316–17; Larry Hancock, *Surprise Attack: From Pearl Harbor to 9/11 to Benghazi* (Berkeley: Counterpoint, 2015), 41.
Fleming, *The New Dealers' War,* 34–35; Dallek, *Franklin D. Roosevelt and*
3 *American Foreign Policy, 1932–1945,* 312–13; and "President Roosevelt's Fireside Chat about the bombing of Pearl Harbor, December 9th 1941, https://www.homeworkforyou.com/static_media/uploadedfiles/source_1_FDR_Fireside_Pearl_Harbor.pdf, accessed December 18, 2024.
Higgs, *Crisis and Leviathan*, 132, 158; and December 9th 1941:
4 "President Roosevelt's Fireside Chat about the bombing of Pearl Harbor: On the War with Japan" https://millercenter.org/the-presidency/presidential-speeches/december-9-1941-fireside chat 19 war japan, accessed December 9th 2024; Wallace, *The Price of Vision*, 24; Fleming, *The New Dealers' War*, 216-17; Folsom and Folsom, *FDR Goes to War,* 161.

5 Folsom and Folsom, *FDR Goes to War*, 161–62; and Fleming, *The New Dealers' War,* 121–22.

6 Fleming, *The New Dealers' War* 98–99; Goodwin, *No Ordinary Time*, 54–55, 314–15; and "Labor: Automobile Armageddon," *Time*, January 18th 1937, https://content.time.com/time/subscriber/article/0,33009,770481-3,00.html, accessed February 12th 2025.

7 Folsom and Folsom, *FDR Goes to War*, 121; Brinkley, *The End of Reform*, 183, 186–87.

8 Higgs, *Crisis and Leviathan*, 208; Fleming, *The New Dealers' War*, 136; Higgs, "Wartime Prosperity? A Reassessment of the U.S. Economy in the 1940s," Higgs, ed., *Depression, War, and Cold War: Challenging the Myths of Conflict and Prosperity* (Oakland: The Independent Institute, 2006), 92–93; Folsom and Folsom, *FDR Goes to War*, 121–22, 166; Davis, *FDR: The War President*, 458.

9 Roosevelt to Biddle, November 17th 1941, PSF, Justice Department, 1940–1944, Franklin D. Roosevelt Presidential Library and Museum, Hyde Park, NY; Stone, Geoffrey R. "Free Speech in World War II: 'When Are You Going to Indict the Seditionists?'" *International Journal of Constitutional Law* 2:2 (2004), 338; Cabell Phillips, "'No Witch Hunts'," *New York Times*, September 21st 1941, SM8; and Patrick S. Washburn, *A Question of Sedition: The Federal Government's Investigation of the Black Press During World War II* (New York: Oxford University Press, 1986), 51.

10 Roosevelt to Hoover, January 21st 1942, PSF Justice Department, 1940–1944, Franklin D. Roosevelt Presidential Library and Museum, Hyde Park, NY; J. Edgar Hoover, Continued, Box 57, Franklin D. Roosevelt Presidential Library and Museum, Hyde Park, NY; Stephen T. Early to Roosevelt, March 20th 1942, PSF, Justice Department, 1940–1944, Franklin D. Roosevelt Presidential Library and Museum, Hyde Park, NY; and Francis Biddle, *In Brief Authority* (Greenwood Press, 1972 [1962]), 237–38; Folsom and Folsom, *FDR Goes to War*, 212.

11 Richard W. Steele, *Free Speech in the Good War* (St. Martin's Press, 1999), 1.

12 Steele, *Free Speech in the Good War*, 232; Laura Weinrib, *The Taming of Free Speech: America's Civil Liberties* Compromise (Harvard University Press, 2016), 11, 265.

13 Biddle, *In Brief Authority*, 238; David M. Kennedy, *Over Here: The First World War and American Society* (Oxford University Press, 1980), 77–78; Steele, *Free Speech in the Good War*, 231.

14 Gene A. Coyle, "John Franklin Carter: Journalist, FDR's Secret Investigator, Soviet Agent?" *International Journal of Intelligence* 24 (2011), 167; Richard Reeves, *Infamy: The Shocking Story of the Japanese Internment in World War II*, (Holt, 2015) 13, 16; Greg Robinson, *By Order of the President: FDR and the Internment of Japanese Americans* (Harvard University Press, 2001), 78; Roger Daniels, *Prisoners Without Trial: Japanese Americans and World War II* (Hill and Wang, 2004 [1993]), 25.

15 Robinson, *By Order of the President*, 77–79, 96; Richard Drinnon, *Keeper of Concentration Camps: Dillon S. Myer and American Racism* (University of California Press, 1987), 32; Reeves, *Infamy*, 17, 33; and Daniels, *Prisoners Without Trial*, 37.

16 Peter Irons, *Justice at War: The Story of the Japanese American Internment Cases* (New York: Oxford University Press, 1983), 39; "Stimson to Ford, January 26, 1942," in *American Concentration Camps* 2 (January 1, 1942–February 19, 1942, ed. Roger Daniels (New York: Garland, 1989), np.; Irons, *Justice at War*, 25, 30; Daniels, *Prisoners Without Trial*, 29–32;Beito, The New Deal's War on the Bill of Rights, 319

17 Robinson, *By Order of the President*, 98–100.
18 Gregory, *New Deal Law and Order*, 14; Lorraine K. Bannai, *Enduring Conviction: Fred Korematsu and His Quest for Justice* (University of Washington Press, 2015), 24; Irons, *Justice at War*, 52; Francis Biddle, *In Brief Authority* (1976 [1962], Greenwood Press), 224.
19 Robinson, *By Order of the President*, 104; Irons, *Justice at War*, 53.
20 Confidential Memorandum of Conversations with Officials at Washington on August 26th, 1942, Dr. Alexander Meiklejohn and Roger Baldwin representing the Union, American Civil Liberties Cases, 1943, Sedition, Correspondence 6., vol. 2501, American Civil Liberties Union Papers, Mudd Library, Princeton University; Daniels, *Prisoners Without Trial*, 44–45; Robinson, *By Order of the President*, 113–15.
21 "Transcript of Executive Order No. 9066: Resulting in the Relocation of Japanese (1942)," accessed August 27th 2022, https://www.archives.gov/milestone-documents/executive-order-9066, accessed December 20th 2024.
22 Robinson, *By Order of the President*, 64, 110–12; Daniels, *Prisoners Without Trial*, 44; Irons, *Justice at War*, 61.
23 "Roosevelt to Frank Knox, Memorandum for the Secretary of the Navy, February 26th, 1942," in *American Concentration Camps*, vol. 3, February 20th, 1942–March 31st 1942, ed. Roger Daniels (Garland, 1989), np.; Daniels, *Prisoners Without Trial*, 48; Robinson, *By Order of the President*, 148–155.
24 Headquarters, Western Defense Command and Fourth Army, Presidio of San Francisco, California, Public Proclamation No. 1., March 2nd 1942, https://en.wikisource.org/wiki/Public_Proclamation_No._1, accessed December 19th 2024.
25 77 *Cong. Rec.*, S2722–26 (daily ed., March 19th 1942); and Western Defense Command and Fourth Army United States, *Final Report*, Japanese Evacuation of the West Coast, 1942 (Washington, DC: United States Government Printing Office, 1943), 30–31.
26 Marc C. Johnson, *Political Hell-Raiser: The Life and Times of Senator Burton K. Wheeler of Montana* (University of Oklahoma Press, 2019), 322; Rachel Pistol, "The Historical Presidency: From Truman to Trump: Presidents' Use and Abuse of the Incarceration of Japanese Americans," *Presidential Studies Quarterly* 51:2, June 2021, 388
27 Daniels, *Prisoners Without Trial*, 55; Reeves, *Infamy*, 48; Robinson, *By Order of the President*, 144.
28 Jason Scott Smith, "New Deal Public Works at War: The WPA and Japanese American Internment," *Pacific Historical Review* 72:1 (February 2003), 70–75, 82–87, 92; Franklin D. Roosevelt, Excerpts from a Press Conference, December 28th 1943, accessed November 22nd 2021, https://www.presidency.ucsb.edu/documents/excerpts-from-thepresscon-ference-8, accessed December 19, 2024; and Franklin D. Roosevelt Letter to the Federal Works Administrator Discontinuing the W.P.A., December 4th 1942, The American Presidency Project, https://www.presidency.ucsb.edu/node/210274, accessed December 19th, 2024.
29 Washburn, *Question of Sedition*, 69–70, 120; Press Conference #814, Executive Office of the President, March 24th, 1942, 231–32, Press Conferences of Franklin D. Roosevelt, 1933–1945, Franklin D. Roosevelt Presidential Library and Museum, Hyde Park, http://www.fdrlibrary.marist.edu/_resources/images/pc/pc0133.pdf, accessed December 19th 2024.

30 Beito, *The New Deal's War on the Bill of Rights*, 215–16; Leo P. Ribuffo, "United States v. McWilliams: The Roosevelt Administration and the Far Right," in *American Political Trials*, ed. Michael R. Belknap (Greenwood Press, 1981) 185; Steele, *Free Speech in the Good War*, 72, 164–66; Arthur Garfield Hays and Roger N. Baldwin to Frank C. Walker, April 15th 1942, American Civil Liberties Cases, 1943, Sedition, Correspondence, 3, vol. 2498, American Civil Liberties Union Papers, Mudd Library, Princeton University.

31 Steele, *Free Speech and the Good War*, 167; Attorney General VI, Seditionists (2), 680. Notebooks, Francis Biddle Papers, Franklin D. Roosevelt Presidential Library, Hyde Park, NY; Washburn, *A Question of Sedition*, 79–80.

32 Washburn, *A Question of Sedition*, 8, 99–100.

33 Washburn, *A Question of Sedition*, 52–53, 80–81, 107.

34 Washburn, A Question of Sedition, 89–94.

35 Washburn, *A Question of Sedition*, 131–32, 135, 139.

36 Washburn, *A Question of Sedition*, 82–84, 130, 140, 163–64.

37 Higgs, *Crisis and Leviathan*, 208; Goodwin, *No Ordinary Time*, 357; David M. Jordan, *FDR, Dewey, and the Election of 1944* (Indiana University Press, 2011), 10; Folsom and Folsom, *FDR Goes to War*, 125.

38 Wallace, *The Price of Vision*, 76; Folsom and Folsom, *FDR Goes to War*, 215.

39 Larrabee, *Commander In Chief*, 357–59; Persico, *Roosevelt's Secret War*, 188–89; and Burns, *Roosevelt: The Soldier of Freedom*, 226.

40 Amanda Smith, *Newspaper Titan: The Infamous Life and Monumental Times of Cissy Patterson* (Knopf, 2011), 412; and Michael S. Sweeney, *Secrets of Victory: The Office of Censorship in the American Press and Radio in World War II* (University of North Carolina Press, 2001), 3, 79–81.

41 Smith, *Newspaper Titan*, 412; Sweeney, *Secrets of Victory*, 3, 79–81.

42 Medoff, *The Jews Should Keep Quiet*, 100–02, 119.

43 Carolyn C. Jones, "Class Tax to Mass Tax: The Role of Propaganda in the Expansion of the Income Tax During World War II," *Buffalo Law Review* 37, January 16th 1988, 686; Davis, *FDR: The War President*, 628; Jordan, *FDR, Dewey, and the Election of 1944*, 15; "Army of 7,500,000 Planned for 1943," *Metropolitan Pasadena Star-News*, October 14th 1942, 1; Goodwin, *No Ordinary Time*, 384; Fleming, *The New Dealers' War*, 155–56.

44 Folsom and Folsom, *FDR Goes to War*, 139; Davis, *FDR: The War President*, 723; Fleming, *The New Dealers' War*, 161; John Morton Blum, *V Was for Victory: Politics and American Culture During World War II* (Harcourt Brace, 1977), 233; Brinkley, *The End of Reform*, 190.

45 Franklin D. Roosevelt, Letter to the Federal Works Administrator Discontinuing the W.P.A., December 4th 1942, https://www.presidency.ucsb.edu/documents/letter-the-federal-works-administrator-discontinuing-the-wpa, accessed February 12th 2025; and Jason Scott Smith, "New Deal Public Works at War: The WPA and Japanese American Internment," *Pacific Historical Review* 72:1 (February 2003), 71, 92.

46 Medoff, *The Jews Should Keep Quiet*, 131–35; Larrabee, *Commander In Chief*, 424.

47 Mark A. Stoler, *The Politics of the Second Front: American Military Planning and Diplomacy in Coalition Warfare, 1941–1943* (Greenwood Press, 1977), 73–76; Burns, *Roosevelt: The Soldier of Freedom*, 318–19.

48 Persico, *Roosevelt's Secret War*, 235; Fleming, *The New Dealers' War*, 425–26.

49 Persico, *Roosevelt's Secret War*, 235.
50 Persico, *Roosevelt's Secret War*, 235–36; Fleming, *The New Dealers' War*, 173, 180; McMeekin, *Stalin's War*, 439-443.
51 Fleming, *The New Dealers' War*, 176, 179.
52 Wyman, *The Abandonment of the Jews*, 82–84, 87.
53 Medoff, *The Jews Should Keep Quiet*, 158, 206; Davis S. Wyman, *The Abandonment of the Jews: America and the Holocaust, 1941–1945* (New York: Pantheon, 1984), 281.
54 Goodwin, *No Ordinary Time*, 411–12; Robert E. Sherwood, *Roosevelt and Hopkins: An Intimate History* (New York: Hopkins Brothers, 1948), 700; Brinkley, *The End of Reform*, 185.
55 Fleming, *The New Dealers' War*, 294–95.
56 Persico, *Roosevelt's Secret War*, 3; Charles Wilson, 1st Baron Moran, *Churchill: Taken from the Diaries of Lord Moran* (Boston: Houghton Mifflin, 1966), 103–04; Fleming, *The New Dealers' War*, 189, 254.
57 Fleming, *The New Dealers' War*, 293–94.
58 Fleming, *The New Dealers' War*, 291, 294–95.
59 "OWI Head Elmer Davis Spread Soviet Katyn Propaganda Lie in World War II Voice of America Broadcasts," Cold War Museum, May 11th 2018, https://www.coldwarradiomuseum.com/owi-head-elmer-davis-promotes-soviet-katyn-propaganda-lie-in-the-us-and-in-voice-of-america-radio-broadcasts/, accessed December 20th 2024; Persico, *Roosevelt's Secret War*, 262–64; Folsom and Folsom, *FDR Goes to War*, 239.
60 Fleming, *The New Dealers' War*, 207; Message of President Roosevelt and Prime Minister Churchill to the People of Italy, July 16th 1943, https://history.state.gov/historicaldocuments/frus1943v02/d297, accessed May 2nd 2025.
61 Stoler, *The Politics of the Second Front*, 101–02; Fleming, *The New Dealers' War*, 207; Persico, *Roosevelt's Secret War*, 279.
62 Roosevelt, Fireside Chat, July 23rd, 1943, https://www.presidency.ucsb.edu/documents/fireside-chat-1, accessed December 19th 2024; Fleming, The New Dealers' War, 207–08.
63 Burns, *Roosevelt: The Soldier of Freedom*, 393–94; Fleming, *The New Dealers' War*, 208–09; Armistice with Italy; September 3rd 1943, https://avalon.law.yale.edu/wwii/italy01.asp, accessed December 19th 2024.
64 Fleming, *The New Dealers' War*, 209–210.
65 Fleming, *The New Dealers' War*, 77–78, 121, 228–29; Jones, *FDR, Dewey, and the Election of 1944*, 49; Folsom and Folsom, *FDR Goes to War*, 162–63; Jesse Jones, *Fifty Billion Dollars: My Thirteen Years with the RFC (1932–1945)* (New York: Macmillan, 1951), 420, 427.

8 The Culmination of a Failed Presidency

1 J.B. Martin to Francis Biddle, February 16th 1944, Folder Ma, Series 4, Box 177, E.H. Crump Collection, Memphis and Shelby County Room, Memphis Public Library and Information Center; Tom C. Clark to Martin, February 26th 1944, 44-72-1, Criminal Division, Department of Justice, National Archives.
2 "A. Philip Randolph, Noted Labor Leader Speaks Here Sunday," *Memphis World*, November 5th 1943, 1; "Memphis City Officials Flayed by Randolph," *New Journal and Guide* (Norfolk, Virginia), November 20th 1943, 18; Elizabeth Gritter, *River of Hope: Black Politics and the Memphis Freedom Movement, 1865–1954* (Lexington: University Press of Kentucky,

2014), 157–58; Jason Jordan, "'We Have No Race Trouble Here': Racial Politics and Memphis's Reign of Terror," in *An Unseen Light: Black Struggles for Freedom in Memphis, Tennessee*, ed. Aram Goudsouzian and Charles W. McKinney Jr. (Lexington: University Press of Kentucky, 2018), 146; "Randolph Defies Boss Crump in Memphis," *Chicago Defender*, November 20th 1943, 3; "Crump Bans Memphis Rally for Randolph," *Chicago Defender*, November 13th 1943, 1.

3 "Memphis City Officials Flayed by Randolph," *New Journal and Guide* (Norfolk, Virginia), November 20th 1943, 18; "Randolph Defies Boss Crump in Memphis," *Chicago Defender*, November 20th 1943, 3; "Randolph Speaks at STFU Conclave-Mass Meeting Cancelled," *Memphis World*, November 12th 1943, 1; Jordan, "'No Race Trouble Here,'" 146; "Crump Warns 'Outsiders' to Stay Out of Memphis," *Chicago Defender*, November 27th 1943, 1.

4 A. Philip Randolph to Eleanor Roosevelt, November 24th 1943, Eleanor Roosevelt to Randolph, December 18th 1943, 100-Personal Letters, Box 790, Eleanor Roosevelt Collection, Franklin D. Roosevelt Presidential Library, Hyde Park, New York. Many thanks to Joel Sturgeon for calling my attention to this correspondence. Also, see Joel Sturgeon, "You Will Be Policed: Boss Crump, the New Deal, and the Price of Black Defiance in FDR's America." *Tennessee Historical Quarterly* 82:1 (Spring 2023), 82.

5 Sherwood, *Roosevelt and Hopkins: An Intimate History* (Harper and Brothers, 1948), 702–03; Medoff, *The Jews Should Keep Quiet*, 192.

6 Medoff, *America and the Holocaust*, 205; Wyman, *The Abandonment of the Jews* 147–48.

7 David S. Wyman and Rafael Medoff, *A Race Against Death: Peter Bergson, America, and the Holocaust* (W.W. Norton, 2002), 34; Wyman, *The Abandonment of the Jews*, 146–49; Medoff, *America and the Holocaust*, 207.

8 Wyman, *The Abandonment of the Jews*, 152; Ben Hecht, "My Uncle Abraham Reports . . . ," *New York Times*, November 5th 1943, 14; Wyman and Medoff, *A Race Against Death*, 41–43.

9 Wyman, *The Abandonment of the Jews*, 193, 204; Wyman and Medoff, *A Race Against Death*, 49.

10 Medoff, *The Jews Should Keep Quiet*, 210.

11 McMeekin, *Stalin's War*, 451; Fleming, *The New Dealers' War*, 203–05.

12 McMeekin, *Stalin's War*, 452; Persico, *Roosevelt's Secret War*, 418; Fleming, *The New Dealers' War*, 205, 371.

13 Franklin D. Roosevelt, Message to Congress on the Progress of the War, September 17th 1943, https://www.presidency.ucsb.edu/documents/message-congress-the-progress-the-war, accessed January 14th, 2025.

14 Robert D. Ubriaco Jr., "Harry S. Truman, the Politics of Yalta, and the Domestic Origins of the Truman Doctrine Ph.D. diss., University of Illinois at Urbana-Champaign, 1992), 48–49; Folsom and Folsom, *FDR Goes to War*, 238.

15 McMeekin, *Stalin's War*, 498–501.

16 G.A. Shepperd, *The Italian Campaign 1943–1945: A Political and Military Re-assessment* (Frederick A. Praeger, 1968), 180; McMeekin, *Stalin's War*, 498–500.

17 Persico, *Roosevelt's Secret War*, 273; Dwight D. Eisenhower, *Crusade in Europe* (Garden City: Doubleday, 1948), 194; McMeekin, *Stalin's War*, 499–504; Folsom and Folsom, *FDR Goes to War*, 238–39.

18 Fleming, *The New Dealers' War*, 315; Wallace, *The Price of Vision*, 283–84.

19 Wallace, *The Price of Vision*, 284; Dallek, *Franklin D. Roosevelt and American Foreign Policy*, 436-37; Burns, *Roosevelt: The Soldier of Freedom*, 408-09; and Fleming, *The New Dealers' War*, 313, 317.
20 Roosevelt, Fireside Chat, December 24th 1943, https://www.presidency.ucsb.edu/documents/fireside-chat, accessed January 13th, 2025.
21 Fleming, *The New Dealers' War*, 327; Jordan, *FDR, Dewey, and the Election of 1944*, 128–29, 131.
22 Fleming, *The New Dealers' War*, 328; Brinkley, *Washington Goes to War*, 261; Jordan, *FDR, Dewey, and the Election of 1944*, 129.
23 Jordan, *FDR, Dewey, and the Election of 1944*, 132; Fleming, *The New Dealers' War*, 328–29; Brinkley, *Washington Goes to War*, 261.
24 Fleming, *The New Dealers' War*, 329; Jordan, *FDR, Dewey, and the Election of 1944*, 133.
25 Fleming, *The New Dealers' War*, 332–33; Jordan, *FDR, Dewey, and the Election of 1944*, 134–35.
26 Roosevelt, Excerpts from the Press Conference, December 28th 1943, https://www.presidency.ucsb.edu/documents/excerpts-from-the-press-conference-8, accessed January 11th 2025.
27 Dallek, Franklin D. Roosevelt and American Foreign Policy, 443; Franklin D. Roosevelt, State of the Union Message to Congress, January 11th 1944, http://www.fdrlibrary.marist.edu/archives/address_text.html, accessed January 11th 2025.
28 Folsom and Folsom, *FDR Goes to War*, 191–92, 202, 206–07; Beito, *The New Deal's War on the Bill of Rights*, 266.
29 Folsom and Folsom, *FDR Goes to War*, 209–210; Franklin D. Roosevelt, State of the Union Message to Congress, January 11th 1944.
30 Irons, *Justice at War*, 271; Reeves, *Infamy*, 220–247.
31 Robinson, *By Order of the President*, 120; Reeves, *Infamy*, 34.
32 Irons, *Justice at War*, 273; Drinnon, *Keeper of Concentration Camps*, 59; Robinson, *By Order of the President*, 221.
33 Ira Katznelson, *When Affirmative Action Was White: An Untold History of Racial Inequality in Twentieth-Century America* (Norton, 2005), 122–26; Rothstein, *The Color of Law*, 167.
34 Katznelson, *When Affirmative Action Was White*, 114–15, 127–28, 140.
35 "Mrs. Dilling, 27 Others Hit by U.S. Grand Jury," *Chicago Daily Tribune*, July 23rd 1942, 1, 11; Lewis Wood, "28 Are Indicted on Sedition Charge," *New York Times* (July 24th 1942), 1, 8.
36 Virgil W. Dean, "Another Wichita Seditionist? Elmer J. Garner and the Radical Right's Opposition to World War II," *Kansas History* 17:1 (Spring 1994), 52–53, 55, 61–62.
37 "House Leaders Back Griffin for Debt Post," *Washington Post*, May 7th 1939, 2; "Urged Griffin for Mayor," *New York Times*, July 24th 1942, 8; "The Enemy Within Our Gates," *National Republic* 31:10, February 1944, 24; "Publisher Fights Removal Order," *Christian Science Monitor*, November 17th 1942, 8; "Griffin Arrested in Hospital Here," *New York Times*, July 25th 1942, 1; "Griffin Defends Trip to Germany," *New York Times*, November 5th 1942, 27; Bureau of Propaganda Investigation, Overall Report of Pending Federal Trial Situation, January 23rd 1943, 6, Folder 24–26, Box 274; Non-Sectarian Anti-Nazi League to Champion Human Rights, Records, Rare Book and Manuscript Library, Columbia University.
38 Beito, *The New Deal's War on the Bill of Rights*, 250–52.
39 James A. Wechsler, "Press Axis Screams 'Frame Up' at Sedition Trial," *PM*,

April 17th 1944, 7; James A. Wechsler, "Chicago-Washington Press Axis Is Mouthpiece—In Headlines—for 30 Accused Seditionists," *PM*, April 30th 1944, 3; "Bring Them to Book," *New Masses* 51:3, April 18th 1944, 9; "The Treason Trial," *Daily Worker*, April 20th 1944, 6; "An 'Innocent' Question," *Daily Worker*, April 22nd 1944, 6; and Percival Roberts Bailey, "Progressive Lawyers: A History of the National Lawyers Guild, 1936–1958" (PhD, Rutgers University, 1979), 299.

40 George S. Schuyler, "Views and Reviews," *Pittsburgh Courier* (Pittsburgh), March 18th 1944, 7.

41 Sam O'Neal, "Mrs. Dilling and 23 Deny Sedition Guilt," *Chicago Sun*, April 18th 1944, 4.

42 Beito, *The New Deal's War on the Bill of Rights*, 254–55.

43 Fleming, *The New Dealers' War*, 343–45.

44 Fleming, *The New Dealers' War*, 378.

45 Jordan, *FDR, Dewey, and the Election of 1944*, 48; Fleming, *The New Dealers' War*, 357.

46 Fleming, *The New Dealers' War*, 360, 401–03; Jordan, *FDR, Dewey, and the Election of 1944*, 50–52.

47 Fleming, *The New Dealers' War*, 356, 391; Jordan, *FDR, Dewey, and the Election of 1944*, 124; Burns, *Roosevelt: The Soldier of Freedom*, 477.

48 Thomas E. Dewey, Address Accepting the Presidential Nomination at the Republican National Convention in Chicago, Illinois, June 28th 1944, https://www.presidency.ucsb.edu/documents/address-accepting-the-presidential-nomination-the-republican-national-convention-chicago-1, accessed January 14th 2025.

49 Wallace, *The Price of Vision*, 362–63; and Jordan, *FDR, Dewey, and the Election of 1944*, 147.

50 Jordan, FDR, *Dewey, and the Election of 1944*, 139.

51 Jordan, *FDR, Dewey, and the Election of 1944*, 144–46, 149–152, 157–58; Steven Fraser, *Labor Will Rule: Sidney Hillman and the Rise of American Labor* (New York: The Free Press, 1991), 530–32; and Fleming, *The New Dealers' War*, 405, 408.

52 Letter on the Vice-Presidential Nomination, July 14th 1944, https://www.presidency.ucsb.edu/documents/letter-the-vice-presidential-nomination, accessed January 14th 2025; Fleming, *The New Dealers' War*, 394, 407–08, 414, 420; Jordan, *FDR, Dewey, and the 1944 Election*, 168–69.

53 Franklin D. Roosevelt, Address Broadcast from San Diego to the Democratic National Convention in Chicago, July 20th 1944, https://www.presidency.ucsb.edu/documents/address-broadcast-from-san-diego-the-democratic-national-convention-chicago, accessed January 14th 2025.

54 Goodwin, *No Ordinary Time*, 434–35, 517–521, 542.

55 Wyman, *The Abandonment of the Jews*, 214, 240–43; Wyman and Medoff, *A Race Against Death*, 13.

56 Wyman, *The Abandonment of the Jews*, 40, 239–240, 245.

57 Medoff, *The Jews Should Keep Quiet*, 271; Wyman, *The Abandonment of the Jews*, 292.

58 Wyman, *The Abandonment of the Jews*, 290–92, 307; Medoff, *The Jews Should Keep Quiet*, 271, 275; Medoff, *America and the Holocaust*, 272.

59 Fleming, *The New Dealers' War*, 373–74.

60 Fleming, *The New Dealers' War*, 369–370, 421; Persico, *Roosevelt's Secret War*, 415.

61 Fleming, *The New Dealers' War*, 422–24.

62 Persico, *Roosevelt's Secret War*, 348–49.
63 John Dietrich, *The Morgenthau Plan: Soviet Influence on American Postwar Policy* (New York: Algora, 2002), 54–58; Persico, *Roosevelt's Secret War*, 348–350; Dallek, *Franklin D. Roosevelt and American Foreign Policy*, 474–75; Fleming, *The New Dealers' War*, 431.
64 McMeekin, *Stalin's War*, 581; Fleming, *The New Dealers' War*, 431–32; Persico, *Roosevelt's Secret War*, 350–51; Dietrich, *The Morgenthau Plan*, 66.
65 McMeekin, *Stalin's War*, 555–566.
66 Brinkley, *Washington Goes to War*, 259.
67 Hal Gordon, "FDR, Orson Welles, and 'the Fala speech'," Pro Rhetoric, September 25th 2020, https://prorhetoric.com/fdr-orson-welles-and-the-fala-speech/, accessed February 23rd 2025; Franklin D. Roosevelt, Address at a Union Dinner, Washington, D.C., September 23rd 1944, https://www.presidency.ucsb.edu/documents/address-union-dinner-washington-dc, accessed January 14th 2025; Dallek, *Franklin D. Roosevelt and American Foreign Policy,* 482; Burns, *Roosevelt: The Soldier of Freedom*, 524; *Jordan, FDR, Dewey, and the Election of 1944*, 270.
68 Robinson, *By Order of the President,* 224; Irons, *Justice at War*, 365.
69 Jordan, *FDR, Dewey, and the Election of 1944,* 321, 327; Fraser, *Labor Will Rule*, 536–37; Fleming, *The New Dealers' War*, 461.
70 Beito, *The New Deal's War on the Bill of Rights*, 254–57.
71 Attorney General V, Seditionists, Notebooks, 636, Francis Biddle Papers, Franklin D. Roosevelt Presidential Library and Museum, Hyde Park, NY; Sam O'Neal, "Death of Justice Eicher Ends Mass Sedition Trial," *Chicago Sun,* December 1st 1944, 12; 79 *Cong. Rec.*, S157 (daily ed., January 1st 1945).
72 Robinson, *By Order of the President,* 226–27; Franklin D. Roosevelt, Press and Radio Conference, November 21st 1944, http://www.fdrlibrary.marist.edu/_resources/images/pc/pc0166.pdf, accessed January 14, 2025; Reeves, *Infamy*, 232.
73 Lorraine K. Bannai, *Enduring Conviction: Fred Korematsu and His Quest for Justice* (Seattle: University of Washington Press, 2015), 105–06; Charles Wollenberg, *Rebel Lawyer: Wayne Collins and the Defense of Japanese American Rights* (Berkeley: Heyday, 2018), 39–40; Roger Daniels, *Prisoners without Trial: Japanese Americans and World War II* (Hill and Wang, 2004 [1993], 72.
74 Burns, *Roosevelt: The Soldier of Freedom*, 455.
75 Fleming, *The New Dealers' War*, 463, 472–79; Wallace, *The Price of Vision*, 382.
76 Fleming, *The New Dealers' War*, 486; Persico, *Roosevelt's Secret War*, 391.
77 Folsom and Folsom, *FDR Goes to War*, 247; Burns, *Roosevelt: The Soldier of Freedom*, 562–72, 576–77; Albert L. Weeks, *Russia's Life-Saver: Lend-Lease Aid to the USSR in World War II* (Lanham: Lexington Books, 2004), 135–37.
78 Persico, *Roosevelt's Secret War*, 391–92; Fleming, *The New Dealers' War*, 322.
79 John Earl Haynes, Harvey Klehr, and Alexander Vassiliev, *Spies, The Rise and Fall of the KGB in America* (New Haven: Yale University Press, 2009), 235–36; Dietrich, *The Morgenthau Plan*, 31.
80 Fleming, *The New Dealers' War*, 319, 383; Folsom and Folsom, *FDR Goes to War*, 243–44; Wallace, *The Price of Vision*, 424.
81 Dietrich, *The Morgenthau Plan*, 24–31.
82 M. Stanton Evans and Herbert Romerstein, *Stalin's Secret Agents: The Subversion of Roosevelt's Government* (New York: Threshold Editions,

2012), 118–121; John Earl Haynes, "Was Harry Hopkins a Spy?" August 15th 2013, *Front Page*, https://www.frontpagemag.com/was-harry-hopkins-soviet-spy-john-earl-haynes/, accessed May 2nd 2025; Haynes, Klehr, and Vassiliev, *Spies*, 6–8, 220–23; McMeekin, *Stalin's War*, 606. *Also see* David L. Roll, *The Hopkins Touch: Harry Hopkins and the Forging of the Alliance to Defeat Hitler* (Oxford University Press, 2013), 276.

83 Franklin D. Roosevelt, Address to Congress on the Yalta Conference, March 1st 1945, https://www.presidency.ucsb.edu/documents/address-congress-the-yalta-conference, accessed January 14th 2025; Fleming, *The New Dealers' War*, 499.

84 Larrabee, *Commander In Chief*, 599–600; Fleming, *The New Dealers' War*, 440, 495–96.

85 Fleming, *The New Dealers' War*, 507–08.

86 Fleming, *The New Dealers' War*, 510.

87 Folsom and Folsom, *FDR Goes to War*, 249.

88 Burns, *Roosevelt: The Soldier of Freedom*, 583; President Roosevelt to the Chairman of the Council of People's Commissars of the Soviet Union (Stalin), April 1st 1945, https://history.state.gov/historical-documents/frus1945v05/d161, accessed January 14th 2025; President Roosevelt to the British Prime Minister (Churchill) https://history.state.gov/historicaldocuments/frus1945v05/d173, accessed January 14th 2025.

89 Fleming, *The New Dealers' War*, 512; Burns, *Roosevelt: The Soldier of Freedom*, 599–600; Goodwin, *No Ordinary Time*, 601–03.

90 Fleming, *The New Dealers' War*, 560; Folsom and Folsom, *FDR Goes to War*, 275; Wallace, *The Price of Vision*, 438.

91 Persico, *Roosevelt's Secret War*, 364; Fleming, *The New Dealers' War*, 543–44.

92 Robert Higgs, "Wartime Prosperity? A Reassessment of the U.S. Economy in the 1940s," Higgs, ed., *Depression, War, and Cold War: Challenging the Myths of Conflict and Prosperity* (Oakland: The Independent Institute, 2006), 88–89; Doris Kearns Goodwin, "The Way We Won: America's Economic Breakthrough During World War II," *The American Prospect*, October 1st 1992, https://prospect.org/health/way-won-america-s-economic-break-through-world-war-ii/, accessed January 14th 2025.

93 Higgs, "Wartime Prosperity?" 81.

94 Higgs, "Wartime Prosperity?" 93.

95 Vedder and Gallaway, *Out of Work*, 151, 157–58, 164; Selgin, *False Dawn*, 258, 265, 288.

96 Higgs, "Wartime Prosperity?" 97–98; Vedder and Gallaway, *Out of Work*, 161.

97 Higgs, *Crisis and Leviathan*, 214; Richard F. Bensel, *Yankee Leviathan: The Origins of Central State Authority in America, 1859–1877* (Cambridge University Press, 1990), 160.

Partial Bibliography

Alter, Jonathan. *The Defining Moment: FDR's Hundred Days and the Triumph of Hope*. New York: Simon and Schuster, 2006.

American Economic Association. *Report of the Organization of the American Economic Association* 1:1 (March 1886). Baltimore: Publications of the American Economic Association, 1886.

Anderson, Benjamin M. *Economics and the Public Welfare: Financial and Economic History of the United States, 1914–1946*. New York: Van Nostrand, 1949.

Annenberg, M.L. The New Dealers Can't Muzzle the Inquirer: A Statement by M.L. Annenberg. *Philadelphia Inquirer*, April 30th 1938, 1.

Baldwin, Roger N. *The Civil Rights Revolution*. Boston: Beacon Press, 1968.

Atkinson, David N. From New Deal Liberal to Supreme Court Conservative: The Metamorphosis of Justice Sherman Minton. *Washington University Law Quarterly* (1975), 361–394.

Ball, Howard. *Hugo L. Black: Cold Steel Warrior*. New York: Oxford University Press, 1996.

Bannai, Lorraine K. *Enduring Conviction: Fred Korematsu and His Quest for Justice*. Seattle: University of Washington Press, 2015.

Barkley, Alben. *That Reminds Me*. New York: Doubleday, 1954.

Beito, David T. *From Mutual Aid to the Welfare State: Fraternal Societies and Social Services, 1890–1967*. Chapel Hill: University of North Carolina Press, 2000.

———. Beito, David T. *The New Deal's War on the Bill of Rights*. Oakland: The Independent Institute, 2023.

———. Beito, David T. *Taxpayers in Revolt: Tax Resistance during the Great Depression*. Chapel Hill: University of North Carolina Press, 1989.

Belknap, Michael R., ed. *American Political Trials*. Westport: Greenwood Press, 1981.

Bensel, Richard F. *Yankee Leviathan: The Origins of Central State Authority in America, 1859–1877*. Cambridge: Cambridge University Press, 1990.

Berg, Scott. *Lindbergh*. New York: Putnam's, 1998.

Bernstein, David E. *Only One Place of Redress: African Americans and the Courts from Reconstruction to the New Deal.* Durham: Duke University Press, 2001.

Bernstein, David E. *Rehabilitating Lochner: Defending Individual Rights Against Progressive Reform.* Chicago: University of Chicago Press, 2011.

Bernstein, Richard. 'Day of Deceit': On Dec. 7, Did We Know We Knew? *New York Times*, December 15th 1999, https://archive.nytimes.com/www.nytimes.com/books/99/12/12/daily/121599stinnett-book-review.html?scp=98&sq=idea%20of%20the%20day&st=cse, accessed December 2nd 2024.

Bernstein, William J. King William's Tontine: Why the Retirement Annuity of the Future Should Resemble Its Past (a review). *Financial Analysts Journal*, Book Review, September 8th 2017, https://rpc.cfainstitute.org/research/financial-analysts-journal/2015/king-williams-tontine, accessed January 31st 2025.

Best, Gary Dean. *The Critical Press and the New Deal: The Press Versus Presidential Power, 1933–1938.* Westport: Praeger, 1993.

Biddle, Francis. *In Brief Authority.* Westport: Greenwood Press, 1972 [1962].

Bjornstad, Fred A. 'A Revolution in Ideas and Methods': The Construction Industry and Socioeconomic Planning in the United States, 1915–1933. PhD dissertation, University of Iowa, 2011.

Blum, John Morton. *V Was for Victory: Politics and American Culture During World War II.* New York: Harcourt Brace, 1977.

Bordo, Michael D., Claudia Goldin, and Eugene N. White, eds. *The Defining Moment: The Great Depression and the American Economy in the Twentieth Century.* Chicago: University of Chicago Press, 1998.

Boulier, Bryan L., H.O. Stekler, and Jeremy Dutra. Measuring the Onset of the Great Depression: Then and Now. *Indian Economic Review* 36:1 (January–June 2001), 141.

Brands, H.W. *America First: The Battle Against Intervention, 1940–1941.* New York: Doubleday, 2016.

Brands, H.W. *Traitor to His Class: The Privileged Life and Radical Presidency of Franklin Delano Roosevelt.* New York: Random House, 2009.

Brindze, Ruth. *Not to Be Broadcast: The Truth about Radio.* New York: Vanguard Press, 1937.

Brinkley, Alan. *The End of Reform: New Deal Liberalism in Recession and War.* New York: Knopf, 1995.

———. *Voices of Protest: Huey Long, Father Coughlin, and the Great Depression.* New York: Vintage, 1982.

Brinkley, David. *Washington Goes to War.* New York: Knopf, 1988.

Brown, Robert J. *Manipulating the Ether: The Power of Broadcast Radio in Thirties America.* Jefferson: McFarland, 1998.

Burns, James MacGregor. *Roosevelt: The Lion and the Fox.* 1956. Reprint, San Diego: Harcourt Brace, 1984.

———. *Roosevelt: The Soldier of Freedom.* New York: Harcourt Brace, 1970.

Budiansky, Stephen. The Truth about Pearl Harbor: A Debate. Presentation, Independent Institute, January 30th 2003, https://www.independent.org/issues/article.asp?id=445, accessed November 30th 2024.

Carson, Jamie L., and Benjamin A. Kleinerman. A Switch in Time Saves Nine: Institutions, Strategic Actors, and FDR's Court Plan. *Public Choice* 113 (December 2002), 301–320.

Chase, Stuart. A New Deal for America. *The New Republic* 77, no. 917 (June 29th 1932): 167–171.

Cook, Blanche Wiesen. *Eleanor Roosevelt, 1884–1933*, Volume 1. New York: Viking, 1992.

Corcoran, David H. Sherman Minton: New Deal Senator, PhD dissertation, University of Kentucky, 1977.

Coyle, Gene A. John Franklin Carter: Journalist, FDR's Secret Investigator, Soviet Agent? *International Journal of Intelligence and Counterintelligence* 24 (2011).

Culbert, David H. 'Croak' Carter: Radio's Voice of Doom. *Pennsylvania Magazine of History and Biography* 97:3 (July 1973), 306–310.

Czaplicki, Michael Stephen. The Corruption of Hope: Political Scandal, Congressional Investigations, and New Deal Moral Authority, 1932–1952. PhD dissertation, University of Chicago, 2010.

Dallek, Robert. Franklin D. Roosevelt and American Foreign Policy, *1932–1945.* New York: Oxford University Press, 1995.

Daniels, Roger, ed. *American Concentration Camps* 2 (January 1st 1942–February 19th 1942). New York: Garland, 1989.

———. *Prisoners Without Trial: Japanese Americans and World War II.* New York: Hill and Wang, 2004 [1993].

Davidson, Eugene. The Black Cabinet in the New Deal. *New York Age*, April 7th 1934, 2.

Davis, Kenneth S. *FDR: Into the Storm, 1937–1940: A History.* New York: Random House, 1993.

———. *FDR: The Beckoning of Destiny, 1882–1928: A History.* New York: G.P. Putnam's Sons, 1972.

———. *FDR: The New Deal Years, 1933–1937: A History.* New York: Random House, 1986.

———. *FDR: The New York Years, 1928–1933.* New York: Random House, 1985.

———. *FDR: The War President, 1940–1943. A History.* New York: Random House, 2000.

Dean, Virgil W. Another Wichita Seditionist? Elmer J. Garner and the Radical Right's Opposition to World War II. *Kansas History* 17:1 (Spring 1994), 52–64.

Delmont, Matthew F. *Half American: The Epic Story of African Americans Fighting World War II at Home and Abroad.* New York: Viking, 2022.

Dickman, Howard. *Industrial Democracy in America: Ideological Origins of National Labor Relations Policy.* La Salle: Open Court, 1987.

Dietrich, John. *The Morgenthau Plan: Soviet Influence on American Postwar Policy.* New York: Algora, 2002.

Doenecke, Justus D. Review of *Day of Deceit: The Truth About FDR and Pearl Harbor* by Robert B. Stinnett. *Journal of American History* 89:1 (June 2002), 281–82.

Dorsett, Lyle W. *Franklin D. Roosevelt and the City Bosses.* Port Washington, NY: National University Publications, 1977.

Drinnon, Richard. *Keeper of Concentration Camps: Dillon S. Myer and American Racism*. Berkeley: University of California Press, 1987.
Dunnebecke, Joanne. The Crusade for Individual Liberty: The Committee for Constitutional Government, 1937–1958. Master's thesis, University of Wyoming, 1987.
Edwards, Sebastian. Gold, the Brains Trust, and Roosevelt. *History of Political Economy* 49:1 (2017), 1–30.
Edwards, Willard. Slaps Revenue Bureau War on Roosevelt Foes. *Chicago Daily Tribune*, September 21st 1937, 13.
Eichengreen, Barry. *Golden Fetters: The Gold Standard and the Great Depression, 1919–1939.* New York: Oxford University Press, 1995.
Eisenhower, Dwight D. *Crusade in Europe*. Garden City: Doubleday, 1948.
Euken, Jamie C. Evil, Greed, Treachery, Deception, and Fraud: The World of Lobbying According to Senator Hugo Black. *Federal History* 6 (January 2014), 73–74.
Evans, M. Stanton, and Herbert Romerstein. *Stalin's Secret Agents: The Subversion of Roosevelt's Government*. New York: Threshold Editions, 2012.
Fine, Sidney. *Laissez-Faire and the General Welfare State*. Ann Arbor: University of Michigan Press, 1956.
Fleming, Thomas. *The New Dealers' War: FDR and the War Within World War II*. New York: Basic Books, 2001.
Flynn, John T. *Country Squire in the White House*. New York: Doubleday, 1940.
———. *The Roosevelt Myth*. New York: Devin Adair, 1948.
Folsom, Burton W. *New Deal or Raw Deal? How FDR's Economic Legacy Has Damaged America*. New York: Threshold Editions, 2008.
Folsom, Burton W., and Anita Folsom. *FDR Goes to War: How Expanded Executive Power, Spiraling National Debt, and Restricted Civil Liberties Shaped Wartime America*. New York: Threshold Editions, 2011.
Fox, A.M. Quantitative and Qualitative Changes in International Trade during the Depression. *American Economic Review* 27:1 (March 1937), 19–25.
Fraser, Steven. *Labor Will Rule: Sidney Hillman and the Rise of American Labor*. New York: The Free Press, 1991.
Frederickson, Kari. *Depression Dynasty: The Bankheads of Alabama*. Tuscaloosa: University of Alabama Press, 2022.
Freidel, Frank. *Franklin D. Roosevelt: The Apprenticeship*. Boston: Little, Brown, 1952.
———. Freidel, Frank. *Franklin D. Roosevelt: The Ordeal*. Boston: Little, Brown, 1954.
Friedman, Milton., and Anna Jacobson Schwartz. *A Monetary History of the United States, 1857–1960*. Princeton: Princeton University Press, 1963.
Gamble, Richard M. *The War for Righteousness: Progressive Christianity, the Great War, and the Rise of the Messianic Nation*. Wilmington: ISI, 2003.
Gellman, Irwin F. *Secret Affairs: FDR, Cordell Hull, and Sumner Welles*. New York: Enigma, 1995.
Gilmore, Glenda E. *Gender and Jim Crow: Women and the Politics of White Supremacy in North Carolina, 1896–1920*. Chapel Hill: University of North Carolina Press, 1996.
Goodwin, Doris Kearns. *No Ordinary Time: Franklin and Eleanor Roosevelt: The Home Front in World War II*. New York: Simon and Schuster, 1994.

———. *The Way We Won: America's Economic Breakthrough During World War II. The American Prospect*, October 1st 1992, https://prospect.org/health/way-won-america-s-economic-breakthrough-world-war-ii/, accessed January 14th 2025.

Grabar, Mary. *Debunking FDR: The Man and the Myths.* New York: Regnery, 2025.

———. Unpublished Manuscript on FDR (in possession of author).

Grant, James. *The Forgotten Depression: 1921: The Crash that Cured Itself.* New York: Simon and Schuster, 2014.

Gregory, Anthony. *New Deal Law and Order: How the War on Crime Built the Modern Liberal State.* Cambridge: Harvard University Press, 2024.

Gregory, William A., and Rennard Strickland. Hugo Black's Congressional Investigation of Lobbying and the Public Utility Holding Company Act: A Historical View of the Power Trust, New Deal Politics, and Regulatory Propaganda. *Oklahoma Law Review* 29:3 (1976), 569.

Gritter, Elizabeth. *River of Hope: Black Politics and the Memphis Freedom Movement, 1865–1954.* Lexington: University Press of Kentucky, 2014.

Gugin, Linda C., and James E. St. Clair, *Sherman Minton: New Deal Senator, Cold War Justice.* Indianapolis: Indiana Historical Society, 1987.

Hall, Thomas E., and J. David Ferguson. *The Great Depression: An International Disaster of Perverse Economic Policies.* Ann Arbor: University of Michigan Press, 1998.

Hamilton, Tikia K. Making a 'Model' System: Race, Education, and Politics in the Nation's Capital Before Brown, 1930–1950. PhD dissertation, Princeton University, 2015.

Hancock, Larry. *Surprise Attack: From Pearl Harbor to 9/11 to Benghazi.* Berkeley: Counterpoint, 2015.

Hanyok, Robert J. 'Catching the Fox Unaware': Japanese Radio Denial and Deception and the Attack on Pearl Harbor. *Naval War College Review* 61:4 (Autumn 2008), 108–111.

Hasiotis, Arthur C. *Soviet Political, Economic, and Military Involvement in Sinkiang from 1928 to 1949.* New York: Garland, 1987.

Haynes, John Earl. Was Harry Hopkins a Spy? *Front Page*, August 15th 2013, https://www.frontpagemag.com/was-harry-hopkins-soviet-spy-john-earl-haynes/, accessed May 2nd 2025.

Haynes, John Earl, Harvey Klehr, and Alexander Vassiliev. *Spies: The Rise and Fall of the KGB in America.* New Haven: Yale University Press, 2009.

Hearden, Patrick J. *Roosevelt Confronts Hitler: America's Entry into World War II.* DeKalb: Northern Illinois University Press, 1987.

Hecht, Ben. My Uncle Abraham Reports . . . *New York Times*, November 5th 1943, 14.

Hetzel, Robert L. *Monetary Policy of the Federal Reserve: A History.* Cambridge: Cambridge University Press, 2008.

Higgs, Robert. *Crisis and Leviathan: Critical Episodes in the Growth of American Government.* New York: Oxford University Press, 1987.

———. Wartime Prosperity? A Reassessment of the U.S. Economy in the 1940s. In *Depression, War, and Cold War: Challenging the Myths of Conflict and Prosperity*, edited by Robert Higgs, 81–98. Oakland: The Independent Institute, 2006.

High, Stanley. No-So-Free Air. *Saturday Evening Post* 211:33 (February 11th 1939), 8–9.

Hill, Nancy Peterson. *A Very Private Public Citizen: The Life of Grenville Clark*. Columbia: University of Missouri Press, 2014.

Hinton, Harold B. *Cordell Hull: A Biography*. New York: Doubleday, 1942.

Hirsh, Richard F. *Powering American Farms: The Overlooked Origins of Rural Electrification*. Baltimore: Johns Hopkins University Press, 2022.

Hofstadter, Richard. *The American Political Tradition*. New York: Vintage Books, 1948.

Holli Melvin G. *The Wizard of Washington: Emil Hurja, Franklin Roosevelt, and the Birth of Public Opinion Polling*. New York: Palgrave, 2002.

Houck, Davis W. *FDR and Fear Itself: The First Inaugural Address*. College Station: Texas A&M University Press, 2002.

Hughes, Jonathan. *American Economic History*. Glenview: Scott, Foresman/Little, Brown Higher Education, 1990.

Hull, Elizabeth Anne. Sherman Minton and the Cold War Court. PhD dissertation, New School for Social Research, 1976.

Hull, Cordell. *The Memoirs of Cordell Hull*, Volume 1. New York: Macmillan, 1948.

Hurston, Zora Neale. A Negro Voter Sizes Up Taft. *Saturday Evening Post* 224:23 (December 8th 1951), 152.

Ickes, Harold L. *The Secret Diary of Harold L. Ickes: The Inside Struggle, 1936–1939, Volume II*. New York: Simon and Schuster, 1954.

Irwin, Douglas A. From Smoot-Hawley to Reciprocal Trade Agreements: Changing the Course of U.S. Trade Policy in the 1930s. In *The Defining Moment: The Great Depression and the American Economy in the Twentieth Century*, edited by Michael D. Bordo, Claudia Goldin, and Eugene N. White, 343–44. Chicago: University of Chicago Press, 1998.

Irons, Peter. *Justice at War: The Story of the Japanese American Internment Cases*. New York: Oxford University Press, 1983.

Jacobsen, Philip H. Pearl Harbor: Who Deceived Whom? *Naval History* 17:6 (December), https://www.usni.org/magazines/naval-history-magazine/2003/december/pearl-harbor-who-deceived-whom, accessed November 30th 2024.

Jeffries, John W. *A Third Term for FDR: The Election of 1940*. Lawrence: University Press of Kansas, 2017.

Johnson, Marc C. *Political Hell-Raiser: The Life and Times of Senator Burton K. Wheeler of Montana*. Norman: University of Oklahoma Press, 2019.

Jones, Carolyn C. Class Tax to Mass Tax: The Role of Propaganda in the Expansion of the Income Tax During World War II. *Buffalo Law Review* 37 (January 16th 1988), 685–736.

Jones, Jesse. *Fifty Billion Dollars: My Thirteen Years with the RFC (1932–1945)*. New York: Macmillan, 1951.

Jordan, David M. FDR, *Dewey, and the Election of 1944*. Bloomington: Indiana University Press, 2011.

Jordan, Jason. 'We Have No Race Trouble Here': Racial Politics and Memphis's Reign of Terror. In *An Unseen Light: Black Struggles for Freedom in Memphis, Tennessee*, edited by Aram Goudsouzian and Charles W. McKinney Jr., 141–159. Lexington: University Press of Kentucky, 2018.

Kahn, David. *The Codebreakers: The Comprehensive History of Secret Communications from Ancient Times to the Internet.* New York: Simon and Schuster, 1996.

Kaplan, Carla, ed. *Zora Neale Hurston: A Life in Letters.* New York: Anchor Books, 2002.

Kassner, Minna F. Radio Censorship. *Air Law Review* 8:97 (April 1937), 104.

Katznelson, Ira. *Fear Itself: The New Deal and the Origins of Our Time.* New York: Norton, 2013.

———. *When Affirmative Action Was White: An Untold History of Racial Inequality in Twentieth-Century America.* New York: Norton, 2005.

Keiler, Allan. *Marian Anderson: A Singer's Journey.* Urbana: University of Illinois Press, 2002.

Kennedy, David M. *Over Here: The First World War and American Society.* New York: Oxford University Press, 1980.

Kennedy, Susan Estabrook. *The Banking Crisis of 1933.* Lexington: University Press of Kentucky, 1973.

Kobrin, Rebecca. Too Big to Fail in 1930: The Failed Bank of United States and the Long Shadow of East European Jewish Immigrant Banking. *American Jewish History* 103:4 (October 2019), 457–483.

Larrabee, Eric. *Commander In Chief: Franklin Delano Roosevelt, His Lieutenants, and Their War.* New York: Harper and Row, 1987.

Lee, Carol. Wired Help for the Farm: Individual Electric Generating Sets for Farms, 1880–1930. PhD dissertation, Pennsylvania State University, 1989.

Lee, David D. Senator Black's Investigation of the Airmail, 1933–1934. *Historian* 53:3 (Spring 1991), 439–441.

Leonard, Thomas C. *Illiberal Reformers: Race, Eugenics, and American Economics in the Progressive Era.* Princeton: Princeton University Press, 2016.

Leuchtenburg, William E. *Franklin D. Roosevelt and the New Deal, 1932–1940.* New York: Harper and Row, 1963.

———. *The FDR Years: On Roosevelt and His Legacy.* New York: Columbia University Press, 1995.

———. A Klansman Joins the Court: The Appointment of Hugo L. Black. *University of Chicago Law Review* 41:1 (Fall 1973), 6–7.

Lyons, Eugene. *Herbert Hoover: A Biography.* 1948. Reprint, New York: Doubleday, 1964.

McChesney, Robert W. *Telecommunications, Mass Media, and Democracy: The Battle for the Control of U.S. Broadcasting, 1928–1935.* New York: Oxford University Press, 1993.

McClure, Marc Eric. *Earnest Endeavors: The Life and Public Work of George Rublee.* Westport: Praeger, 2003.

McElvaine, Robert. *The Great Depression, America, 1929–1941.* New York: Times Books, 1984.

McKean, Dayton David. *The Boss: The Hague Machine in Action.* Boston: Houghton Mifflin, 1940.

McMeekin, Sean. *Stalin's War: A New History of World War II.* New York: Basic Books, 2021.

McMillen, Neal R. *Dark Journey: Black Mississippians in the Age of Jim Crow.* Urbana: University of Illinois Press, 1990.

Magness, Phil. The Problem of the Tariff in American Economic History, 1787–1934. *Cato Publications*, September 26th 2023, https://www.cato.org/publications/problem-tariff-american-economic-history-1787-1934#protectionism-income-tax-era, accessed February 3rd 2025.

Mangione, Jerre. *An Ethnic at Large: A Memoir of America in the Thirties and Forties.* New York: Putnam's, 1978.

Markoe, Arnold. The Black Committee: A Study of the Senate Investigation of the Public Utility Holding Company Lobby. PhD dissertation, New York University, 1972.

Marrus, Michael R. The Strange Story of Herschel Grynszpan. *The American Scholar* 57:1 (Winter 1988), 70–73.

Martin, Isaac William. *Rich People's Movements: Grassroots Campaigns to Untax the One Percent.* New York: Oxford University Press, 2013.

Medoff, Rafael. *The Jews Should Keep Quiet: Franklin D. Roosevelt, Rabbi Stephen S. Wise, and the Holocaust.* Philadelphia: Jewish Publication Society, 2019.

———. Op-Ed: Recalling a Mormon Senator Who Tried to Save Anne Frank's Life. *Jewish Telegraphic Agency*, February 26th 2012, https://www.jta.org/2012/02/26/ideas/op-ed-recalling-a-mormon-senator-who-tried-to-save-anne-franks-life, accessed November 17th 2024.

Meier, August, and Elliott Rudwick. The Rise of Segregation in the Federal Bureaucracy, 1900–1930. *Phylon* 28:2 (2nd Qtr., 1967), 178–184.

Michaelis, David. *Eleanor.* New York: Simon and Schuster, 2020.

Moe, Richard. *Roosevelt's Second Act: The Election of 1940 and the Politics of War.* New York: Oxford University Press, 2013.

Moley, Raymond. *After Seven Years.* New York: Harper and Brothers, 1939.

———. *The First New Deal.* New York: Harcourt Brace, 1966.

Monroe, Dan. *Hemingway, the Left, and Key West.* In Kirk Cornutt and Gail D. Sinclair, eds., *Key West Hemingway: A Reassessment.* Gainesville: University Press of Florida, 2009.

Moreno, Paul D. *Black Americans and Organized Labor: A New History.* Baton Rouge: Louisiana State University Press, 2006.

Moser, John E. *Right Turn: John T. Flynn and the Transformation of American Liberalism.* New York: University Press, 2005.

Murphy, Lawrence R. *Perverts by Official Order: The Campaign Against Homosexuals by the United States Navy.* New York: Harrington Park Press, 1988.

Nekrich, Alexandr M. *Pariahs, Partners, Predators: German-Soviet Relations, 1922–1941.* New York: Columbia University Press, 1997.

Newman, Roger K. *Hugo Black: A Biography.* New York: Fordham University Press, 1994.

Offner, Arnold A. Appeasement Revisited: The United States, Great Britain, and Germany, 1933–1940. *Journal of American History* 64:2 (September 1977), 373–398.

Olson, Lynne. *Those Angry Days: Roosevelt, Lindbergh, and America's Fight Over World War II, 1939–1941.* New York: Random House, 2013.

O'Neal, Sam. Death of Justice Eicher Ends Mass Sedition Trial. *Chicago Sun* (December 1st 1944), 12.

Oursler, Fulton. *Behold This Dreamer! An Autobiography.* Boston: Little, Brown, 1964.

Patterson, James T. *Congressional Conservatism and the New Deal: The Growth of the Conservative Coalition in Congress, 1933–1939.* Lexington: University of Kentucky Press, 1967.

Persico, Joseph E. *Roosevelt's Secret War: FDR and World War II Espionage.* New York: Random House, 2002.

Polenberg, Richard. The National Committee to Uphold Constitutional Government, 1937–1941. *Journal of American History* 52:3 (December 1965), 582–598.

———. *Reorganizing Roosevelt's Government: The Controversy Over Executive Reorganization, 1936–1939.* Cambridge: Harvard University Press, 1966.

Powell, Jim. *FDR's Folly: How Roosevelt and His New Deal Prolonged the Great Depression.* New York: Three Rivers Press, 2003.

Procter, Ben. *William Randolph Hearst: The Later Years, 1911–1951.* New York: Oxford University Press, 2007.

Quinn, Susan. *Furious Improvisation: How the WPA and a Cast of Thousand Made High Art in Desperate Times.* New York: Walker and Company, 2008.

Rable, George C. The South and the Politics of Antilynching Legislation, 1920–1940. *The Journal of Southern History* 51:2 (May 1985), 201–220.

Ransom, Roger L., and Richard Sutch. Tontine Insurance and the Armstrong Investigation: A Case of Stifled Innovation, 1868–1905. *Journal of Economic History* 47:2 (June 1987), 379–390.

Reeves, Richard. *Infamy: The Shocking Story of the Japanese Internment in World War II.* New York: Holt, 2015.

Ritchie, Donald A. What Makes a Successful Congressional Investigation? *OAH Magazine of History* 12:4 (Summer 1998), 21.

Robbins, Lionel. *The Great Depression.* London: Macmillan, 1934.

Robinson, Greg. By Order of the President: FDR and the Internment of *Japanese Americans.* Cambridge: Harvard University Press, 2001.

Rodgers, Daniel T. *Atlantic Crossings: Social Politics in a Progressive Age.* Cambridge: The Belknap Press of Harvard University Press, 1998.

Roll, David L. *The Hopkins Touch: Harry Hopkins and the Forging of the Alliance to Defeat Hitler.* New York: Oxford University Press, 2013.

Roosevelt, Elliott, and James Bough. *A Rendezvous with Destiny: The Roosevelts of the White House.* New York: Putnam's, 1975.

———, ed. *FDR: His Personal Letters, 1905–1928.* New York: Duell, Sloan, and Pearce, 1950.

Roosevelt, Elliott, ed. *FDR: His Personal Letters, 1928–1945.* New York: Duell, Sloan, and Pearce, 1950.

Roosevelt, Franklin D. A Social Security Program Must Include All Those Who Need Its Protection, August 15th 1938, https://www.ssa.gov/history/fdrstmts.html#message1, accessed February 2nd 2025.

. Acceptance Speech for the Renomination for the Presidency, Philadelphia, June 27th 1936, https://www.presidency.ucsb.edu/documents/acceptance-speech-for-the-renomination-for-the-presidency-philadelphia-pa, accessed September 6th 2024.

———. Address Accepting the Presidential Nomination at the Democratic National Convention in Chicago. https://www.presidency.ucsb.edu/documents/address-accepting-the-presidential-nomination-the-democratic-national-convention-chicago-1, accessed June 18th 2024.

———. Address at Barnesville, Georgia, August 11th 1938, https://www.presidency.ucsb.edu/documents/address-barnesville-georgia, accessed August 21st 2024.

———. Address at Chautauqua, N.Y., August 14th 1936, https://www.presidency.ucsb.edu/documents/address-chautauqua-ny, accessed September 7th 2024.

———. Address at Madison Square Garden, New York City, https://www.presidency.ucsb.edu/documents/address-madison-square-garden-new-york-city-1, accessed February 3rd 2025.

———. Address to Congress on the Yalta Conference, March 1st 1945, https://www.presidency.ucsb.edu/documents/address-congress-the-yalta-conference, accessed January 14th 2025.

———. Annual Message to Congress, January 3rd 1936, https://www.presidency.ucsb.edu/documents/annual-message-congress-2, accessed September 7th 2024.

———. Campaign Address on Agriculture and Tariffs at Sioux City, Iowa, September 29, 1932, https://www.presidency.ucsb.edu/documents/campaign-address-agriculture-and-tariffs-sioux-city-iowa, accessed January 22nd 2025.

———. Campaign Address on Progressive Government at the Commonwealth Club in San Francisco, California, September 23rd 1932, https://www.presidency.ucsb.edu/documents/campaign-address-progressive- government-the-commonwealth-club-san-francisco-california, accessed June 18th 2024.

———. Campaign Address on the Federal Budget at Pittsburgh, Pennsylvania, October 19, 1932, https://www.presidency.ucsb.edu/documents/campaign-address-the-federal-budget-pittsburgh-pennsylvania, accessed June 16, 2024.

———. Executive Order 6261—Relating to the Sale and Export of Gold Recovered from Natural Deposits, August 29th 1933, https://www.presidency.ucsb.edu/documents/executive-order-6261-relating-the-sale-and-export-gold-recovered-from-natural-deposits, accessed August 1st 2024.

———. Executive Order 7037, Establishing the Rural Electrification Administration, May 11th 1935, https://en.wikisource.org/wiki/Executive_Order_7037, accessed August 25th 2024.

———. Fireside Chat, September 31st 1934, https://www.presidency.ucsb.edu/documents/fireside-chat-20, accessed January 31st 2025.

———. Fireside Chat 3: On the National Recovery Administration, July 24th 1933, https://millercenter.org/the-presidency/presidential-speeches/july-24-1933-fireside-chat-3-national-recovery-administration, accessed January 26th 2025.

———. Fireside Chat, December 24th 1943, https://www.presidency.ucsb.edu/documents/fireside-chat, accessed January 13th 2025.

———. First Inaugural Address of Franklin D. Roosevelt, March 4th 1933, https://avalon.law.yale.edu/20th_century/froos1.asp, accessed August 1st 2024.

———. Roosevelt, Franklin D. *Looking Forward.* London: William Heinemann, 1933.

———. Message to Congress on Social Security, January 17th 1935, https://www.presidency.ucsb.edu/documents/message-congress-social-security, accessed August 19th 2024.

———. Message to Congress on the Progress of the War, September 17th 1943, https://www.presidency.ucsb.edu/documents/message-congress-the-progress-the-war, accessed January 14th 2025.

———. Press Conference, April 12th 1933, http://www.fdrlibrary.marist.edu/_resources/images/pc/pc0185.pdf, accessed January 26th 2025.

———. Press Conference, May 31st 1935, https://www.presidency.ucsb.edu/documents/press-conference-23, accessed August 17th 2024.

———. Press Conferences of President Franklin D. Roosevelt, 1933–1945, Series 1: Press Conference Transcripts, April 29th 1938, 399–400, and May 10th 1938, 407–08, Franklin D. Roosevelt Presidential Library and Museum, http://www.fdrlibrary.marist.edu/archives/collections/franklin/?p=collections/findingaid&id=508, accessed October 7th 2024.

———. Proclamation 2039, March 6th 1933, https://www.lawandfreedom.com/site/executive/execorders/Roosevelt.pdf?88;a79e, accessed August 1st 2024.

———. Radio Address on the National Democratic Platform From Albany, New York, July 30th 1932, https://www.presidency.ucsb.edu/documents/radio-address-the-national-democratic-platform-from-albany-new-york, accessed June 16th 2024.

———. Roosevelt, Franklin D. Statement on N.I.R.A., June 16th 1933, https://www.presidency.ucsb.edu/documents/statement-nira, accessed August 9th 2024.

———. Statement on Neutrality Legislation, August 31st 1935, https://www.presidency.ucsb.edu/documents/statement-neutrality-legislation, accessed August 19th 1935.

Rothbard, Murray, *America's Great Depression.* New York: Van Norstand, 1963.

Rothstein, Richard. *The Color of Law: The Forgotten History of How Our Government Segregated America.* New York: Norton, 2017.

Schivelbusch, Wolfgang. Three New Deals: Reflections on Roosevelt's America, Mussolini's Italy, and Hitler's Germany, 1933–1939. New York: Henry Holt, 2006.

Schlesinger, Arthur M., Jr. *The Age of Roosevelt: The Coming of the New Deal.* Boston: Houghton Mifflin, 1959.

———. *The Age of Roosevelt: The Politics of Upheaval.* Boston: Houghton Mifflin, 1960.

Schumpeter, Joseph A. *Business Cycles: A Theoretical, Historical and Statistical Analysis of the Capitalist Process.* New York: McGraw-Hill, 1939.

Seiler, Christine Kay. The Veteran Killer: The Florida Emergency Relief Administration and the Labor Day Hurricane of 1935. PhD dissertation, Florida State University, 2003.

Selgin, George. *False Dawn: The New Deal and the Promise of Recovery, 1933–1947.* Chicago: University of Chicago Press, 2025.

Shepperd, G.A. *The Italian Campaign 1943–1945: A Political and Military Re-assessment.* New York: Praeger, 1968.

Sherwood, Robert E. *Roosevelt and Hopkins: An Intimate History.* New York: Harper and Brothers, 1948.

Shesol, Jeff. *Supreme Power: Franklin Roosevelt vs. the Supreme Court.* New York: Norton, 2010.

Shlaes, Amity. *The Forgotten Man: A New History of the Great Depression.* New York: Harper Perennial, 2007.

Shlaes, Amity, ed. *New Deal Rebels.* Great Barrington: American Institute for Economic Research, 2023.

Smiley, Gene. *Rethinking the Great Depression.* Chicago: Ivan R. Dee, 2002.

Smith, Amanda. *Newspaper Titan: The Infamous Life and Monumental Times of Cissy Patterson.* New York: Knopf, 2011.

Smith, Jason Scott. New Deal Public Works at War: The WPA and Japanese American Internment. *Pacific Historical Review* 72:1 (February 2003), 63–92.

Smith, Jean Edward. *FDR.* New York: Random House, 2007.

Spear, Sheldon. The United States and the Persecution of the Jews in Germany, 1933–1939. *Jewish Social Studies* 30:4 (October 1968), 215–242.

Steel, Ronald. *Walter Lippmann and the American Century.* Boston: Little, Brown, 1980.

Steele, Richard W. *Free Speech in the Good War.* New York: St. Martin's Press, 1999.

———. *Propaganda in an Open Society: The Roosevelt Administration and the Media, 1933–1941.* Westport: Greenwood, 1985.

Stein, Leon Seymour. Editorializing by Broadcast Licensees: A Developmental Analysis of the Problem of Federal Regulation of Editorializing by Broadcast Licensees. PhD dissertation, New York University, 1965.

Stinnett, Robert B. *Day of Deceit: The Truth About FDR and Pearl Harbor.* New York: Simon and Schuster, 2000.

Stoler, Mark A. *The Politics of the Second Front: American Military Planning and Diplomacy in Coalition Warfare, 1941–1943.* Westport: Greenwood, 1977.

Stone, Geoffrey R. Free Speech in World War II: 'When Are You Going to Indict the Seditionists?' *International Journal of Constitutional Law* 2:2 (2004), 334–367.

Sturgeon, Joel. You Will Be Policed: Boss Crump, the New Deal, and the Price of Black Defiance in FDR's America. *Tennessee Historical Quarterly* 82:1 (Spring 2023), 68–95.

Sweeney, Michael S. *Secrets of Victory: The Office of Censorship in the American Press and Radio in World War II.* Chapel Hill: University of North Carolina Press, 2001.

Trohan, Walter. Political Animals: Memoirs of a Sentimental Cynic. New York: Doubleday, 1975.

Tuccille, Jerome. *The War Against the Vets: The World War I Bonus Army During the Great Depression.* Lincoln: University of Nebraska Press, 2018.

U.S. Senate, 77th Congress, Second Session, Document 159. *Report of the* Commission Appointed by the President of the United States to Investigation and Report the Facts Relating to the Attack Upon Pearl Harbor in the Territory of Hawaii on December 7th 1941. Washington, DC: Government Printing Office, 1942.

Ubriaco, Robert D., Jr. Harry S. Truman, the Politics of Yalta, and the Domestic Origins of the Truman Doctrine. PhD dissertation, University of Illinois at Urbana-Champaign, 1992.

Vedder, Richard K., and Lowell E. Gallaway. *Out of Work: Unemployment* and *Government in Twentieth-Century America*. New York: New York University Press, 1997.

Vickers, Kenneth W. John Rankin: Democrat and Demagogue. MA thesis, Mississippi State University, 1993.

Vieth, Jane Karoline. Joseph P. Kennedy: Ambassador to the Court of St. James's, 1938–1940. PhD dissertation, The Ohio State University, 1975.

Wallace, Henry A. *The Price of Vision: The Diary of Henry A. Wallace, 1942–1946*. Edited by John Morton Blum. Boston: Houghton Mifflin, 1973.

Washburn, Patrick S. *A Question of Sedition: The Federal Government's Investigation of the Black Press During World War II*. New York: Oxford University Press, 1986.

Weaver, Carolyn L. *The Crisis in Social Security: Economic and Political Origins*. Durham: Duke University Press, 1982.

Weeks, Albert L. *Russia's Life-Saver: Lend-Lease Aid to the USSR in World War II*. Lanham: Lexington Books, 2004.

Weinrib, Laura. *The Taming of Free Speech: America's Civil Liberties Compromise*. Cambridge: Harvard University Press, 2016.

Weiss, Nancy J. *Farewell to the Party of Lincoln: Black Politics in the Age of FDR*. Princeton: Princeton University Press, 1983.

Whalen, Richard. *The Founding Father: The Story of Joseph P. Kennedy*. Washington, DC: Regnery Gateway, 1993 [1964].

White, Graham J. *FDR and the Press*. University of Chicago Press, 1979.

Whitman, James Q. Of Corporatism, Fascism, and the First New Deal. *American Journal of Comparative Law* 39 (1991), 747–778.

Wilson, Charles, 1st Baron Moran. *Churchill: Taken from the Diaries of Lord Moran*. Boston: Houghton Mifflin, 1966.

Wilson, Joan Hoff. *Herbert Hoover: Forgotten Progressive*. Long Grove: Waveland, 1992 [1975].

Wilson, Woodrow. *A History of the American People*, Volume 5. New York: Harper and Brothers, 1918, reprint of the 1910 edition.

Witham, Barry B. *The Federal Theater Project: A Case Study*. Cambridge: Cambridge University Press, 2003.

Wolgemuth, Kathleen L. Woodrow Wilson and Federal Segregation. *The Journal of Negro History* 44:2 (April 1959), 158, 173.

Wollenberg, Charles. *Rebel Lawyer: Wayne Collins and the Defense of Japanese American Rights*. Berkeley: Heyday, 2018.

Wright, Gavin. The Political Economy of New Deal Spending: An Econometric Analysis. *Review of Economics and Statistics* 56:1 (February 1974), 30–38.

Wright, Robert E. *FDR's Long New Deal: A Public Choice Perspective*. New York: Palgrave Macmillan, 2024.

Wyman, David S. *The Abandonment of the Jews: America and the Holocaust, 1941–1945*. New York: Pantheon, 1984.

Wyman, David S., and Rafael Medoff. *A Race Against Death: Peter Bergson, America, and the Holocaust*. New York: Norton, 2002.

Zanagrando, Robert L. *The NAACP Crusade Against Lynching, 1909–1950*. Philadelphia: Temple University Press, 1980.

Zane, Sherry. 'I Did It for the Uplift of Humanity and the Navy': Same Sex Acts on the Origins of the National Security State, 1919–1921. *The New England Quarterly* 91:2 (June 2018), 279–308.

———. The Newport Sex Scandal and the Early-Twentieth-Century Origins of the U.S. National Security State. PhD dissertation, University of Connecticut, 2012.

Index

Adkins v. Children's Hospital, reversed by West Coast Hotel Co. v. Parrish, 105
A Farewell to Arms (Hemingway), shaped antiwar sentiment, 76
Abt, John J., admitted political mission in Key West, 78
African Americans (and FDR), 7–8, 10–11, 27–28, 98–100, 140–44; New Deal and, 38, 52–55, 60, 68, 121, 134; Marian Anderson controversy, 148–49; World War II and, 148–49, 170–71, 195
Agricultural Adjustment Act (AAA), 38–39, 85; used politically in 1936 election, 96–97; increased spending in 1938, 114; rushed payments in 1940, 139; harmed Black workers, 99
A.L.A. Schechter Poultry Corp. v. United States, 64
Allen, Robert, mocked Heller and Schechters, 65
All Quiet on the Western Front (Remarque), influenced antiwar sentiment, 76
Alter, Jonathan, on FDR's intentional economic decline during transition, 31
Amalgamated Clothing Workers, supported FDR's campaign, 97
American Bar Association (ABA), Strawn's past presidency, 86; formed Bill of Rights Committee, 120–22
American Civil Liberties Union (ACLU), demanded Black Committee's seized telegrams, 90–91; opposed targeting National Woman's Party, 90–91; targeted by Black Committee, 90; shifted to federal courts, 122; opposed Black Committee surveillance (Celler, McCormack), 91; opposed Minton Committee, 116; challenged Hague's actions, 118, 122; Baldwin on Social Justice prosecution, 169; reported internment disapproval, 165
American Communist Party, opposed Wagner Act, 68
American Construction Council, 16–17
American Federation of Labor (AFL), 42, 53, 68, 97
American Jewish Congress, criticized delayed "rescue through victory" policy, 185
American Legion, Aided Key West hurricane response, 78; FDR praised for Centralia mob role, 14
American Newspaper Publishers Association (ANPA), noted media criticism of FDR, 79; Hanson's role, 88; criticized Minton Committee, 116
American Rhetoric, ranked FDR's inauguration address, 33
America First Committee (AFC), non-interventionist group, members included Brewster,

Ford, Kennedy, Longworth, Roosevelt Jr., Shriver, Stewart, Stuart, Thomas, Vidal, Wood, 141; opposed Selective Service Act, 139–141; disbanded post-Pearl Harbor, 158; FDR pushed for investigation, 162

American Veterans Committee, noted racial disparities in GI Bill benefits, 194

Anderson, Benjamin, criticized New Deal's economic failures, 107

Anderson, Marian, excluded from Constitution Hall (DAR) and Central High School, 129–130; NAACP defense, 129–130; Hurok's concert suggestion, 129–130; Eleanor Roosevelt resigned from DAR, 129–131; *Washington Tribune* editorial, 129–130; Weiss on FDR's political benefits, 130–131; Lincoln Memorial concert, 130–131

Anschluss (1938), German annexation of Austria, 111, 126

Arnold, Ervin, 11–12

Astor, Vincent, dined with FDR during WWI tour, 96

Atkinson, David N., on Minton's bill origins, 117

Avery, Sewell, defied War Labor Board in Montgomery Ward incident, 196; Gallup poll upport, 196

Axis Powers, formed via Tripartite Pact (Germany, Italy, Japan), 141; Soviet Union considered, 141; surrendered in North Africa, 178; FDR refused to negotiate with dissidents, 183

Bacon, Francis, source of "fear itself" phrase, 33

Badoglio, Pietro, Italian leader; negotiated armistice, resisted unconditional surrender, 181–82

Baker, Newton D., deployed troops during Red Summer, 11; condemned Black Committee, 86

Baldwin, Roger N., demanded Black Committee's seized telegrams, 90; opposed Social Justice prosecution, 169

Ballantine, Arthur, 34–35

Baltimore Sun, criticized Black Committee, 86; Mencken's Jewish immigration proposal, 128

Baltimore-Afro American, criticized FDR's military promotions, 143; GOP ad on Davis Sr.'s promotion, 143; cited for seditious implications (MacLeish), 170

Bank Holiday (1933), declared by FDR, 34

Bank of United States, collapse and Scandal, 22–24

Banking Crisis (1933), accelerated pre-inauguration, 30–31; FDR's indifference, 30–31; state bank holidays, 31; Emergency Banking Act, 34

Barkley, Alben, 138, 192, 198

Baruch, Bernard, 41, 178, 186

Battle of Britain (1940), RAF effectiveness, possible Willkie campaign impact, 142

Battle of Midway (1942), Nimitz's victory, 172; *Chicago Daily Tribune* story investigated for Espionage Act violation, 172–73

Bellows, Henry A., CBS VP; supported FDR, 48

Bensel, Richard F., on Union's Civil War mobilization model, 214

Bergson, Peter (Hillel Kook), opposed "rescue through victory", 185; led Emergency Committee to Save Jewish People, 185; arranged Rabbis' Capitol pilgrimage, 186; FBI investigation ordered, 186

Berle, Adolf, Assistant Secretary of State, 24–25, 145–46, 153, 209

Bermuda Conference (1943), reaffirmed "rescue through victory", 177; rejected quota use, Liberty Ships for refugees, 177

Bernstein, David E., on Wagner Act's harm to Black workers, 68

Best, Gary Dean, 112

Bethune, Mary McLeod, popularized Black Cabinet, 54

Biddle, Francis, opposed Fifth Column rhetoric, 136; pressured by FDR for sedition trials, 162; opposed Japanese American internment, 165; called U.S. v.

McWilliams a "dreary farce", 205; resisted prosecuting non-interventionists, 161–62; targeted Social Justice, McCormick-Patterson papers, 169; met Sengstacke on Black press, 170; analyzed *Chicago Daily Tribune* articles, 169; weakened by Stimson in internment debate, 164; demanded Montgomery Ward's books, 196; warned FDR on internment dangers, 192; received Martin's plea against Crump, 183

Bill of Rights Committee (ABA), challenged Hague's actions, 120; formed by Vanderbilt, Hogan, 120

Bill of Rights Day, commemorated by MacLeish, 170

Bismarck (German Battleship), Berle on unlikelihood of German invasion post–sinking, 146

Bismarck, Otto von, influenced progressive ideas, 2

Black, Hugo L., led airmail scandal, Black Committee investigations, 50, 71–73, 83–92; defended by Rankin, 87, 91; exposed for Klan ties, 106–07; tax shelter controversy, 105–06; Ickes on FDR's Senate committee consideration, 91; opposed anti-lynching bill, 105; Supreme Court nomination, 106–07

Black Cabinet, 54–55

Black Committee, led by Black, 71–73, 83–92, 100–01; investigated fake telegrams (Driscoll), 72–73; accessed tax returns, 73; targeted utility executives, Lawrence, McSwain, 72–73; Gadsden's testimony, 72; surveilled telegrams with Western Union, 84–92, 100–01; targeted ACLU, National Woman's Party, 90–91; supported by FDR, Rankin, 87, 91–92; opposed by Celler, Cochran, McCormack, May, Longworth, Moley, 87, 89–91; criticized by newspapers (*Chicago Daily Tribune*, Krock, McCormick, *Washington Post*), 86, 89, 92; Strawn, Wheat limited leverage, 91–92

Black Press, harassed by federal authorities, 170; Biddle-Sengstacke meeting, 170; Double V campaign, 170; reduced criticism post-agreement, 170–71; limited federal access, 171

branch banking, FDR fails to endorse, 29–30, 36–37

Blondell, Joan, in *Footlight Parade*, 44

Blum, John Morton, on Blue Eagle (NRA emblem), 41–44; on Kaiser's wartime mobilization role, 214

Borah, William E., opposed NRA, 51; criticized New Deal, 104; coined "Phony War", 133

Brain Trust, 24–25

Braley, Berton, 90

Brandeis, Louis, opposed NRA in Schechter, 66; anti-centralization message to Cohen, Corcoran, 66

Brands, H.W., on FDR's differences from TR, 9; on banking crisis acceleration, 31; noted FDR's Greer misrepresentation, 152

Brereton, Lewis, requested MacArthur's counterattack against Japan, 158

Brindze, Ruth, on radio censorship, 49

Brinkley, Alan, 50, 115, 174, 178

Brinkley, David, on LaGuardia's OCD leadership, 148; on FDR's health decline, 190

British Security Coordination (BSC), FDR's cooperation, 135; propaganda campaign, 135–36; faked Nazi documents, 153; Stephenson's leadership, 135; Cull on covert campaign, 135; Sherwood on FDR's secret alliance, 135; Ignatius on media manipulation, 135; based in Rockefeller Center, 135

Brookings Institution, criticized NRA, 67

Brown and Root, funded Democratic campaigns via naval base, 139; role in Corpus Christi naval base, 139

Bruenn, Howard, diagnosed FDR's severe hypertension, heart issues, 190
Bryan, William Jennings, antiwar Secretary of State; FDR's criticism, 8
Bureau of Economic Warfare (BEW), renamed from Economic Defense Board, 159; Wallace's leadership, 159; clashed with Jones over rubber production, 159–160, 182
Bureau of Internal Revenue, granted Black Committee tax return access, 73
Bureau of Labor Statistics, FDR suggested manipulating cost of living figures, 172; Lubin's role, 172
Burns, James MacGregor, on FDR's moderate governorship, 19; criticized Japan negotiations, 151; on Civilian Conservation Corps, 35; on Economic Bill of Rights as radical, 191
Bush, George W. ,165
Butler, Nicholas Murray, joked about FDR's law school dropout, 4
Byrnes, James, 54, 178, 198–99

Cagney, Jimmy, in *Footlight Parade*, 44
Canaris, Wilhelm, 136, 177, 186–87, 201, 211
Capital Strike, FDR's claim of business conspiracy, 108; condemned by Ickes, 108
Cardozo, Benjamin, opposed NRA in Schechter, 66
Carter, Boake, 106, 112–14
Carter, John Franklin, 163–64
Casablanca Conference, FDR's unconditional surrender policy, 175–76; Churchill's discomfort, 176; FDR's health concerns, 178
Catledge, Turner, shocked by FDR's health decline, 190
CBS, rejected Fletcher's skits, 85; cut Vandenberg's debate, 94–95; Bellows supported FDR, 48; discontinued Carter's program, 114
Celler, Emanuel, opposed Black Committee's surveillance, 91
Centralia, Washington, FDR praised American Legion mob's attack on Wobblies, 14
Chamberlain, Neville, pressured by Kennedy at FDR's urging, 131; negotiated Munich Pact, praised by FDR, 123; abandoned appeasement, 128; Polish guarantee, 128; Davis on miscalculation, 128
Chambers, Whittaker, revealed Hiss's espionage, 209
Chandler, Albert B., challenged Barkley in Kentucky primary, 124
Chase, Stuart, New Republic article on Soviet planning; Coined "New Deal", 26
Chicago Daily Tribune, Criticized Black Committee (Klan cartoon), 92; opposed Court Packing, 104; criticized Key West hurricane response, 78; post-Pearl Harbor FDR support, 157; investigated for Midway story, 172–73
Chicago Defender, 52–54, 170
Chicago Sun, 172, 195
Churchill, Winston S., 134, 137, 144, 150–52, 175, 181, 184–89, 202, 203, 207–08, 212
City Trust, collapsed in 1929; FDR's grudge against Moses, 23; Lehman's investigation, 23
Civilian Conservation Corps (CCC), established, 35, 38–39; used politically in 1936 election, 96–97; spending in 1938, 114
Clark, Bennett Champ, sponsored Clark Amendment, 75
Clark, Grenville, 4, 105, 116
Clark, Mark, lamented Italian campaign weakening, 188
Clark Amendment, Social Security Act provision, 75–76; Douglas on, 76
Coast Guard, aided Key West hurricane response, 78; *S.S. St. Louis* intervention, 131
Cochran, John J., opposed Black Committee's telegram seizures, 87
Code of Wartime Practices, governed censorship, 172; *Chicago Daily Tribune* compliance, 172–73
Cohen, Benjamin, Brain Truster, 25; received Brandeis's anti-centralization message, 66; worried about Court Packing hubris, 103;

managed third-term campaign, 134
Congress of Industrial Organizations (CIO), 199, 205; supported FDR's campaign, 97; linked to Flint sit-down strike, 108; targeted by Hague, 118
Coolidge, Calvin, 13–14
Coolidge, Grace, pledged to care for Jewish refugee children, 128
Corcoran, Thomas, received Brandeis's anti-centralization message, 66; lobbied for Wheeler–Rayburn Bill, 71; received Wheeler's FDR critique, 104
Coughlin, Charles E., radio support for FDR, 49–50; met FDR, 80–81; opposed FDR, 104; Social Justice shutdown, 169; accused of Espionage Act violation, 169
Court-packing plan, FDR's proposal, 103–06, 109, 115, 120–22, 124; blocked, 125; opposed by Wheeler, Garner, Lehman, NCUCG, 104–05, 119; linked to Stalin, Hitler, Mussolini, 112, 122; Cohen's concerns, 103; Hughes denied backlog, 104
Covenant speech, FDR's sound money promise, 28
Cox, James M., 1920 Democratic nominee, chose FDR as running mate, 13–14
Cramer, Lawrence, proposed Jewish refugee admission in Virgin Islands, 126
Crisis (NAACP), Du Bois's NRA critique, 52
Croly, Herbert, defined New Nationalism, 3
Crump, Edward H., Memphis boss; targeted J.B. Martin, 142–43, 183; supported FDR, 143; blocked Randolph's speech, 184; compared to Nazis by Simmons, 142–43
Cull, Nicholas, on BSC's covert campaign, 135
Cummings, Homer, evasive on anti-lynching probe, 98
Currie, Lauchlin, 114, 209
Czaplicki, Michael Stephen, on Black's FDR relationship, 71–72
Daily Worker, supported U.S. v. McWilliams, 195
Daniels, Josephus, appointed FDR to Navy, 6–7; racist policies, 7–8; fired Lucy Mercer, 10–11; rejected FDR's infantry volunteering, 9; warned FDR of Senate report, 15
Darlan deal, 175, 189
Darlan, François, Vichy commander; negotiated ceasefire with Eisenhower, 175
Darrow, Clarence, criticized NRA as National Recovery Review Board head, 52
Daughters of the American Revolution (DAR), excluded Marian Anderson, 129–130; Eleanor Roosevelt resigned, 129–131; Hurston's critique, 129–131
Davidson, Eugene, on Black Cabinet as mythical, 55
Davies, Joseph, 113,179–180, 207
Davis, Benjamin O. Sr., GOP ad on delayed promotion, 143; promoted by FDR, 143
Davis, Elmer, on FDR's vague campaign speeches, 26; belittled Katyn massacre reports, 180
Davis, John W., 1924 Democratic nominee, 18
Davis, Kenneth S., 10, 13–16, 32, 128
DC Board of Education, excluded Marian Anderson, 129–130; cited 1906 segregation law, 129–130
De Gaulle, Charles, at Casablanca Conference, 175
Debs, Eugene, 194
Delano, Warren, 2
Delco-Light, sold lighting plants, 63
Democratic National Committee (DNC), Hurja's polling, 57; Hague's role, 118, 120; FDR's purge, 121; Hannegan's anti-Wallace role, 197; controlled 1944 convention, 199
Democratic National Convention (1932), FDR's nomination, 25–26; Garner released delegates, 26
Democratic National Convention (1940), FDR's third–term strategy, 134, 137–39; Barkley's statement, 138; Garry's "voice

from the sewers", 138; Wallace nominated, 138–39
Dennis, Lawrence, U.S. v. McWilliams defendant, 194; compared to Rosenberg, 196
Dewey, Thomas E., 198–205
DeWitt, John L., 164–67
Dickman, Howard, on Italian labor law influence, 47; on Wagner Act's Fascist influence, 68
Dies, Martin, 101
Dilling, Elizabeth, U.S. v. McWilliams defendant, 194
Dodd, William, 47, 94
Donovan, William, partnered with BSC, 135; shared fake Nazi documents, 153; FDR's law school classmate, 135; appealed on Canaris's anti-Hitler plot, 187
Double V campaign, popularized by Pittsburgh Courier, 170; reduced post-Biddle agreement, 170–71
Douglas, Lewis, 44
Douglas, Paul H., on Clark Amendment, 76
Douglas, William O., considered for 1944 VP nomination, 198
Dresden Bombing (1945), allied bombing of civilians, 211
Driscoll, Denis J., reported fake telegrams in Black Committee, 72
Du Bois, W.E.B., criticized NRA's impact on Black workers, 52; advocated "Close Ranks" in WWI, 170
Duces Tecum Subpoenas, used by Black Committee, 71
Duggan, Lawrence, 209
Dulles, Allen, reported anti-Hitler posters in Germany, 187
Dunkirk Evacuation (1940), 137
Dunn, Herbert O., naval board inquiry into Newport Sex Scandal, 13–15
Durante, Jimmy, in *Give a Man a Job*, 44
Earle, George, warned FDR about Stalin, 211; met Canaris in Istanbul, 186; brought Katyn massacre evidence, 197
Early, Stephen, 48, 54, 94, 112–13, 123
Economic Bill of Rights, FDR's proposal, 191–92; racial disparities, 192; Burns on radical speech, 191
Economic Defense Board, renamed BEW, 159
Economic Royalists, FDR's term for New Deal opponents, 94
Eicher, Edward C., 195–96, 206
Eisenhower, Dwight D., 101, 175–76, 181
elections, (1904), 3; (1912), 6; (1920), 12–14; (1924), 12–14; (1928), 18; (1930), 33; (1932), 23–28; (1934), 57–58; (1935), 81; (1936), 93–100 (1938), 122–24 (1940), 133–144; (1942), 174; (1944), 198–205
Ely, Richard, 3
Emergency Banking Act (1933), drafted by Ballantine, 34; Fireside Chat, 34
Emergency Committee to Save the Jewish People of Europe, proposed refugee agency, 185; supported by Eleanor Roosevelt, Ickes, Hoover, Hearst, 185; led by Bergson, 185; organized "We Will Never Die", 185
Espionage and Sedition Acts, FDR supported in WWI, 10; precedent for U.S. v. McWilliams, 194; used against Social Justice, 169
Evans, M. Stanton, 209
Evian Conference (1938), Taylor as FDR's refugee spokesman, 111–112; FDR's limited response, 126
Executive Order 6102 (Gold Ban, 1933), issued by FDR, 35
Executive Order 9066, authorized Japanese-American internment, 166–167; upheld in Korematsu, 206; rejected for Italian, German aliens, 166; proposed for Hawaii, 166–67
Executive Order 8802 (1941), Countered war industry discrimination, 149; criticized by Hurston, 149; weak enforcement, 149

Fair Employment Practice Committee (FEPC), established by Executive Order 8802, 149; limited impact, 149
Fair Labor Standards Act (1938), set national minimum wage,

impacted Southern employment, 121
Farley, James A., 23, 57–58; reassured on Court Packing, 104; proposed prosecuting Hague, 118–19; tested presidential candidacy, 131–32, 134, 137–38; on Garner's anti-lynching shift, 134; on FDR's health decline, 190
"Fear Itself" Phrase, sourced from Bacon, Katznelson, Moley, Eleanor Roosevelt, 33; omitted by Hearst Metrotone, 34
Federal Communications Commission (FCC), 48–49, 89, 91, 94–95, 100
Federal Council of Churches, supported King-Havenner Bill, 134
Federal Emergency Relief Administration (FERA), established, 35–36
Federal Housing Administration (FHA), established, 53–54; Rothstein on racial segregation role, 54
Federal Radio Commission (FRC), regulated radio, 48–49; Pettey's role, 48
Federal Reserve, 23
Federal Theatre Project (FTP), produced *Power*, 61–62
Federal Writers Project, 113
Feis, Herbert, 152
Ferguson, J. David, on Wagner Act's exclusionary effects, 69
Fifth Column, FDR's exaggerated Nazi espionage threat, 135–36; opposed by Biddle, Jackson, 136; Democratic accusations against Willkie, 142
First Amendment, FDR's violations, 112–13, 116–120; Four Freedoms Speech, 144–45; Public support grew, 103, 117–122, 124; wartime violations, 161–62; Crump's violations, 183–84
First New Deal, policies, 34–58
Fish, Hamilton, 105–06, 111, 147, 157
Fleming, Ian, 135
Fleming, Thomas, 158, 176–77, 182
Fletcher, Henry P., rebuffed by CBS, NBC, 85
Flynn, Ed, received New Deal funds, 97; anti-Wallace cabal, 199
Flynn, John T., on FDR as country squire, 5–6; on banking commission, 23; on American Construction Council, 17; on NRA enforcement, 43; on Neutrality Act, 77, 110
Folsom, Anita, on naval base's political bonus, 139
Folsom, Burton W., on excise taxes, 70; on New Deal spending, 100; on naval base's political bonus, 139
Footlight Parade (Warner Brothers), NRA promotion film, 44; featured Blondell, Cagney, Keeler, 44
Ford, Gerald, AFC member, 141
Ford, Henry, announced wage increase post-1929 crash, 21
Ford, Leland M., proposed internment of all Japanese, 164
Fortune, polled business executives on New Deal, 107
Four Freedoms Speech (1941), delivered by FDR, 144–145; irony given First Amendment record, 145
Franco, Francisco, 95, 111
Frank, Anne, 135
Frank, Jerome, on AAA meat distribution, 39
Frank, Otto, attempted U.S. immigration, 134
Frankfurter, Felix, received FDR's airmail complaints, 50, 208
Freidel, Frank, on New Deal's ideological origins, 6
Friedman, Milton, on Canadian banking model, 22
Front of Decent People, anti-Hitler resistance; FDR rejected negotiations, 186–187; members executed, 211
Fushimi, Hiroyasu, warned of Japan's oil needs, 151
Gadsden, Philip H., testified in Black Committee, 72
Gallup Poll, 94, 104, 141–42, 147–48, 196, 198

Gallaway, Lowell E., supported Wallace in 1944, 198; on postwar recovery, 213
Gannett, Frank, founded NCUCG, 104
Garner, Elmer J., U.S. v. McWilliams defendant, 194
Garner, John Nance, 25–26, 104, 132, 136–37
Garrett, Garet, observed FTP propaganda, 61–62
Garry, Thomas D., "Voice from the sewers" at 1940 convention, 138
Gellman, Irwin F., on FDR's Newport Sex Scandal views, 12
General Foods, 113
German American Bund, failed 1939 rally, 136; limited membership, 136
German Declaration of War on the U.S., 158
German invasion of Poland (1939), triggered WWII, 132–33
German-Soviet Non-Aggression Pact (1939), divided Poland, Baltics, 132; defended by Davies, 179
German-Soviet Treaty of Friendship, divided Poland, Baltics, 132
GI Bill, supported by FDR, 193; racial disparities, 193–94; Rankin's Jim Crow provisions, 193
Geisel, Theodor ("Dr. Seuss"), 165
Gillette, Guy M., proposed refugee bill, 186; declared premature victory, 186
Give a Man a Job (MGM), NRA promotion film, 44
Gladden, Washington, 2
Glass, Carter, proposed banking bill, 22, 230; on gold standard, 35; criticized NRA, 51
Glass-Steagall Act (1933), established, 36–37
Goebbels, Joseph, 176–77, 203
gold inflow to the U.S., 56–57
Gold Standard, 27, 35
Good Neighbor Policy, Latin American relations, 61
Goodwin, Doris Kearns, on wartime mobilization, 213
Grabar, Mary, on "national consecration", 34
Granger, Lester, criticized Wagner Act, 68
Grant, Ulysses S., FDR's model for unconditional surrender, 175–76
Great Depression, 18–124
Green, William, consulted Fascist Italy's labor laws, 47
Gregory, Anthony, on Eleanor's civil rights impact, 60; on TVA's racial impact, 38
Greer Incident (1941), FDR's misrepresentation, 152
Grew, Joseph, 111, 151
Griffin, William, dropped from U.S. v. McWilliams, 195; pledged FDR support, 195
Grynszpan, Herschel, sparked Kristallnacht, 125–26
Guadalcanal, Allied victory, 178

Hague, Frank, 118–121
Haiti Constitution, FDR's false authorship claim, 13
Halifax, Lord, on FDR's war strategy, 150, 154
Hannegan, Robert E., anti-Wallace cabal, 197–99; controlled 1944 convention, 199
Hansen, Alvin, predicted postwar unemployment, 214
Hanson, Elisha, on FDR media criticism, 79; ANPA role, 88
Harding, Warren G., 14, 20–21, 53
Harlem Hospital, named for FDR support, 99
Harriman, W. Averell, appealed to Stalin on Warsaw Uprising, 204
Hart, Lorenz, in *Give a Man a Job*, 44
Harvard Board of Overseers, FDR supported Jewish quotas, 16
Hassett, William D., on FDR's racial comments, 193
Havenner, Franck, co-sponsored King-Havenner Bill, 134
Haynes, John Earl, disputed Hopkins as spy, 209
Hearst, William Randolph, 25–26, 88, 91, 169, 185
Hearst Metrotone, omitted "fear itself", 34
Hecht, Ben, pressured for Romanian refugee proposal, 177; criticized FDR's inaction, 186

Heller, Joseph, 65–66
Hemingway, Ernest, criticized Key West hurricane response, 78–79; *A Farewell to Arms*, 76
Henderson, Leon, 114, 148, 160
Henning, Arthur Sears, approved Midway story, 172
Herk, Izzy, NRA burlesque code, 44
Hickok, Lonera, 10
Higgs, Robert, 107, 171, 213–14
Hill, Herbert, on NRA's harm to Black workers, 53
Hill, T. Arnold, pressed FDR for military desegregation, 140
Hillman, Sidney, 148, 199
Hiroshima and Nagasaki, James Roosevelt on FDR's bomb willingness, 212
Hirsh, Richard F., on REA's impact, 64
Hiss, Alger, Soviet spy at Yalta, 208–210
Hitler, Adolf, 44–45, 48, 57, 112, 122, 132–33, 147, 175
Hofstadter, Richard, on FDR's Bank of United States stance, 24
Hogan, Frank J., Strawn's lawyer, 86; Formed ABA Bill of Rights Committee, 120
Holocaust, evidence mounted, 131, 150, 173; FDR's inaction, 177–78, 200
Home Owners Loan Corporation (HOLC), established, 37
Hoover, Herbert, 12, 16, 18, 20, 43, 69–70, 99, 185
Hoover, J. Edgar, surveilled Lindbergh supporters, 135; opposed internment, 164
Hoover Dam, renamed by Ickes, 37
Hopkins, Harry, 35, 61, 78–79, 93–94, 114, 118–19, 123–24, 147, 168, 176, 209–210
Horthy, Nicholas, Hungarian refugee proposal, 200–01
Houck, Davis, on "national consecration", 34
Houston, Charles, defended Marian Anderson, 129–130
Howard University, received New Deal funding, 99; Ickes's speech, 98–99
Howard, Moe, in *Give a Man a Job*, 44
Howe, Louis, 6, 10, 22, 49
Hrdlicka, Aleš, FDR inquired about Japanese skull correction, 193
Hughes, Charles Evans, Denied Supreme Court backlog, 104; Upheld New Deal laws, 105
Hull, Cordell, 35, 45–46, 55–56, 60–61, 155
Hurja, Emil, guided New Deal spending, 57, 80, 94, 96
Hurok, Sol, Anderson's manager; suggested Lincoln Memorial concert, 129–130
Hurston, Zora Neale, criticized Eleanor's DAR focus, 129–131; criticized Executive Order 8802, 149
Huston, Walter, 179

Ickes, Harold, 37, 91, 106, 108, 126, 129–130
Ijams, George E., Key West hurricane investigation, 78
Ignatius, David, on BSC's media manipulation, 135
Inauguration Address (1933), ranked highly, 33; "fear itself" phrase, 33
Industrial Workers of the World, attacked by American Legion, 14
Ingersoll, Ralph, supported BSC propaganda, 135
Insull, Samuel, utility executive in *Power*, 62
International Ladies Garment Workers Union, supported FDR, 97
International Red Cross, proposed monitoring Jewish prisoners, 185
Italian Campaign (1943–1944), slowed by unconditional surrender, 181–82; Clark's lament, 188

Jackson, Robert H., managed third-term campaign, 134; questioned Fifth Column, 136
Japanese Americans, 18, 162, 164–68, 174, 204–06
Jewish Socialist Bund, reported Nazi gas vans, 173
Jewish Telegraphic Agency, reported Nazi massacres, 150
Jews, FDR and, 16, 106, 111–12,

125–28, 120–21, 134
Johnson, Edwin, 186
Johnson, Hiram, opposed Selective Service Act, 139
Johnson, Hugh S. 41–46, 55
Jones, Jesse, gold-buying spree, 46; clashed with Wallace, 159–160, 182

Kaiser, Henry J., wartime mobilization role, 214
Kaltenborn, H.V., on AAA bureaucracy, 39
Katznelson, Ira, 33, 38, 193
Katyn Forest massacre, Stalin's responsibility, 180, 189, 197
Keeler, Ruby, in *Footlight Parade*, 44
Kelly, Edward J., recruited Garry for 1940 convention, 138; anti-Wallace cabal, 199
Kennan, George F., criticized FDR's Japan policy, 155
Kennedy, David M., on New Deal's recovery failure, 38, 157
Kennedy, John F., AFC member, 141
Kennedy, Joseph P., Major FDR donor, 126; first SEC head, 126; ambassador to UK, 126
Kennedy Plan, Rublee's authorship, 126–27; Nazi emigration negotiations, 127–28
Kent, Frank R., 28, 61
Kent, Samuel N., prosecuted in Newport Sex Scandal, 12–13
Key West Hurricane (1935), 77–79, 93–94; Hemingway's critique, 78–79
Key West Hurricane investigation (1936), Rankin's chairmanship, 93–94
Keyes, Henry W., 15–16
Keynes, John Maynard, 46, 108–09
Kimmel, Husband, underestimated Pearl Harbor risk, 154–55
King, Martin Luther Jr., 'I Have a Dream' speech ranked, 33
King, William H., co-sponsored King-Havenner Bill, 134
King-Havenner Bill, FDR's indifference, 134–35; supported refugee admission, 134
Kintner, Robert, compared 1940 convention to puppet show, 138
Klaw, Spencer, AFC member, 141
Klehr, Harvey, disputed Hopkins as spy, 209
Knox, Frank, 137, 140, 166
Knudsen, William, led OPM, 148, 159–160
Konoe, Fumimaro, proposed FDR summit, 151; replaced by Tojo, 152
Korematsu v. United States, upheld Executive Order 9066, 206
Kristallnacht (1938), Nazi response to vom Rath's murder, 125–26; FDR's timid response, 126
Krock, Arthur, 123
Ku Klux Klan, 7, 92, 106–07

LaFollette, Philip, 28
LaFollette Robert, M. 3
LaFollette, Robert Jr., 70, 76
LaGuardia, Fiorello, OCD leadership, 148
Lafount, Harold A., on NRA compliance, 49
Landis, Kenesaw M. II, lost faith in U.S. v. McWilliams, 196
Lane, Franklin K., 9, 16,
Landon, Alfred E., 93–95, 98–100, 119
Larrabee, Eric, on Nimitz's Midway victory, 172
Lawrence, David, 73, 100
League of Industrial Rights, opposed Wagner Act, 67
Lee, Robert E., 176
Lehman, Herbert, investigated City Trust, 23; opposed Court Packing, 105–06
Lend-Lease, 144–46, 202–03, 208
LeMay, Curtis, role in Tokyo bombing, 211
Lenin, Vladimir, referenced for Soviet totalitarianism, 47
Leslie, Harry G., 28–29
Leuchtenburg, William E., on FDR's 1936 reelection doubts, 85; on anti-business rhetoric, 107
Lewis, John L., supported FDR, 97
Life, Praised Kennedy Plan, 127

Lincoln Memorial concert, Anderson's performance, 129–130
Lindbergh, Charles, 51, 135
Lippmann, Walter, criticized Black, Minton Committees, 87, 91, 116, 119
Literary Digest, inaccurate 1936 poll, 100
Lohr, Lennox, rejected Fletcher's skits, 85
London Economic Conference, FDR scuttled, 44–46
Long, Breckinridge, on Italian labor law influence, 47
Long, Huey, 25–26, 69–70, 75, 80–81
Longworth, Alice Roosevelt, criticized Black Committee, 89–90; AFC member, 141
Lonergan, Augustine, chaired Campaign Expenditures Committee, 91
Loyless, Thomas Wesley, persuaded FDR for *Macon Telegraph*, 18
Lubin, Isador, FDR suggested manipulating cost of living, 172
Lusitania sinking (1915), influenced Neutrality Act, 133

MacArthur, Douglas, 27, 158
MacLeish, Archibald, 27, 170
Macon Telegraph, FDR's "Roosevelt Says" column, 18–19
Maged, Jacob, jailed for NRA violation, 51
MAGIC Intercepts, FDR's access, 145; role in Midway, 172
Maloney, James Loy "Pat", approved Midway story, 172
Mangione, Jerre, on FDR's vindictiveness, 113–14
March on Washington (1941), organized by Randolph, 149; cancelled post-Executive Order 8802, 149
Marshall, George, 166, 203
Marshall, Thurgood, criticized FDR's civil rights record, 98
Martin, J.B., 142–43, 145, 183
McCarthy, Joseph, 101
McCloy, John J., supported ending internment, 193
McClure, S.S., NCUCG supporter, 104
McCormick, Anne O'Hare, on 1932 tax revolt, 28
McCormick, Robert, 86, 157, 172–73
McCormack, John, opposed Black Committee surveillance, 91
McElvaine, Robert, on FDR's political calculations, 39
McFadden Act (1927), prohibited interstate banking, 20
McIntire, Ross T., covered up FDR's condition, 190
McMeekin, Sean, on Allied plans against Soviet Caucasus, 133
McMillen, Neal R., on lynching impunity, 53
McReynolds, James Clark, questioned NRA poultry code, 66
McSwain, John J., 88
McWilliams, Joseph, U.S. v. McWilliams defendant, 194
Means, Gardiner C., co-authored *American Economic Life*, 25
Medoff, Rafael, on Nazi extermination plans, 173
Melman, Seymour, on wartime mobilization, 213
Memphis Red Sox, owned by J.B. Martin, 142
Mencken, H.L., proposed admitting 400,000 Jews, 128
Menzies, Stewart, Canaris's conditional surrender appeal, 201
Mercer, Carroll, Lucy Mercer's father, fought with TR in Cuba, 9
Mercer, Lucy, affair with FDR, 9–10; resumed relationship, 200
Merritt, Walter G., criticized Wagner Act, 67–68

Michaelis, David, 4, 15
Michelson, Charles, on FDR's banking crisis strategy, 31
Mills, Ogden, drafted Emergency Banking Act, 34
Minton, Sherman, led Minton Committee, 115–16, 119–120; press gag bill, 115–120
Minton Committee (1938), investigated press, 115–16, 119–120; criticized by multiple outlets, 116–17, 119–120

Mission to Moscow, FDR praised, 179–180; pro-Soviet film, 179
Moe, Richard, on FDR's third-term subterfuge, 134
Moley, Raymond, 24–25, 29–30, 46, 91
Molotov-Ribbentrop line, drawn in 1939, 188; FDR endorsed, 188
Montgomery Ward, 52, 196
Morgenthau, Henry, 17, 46; 73, 107–08, 203–04, 212
Morgenthau Plan, 202–03
Moseley, George Van Horn, named in U.S. v. McWilliams, 196
Moses, Robert, investigated City Trust, 23; FDR's grudge, 23
Mundelein, Cardinal George William, 110, 131
Muni, Paul, 134, 185
Munich Pact (1938), negotiated by Chamberlain, 123; violated by Germany, 128
Murphy, Frank, did not intervene in UAW strike, 108
Mussolini, Benito, 45, 47–48, 77, 180
mutual-aid societies, declined during Depression, 19–20

The Nation, warned of FDR's vindictiveness, 112; criticized Hague, 120
National Association for the Advancement of Colored People (NAACP), 8, 68, 98
National Association for Manufacturers, 42
National Association of Broadcasters (NAB), supported FDR, 48
National Committee for Independent Courts (NCIC), targeted by FDR, 105
National Committee to Uphold Constitutional Government (NCUCG), opposed Court Packing, 104
National Consecration, in FDR's inauguration address, 34
National Constitution Center, ranked inauguration address, 33
National Industrial Recovery Act (NIRA), 40–44, 52–53
National Labor Relations Act (Wagner Act), sponsored by Wagner, 67–69; harmed Black workers, 68–69
National Newspaper Publishers Association (NNPA), Sengstacke's leadership, 170
National Recovery Administration (NRA), established, 35, 40–44; struck down in *Schechter*, 64–66
National Recovery Review Board, led by Darrow, 52
National Woman's Party, targeted by Black Committee, 90–91
Neal, Claude, 54
Nelson, Donald, 160, 178
Neutrality Act, 77, 109–110, 131, 133
New Freedom, 6
New Nationalism, 6
New Masses, published Hemingway's critique, 79; supported U.S. v. McWilliams, 195
New Republic, on Court Packing, 112; on Hague, 120
New York Daily News, targeted by FDR, 168–69
New York Enquirer, published by Griffin, 195
New York Herald Tribune, criticized Minton Committee, 116–17
New York Post, criticized Minton Committee, 116–17
New York Times, supported FDR's free speech, 121
New York Times Magazine, on Nelson's WPB power, 160
Newport Sex Scandal, 1, 11–12, 14–15
Newsweek, criticized Key West response, 78; linked Minton's bill to FDR, 117
Nicolaides, Betty, on New Deal favoritism, 95
Nimitz, Chester, Midway victory, 172
Nock, Albert Jay, 122
Nogués, Charles, discussed Jewish restrictions with FDR, 175
Normandy Landing (Operation Overlord), Allied success, 198
Norris, George, on public power, 36–38, 61–62
Norris, Tennessee, TVA's "sundown town", 38
Nye, Gerald, proposed lifting Spanish embargo, 111

Office of Civilian Defense (OCD), LaGuardia's leadership, 148
Office of Price Administration and Civilian Supply (OPACS), Henderson's leadership, 148, 160–61, 171–72
Office of Production Management (OPM), Knudsen, Hillman leadership, 148
Office of War Mobilization, Byrnes directed, 199
Operation Torch (1942), Allied landing in North Africa, 175

Paley, William S., rejected Fletcher's skits, 85
Palmer, A. Mitchell, 12, 14
Panay sinking, 110, 113
Patterson-McCormick Axis, FDR's term for targeted publishers, 168–69
Patterson, Cissy, FDR noted "subversive mind", 169
Patterson, Robert, Clashed with Nelson, 160
Pauley, Ed, anti-Wallace cabal, 199
Pavlov, Vitaly, influenced Harry Dexter White, 209
Peale, Norman Vincent, supported NCUCG, 104
Pearl Harbor, Japanese attack, 153–55
Pearson, Drew, 65
Peek, George, 55–56, 60–61
Pepper, Claude, on Revenue Bill veto reaction, 192
Perkins, Frances, 73, 113, 134
Perkins, Fred, 51
Perry, Oliver, blocked Randolph's speech, 184
Persico, Joseph, 145
Pettey, Herbert L. 48
Phony War (1939–1940), coined by Borah, 133
Pinchot, Gifford, NCUCG supporter, 104
Pittsburgh Courier, Double V campaign, 170; on GI Bill disparities, 194
Pittsburgh Post-Gazette, exposed Black's Klan ties, 106
PM, supported BSC propaganda, 111, 125, 128, 131–33
Poland, 173, 189, 203, 211
Polish Guarantee (1939), Britain's pledge, 128, 133
Polk, Frank, 11
Poll Tax, Wallace's repeal call, 199
Post, Merriweather Marjorie, pressured Carter, 113; married to Davies, 179
Power (FTP play), produced by Federal Theatre Project, 62
private pensions, 74–75
Prohibition, 24
Progressive movement, 2–6
Proskaner, Joseph M. 17
Providence Journal, criticized Newport Sex Scandal, 12–13, 14
Prussian Military Junkers, FDR opposed in unconditional surrender, 187
Public Law 503 (1942), penalties for violating Executive Order 9066, 167–68
Public Works Administration, 36
Publicity (Wichita weekly), published by Garner, 194

Quarantine Speech, 110–11

Rabbis' Capitol Pilgrimage, arranged by Bergson, 186
radio, FDR's use of, 48–50, 84–85, 94–95
Rainer, John, supported King-Havenner Bill, 134
Rainer, Luise, 134
Rand, Jr., James, 30
Randolph, A. Philip, 140, 148–49, 184
Rankin, Jeannette, opposed war declaration, 158
Rankin, John E., 78, 87, 93–94, 193
Ransom, Roger L., on tontine insurance ban, 74
Rathom, John, criticized FDR's Newport methods, 12–13, 14
Rauschenbush, Walter, Social Gospel advocate, 2
Rayburn, Sam, considered for 1944 VP, 198
Reagan, Ronald W., "Tear Down This Wall" speech ranked, 33

Reams, R. Borden, on Jewish refugee risks, 184–85
Reciprocal Trade Agreement Act (RTAA), established, 55–56
Red Cross, aided Key West response, 78; monitored Jewish prisoners, 185
Red Summer (1919), FDR's inaction, 11
Reid, Helen, BSC media role, 135
Republic of China, 153–54, 189
"Rescue through Victory", FDR's policy, 157, 184–85; Reaffirmed at Bermuda, 177
Revenue Act (1935), established, 69–70
Revenue Act of 1932, Hoover's tax increase, 22
Revenue Bill (1944), FDR's veto overridden, 192
Rice, Walter Lyman, 65
Rickenbacker, Eddie, Criticized airmail scandal, 50
Richberg, Donald, NRA Chief Counsel, 41
Riegner, Gerhart, reported Nazi extermination, 173
Ringle, Kenneth, opposed internment, 166
Roberts Commission, investigated Pearl Harbor, 155
Roberts, Owen, upheld New Deal laws, 105
Robinson, Edward G., in "We Will Never Die", 185
Robinson, Greg, on FDR's internment decisions, 165
Robinson, Joe, died during Court-packing debate, 106
Robbins, Lionel, critiqued NRA wage policies, 42
Roerich, Nicholas, ties to Wallace, 182
Rogers, Edith Nourse, 93, 128
Rogers, Will, on Revenue Act, Long, 70
Rogers, Will Jr., co–sponsored refugee bill, 186
Romanian refugee proposal, offer to transport Jews, 177
Rommel, Erwin, cooperated with Canaris, 201
Roos, Charles F., 67
Roosevelt, Anna, insisted on FDR's medical exam, 190; facilitated Mercer meetings, 200
Roosevelt, Eleanor, traumatic childhood, 4; marriage to FDR, 4; and Lucy Mercer, 9–10; relationship with Lorena Hickok, 9–10; role in civil rights, 59–60, 98, 105, 148–49, 159–160, 185
Roosevelt, Elliott, (Eleanor's father), suicide, 4
Roosevelt, Elliott (son), 8, 43, 47, 50, 88
Roosevelt, Franklin D., early life, 1–2; progressive influence, 2–3; Assistant Secretary of the Navy, 6–9; Newport Sex Scandal, 12, 14–15; 1920 campaign, 12–13; polio, 15–18; business investments, 16; support for quotas on Jews while on Harvard Board of Overseers, 16; Construction Czar, 16–17; articles for *Macon Telegraph*, 17–18, 1924 convention speech endorsing Smith, 17; Governor, 18, 21–23; presidential campaign (1932), 23–28; presidential transition, 28–32; First New Deal, 34–58; Second New Deal, 59–81; pre-war foreign policy, 109–112; World War II, 132–212; death, 212; assessment, 212–215
Roosevelt, James (father), 1–2
Roosevelt, James (son), On FDR's atomic bomb willingness, 212
Roosevelt, John (son), 161
Roosevelt, Sara Delano, 2–4, 10
Roosevelt, Theodore (TR), 2–3, 8–9
Roosevelt, Theodore Jr., AFC member, 141
Rosenman, Samuel, speechwriter, racial views, 54
Rothstein, Richard, 53–54
Rublee, George, authored Kennedy Plan, 126–27
Rumpf, Hans, authored *The Bombing of Germany*, 210
Rural Electrification Administration, 62–64, 70
Rutherford, Lucy Mercer, See Mercer, Lucy

Samuelson, Paul, predicted postwar unemployment, 214
San Francisco Daily News, 163
Schechter brothers, 64–66
Schilke, Charles, 112
Schlesinger, Arthur Jr., on London Economic Conference, 45
Schumpeter, Joseph, critiqued New Deal, 42
Schuyler, George S., criticized sedition trial, 195
Second New Deal, policies, 59–76
Second Quebec Conference (1944), Morgenthau Plan discussion, 202–03
Section A (Newport Sex Scandal), FDR's leadership, 12, 15
Securities and Exchange Commission, 70
Sedition Prosecutions, 161, 163, 195–96, 205–06
Seiler, Christine Kay, 93
Selective Service Act, 139, 173
Selgin, George, 56–57, 115
Senate Committee (Newport), reported FDR's actions, 15
Sengstacke, John H., met Biddle, 170
Sherwood, Robert E., on FDR's BSC alliance, 135
Shlaes, Amity, 38, 56
Shirer, William, on "Phony War", 133
Short, Walter C., uninformed about Pearl Harbor, 155
Shriver, R. Sargent, AFC member, 141
Sicily landing (1943), Allied operation, 180
Simmons, Roscoe Conkling, compared Crump to Hitler, 143
Smith, Al, 17–18, 137
Smith, Jason Scott, on WPA's internment role, 168, 174
Smith Act (1940), basis for U.S. v. McWilliams, 194
Smith, Jean Edward, 4
Smoot-Hawley Tariff (1930), signed by Hoover, 21
Social Gospel, 2–3
Social Justice, Shutdown, 169
Social Security Act (1935), established, 73–76
South Memphis Drug Store, owned by Martin, 142
Spanish Civil War (1936–1939), Neutrality Act applied, 95, 110–11
Special Senate Committee to Investigate Campaign Expenditures, chaired by Lonergan, 91
S.S. St. Louis, 130–31
Stalin, Joseph, 47, 57, 132, 147, 180, 189, 197, 208–09, 211–12
Stauffenberg Plot (1944), 201–02
Steele, Richard W., 112, 162
Steinbeck, John, on FDR's intrigue fascination, 11
Stephenson, William, led BSC, 135, 153
Stern, J. David, 49, 120
Stettinius, Edward, supported ending internment, 193
Steward, Luther, FDR's letter on bargaining, 69
Stewart, Potter, AFC member, 141
Stimson, Henry, 31, 137, 163–64, 167, 202
Stinnett, Robert B., claimed FDR knew of Pearl Harbor attack, 154
Stokes, Thomas L., exposed WPA abuses, 124
Strawn, Silas H., 90–92
Stuart, R. Douglas, AFC member, 141
Sudetenland, Hitler's agitation, 123
Sulzberger, Arthur, supported BSC propaganda, 135
Sutch, Richard, 74

Taft, Robert A., 74, 137, 144, 186
Tax Delinquency and Revolt (1932), 18–19, 29
Taylor, Maxwell, clandestine mission to Rome, 181
Taylor, Myron, Evian Conference spokesman, 112
Tehran Conference (1943), FDR's health decline, 189–190
Tennessee Valley Authority, 37–38
Thomas, Norman, arrested by Hague, 119–120; AFC member, 141
Thompson, Dorothy, supported BSC propaganda, 135

Thoreau, Henry David, possible "fear itself" source, 33
Time, on OPA as "kitchen Gestapo", 161
Tojo, Hideki, replaced Konoe, 152
Tolischus, Otto, reported Kristallnacht, 125
tontine insurance, banned by New York, 74
Townsend, Francis, 75
Trading with the Enemy Act, 30–31, 34–35
Tripartite Pact (1940), 141, 153
Triple A—Plowed Under (FTP play), 153
Truman, Harry S., 168, 198–99, 212
Trump, Donald J., referenced for tariff powers, 56
Tugwell, Rexford, Brain Truster, 24–25, 31, 47
Tyler, Ralph W., purged by Daniels, 8

Unit Banking, role in bank failures, 20
United States v. Butler, struck down AAA, 85
U.S. v. McWilliams, sedition trial, 194; Biddle called "dreary farce", 205
Unconditional Surrender policy, FDR announced, 175–76
Urban League, Opposed Wagner Act, 67–68

Vance, Rupert B., 39
Vandenberg, Arthur, 94–95, 131
Vanderbilt, Arthur T., formed Bill of Rights Committee, 120
Vassiliev, Alexander, disputed Hopkins as spy, 209
Vedder, Richard K., on postwar recovery, 213
Venona documents, revealed Soviet espionage, 208
Veterans Administration, GI Bill disparities, 193–94
Vidal, Gore, AFC member, 141
Viner, Jacob, criticized FDR's business warfare, 109
Villard, Oswald Garrison, criticized Hague, 120; AFC member, 141
vom Rath, Ernst, murder sparked Kristallnacht, 125

Wagner, Robert, sponsored Wagner Act, Wagner-Rogers Bill, 67–69, 128
Wagner-Rogers Bill (1939), supported refugees, 128
Wakasugi, Kaname, proposed China withdrawal, 151–52
Walker, Frank, anti-Wallace cabal, 199
Wallenberg, Raoul, saved Hungarian Jews, 200
Wallace, Henry A., 138–39, 159–160, 182, 212
War Labor Board, Montgomery Ward incident, 196
War Production Board (WPB), created by FDR, 160
War Refugee Board, created in response to Emergency Committee, 186, 200
Warburg, James, opposed gold buying spree, 46
Ward, Geoffrey C., 11
Warm Springs Georgia, FDR's polio treatment, 18
Warner, Jack, produced *Mission to Moscow*, 179
Warner Brothers, produced *Footlight Parade*, 44
Warren, Charles, responded to FDR's prosecution request, 10
Warren, George Frederick, influenced gold buying spree, 46–47
Warsaw Uprising, Harriman's appeals to Stalin, 204
Washburn, Lois de Lafayette, U.S. v. McWilliams defendant, 196
Washburn, Patrick S., on Black press harassment, 170
Washington Post, on Maged's NRA case, 51; criticized Key West response, 78
Washington Times-Herald, on Wallace's Roerich ties, 182
Washington Tribune, Anderson controversy editorial, 129–130
Watson, Edwin "Pa", anti-Wallace cabal, 197
We Will Never Die, dramatization with Robinson, 185

Weaver, Carolyn L., 209–210
Weinrib, Laura, 122
Weiss, Nancy J., on Anderson controversy benefits, 130
Welles, Orson, suggested Fala speech, 204
Welles, Sumner, supported refugees, 126; attested to Nazi extermination, 173
West Coast Hotel Co. v. Parrish, Reversed Adkins, 105
Western Union, 84–86, 87–89, 98
Wheat, Alfred A., Limited Black Committee's leverage, 92
Wheeler, Burton K., 71, 87–88, 104, 119
Wheeler-Rayburn Bill, supported by Browning, Corcoran, 71, 73
White, Walter, 54, 60, 105, 140
White, William Allen, on FDR's health decline, 178
Williams, Aubrey, 78, 114
Williams, James T. Jr., targeted in Black Committee, 88
Willkie, Wendell, 72, 137–144; supported Selective Service Act, 139
Wilson, Woodrow, 3, 6–12, 162
Winchell, Walter, warned FDR about Hiss, 209
Winfield, Betty Houchin, on Fireside Chats, 49
Wise, Stephen S., 111, 173
Wood, Robert, AFC member, 141
Woodin, William, on gold standard, 35
Works Progress Administration (WPA), established, 70–71; political use, 96–97, 114, 139
World Jewish Congress, reported Nazi extermination, 173
World War I Veterans, 27–28, 36, 77–79
Wright, Gavin, 114
Wright, Robert E., 63
Wyman, David S., on War Refugee Board's limited impact, 199–200

Yalta, Confrtence, 209–210
Yamamoto, Isoroku, ordered Midway withdrawal, 172
Yates, Paul C., described Black Committee procedures, 84
Young, Jack, FDR voice imitator, 179
Young, Owen D., on Bank of United States collapse, 24